ROUGH BEAST

MÁIRÍA CAHILL
ROUGH BEAST

My Story and the Reality of Sinn Féin

An Apollo Book

First published in the UK in 2023 by Head of Zeus Ltd
This paperback edition first published in 2024 by Head of Zeus Ltd,
part of Bloomsbury Publishing Plc

Copyright © Máiría Cahill, 2023

The moral right of Máiría Cahill to be identified
as the author of this work has been asserted in accordance with
the Copyright, Designs and Patents Act of 1988.

All rights reserved. No part of this publication may be reproduced,
stored in a retrieval system, or transmitted in any form or by any means,
electronic, mechanical, photocopying, recording, or otherwise,
without the prior permission of both the copyright owner
and the above publisher of this book.

Every effort has been made to trace copyright holders and to obtain
permission for the use of copyrighted material. The publisher apologises for
any errors or ommisions and would be grateful if notified of any corrections
that should be incorporated in future reprints or editions of this book.

9 7 5 3 1 2 4 6 8

A catalogue record for this book is available from the British Library.

ISBN (PB): 9781804540138
ISBN (E): 9781804540107

Printed and bound in Great Britain by
CPI Group (UK) Ltd, Croydon CR0 4YY

Head of Zeus Ltd
First Floor East
5–8 Hardwick Street
London EC1R 4RG

WWW.HEADOFZEUS.COM

For my parents, Noreen and Philip, whose lives have been greatly impacted by the events in this book and yet never once told me not to use my voice.

For my daughter, Saorlaith, the loveliest, kindest teenager I know and love, and who I will always be proud of.

And in memory of all of my grandparents, but particularly my Granny Nora, who taught me that no matter what life throws at you, get up, keep going and never lose your sense of humour.

Prologue

The glow from the streetlamps bathed the boys playing on the road in amber hue as I hurried past them, hands in my pockets. The ball hit the kerb, then skittered across the pavement in front of me, spinning as it moved, throwing quick oval shadows on the green electric box as it hit – shadows that dissipated almost immediately as it rolled back in the opposite direction to connect with small feet. Ordinarily, I wouldn't even notice a game like this, but afterwards, this trivial event was seared in my mind as I replayed the events of that night over and over, in an effort to make sense of what had occurred.

It was a five-minute walk to the top of my estate, and my trainers made no sound on the dry October ground. I wanted to run a mile in the other direction but felt there was little point. They would only catch up with me anyway.

I had woken up that morning feeling okay, until that woman arrived at my workplace. When the IRA* came looking for me, I was waiting for a lift to Stormont. Although the Northern Ireland Assembly wasn't sitting, the offices were still functioning and I had agreed to meet Denis Donaldson, Sinn Féin's administrator, to help him with his work. I was in a tizzy because in the rush to get ready for the car which was picking me up from the Sinn Féin Six County office, the hem on my blue trouser suit had caught in the heel of my boot and I had tripped

---

* Irish Republican Army

over it and fallen. The office was behind a security door on the second floor of an old stone linen mill in Conway Street. 'The Mill', as everybody called it, also housed an education centre. My grandfather Frank had founded the centre, and some other social enterprise businesses for local people. The floor was covered in dusty, damp fabric tiles, and I quickly tried to brush the dust off my trousers and see if the burn to my knee was going to bleed and stick to the lining.

It was 1999. This was still a dangerous time in Northern Ireland and republicans felt vulnerable to attack, hence the full-time security man, Sean, whose job it was to watch the CCTV cameras and operate the big olive green steel door.

The buzzer sounded and Sean let the blonde woman in. She was in her forties and pleasant looking, but with a noticeably inflamed nose. I didn't know her personally, but had seen her a few times before and suspected by observing her hushed tones while speaking with other known republicans that she was probably an IRA member. That's the strange thing about west Belfast. The IRA is supposed to be the most secretive terrorist organisation in the world, but its members are made up of two kinds of people: those who want you to know they're in it – the kind of people (men usually) who hold court in the pub on a Friday evening – and those who don't but still behave weirdly, so much so that you can spot one (usually female) a mile off. So, when the older woman had come in a few times previously to talk to people in the Sinn Féin office, she had often poked her head around the door and said to someone: 'Can I have a wee word with you?' and the two of them would go and whisper together in the next room. It was unheard of for anyone not important within Belfast republicanism to have that level of access to the Sinn Féin floor.

I was still laughing at tripping over my hem when she arrived, but stopped abruptly when she addressed me by my first name and asked if I had a minute.

'I'm on my way to Stormont,' I said, and felt the colour draining from my face.

'It will only take a few seconds,' she replied, turning on her heel and beckoning me to follow her into the empty office next door. I felt immediately this was not going to be a good conversation.

The door closed behind me, and I leaned my back against it.

'We need to see you about something,' she half-whispered, standing close to my face. 'Tonight.' There was no need to ask who the 'we' was, and she knew I knew.

I asked what it was about.

'I can't tell you that but we need to see you. It's important,' she said.

'Tell me now,' I replied, my voice rising. My face was flushed and I could feel a trickle of sweat running down my back, my lilac shirt sticking to the damp fold under my armpits. I was frightened, and she saw my fear. She put her hand on my shoulder and smiled. Three or four times I urged her to tell me what it was about, and each time she repeated that she couldn't tell me but that I had to see 'us' that night. She also told me not to worry, but I wasn't convinced.

At that point Sean shouted that the car was outside, and I told her I had to go. She said she would collect me that evening at seven thirty from outside the Xtra-vision film rental shop on the Andersonstown Road. I didn't think to ask her how she knew I lived near there. I assumed the IRA knew everything.

I don't think any words can describe the feeling when you are summoned to a meeting by the IRA. I lived in west Belfast and was working voluntarily for Sinn Féin, its political wing, so meeting members of the IRA wasn't unusual for me. I worked and drank with them. Some of them were family members, so I had no feeling of fear being around them – until I became the focus of their attention. That changed everything. It was okay to be on the periphery of danger, to flirt with it even at protests during the marching season in Belfast, but being on the IRA's radar was a very different and more perilous thing.

I walked around Stormont in a daze for most of the day. I was scared but went through the motions, photocopying papers and eating with Denis Donaldson in the canteen while he cracked jokes and pointed out members of other political parties who sat in their own groups. It is perhaps indicative of the precarious nature of republicans' interpersonal relationships that Donaldson, who was in a hugely influential position in 2000, was murdered in 2006 when he was exposed as a British agent. That's the other thing about west Belfast: the rule of republican secrecy. As the former Sinn Féin president Gerry Adams coldly told a television news crew after the 1987 murder of west Belfast man Charlie McIlmurray: 'I think Mr McIlmurray, like anyone else living in west Belfast, knows that the consequence for informing is death.' Donaldson, like McIlmurray, paid the price.

I wasn't an informer, but the prospect of meeting the IRA that night still filled me with dread. I knew that I had no option but to meet them and I was running scenarios in my head. I didn't know what they wanted and I began to visualise every detail of the previous weeks in my mind. I had had no rows with anyone that I could remember. Growing up, I had seen plenty of street fights and republican family feuds. The larger the family, the more mafia-like they behaved. I even once saw someone having their ear bitten off in the street. I came from a large family, but we did not lower ourselves to the laws of the concrete jungle. Neither did we fall foul of the 'community', in other words, the IRA. Where I come from, people have been beaten, abducted and shot for having affairs with the spouses of IRA members. I've been in living rooms where IRA members turned up to ask a woman to take back her alcoholic husband. Another friend was visited and told that she would not be allowed to leave her jailed male partner, because it would affect 'prisoner morale'. I've seen young people shot in the knees at night, and others taken out and punched in the face for not standing up for the playing of the Irish national anthem in a bar.

So not knowing which IRA members I was being taken to meet, where I was going, or what exactly it was about was terrifying. Maybe they were trying to recruit me? How would I get myself out of *that*? A few weeks earlier, the former IRA leader of the H Blocks, Brendan 'Bik' McFarlane, whom I knew well, had come quietly to let me know that the IRA were asking questions to try and build up a picture of my private life. Surely that was none of their business? But in west Belfast, everything was their business, so I couldn't rule it out.

The uncertainty meant that I also didn't know what the IRA would do to me. I had heard stories of people who had fallen foul of the organisation being beaten and tortured and dumped by the roadside. I thought I might be about to join them. That may sound ludicrous now, so many years after the Good Friday Agreement, but at that time, a year after the peace accord was signed, the fear was still very real. The IRA was still killing people, and still in near-total control of the area I lived in. In a normal world, if an armed organisation ordered you to meet them at night and you had a few hours' grace, I imagine you would run like hell, or tell the police, or at least your family. I did nothing except torment myself. I wrote a note to my parents and hid it under my pillow. 'The IRA did it and one of their names is xxxxxx. Ask R... who she is.' Then I walked down the stairs, looked into the kitchen where my mum was standing at the sink washing the dishes, and closed the front door behind me.

The woman who had summoned me was late. I stood at the corner of Andersonstown Road and Stockmans Lane feeling exposed and eyeing every car with suspicion. It was one of the longest ten minutes of my life.

A small maroon car pulled into the layby and the driver leaned across the passenger seat and opened the door. I got in. The car radio was on, playing pop music. She apologised for being late.

'It's all right,' I said, as if we were on our way to some harmless social occasion.

She drove up the Andersonstown Road, past the housing estates of Mooreland and Owenvarragh and the GAA ground, Casement Park. I put my hand on the internal door handle and wondered what would happen if I opened it and jumped out into the busy traffic.

'There is still time,' I was telling myself, but I knew there wasn't.

'Where are we going?'

'Not far,' she replied. I kept my hand on the door handle, though I was frozen to the seat in fear.

'Do you know what this is about?' she asked, turning the radio down.

'I think I have a fair idea,' I replied. I was doing what I always did when under pressure and scared. I became cheeky and tried to appear confident. I didn't want to let her know how frightened and anxious I was. I wanted her to think I did know why I was in that car so I could find out from her what was awaiting me. A few seconds of uncomfortable silence hung in the air between us. The smell of pine air freshener was making me nauseous.

'Is it a problem for you?' she asked.

'Well, you tell me what you want me here for and I'll tell you if it's a problem or not,' I countered.

She laughed and kept driving.

Part One

1

I was born in 1981, three days before Bobby Sands, the first IRA hunger striker, died. It was a troubled entry into the world at a turbulent time. I was taken away after birth and put into a room down the corridor with the other babies. My mother still recalls hearing my cries, being forbidden to go down and pick me up, and arguing with the nurse. Chaos erupted outside the hospital and across Northern Ireland after Sands's death — roads were blocked, riots raged, and when we were discharged we made it home eventually through streets thick with smoke from burning hijacked cars and buses.

My mother Noreen had escaped the conflict in her teenage years when she left to study teaching in Manchester before returning to take up a post in a primary school, and my father Philip ran his own picture-framing business. My childhood was happy enough. My sister arrived when I was five, and my parents made sure to read to us every night, encouraging our love of authors like Roald Dahl and Enid Blyton. They also took us on holidays, mostly camping around Ireland, and the happy part of my brain is filled with the sounds of the Atlantic Ocean crashing in around our bare feet as we jumped frothy white waves, the salty taste of my long blonde hair whipping around my face, and the soothing patter of rain on our canvas tent roof. Ireland has never been known for its great weather, but it has many beautiful places — particularly when you want to escape the concrete jungle in which I grew up, littered with death and destruction.

As a child, with both parents working, I spent most of my time at my maternal grandparents' house in Turf Lodge and I visited my father's parents in Ballymurphy at the weekends – two working-class housing estates at the top of the Whiterock Road, the feeder route off the Falls Road. I was not allowed outside the door in Turf Lodge, where I spent every weekday after school, since my grandmother Nora thought it was too rough for her only daughter's child. Nora was born in 1928 in Cork, and moved to Belfast when her father left the Irish Army to join the British Army as the Second World War started and relocated the family to Ardoyne in north Belfast. She was brilliant craic,* quick-witted and stubborn, and I was closer to her than anyone else in the family. My Granda Joe worked as a bus driver and later in Mackie's factory, and was Chief Ranger in the Irish National Foresters, an old nationalist-friendly society that promoted Irish culture. He loved gardening and singing, and one of my earliest memories is sitting as a two-year-old being taught the Harry Dacre song 'Daisy Bell'. I can still see his smile as he put his glasses on the top of his head and chuckled as I sang back in a baby voice: 'Daisy, Daisy, give me your answer, do, I'm half-crazy all for the love of you…'

I had more freedom in Granny Tess and Granda Frank's house in Ballymurphy if visiting at the weekends. Frank was a small bespectacled man whose family had been committed republicans for decades, at one stage living beside the 1916 leader James Connolly's family in Belfast. His father had been a printer and compositor, and he and his wife spent a lot of time instilling republican values in their children.

Their teaching worked. Granda Frank was interned three times without charge, which left my Granny Tess raising eight boys and one girl on her own. Tess, who had been born a Protestant in a

---

* *Craic* means 'enjoyable social activity' and by extension describes someone who embodies this.

home for unmarried mothers, was raised a Catholic when she was eventually fostered. She was a beautiful singer, seamstress and knitter, and I have many fond memories of sitting with her as she simultaneously knitted, held a cigarette with a long ash tip until it fell off, and singing all the while. She had an easy-going manner, and as long as we came home to eat something, she didn't mind us playing on the streets, which we did frequently. Our street games mostly consisted of sitting on a rope with a cushion taken from her house on top so it wouldn't hurt our backsides, and after a local boy spat on his hands and scaled a lamp-post to tie the rope to the top, it became a great swing. We would walk around the lamp-post until the rope curled taut and then launch ourselves in the opposite direction, so that the laws of motion would propel us at speed, whooping, squealing and laughing as the landscape became a blur in our spinning eyes.

It wasn't unusual for me from early childhood to pick up my grandparents' dog's lead and take her walking around the large estate on my own. I remember it as always a grey, cold place, brightened by the warmth and the craic of the people who were in and out of Granny's throughout the day. People in 'the Murph' didn't stand on ceremony, and they didn't lock their doors. They lived on top of one another, knew each other's business, stayed within the area even when they grew up and had children of their own, and created their own insular, almost self-sufficient community. I loved it. Although from west Belfast, I didn't know what the IRA or Sinn Féin was until I was in Primary Seven, aged ten. It wasn't unusual to see the Sinn Féin president Gerry Adams coming into my grandmother's house and joining my grandfather in the kitchen for a quiet talk. Though I knew even then that he was somehow a high-profile figure, it seemed normal at the time, and I didn't pay much attention to it.

One day after school I mentioned to my mother that a substitute teacher had asked me, 'Are you related to Joe Cahill?' My father's brother is also called Joe and, thinking he was talking about him, I said: 'Yes, he's my uncle.' I was puzzled when his reaction was one of delight, for – no offence to my younger uncle

Joe – he didn't seem to be the living legend that the teacher was enthusing about to me. My mother gave me one of her looks and followed me up to my bedroom.

Light was coming through the venetian blinds, causing the dust to dance – invoking an image of little glittery fairies, dive-bombing off each line of cream aluminium, in a race to the pink carpet below. I frequently went to such places in my head when the adults started to talk, and so, as my mother sat on the bed next to me, I was more interested in my imaginary world than anything she was going to say. My father, standing in the landing, leaned up against the architrave on his arm, his elbow poking over the door frame.

'Máiría," my mum said. 'Do you know when someone asks you about your Uncle Joe again? Well, you're better telling people you don't have an Uncle Joe.'

I was confused and asked her why.

'Well, it is better that people don't find out where your Uncle Joe is.' This did not clear up my confusion, and so my mother had to explain what 'being on the run' meant, and how he was once convicted of murder. This news made me break my gaze from the dust fairies, who by now were pirouetting rather than dive-bombing. This was the moment I learned that Joe Cahill, my paternal great-uncle, was a senior IRA man.

'Your Uncle Joe's a murderer' is what I heard, though I imagine my mother might have been a bit more nuanced than that. My father, whose voice was always calm, tried to explain the history of the IRA, and Joe's role in it, in a few sentences, but how does a child take in information like this? It wasn't unusual for other children to have family members who were republicans, but at that moment, this was news that turned my head upside down. How could Joe Cahill, the kindly older man we sometimes visited in Dundalk, have shot someone else? I understood though, that in order to make sure that he wasn't put in danger (or that I wasn't treated badly because someone didn't like him), that I should refrain from talking about him to anyone who asked again. And so I didn't.

Joe's childhood and his early time in the IRA included lots of mixing across the traditional sectarian divides, as he explained later in an interview for West Belfast Festival Radio:

> There is a tremendous affinity between all religions on this island, but particularly in the North through culture. And I can think back to when the All-Ireland dancing champion was a young lad from the Shankill road – Bertie. Or Yvonne Hood, who was the senior girl champion. There were lots of people like that. There were special classes throughout Belfast, the Ardscoil had a special class for Protestants, and it was well attended, learning the language. There was one famous programme that went for years on Radio Éireann, *If You Must Sing, Sing an Irish Song*, on a Saturday afternoon, and you would have heard that blaring out on the Shankill road.[1]

As I grew, I understood his history better and learned how Joe had been sentenced to death in 1942 along with five others for the murder of Constable Murphy, and how he escaped the hangman's noose due to a public campaign for clemency which included letters from Pope Pius XII and Éamon de Valera, and a confession from Tom Williams, who, as the commander of the IRA unit involved and thinking he was doomed to die anyway, admitted to firing the shots that killed the constable. In the early 1970s Joe became an important founder of the Provisional IRA and was Chief of Staff of the IRA for a period of about a year, and spent 23 days on hunger strike in Mountjoy Prison in Dublin.

He spent a long period 'on the run', and when we visited him in Muirhevnamor, a housing estate in Dundalk, he would sit in the armchair, elbow on the rest, hand in the air, as he spoke quietly, slowly and deliberately choosing his words. His wife, Annie, always seemed to have a pot of soup made with beef shin on the go, and as I became closer to the two of them when they moved back to Andersonstown in west Belfast in 1998, I would delight at Annie's beautiful singing, which Joe described as 'one of the things that helped me along a difficult road', and the craic with both of them as Joe would sometimes bark at Annie, who was hard of hearing, if she misheard what he was saying.

On one occasion Joe said to me: 'Well, are you doing any romancing?'

I was about to answer when Annie chimed in: 'Dancing, I love dancing, where are you dancing?'

'For fuck sake Mrs, I said RO-MAN-CING!' he shouted with a half-smile on his face. I was then given a waltzing lesson on the living-room floor, as she taught me how not to step on her toes.

I was very fond of them both, which was reciprocated, and I often would call at their house or meet him at Sinn Féin events. At a press conference on the decommissioning of IRA weapons in Conway Mill he took me aside and told me doctors thought he had a brain tumour. I cried and he cried as he hugged me. In a nod to his legendary stinginess with republican funds – he was for many years the treasurer of Sinn Féin – and in an effort to raise a smile, I said: 'Will you leave me all your money when you die?'

He took a twopence piece out of his pocket and handed it to me. 'You might as well have it now,' he said, laughing. I still have the coin he gave me.

As I became older, and radicalised by the republican movement, I became proud of Joe. I watched how others looked up to him, how he became a legendary figure – a wise old man to some, a useful propaganda tool for others. I loved him, and the relationship I had with him. He became a surrogate grandfather – both my own had died in the 1990s – and he regaled me with interesting stories. He had a forensic memory, though if he ever forgot anything – an unusual occurrence – he would laugh and say he was 'suffering from CRAFT disease', the acronym for 'can't remember a fucking thing'.

Others were not fond of him at all. They saw an unrepentant old IRA man, a hard-liner, a caricature, the two-dimensional figure of a ruthless murderer. As access to the internet became easier in the late 1990s, I would see comments like 'murdering bastard' frequently appear under news stories about him.

The journalist Gail Walker once wrote in an article in the *Belfast Telegraph*: 'You could say he's the nearest thing the Provos have to Sir Cliff Richard – a man with a hit in every decade.' Two decades later, Gail became my editor and later my friend, and we laughed at that line, which was fair comment, and I think would have amused him.

He was revered within Sinn Féin and reviled by some outside the republican movement, who saw him only as a killer, though Joe did not see himself as sectarian, believing that the IRA he joined was in the business of fighting the British. In an interview, Joe was asked in the West Belfast Festival Radio version of *Desert Island Discs* to imagine that he was sitting on an island outside Andersonstown barracks, and which Protestant he would like to have with him:

> The island wouldn't be able to hold all the Protestants I would want to have on it, you know? It is not so much the part that they have played in my life, I think it's the part that they played in Ireland. And sadly a lot of our history is forgotten. And if I was sitting on this island I'd like to do a bit of reflection and I think back to the 1940s and I think of a group of people under the banner of a man, to me he was a hero, Denis Ireland. He formed a group called the Ulster Union Club and they believed in the reunification of Ireland albeit by peaceful means ... it was only open to Protestant people, I remember that, they held their cultural sessions, language, dancing, music, all that sort of thing in the YMCA in the Mountpottinger road. A lot of Protestants joined that organisation but alas quite a lot of them found that because of the situation in the North of Ireland, it was impossible to pursue and look for the reunification of Ireland through peaceful means so I think the natural projection for them was to join the IRA. And I think of some of those people today and I think of one man in particular, who was involved in a gun battle, in Crumlin Road in 1942 just after the execution of my comrade Tom Williams, he was along with a Kerryman

called Davy Fleming who did over 100 days' hunger strike in Belfast prison. That man was John Graham … he got 16 years in jail and he was a great debater, and he was a very convincing Protestant. He would debate from morning to night on the rights and wrongs of religion – who was right and who was wrong. And he would point out that the Church of Ireland was the true Christian church, they were the continuity of St Patrick and all that sort of thing. He would also go on to say that Brigid and Colmcille were all in the hands of the COI [Church of Ireland], which is true, if you take Tara, and you take Downpatrick, Slane, no matter where you go in Ireland. He would be very convincing in his arguments that Catholics had gone astray, not them. There was maybe a sad end to this tale … when I came out of prison I would always have held up John as a typical republican, here was a true follower of Tone, a Protestant who adopted republican principles, and preached them and actively sought to free Ireland by the same means as Tone. To me, he was my hero as far as Protestants were concerned. But at the end of the day, he let me down badly. He became a Catholic.[2]

While I may not have taken much notice as a child of people like Gerry Adams, I did however notice the British soldiers on the streets. It was impossible to be unaware of them. I was warned not to speak with them, and if I was being sent to the nearest house shop for 'fegs' for Granny, I was told to hide them up my jumper and not to let the 'Brits' see them. They seemed to be everywhere. There was always a patrol in Ballymurphy Drive, British soldiers in their green and brown khaki. I almost tripped over one of them when I opened the gate to the bit of yard at the front of the house, or I'd see them crouching outside the wall, hunched down and looking through the scope of their guns or surrounded by a clatter of curious young children asking to peer down their rifles. Soldiers would steal your football and have a bit of fun with it between themselves, until one of the adults roared at them to give it back. These were young lads, who seemed old to me at the time, with funny accents, who didn't belong and who were universally hated by the Ballymurphy residents of whichever street they were walking through. I didn't hate the soldiers, although I feared them with an intensity that had the potential to turn into anger at a later stage. My father's parents did hate them, and saw the army as an oppressive, malevolent force. My mother's mother took no notice of them except when their radios interfered with her RTÉ television signal, though some of her sons, who were not political, were badly beaten by the Paras (an abbreviation for the Parachute Regiment) in the early years of the Troubles. I was frequently stopped by army patrols while in the back of my parents' car. I could sense the fear coming from the front seats, especially from my mother, any time the army torchlight lit up the car and signalled it to stop. I remember once squealing when a plastic bullet ripped past our stopped car during a confrontation between the army and local republicans.

I remember the antagonism of the army towards my father once the radio-check of his surname came crackling back through the soldier's walkie-talkie. 'Out of the car, sir,' in an English or Scottish accent, and a search would ensue while the torch was shone around the inside of the car. I was patted down even as a child sitting in the back seat, around the sides of my coat and the seat belt. I remember the matter-of-factness of my father's tone as he explained – sometimes for the second time in a 600-yard journey – where he was going to and where he was coming from. My father was a quiet, mild-mannered man, and I remember only one occasion when he became enraged at the army, seeking out the sergeant in charge to complain about the treatment of his family. I was thirteen and walking with him to the chip shop on the Andersonstown Road. One of the squaddies from a Scottish regiment wolf-whistled at me on the way past, and my father lost his temper, embarrassing me in the process, and complained to the NCO. He said he did not think it was acceptable behaviour for any man to feel such a sense of entitlement or to treat any girl as an object in that manner. We received an apology on the spot.

We made trips to Dundalk in the Irish Republic to see Joe, and another of my uncles who was 'on the run' in the 1980s and 1990s. Once again I was warned I couldn't tell anyone I had been there, but that was now normal to me, and I never questioned it. I also didn't question anyone's membership of the IRA. In the place where I grew up it was almost akin to knowing someone in the Boy Scouts or the Girl Guides. The IRA or republicanism didn't feature much as a topic of discussion in my parents' house. As a child I was more interested in my toy Skeletor and Battle Cat than in what was going on around me. A memory comes to mind of when I was five, of my grandfather Frank laughing as he took me down through the estate with him to a meeting in Springhill Community House. I'd asked him if he was famous because everyone we passed said hello to him, and I can still remember his chuckle as he relayed the story to the people he was going to meet. I just accepted everybody for who they were, and not what they did for a living or had done in the past. Militant republicanism didn't register because it was routine.

That's not to say that I didn't undergo a sea change when I hit my teenage years and began to have actively political views – radicalisation, I believe it is called. I can't pinpoint when exactly I became a Sinn Féin supporter, and by virtue of the fact Sinn Féin was its political wing, of the IRA too. It wasn't that I supported killing – far from it – but I desensitised myself to it. People were murdered during most of my childhood almost every day or week, and the news was an ever-constant cacophony of mayhem. I grew up listening to pro-IRA songs and sang them too. I was surrounded by people on my father's side of the family who, although not themselves sectarian, supported the use of armed force to free Ireland. Friends of the family were imprisoned, or were murdered by loyalists. I grew up knowing that my father, simply by virtue of his relations, was himself a target. My grandfather and uncle were bombed, my great-uncle Tom, the IRA's finance director, was shot during a republican feud and survived, I had other uncles in jail, and two more on the run. My second cousin, Siobhán, was jailed for making bombs, and I don't think any child escapes that level of tension in a family, no matter how hard their parents try to shield them.

This change in me was largely organic, but the real turning point for me was when at the suggestion of Aunt Ellen (my father's sister) in 1996 I volunteered to answer phones and help out at the community radio station of Féile an Phobail, the West Belfast Festival. My parents agreed on the condition that I would leave after two weeks and go to the Gaeltacht in Donegal to learn Irish. I was fifteen, and very excited.

The first day was difficult. I was incredibly shy. However, after we all broke the ice, and I got into the swing of things, I loved it. Community radio was so unpredictable, and I required a crash course from the other girls answering the phones on what were acceptable requests to give to the presenters on air – and what were not. I was caught out a few times with wind-ups, where I would innocently write down ribald plays on words and then hear the laughter coming from the production booth as a presenter would equally naively read an inappropriate message out on air – and then realise too late what it sounded like. One memorable one said 'To Sean De Leer, hope you have had a light bulb moment, all the best, from Mike Hunt.' There was nothing we could do once something went over the airwaves. Unlike mainstream radio stations we didn't have a delay switch, so we usually made things up and apologised automatically if we were caught out. More often than not, though, we would just fall about laughing.

The radio operated on a twenty-eight-day licence, and mostly played a mixture of rebel songs and rock music. I recall, for example, that we encouraged people to boycott a particular brand of local bread, as the bakers had been suspected of supplying Orangemen* protesting at Drumcree after they were banned from marching down the nationalist Garvaghy Road, and that

---

* Orangemen are members of the Orange Order, an exclusively Protestant cultural organisation, whose annual march celebrates the 1690 Battle of the Boyne, and King William III's victory over the deposed King James II.

there were a lot of political broadcasts. Everyone was clear from the outset that this was a republican radio station.

I landed a presenting role accidentally. One of the presenters hadn't shown up for their shift, and Mart, a forty-something man with a rock-cum-hippy persona, came out, grabbed me by the shoulders and boomed: 'You! You'll do, come on for yer big break.'

He sat me in front of the microphone, told me I had thirty seconds left, shoved the radio station advertising poster in my face and told me to read out the contact details, say hello and play music.

'But I don't have any music,' I pleaded.

'Do I fucking have to do everything here myself?' he bellowed, jokingly, shaking out his long dark ringlets and moving his trademark roll-up behind his ear. 'Here'. And he shoved five CDs down in front of me. I picked up the CD of the Irish republican band, The Wolfe Tones, and shouted across to him with about five seconds to go. 'Mart, is it ok to play Celtic Symphony?'

'Course,' he said with a wink, 'may as well give the great unwashed a bit of culture,' and he smiled and walked off, leaving my heart in my mouth.

I was cued in and started waffling. 'Welcome to Triple FM, 105.4. If you have any requests or dedications, phone in and I'll read them out for the craic. And now, Mart says I've to give you, the great unwashed, some culture. Take it away, Wolfe Tones!' I hit the play button on the CD, as the sound guy, Rab, turned the fader up. It lasted less than a minute. Until the chorus to be precise –

Graffiti on the wall which says we're magic, we're magic
Graffiti on the wall, graffiti on the wall,
And it says OOH AAH UP THE 'RA, SING OOH AAH UP
  THE 'RA* ...

Mart came flying in like a lunatic, and my eyebrows shot up.

'Get it off to fuck, off to fuck!' he roared, running over to hit the stop button, leaving us with dead air until he stuck in an

---

* 'RA is an abbreviation for IRA.

innocuous CD. 'Jesus, wee girl!' he said, 'are you trying to get us both shot? The 'RA's been on, squealing to get that off or we will lose our licence. '

'You said it was ok,' I said accusingly. 'I asked you and you said to give the great unwashed some culture.'

'When you said Celtic Symphony, I thought you meant something like Micheal Ó Súilleabháin and the fucking RTÉ Orchestra!' he squealed, exasperated. 'Not let's bring Mart and Máirías's kneecapping on quicker by playing 'Ooh aah up the 'RA !'

We both laughed, slightly hysterical. Even when an older well-known republican arrived, and started giving off, we were still trying our best to keep the smirks off our faces. Requests were made for that song the rest of the day, and complaints about it being cut, and I got a regular show because of it. I loved the electric feeling of excitement as you cued in your mike and talked about whatever came into your head. I never really planned a show, preferring instead to take a few newspapers in and use them for inspiration, or just make it up as I went along.

Winging it normally worked. I never really stayed out of trouble though and had a few close scrapes. I once read the Taoiseach's private secretary's mobile number out live on air and told everyone to get a pen and ring the official and complain about whatever the Irish prime minister had done that day. That prompted a laughing phone call from my cousin Siobhán O'Hanlon, Gerry Adams' secretary, giving me the Taoiseach's own mobile number. I probably broke every rule under the sun in the journalistic ethical code, but that was the point. We weren't journalists. We were just larking around with a microphone in front of us, not realising that there were people actually listening at the other end in their houses and cars. That's what made 'the radio', as we referred to it, so unique.

There were some madcap community presenters and shows over the years, which added to the thrill of it. Fra Coogan was a particular favourite. An ex-prisoner, Fra had developed a problem with alcohol, and he would abstain for some shows, and show up drunk for the others. We either knew by the smell of the drink as he walked into the unventilated studio, or else he would play the hunger strike song 'Joe McDonnell' and become drunkenly melancholic. He was a Jerry Vale and Perry Como fan, and he was our alternative to the BBC's presenter Hugo Duncan, who played country music. Fra was a big hit, mostly because older people liked the music he played, while the younger age group enjoyed it when he would forget himself and start cursing on air. I was very fond of him.

We had other republican presenters too, people like Tommy Gorman and Jake Jackson, both ex-IRA prisoners, who would read the newspapers on air with deadpan Belfast humour. We also had representatives from the loyalist community, and later, the Shankill Women's Centre were given a weekly slot. There were great Belfast characters too, such as Brian Moore, the cartoonist for Sinn Féin's paper, the *Republican News*, who always dug up obscure but interesting music, while other shows were dedicated to broadcasting directly to the prisoners at Long Kesh.

Such was the attempt to frustrate the licence regulators that we had not-so-subtle codes for the prison such as 'The Ranch' or 'The Lazy K'. Most of the families who listened had a relative in prison, so they would telephone requests for the prisoners, and we would read them out. We would receive calls from 'The Blocks' daily, telling us where they could get a signal and prisoners usually congregated in a cell that had reception. There was a guy whom we called 'the dirty-grey-haired engineer from Lisburn', a prisoner who would call to tell us that he had put a coat hanger with tinfoil wrapped around it out of the cell window, which he moved until he got a signal. The prisoners' slot was renamed 'Jailhouse Rock', and lasted until the remaining prisoners were released early under the terms of the 1998 Belfast / Good Friday Agreement.

On another occasion, a Mexican mariachi band who flew over for Féile walked into the studio with festival director (later Sinn Féin MLA), Caitriona Ruane, and we turned up the mikes and let them play for a half an hour while we danced round the room.

With a man known as 'Nuts', I used to drive around Belfast and phone into the studio with an 'outside broadcast'. Once, Nuts stopped a British Army foot patrol in Ballymurphy and asked a young squaddie if he could interview him. He readily agreed. He got dog's abuse from the radio studio, with the presenters getting in on the act and jokingly asking him if he would not like to go home to his mammy. It was going well until his superiors realised what was happening, and swiftly put a stop to it.

In later years, we set up our own news team, which was trained by journalist Ann Cadwallader. I enjoyed having to go out, record, edit and present the news, sometimes all in the space of an hour. On occasion I would be the only person in the news team for the day, which meant I had to find material for news, weather and sports on my own. Knowing nothing about sport, I would just copy the teletext. The weather was easy, as it was nearly always raining. The news changed rapidly, and I found myself still writing segments with a minute or so to go before we went on air. This changed later, when most of the news was pre-recorded, and people just regurgitated what they heard on other news stations. It lost its edge then. But the first few years were electrifying.

The radio moved to different locations over the years, broadcasting from Springvale Learning Campus, the Blackstaff Mill, the Festival Office, the Upper Springfield Development Trust and even from above Coopers Chemist in Andersonstown. I volunteered there for a decade, until summer 2004. I picked up some confidence and skills along the way, and it also developed my political thinking. I'm convinced that I would never have got involved in Sinn Féin had I not been introduced to it through the people I worked with at the station. My first introduction to the party's youth wing came as a direct result of working with Eoin Ó Broin, now a TD* and at the time of writing the party's housing spokesman, who presented the Scéalta current affairs programme. I liked Eoin, he was charismatic and intelligent and I readily agreed with most of what he said. Joining the party was

---

* *Teachta Dála*, a Member of the Irish Dáil.

a decision that shaped my life. There was no official ceremony. I was simply asked to go along to a meeting, and then another and another, and before long, I was elected as the national secretary of Sinn Féin Youth in Dublin, without knowing I had even stood for election. The first I knew of my appointment was when two senior IRA men, Bobby Storey and Gerry Kelly, sent me a pint in a bar in Belfast to congratulate me. Others on the National Executive included Pearse Doherty, now Sinn Féin's finance spokesperson, Matt Carthy, now a TD, and Toireasa Ferris, who later became a councillor in Kerry. Eoin O'Broin clearly had an eye for picking future politicians.

2

The IRA woman, Breige, turned the car up streets I knew very well, past the Busy Bee shops, past the library near the primary school I had attended, up the hill and then veered right at the Christmas Tree street, so-called because the neighbours all put their twinkling lighted trees in the front windows in December. I knew the area – it was near Ramoan Gardens where I had stayed for a while with my cousin Siobhán O'Hanlon, Gerry Adams's secretary. We stopped at a house split into two in Kenard Avenue, although I didn't know the street name at the time. The area, built at the foot of Divis mountain, had once been a social housing estate, though a lot of the houses were now owned privately.

We walked to the door, which she opened with a key and left off the latch, and up a dark flight of narrow stairs which led to a small hallway and living room. It smelled as if someone had cooked dinner a short while before. She showed me to a chair in a tiny kitchen to the right of the living room, connected by a door. I sat down. She filled the kettle and in my frightened state I thought for a moment she was going to pour boiling water over me. I watched the steam rise and as it hit the cupboards above the kettle, billow out in a ghostly shape, and move along the countertop in slow motion. Relief irrationally flooded me when she asked if I wanted a cup of tea. She said she was starving, so I knew the dinner had not been hers and realised that it must be someone else's flat.

I heard footsteps coming up the stairs. Seamus Finucane appeared, and I went to pieces inside. I knew from his reputation on the street that he was a senior IRA member and that this was not good. I also knew because of his presence that something extremely serious was going on. And I was thinking that there were no escape routes from this small apartment. We were in a tiny kitchen with a window looking out into darkness. I could see the house lights of the street behind where Siobhán lived and tried to estimate how far away we were. Finucane was blocking the exit as he stood in the kitchen door frame, no more than a metre away from me with his arms folded. He was wearing navy tracksuit bottoms and a tracksuit jacket and white trainers. Typical jail attire. When I asked what I was here for, Seamus said I would find out in a minute. I had met him before, at Sinn Féin meetings where he was brought in to give the 'Army' line, but I didn't know him personally. He had small beady eyes, cold eyes, behind his glasses. Breige sat down on the chair next to me at the pine table, and he remained in the doorway.

'Do you know what we are here for?' she said.

'No, do you want to tell me?' I was still doing my cocky routine, as I wouldn't give Finucane the satisfaction of knowing I was shitting myself. I also thought I had a better chance at survival if I brazened it out.

She announced that they were there on behalf of Óglaigh na hÉireann though she couldn't actually pronounce the Irish words and gave up, saying simply that they were 'the Army'.* They had heard I had spoken to people about Marty Morris, my father's sister Ellen's partner, and my heart sank. I couldn't understand where they had got that information from and in an attempt at completely mad bravado I said: 'See, without sounding like a cheeky bastard? That's none of your business.'

She snapped and retorted: 'Without sounding like a cheeky bastard back, it's everything to do with our business.' I could feel

---

* is Irish for the Irish Republican Army, or IRA. 'The Army' is a common republican codeword in English for the same organisation.

the blood pumping in my head, and the room spun a bit. I left the tea sitting and sat on my hands, digging my fingernails into my skin to focus. I was in deep shit, no doubt about it. I had no option but to listen to the rest of what they had to say.

3

I was asked to join the IRA on four separate occasions, and said no every time. On one occasion, I was asked by a woman who worked with their 'intelligence unit', though she can't have been that clever because she herself ended up doing time in jail; another invitation was from a woman on their Northern Command, who was also imprisoned; then Denis Donaldson, the man I had met in Stormont, who was later outed as an MI5 spy and had his arm severed by a shotgun blast when they shot him dead in a remote cottage in Donegal in 2006. Thankfully, I declined all these offers. The very first approach from the IRA, however, came from my aunt's then partner Martin Morris and a friend of his, when they asked me as a sixteen-year-old to move guns around Belfast for them.

I didn't like Morris, from the moment I met him. He was bony and thin and there was nothing good-looking or charming about him. He was loud-mouthed, vulgar, and smelled of sweat and roll-up cigarettes. I was also afraid of him since the time I had seen him years earlier playfully but forcefully kick my younger male cousin in the back with his bare foot in my granny's living room. He was painting the room at the time; he had just been released from prison, where he had served time for robbery. All he could talk about was his time in Long Kesh jail, what he had done, what the other prisoners did. He didn't really have much to say about anything else except politics. He was part of the IRA's 'Civil Administration Unit' – more commonly known as punishment squads, the IRA's answer to criminal or anti-social behaviour, since they had made west Belfast a 'no-go' area for the state's police service. The Civil Administration's role was to threaten, beat or shoot young people who had committed petty crimes, often maiming them by shooting out their kneecaps. Morris' nickname was 'Blood-on-the-Boots,' and he earned a fearsome reputation among teenagers, who thought he was a psychopath. I tried to stay out of his way, though he made a real effort with me. He used to tell me that I was smart and ask whether I had boyfriends, the kind of stuff that makes you cringe with embarrassment when you are a teenager. But my father's sister Ellen adored him and, since she was like an older sister to me, I felt obliged to tolerate him.

In July and August of 1997, I began to see a lot more of Morris because we were both working together on the festival radio station. He was on the management committee, and he seemed to be on the management committee of everything in west Belfast that year. Republicans put their people into key positions in the community as a strategy to gain control and people were unlikely to challenge the local hard men. Morris was becoming influential, and he was feared. Given the unpredictability of the station that year, which included amongst the ordinary volunteers, a mad mix of marijuana smokers, drinkers, ex IRA prisoners, and Sinn Féin personnel, along with live bands and musicians, it was a chaotic environment, and I regularly found myself working from six or seven in the morning through to midnight or even two the next morning. Long shifts were taking their toll on me, and my parents were concerned about the amount of time I was spending there. Morris assured them he would keep an eye on me and suggested that while I was doing shifts at the station I stay with him and Ellen at their new house in Ballymurphy, as my parents were at their house in Donegal.

A few days later, Morris came into the living room with a friend of his who I knew. Ellen was out on some errand. They sat on the settee near the window, and I sat on the armchair nearer the kitchen. Morris got up to take the phone line out of the wall and said that they wanted to talk to me. I became concerned.

Many people believed that the British were using phone lines to monitor conversations, and unplugged their land line when they wanted to speak privately, or when they wanted to show off their IRA credentials. I guessed it was the latter. He explained that they were there representing Óglaigh na hÉireann. One of them said; 'You're a clever girl, you know who we are and we wanted to ask you a few questions.'

Morris explained that they were 'working in' the Upper Springfield area and that they were 'red lights', meaning that the police and army had their names and descriptions, so they had more chance of being arrested than your average Joe. He explained that people had noticed how smart I was, that I came from a line of republicans, and that they wanted me to come and work for them. They explained they would be able to look after me and make sure I wasn't 'scooped'. They said they needed to move guns around Belfast, and told me how they would make sure there were no traces on the weapons by stripping them down, and dousing them in washing-up liquid before putting them back together. They would give me clothing on which the traces of firearms could not be detected easily. One of them spoke about white gloves, and, though now I imagine they were talking about the type of thin rubber gloves you find in a hospital, in my mind I was picturing white furry ones, and thought to myself that they would be very obvious, and ridiculous if someone was trying not to draw attention to themselves.

They said they wanted me to carry the first gun in a black taxi to Ardoyne, that they would put it in a bag with swimming gear, and that if I was walking through Ballymurphy with it and I saw the 'peelers',* I was to drop it in a garden or rap the nearest door and ask the occupier to let me in. I was picturing this in my head as they were speaking, and wasn't convinced that any neighbour would just let me into their house with a bagful of guns.

I said little during this conversation, but the hairs on the back of my neck stood up. All I could initially say was that I was

---

* Slang for the police – in this case the Royal Ulster Constabulary, or RUC.

in the middle of schooling, and I needed time to think. I had just finished my GCSEs, and intended to do my A-levels, and I certainly didn't want to jeopardise my education – or my freedom – by moving guns for the IRA. They said they did not want me to be arrested, as 'the Army' needed brains, so they would look after me. They spoke about a young girl, Teresa, who had been caught, but said she didn't get a lot of prison time and that they would train me in how to behave in case I was brought to Castlereagh to be interrogated. Fright coursed through me, and I refused to consider their offer.

Despite my saying no, they said they would leave me to think about it, but I never heard from the two of them again about that particular idea, and nor did I ever join the IRA. Although the conversation was alarming at the time, it was routine for the IRA to seek out new recruits, and I probably should have expected it.

Within a few days of that conversation, Morris offered me a tin of Harp lager and a cigarette. I said no, not wanting to drink or smoke in front of my aunt – I had just turned sixteen. He waited until she went to the bathroom and said, 'You're a big girl, not a child, I'll sort it out with Ellen.' When she came back into the room, he laughed and explained that he would rather have me drinking in the house than on a street corner. I hated the taste of the Harp, it was bubbly and gassy and I was tired from a long day at the radio station, but I wanted to look like I could keep up with him, so I was drinking half a tin and then opening another one when he handed it to me, and drinking some of that.

I had two or three tins, leaving some of the beer in each one, but it was making me feel dizzy and befuddled and I was tired. I fell asleep on the blue settee near the wall. I woke up to find someone tugging at my trousers. I was groggy, that unpleasant feeling of drifting unreality. The trousers I was wearing were unusual, because the zip was at the back. It took quite a while before he realised that. And in those first few seconds, I froze while trying to work out what was going on, and then I knew immediately who it was because of his distinctive smell and breathing, and panic hit. I thought about screaming, but I was afraid that he would strangle me to keep me quiet, then I thought about opening my eyes to try telling him to go away, but I was too embarrassed and overwhelmed, and I made a quick decision which I will regret for the rest of my life. I decided to pretend that I was asleep. I was feeling uncontrollable fear and confusion, like white noise. And then, in the time it takes to click your fingers, I said goodbye to the life I had known beforehand.

I thought that if I stayed asleep and pretended to be waking up, he might get scared and stop, then I could go into granny's house next door and tell them. Ellen was upstairs sleeping, but I didn't want her coming down and seeing this. I thought that if I coughed and moved a bit, he might think she would come down and stop. When I realised despairingly that he had no intention of stopping, I fought to find ways of stopping it before it got worse, but I was too ashamed and too scared to do it. I gave up and became almost like a rag doll. That's the only way I can describe it, I was lying there and if he moved me I stayed still until he moved me again. I tried to stop myself from screaming.

Instead I screamed inside my head.

There is nothing worse than that feeling of powerlessness when you realise your life is in someone else's hands and you are too afraid to face it down. After a while, he lifted my hand and I immediately let my arm go limp because I was pretending to be sleeping and he put it on his penis and gripped his hand over it tightly to hold it in place. The smell is the thing I still recall most acutely, that and the sound of his breathing. And those feelings of shame and fear. I wanted to be sick and, flooded with shock, I was still trying to make sense of what was happening. I had my left arm tucked up under my neck – I remember that because it stopped me from screaming when what he was doing became too painful – and I dug my fingernails into my skin either to distract from the pain or to help me not to react to what he was doing, because I was keeping up the pretence of being asleep.

When he finished, he went into the kitchen, which was beside where I was lying on the sofa, and I could hear him ripping kitchen roll, and he came back and sat beside me still lying motionless in the same position, and calmly smoked a cigarette. I was nauseated by the physical feelings – I could feel the gloop on my stomach pulling my skin as his semen started to dry, and I was sore, and I wanted to either scream or cry, or both, and I was afraid he would start again.

One of the things that demonstrates how brazen he was is that he wiped the settee with the kitchen roll and he didn't wipe me, and I felt like dirt because of that. The furniture was more important than I was. In hindsight, he must have been absolutely confident that I would say nothing, because had I done so he would have been trapped: his DNA was all over me. He finished his smoke, and then walked out of the room and went to the downstairs bathroom. I heard running water, and then he went upstairs to bed. I was stunned, I think, and I waited for about twenty minutes, half an hour maybe, before I tried to move. I was in pain, bruised, and my head was spinning with confusion. I went into the bathroom, and tried to go to the toilet but couldn't. I saw a little blood as I wiped myself, filled the sink up and washed as best I could, and went back and lay on the settee. Tears came then. I didn't make a noise, water just flowed out of my eyes and into the cushion.

I started dozing again. He came downstairs in the early morning, and while I was struggling to wake he kicked me hard in my lower back and said, 'Put the kettle on and make me a cup of coffee.' I couldn't walk properly because of the pain of what he had done the night before, and the additional pain left by his kick, and I told his wife he had kicked me in the back and that's why I was sore. She thought he was joking. But the fact that sickens me to this day is that I got up while he watched me and stood in the kitchen and made his coffee with one sugar and handed it to him as if nothing had happened.

I am confident that Morris used the IRA recruitment conversation to frighten me, so that I would not disclose my sexual abuse once it started. I now knew he had access to weaponry and that he was potentially dangerous, and the aura of the 'RA' was intimidating in ways that people born later can barely understand. You simply didn't report IRA men to the RUC at that time, unless you wanted to end up badly beaten or dead on a border road. And so, when the abuse started, and since I had pretended to be sleeping, I found myself trapped in a cycle which I was unable to escape. When I found myself in the bathroom that first night trying mentally and physically to cleanse myself of what had just happened, I was already unconsciously keeping a secret that poisoned my mind against myself, and fractured any sense of self-esteem that I still had. That secret, and his role in the IRA, served to empower him to abuse further. I became a walking shell. It was a long time before I started to be able to put the pieces back together.

I wish now I had gone to the nearest army barracks that night and not washed the evidence away, but hindsight is not helpful, and I couldn't have gone to the police. Sinn Féin had made it clear for decades that the RUC was not acceptable in nationalist communities. To go to them was seen as a betrayal, and I would have been at risk. Name an IRA man to the RUC? I had grown up knowing that this was to violate the ultimate taboo, the community's solidarity against the British state. My family was steeped in republican politics, and I had absorbed their attitude to the official institutions. The consequences were too frightening to contemplate properly.

Morris's abuse continued for over a year. That first night, an event that the criminal justice system clinically refers to as digital penetration, was followed by more of the same, then rapes in that house in Ballymurphy. I was still engaged in a battle of wits. He would do what he wanted, and I fought him in my head, while still pretending to be sleeping, because I was no match for him physically. It was a herculean effort not to react, and I would talk to myself in my head to try and keep calm. He never uttered a word, and for that reason, I convinced myself that he thought I was still sleeping too. The reality was otherwise unbearable. I don't know how many times it happened – I shoved it to the back of my head and that allowed me to function. Sometimes sounds distinguish the memories: once a man was sleeping on the other sofa in the room after a house party; another was hearing news coverage in the background on the night Princess Diana was killed in a Paris tunnel, and another was a drunk man walking up the street outside shouting to himself.

Abuse is a strange thing, because the victim takes on all of the responsibility and shame, and becomes completely trapped. I was acutely aware that I had younger cousins, and that there were children coming in and out of the house, and I took on the responsibility for them also. One of the main reasons for going back to that house after the first time was because I stupidly thought if it was happening to me, then it wouldn't be inflicted on anyone else. The damage had already been done to me as far as I was concerned, and I didn't want anyone else suffering the same fate. And, had I stopped staying with them, it would have raised questions within the family. I was close to my aunt. I wanted things to remain as normal as possible with her, despite the horrendous circumstances.

After a few months I thought I might be pregnant. I was terrified. Abortion wasn't available in Northern Ireland, and my thinking was so damaged at the time that I was already working out ways to kill myself before I even thought of taking a pregnancy test. My cousin Siobhán O'Hanlon was the first person I told. I was in the Hercules bar in Castle Street in Belfast with my friend Aine, and Siobhán was at the bar with a friend of hers. We spoke for a while, and I discovered I had left my keys behind and locked myself out. She offered to let me stay at hers, and, noticing something was wrong with me, we sat up and talked once we got back to her flat. I edged around telling her but I was so obviously distressed that she guessed what was happening, and I confirmed that it was, and who was responsible. It was Siobhán, later, who bought a pregnancy test for me. It was negative.

Siobhán was a tiny but fierce woman. She joined the IRA in the 1970s, had a ferocious reputation, and was nicknamed 'The Poison Dwarf', a moniker bestowed by some republican men who didn't like her air of authority. My father's cousin, she was more like an older sister to me in the late 1990s. She was a typical no-nonsense republican who was afraid of nothing except, oddly, pigeons, and she always laughed to herself when Ian Paisley* came on the radio. She was imprisoned in Armagh jail in 1983 for her part in setting up an IRA bomb-making factory, and after her release was part of an IRA unit that travelled to Gibraltar intending to bomb the British garrison on the rock. Three unarmed members of the unit were shot dead in the street by the SAS in March 1988. Siobhán never talked about Gibraltar and never admitted her role in the incident, but she had a hand-painted portrait of one of those who was killed, Dan McCann, hanging in her hall. After her death MI5 released surveillance photographs they had taken of her staking out the scene in Gibraltar, her long brown curly hair blowing behind her in the wind. She looked like a regular tourist. But Siobhán, instead of taking in the sights, was noting the precise times the military parade took place. She also worked later as Gerry Adams' secretary and was Sinn Féin's notetaker during negotiations with the British Government. Cancer later ravaged her breasts, and then her lymph nodes, before travelling to her brain and eventually claiming her in April 2006.

At the funeral, Adams, acting on advice from her friend and comrade Rita O'Hare, read from a poem by William Butler Yeats.

> ... For all that is done and said.
> We know their dream; enough
> To know they dreamed and are dead;
> And what if excess of love
> Bewildered them till they died?
> I write it out in verse –
> MacDonagh and MacBride
> And Connolly and Pearse
> Now and in time to be,
> Wherever green is worn,
> Are changed, changed utterly:

---

* Leader of the Unionist DUP during 'the Troubles' (the Northern Ireland conflict).

A terrible beauty is born.[3]

She would probably have scoffed at the poetry but it suited her well. Direct, frank, articulate, inherently stubborn but with a soft side too, she was indeed a terrible beauty.

There were two other occasions when I got drunk and disclosed in confidence what was happening to me to two other women, both of whom were connected with Sinn Féin, though that wasn't a consideration for me at the time. I knew them through the radio, and Sinn Féin's youth wing, and I needed a sympathetic ear. None of the three women suggested that I tell my family, or the police. One of them, Sue Ramsey, had seen the fright on my face as Morris gripped me by the throat in the festival office one time, and asked me why I was afraid of him. Siobhán did make some suggestions as I gradually stayed more at her flat during the weekends. I should down a few Rumplemintz for Dutch courage and tell him outright to stop, or she herself could tell him to stop doing it. Neither option was very helpful to me. I didn't have the mental or physical confidence to confront him and I was also mortally embarrassed, as the abuse had taken place when I was pretending to be sleeping, and I was still under the illusion that he did not think I was awake. In a strange way, I was more distressed about the fact that he would think I knew what he had done to me, that he would know I was alert throughout, so I buried it and tried to keep myself afloat instead. I had an ability to get through life by just keeping busy – I was trying to work my way through my A-levels, which was tough, and I had no option but to keep going.

And so, in 1999, a year after I disclosed what Morris was doing to me to Siobhán and the other women, I found myself facing the IRA, who had now obviously got wind of what had happened to me.

4

Volunteers should be well versed in General Army Orders and Court of Inquiry and Court Martial Procedures. They should understand that they are aimed not only at ensuring the IRA runs smoothly within these agreed disciplinary codes, but also at protecting the rights of Volunteers. While everyone is accountable to disciplinary process under General Army Orders, this is not their only function. They are there to protect the Army and as the Army is its Volunteers, they must serve to protect the Volunteers as well.[4]

As we sat in the flat in Kenard Avenue, Breige said: 'It is our business, he's a volunteer in the IRA and as far as we are concerned we can't have abusers in our ranks if that is true, and we need to work out whether this is true or not, whether you are telling the truth or not.'

I put my head down and stared at the table. My face was burning and I couldn't think. I tried to control my breathing, but my heart was pumping in my chest so hard I could feel the pulsing in my ears.

I died inside that night for a while. I had had a similar experience when the abuse happened, where I just couldn't take in what was happening, and I numbed out. I did it again once she said those words. That probably saved me, because what it allowed me to do was think quickly, and try and preserve myself. I remained scared and frightened, but my head took over and I tried to race ahead to see where they were going next. I tried to shut down, not to let them see I was surprised, not to cry or give them anything. It was what I imagine their own members did under interrogation. I played them unconsciously at their own game.

The woman asked me how many people I had told, what I had said, and what had happened with Morris. I thought to myself: 'Jesus Christ, where did they get this from?' I had only told a few people a good year before this meeting, if that's what it was, and I couldn't understand why they were coming to me now. Which of the women I'd confided in had told them, and were they going to try and get information from me and then punish me? Was Morris more important to them? Their reputation? What if they didn't believe me? I didn't answer her questions; I just sat there and looked between her and the table.

Finucane, who hadn't really said anything until then, interjected in a sing-song and rather effeminate voice: 'We are viewing this as very serious.'

I interpreted this as a threat, though I have no idea if he meant it as such. But how else could I have interpreted it? Here was the IRA picking me up and taking me to a safe house, telling me I had to speak to them about something deeply personal, so they could decide whether it was true or not. The IRA in 1999 was still killing people, despite the Good Friday Agreement. In January of that year, Eamon Collins, a former IRA man turned repentant informer, who later wrote a book about his experiences in the IRA, was battered and stabbed to death near his home in Newry. In July, twenty-two-year-old Charlie Bennett was found in a ditch in the car park of a west Belfast GAA club. He had been beaten so badly that he was unrecognisable, then shot in the head from two inches away. Both of these murders were deliberately gruesome and meant to silence 'traitors'. This was an organisation you did not cross, and I certainly did not want to be sitting facing their inquisitors as an eighteen year old, even if I did come from a republican family. At this moment my family and loved ones had no idea where I was.

Breige fired deeply personal questions at me. I was embarrassed and I wanted the man Finucane to leave. I had taken an instant dislike to him but I thought I might be able to get some information out of her if she were on her own. I tried to exude confidence, which was fabricated to mask how afraid I was. I thought if they couldn't sense fear then I had a chance of surviving. The only thing that let me down was the cup of tea. I lifted it, but couldn't hold it while my hands were shaking. I sat on my hands and let the tea sit there until it stopped leaking steam.

My cheeky fuckerness took over.

'Do you not think it's highly insensitive having him here?' I raised my voice, and my eyes to look at her. 'He's a man, you're asking me about personal stuff and I don't want him here.'

It was a gamble, but I was trying to stall for time, to think about what I was going to do next.

He looked angry. 'It's my business to be here!' he said.

I said that I wouldn't talk if he stayed and they were getting no information out of me. He rolled his eyes and made some remark about how no one ever wanted to speak to him and then they both took a few steps to the living room and had a short whispered discussion and he came back in.

'Right, okay, this is against procedure, you're breaking our procedures, there is not supposed to be just one person with you ... but I'm going to go for a while, you make sure you talk to her and I'll be back in a while and she can tell me what you have said.'

Breige was a bit more easy-going when she sat down again and explained they didn't mean to freak me, and by bringing him in they wanted me to understand that it was serious, that they were taking it seriously. That insistent repetition of the word serious, as if I needed telling.

I was still angry. I said I thought that this was the most ludicrous thing in the world. 'Youse have press ganged me, got me to meet you, sprung this on me, brought me to this room ...'

She took out a notebook and a pen and started writing away and she asked me questions.

'Were you abused?'

I nodded.

'By Marty Morris?'

I nodded again.

'Was it sexual assault or sexual abuse?'

Confusion. I didn't know the difference. I didn't answer. Instead I asked if he knew they were talking to me, because all hell would break loose and I was concerned at my parents finding out and not being able to find me.

'No, we haven't told him and we haven't suspended him either. He has rights.'

I began to think about my own rights, and at that moment it felt like I had none.

'We needed to speak to you first before going to him, we are starting an investigation, a court of inquiry. We need statements from you so we can move to the next bit.'

'You're not getting them,' I said. I felt sick.

'What do you mean we are not getting them? Come on Máiría, you are giving them, you don't have an option, we need the statements.' She shrugged her shoulders and put her hands on the table.

'You can't expect me to sit there and talk to you.' I looked out the window and thought I could see Siobhán O'Hanlon's bathroom window in Ramoan Gardens, the street around the corner. I took another gamble.

'I can't talk about this stuff. Go and speak to Siobhán, because she will tell you it is true.'

First mistake. I had given too much information. She raised her eyebrows as if that was news to her. She went back and clarified the difference between sexual assault and sexual abuse. Second mistake. I told her I had been sleeping while he forced himself on me. She filled in the gaps herself.

She asked me if I had been raped. I said yes. Third mistake. Again I had given away deeply personal information. The IRA had now confirmation from me that I had been raped – and they now wanted the details.

I asked her what if I said no to all of this, not denying that it happened but no to giving them the information they sought. I thought that if I refused to talk then they couldn't proceed. She said no, that was definitely not an option and she became frustrated with me. She said that by speaking to people outside 'the Army' about it, I had put it in the public domain. I said to her that it wasn't public.

'Oh but it is, Máiría, it is in the public domain and we need to make sure that what you are saying is the truth and if it's true then he won't be able to do it again as a volunteer.'

I realised then that I was being questioned to determine if I was truthful, and so that the IRA could protect its reputation. I was still taking this information in when Finucane returned. They had a general chit-chat about stupid things; he came in with his clothes wet and seemed annoyed that it had been raining.

'You can't be discussing this with anyone, we need to protect this information, we can't be seen to be having alleged abusers in our ranks, do you understand the seriousness of this, do you want to say this didn't happen?' he asked.

'Why the fuck would I say that?' I answered.

He smirked, and I couldn't work out where this was going next. I presumed that if he was telling me I couldn't speak to anyone, that they were going to let me go home. All I needed to do was sit it out for a while.

I told them that if they were going to make me talk I didn't want to talk to him, but they should get me another female. I was trying to stall for time again. He said he would go away and consider the 'request' then he got close to my face and warned me that I was not allowed to speak to anyone about what had just happened, about who had been in the room, or about Marty Morris. He then walked out.

Breige gave me a lift down the road in silence until I was getting out of the car at the top of Stockmans Lane. 'We will be back in touch,' she said. Another surge of anxiety and fear.

Fourth mistake. I went home and went straight up to my room. I should have told my parents that night, but I was too afraid.

I got into bed and pulled the duvet up over my head. I could feel the goose-feather pillow moulding itself around my skull, and I felt cocooned. I lay in bed with my eyes closed and thought hard. I was still convinced that at some point I would be harmed, if not killed. I thought that they would think Morris and their army needed to be protected. He was one of them. I wasn't. They had been angry and impatient, that much was obvious. But I had been allowed to go home. Why do they want to do this? Why have they let me go? Why now? What am I going to do? I zoned out, and listened to my parents going to bed. I kept the light on, because I was too scared to sleep in the dark. I thought about running away but I had no money and they would find me. I believed that the IRA were omnipresent, that no place was safe.

I didn't have to wait long to hear from them. The next morning, they came to my workplace and I was instructed to go to a building at Mulholland Terrace in west Belfast later that evening.

5

If I thought being questioned and browbeaten by Seamus Finucane was traumatic, I had no idea what was in store. When I went into the room of the old Falls Women's Centre building, I had no idea who Maura McCrory was. Now I can't get her out of my head. Sitting in a chair that looked too small for her with her legs apart and her tights wrinkled at the ankle, McCrory could have been mistaken for a stern old grandmother and not a respected member of the republican movement. Grey badly permed hair and glasses, woolly cardigan, a hard-nosed face, and a bark as bad as her bite, I imagined her leaning over a gate castigating children for making a noise outside her house. I knew nothing of her role in the 1981 Hunger Strike Relatives' Action Committee, when she and other women wore blankets and protested against Margaret Thatcher's prison policy which led to ten men dying, and that was probably just as well. Not knowing her background gave me an advantage, I think had I done so I might have seen her as a human being, instead of the monster she became to me.

I was immediately terrified of her, so I depersonalised her. That saved me, and helped me to escape her in my head when she was giving me lectures about how I was making the whole thing hard for them. She of course meant that because I couldn't tell her what Morris did to me I was inconveniencing 'the Army'; I was simply too frightened and confused to open my mouth.

I find it hard to remember these 'meetings' coherently. There were so many of them. But I remember my thoughts and feelings. Abject terror. Confusion. Deadness. Frustration. Nerves in my belly. Fight, flight and 'fuck away off'. The downstairs room was full of posters and leaflets on domestic violence, benefits, community events and rape. I used to focus on them when I was there to block out what they were saying at me. At me. Not to me. These were no ordinary conversations.

She was introduced to me simply as 'Maura'. She didn't speak to me when she was introduced, just nodded sternly. There was the usual veiled warning about how I was not to tell anyone about them, that although we were in a women's centre and she worked there by day, the other staff members did not know she was 'involved', or that they were questioning me for the IRA. That night, Breige Wright, the woman from the first night, was the good cop and Maura the scary cop.* Again, Breige asked me to describe the details of what had happened. Again I clammed up. Even if I had wanted to, I could not have spoken. I was reliving what Morris had done to me. With every question they fired, I retreated a bit more. I couldn't get it from my head to my mouth. They chastised me for having 'a cheeky look on my face'. I was trying not to cry. I dug my fingernails into my palms to stop the tears.

I pulled my knees up to my chest on the chair and assumed the fetal position and stayed like that for about twenty minutes. Constant talking. Burning my ears.

"I can't do this, I can't do this, I can't do this, I can't do this, I can't do this.' I was rocking now, my hands cupped around the top part of my head, pulling my hair.

'Máiría you have to and you can, come on, love, you have to start, we have been here an hour now, you need to start talking.' Breige's voice was softer now.

---

* McCrory died in 2021. Her funeral was a small affair due to Covid, and her tricolour-adorned coffin was driven from her home in Dermott Hill to Corpus Christi church in Ballymurphy. As the hearse crawled along the streets in February sunshine, six women dressed in white shirts, black ties and black trousers acted as a guard of honour. At the front, alongside the hearse, was Breige Wright.

'Why are you doing this to me? Leave me alone, leave me alone, leave me alone!' My hands flew down to my knees and I pulled at the skin on my hand and tried to get a mental grip.

'You know why, love.' She had a habit of calling me love. 'You're wasting our time, love; we can't sit here all night. When did he first touch you?'

No answer. I closed my eyes and felt the first time. I said nothing.

'When did he first touch you?'

No answer.

Maura shifted in her seat. 'How long ago? Are you saying he didn't touch you?'

I snapped my eyes open. 'I'm not a liar! Fuck you!'

'Watch your language! We have to go back and tell people, and unless you start giving us details we will have to go back and tell them that you won't tell us anything and that Morris is innocent.' McCrory wasn't raising her voice, but the threat was clear. They were telling me that if I didn't give them anything I was in trouble, that the senior people in the IRA would assume I had made it up.

I needed time to think. I stalled and said to McCrory. 'Go you away, and I'll talk to her. I know her from last night, I don't know you,' I pointed at McCrory. 'This is embarrassing for me and I want you to go.'

'I'm going nowhere,' she said, but when I had sat mute for another half an hour, she said she would give us ten minutes. She went up the stairs of the Centre and I could hear the floorboards creaking as she walked the room above our heads.

Breige was sitting at the end of a square desk with a notepad and pen. I was at the other end. I was exhausted. I just wanted it all to go away.

She softened. 'Look, I can see this is hard for you love, but you need to start talking.'

'I can't get the words out of my mouth.' My hands went back to my head again.

'Will I guess, can you mime?' The attempt at humour revolted me, but in a strange way it worked.

She asked me what age I was when he first abused me.

'Sixteen.'

'When he touched you? Not a paedophile then.'

I didn't even know what she meant, I knew what a paedophile was but I didn't know the age definition. I thought she was saying he hadn't abused me.

She again cited the difference between sexual assault and abuse. 'Did it happen more than once? How many times … do you know how many times, Máiría?'

I shook my head. Tears were burning at the back of my eyeballs, threatening to roll down my cheeks, but I snapped out of it fairly quickly.

'You said yesterday you were sleeping, did you say no?'

'I was too afraid to.'

'Did he threaten you?' I shook my head. In my head I was saying he didn't need to. I couldn't say that to her, I didn't think she would understand.

'What did he do?'

I opened my mouth and I couldn't do it, I couldn't get the words out. I could feel my face burning with embarrassment.

She got up and pulled the chair Maura had been sitting on to right beside me. She lowered her voice. 'I am trying my best to help you here, but you need to tell me what he did.'

'I can't.'

'Why?'

'Because it's too embarrassing.'

'I'm in my forties Máiría, I've been having sex for a long time, you can't embarrass me.'

She smiled and missed my point.

'Did he wear condoms?'

I shook my head. I would have felt it or heard it if he had. I was sure that he hadn't.

'Did he just put it in your vagina or did he put it anywhere else?'

'I want to be sick.'

She allowed me to go to the bathroom and I vomited in the toilet, as quietly as I could. I didn't want them to hear it.

When I came back, Maura was sitting in her chair again.

'We are going to let you go home now and we will be back in touch. We have to go and speak with people to see how we are going to proceed. It would be better for you if you give us details,' she said.

I looked at her in disgust. They told me if I could think, and write it down, good cop would phone me in an hour or two. Not really feeling that I had much of a choice, I nodded.

I left that building a shell of a person. I had to go to a café where I was helping out as a waitress to help clear the place at the end of the night. It wasn't that far away, but I have no memory of walking there. I do remember that when I got in there the manager was already clearing the tables. I asked her if she had a pen. I had a small hardback book, the cover was green, white and orange like the Irish flag, and I sat on the table and wrote quickly. Three incidents. Very little detail. That was all I could do.

Breige phoned dead on the hour. I told the manager I would lock up and meet her afterwards at her house with the keys. I met the IRA woman at the corner of Beechmount Avenue on the Falls Road. It was raining heavily, and I tore out the three bits of paper and handed them over. She put them in the pocket of her black leather jacket. 'Good girl,' she said.

6

Being abused was upsetting and confusing. Everything I had trusted was turned on its head, instantaneously. I pushed away those I loved the most, almost unconsciously. I didn't want to be touched. I began to wear baggy clothes so no one would look at my figure. I believed I had brought it on myself. I over-analysed everything I had said that first night, every time I smiled, every word that had come out of my mouth. I couldn't work out what I had done wrong, apart from drinking the beer I had been offered, and I became very angry with myself. And, because I was angry at myself, I also became sharp with others. My mother later recalled in her police statement a child who went from being 'demonstrative' to 'withdrawing into herself, and moving away when anyone tried to hug her …' It was obvious that something wasn't quite right, but no one was quite sure what was amiss.

I became part of the secrecy in which sexual abuse thrives, simply because I was too scared to disclose it to anyone. I geared myself up many times to tell those I loved – my parents, a close friend – fought with myself to do it, but when push came to shove, I was unable to speak. I hated myself for that.

I don't think anyone, unless they have been in the same position, can explain this reticence properly or rationally. You will yourself to do something and you work out scenarios for doing it, and you mentally try to force yourself. And right at the point where you feel it just may be on the tip of your tongue, something happens, as if an invisible gag has been placed on your mouth. As the reality of the potential consequences of disclosure sinks in, you feel icily cold and hot all at once. Your heart starts to race and you sweat, at first without noticing, and then guilt takes over. And then sadness, waves and waves of it, like the onset of immediate grief for the childish innocence that you once had.

In short, I was petrified of the unknown outcome of telling the truth, and terrified of him.

It all went back to the moment Morris laid a finger on me. When I didn't say anything after the first time, and I was standing in my aunt's bathroom quietly washing his semen off my stomach, I became automatically, if unwillingly, complicit. I was in shock, but I didn't know it at the time. I did what I felt I should do, which was to try and get him off me. I wanted the smell and the feel of him gone. I wanted the memory of what had just happened erased from my head. I wanted to be able to think straight and for the bruising pain to stop. And I wanted life to go back to a time before anything on that settee had happened. Washing off the evidence was like cleansing myself, and if I could have turned the shower on without waking up the house, I would have done that too. The next morning when I eventually had a proper opportunity to wash, I scrubbed my skin raw in an attempt to rid myself of him. But I still didn't feel clean. I still do this at times; when I want to wash my day down the plughole, a hot shower gives me the opportunity to both lose myself and collect my thoughts and get whatever is contaminating my head out of my system. Old habits die hard.

There were a few occasions when I came very close to speaking – and when, looking back, I wish I had had enough strength to do it. Once when I was sitting with my granny I became overwhelmed with an urge to tell her and be comforted. An uncle walked into the house just as I opened my mouth to speak, and the moment was lost. I twice tried to tell my Aunt Ellen. I went up to her house one night when I knew Morris would be at work, and panicked as I tried to say the words. I couldn't hurt her that much, and the moment passed.

Once I informed Siobhán that I was going to have to tell my aunt before she and Morris were married. They had asked me to be their bridesmaid and I was put in an impossible position. If I had said no, then everyone would have wanted to know why. So I went through the grotesque motions of the dress fittings and the endless wedding talk. I was seventeen years of age, part of a large, affectionate and respected family, but feeling deranged because of his abuse, and I had no idea what would happen if I opened my mouth. Most of all though, I just didn't want to hurt my aunt. But then I decided that enough was enough. I was due to be sleeping over with my aunt in Granny's the night before the wedding, we would be more or less alone, and I decided to tell her then. Siobhán asked me if I was 'fucking nuts'. She poured a glass of wine and then remarked about how my life would give *Eastenders* a run for its money. I smiled grimly, but I knew she was right. I was hardly going to do it on the eve of the wedding, it just wasn't the right time.

I spent the evening with my aunt, and when I eventually went to bed, I heard a shot from the alleyway behind the house in the early hours of the morning. I automatically connected the shooting – probably some poor unfortunate's kneecap being blasted to fragments – with the IRA. Morris was a dangerous individual, that stark fact was never out of my mind. I'd felt his rage. He pushed me past the point of pain sometimes. Here I was lying beside my aunt, who was about to marry this madman, and I thought to myself that I was disgusting for not opening my mouth. I was going to let her walk down the aisle, and time was running out, and I couldn't do it. I couldn't break her world.

I went through the motions the next day and stayed as far away from him as possible. He gave me a gift from him and his wife on the morning of the wedding. A gold Claddagh bracelet, with a heart inside two hands under a crown. I went to the bathroom and vomited.

I'd like to think that if I had known what I've learned since then I would have disclosed the truth after the first incident, but thinking about the shock that I felt at the time, I am unsure if

I would have. That's how abuse survives and abusers get away with it. Silence envelops it and keeps it secret. Shame compounds every thought that the abused person has. And abusers know it. They latch on to it and they seek out vulnerability and they use it for their gratification. They take their chances and they groom and they embarrass and they turn the person they are harming from a human being into a fragile shell. And, not content with that, they keep cracking at that shell until it starts to fracture into little splinters. Once the splintering happens, it's almost impossible to put the pieces back together.

7

Getting through each day at school was becoming much more difficult as September 1998 began – a year before the IRA came to me. Morris was regularly abusing me throughout that summer, and I was also trying to dodge other IRA ex-prisoners, some of them well known, who came out of jail on early release due to the Good Friday Agreement and gravitated towards young women like, as my granny would say, 'flies round shite'. I was mixing in older circles with people who had their own set of morals, had spent decades behind bars, were desensitised to death and excited by the exuberance of youth, and whose idea of flirtation ('intellectual conversations', to them) was drunkenly discussing Leonard Cohen or the philosopher Paulo Freire while trying to put their hands on your ass in the pub. Life was becoming increasingly claustrophobic.

Northern Ireland was now supposedly at peace, though it was a strange and volatile kind of peace. One month before, the Real IRA had murdered 29 people, including a mother pregnant with twins, in the market town of Omagh in County Tyrone, by detonating a car bomb in the small town's main street. Another 220 people were injured. A month before Omagh, the mainstream IRA shot thirty-three-year-old Andrew Kearney in the New Lodge area of Belfast, and left him to bleed to death. In July, three little children, Richard, Mark and Jason Quinn, were killed by loyalists, who firebombed their home at the height of the Drumcree marching dispute.*

The IRA was also still carrying out so-called 'punishment' attacks, mostly on young people engaging in anti-social behaviour, though republicans were also attempting to establish Community Restorative Justice (CRJ) as an alternative. My abuser was a senior community worker for CRJ in the Upper Springfield area, where, ironically, he had previously been part of a unit which administered the IRA's more brutal form of discipline against some of the very young people CRJ was trying to reach. †

I was drinking a lot by then and had developed an addiction to codeine, although I had convinced myself that I really needed the pills because of the constant headaches I was getting. Day-to-day school life was beginning to become unreal for me, and I drifted, existing from one day to the next. It was as if I had two heads for dealing with Marty Morris – the head that conversed with him if I saw him during the day, and the head that feared him and his approaches at night. It consumed all of my energy. When I wasn't being abused, I was remembering it. I began acting out, my clothes got baggier still, and I developed a razor-sharp tongue if people got too close for comfort. I bristled if someone invaded my space; it made me feel uncomfortable. Hugs were fine, mostly, because they were a safe form of contact for me, though I moved away if my parents reached out. Looking back, I was afraid that if I let my guard down with them, it would all come tumbling out. My parents were also starting to notice a change in me. I was

---

* Drumcree was a tinderbox of violence when Orangemen were stopped from walking through the nationalist Garvaghy Road in 1996. The confrontations continued for years until the parade was eventually banned. Every year, the Orange Order still hands a token letter of protest to police.
† Community Restorative Justice was established in Northern Ireland in 1998 to provide an alternative means of dispute resolution to paramilitary attacks on people. Traditionally, republicans carried out their own forms of rough justice on those who were deemed to be 'anti-social', frequently shooting people in the kneecaps. Community leaders knew an alternative was needed to move republicans away from physically attacking members of their own community.

becoming rebellious. I was seventeen, and didn't appreciate the rules and curfews my parents laid down. I argued constantly with my mother over Sinn Féin. She was worried that I would become involved in the IRA, and no matter how many times I told her I wouldn't join 'the Army', I couldn't convince her. It was the one topic that would guarantee an argument at home.

The last straw was added when I announced that I wanted to leave school. It was becoming too difficult for me to pretend that everything was all right, day after day. I was dangerously thin, my classmates noticed the loss in weight when I returned to school, the teachers were getting up my nose asking if I was okay, my parents were laying down the law and telling me I couldn't go out on school nights, and I snapped. I knew how much my mother in particular believed in education, and I needed some control. I announced I wasn't going back to school, lifted a spare shirt and walked out in tears with twenty pence in my pocket.

I lasted two weeks sofa-hopping with friends, until I decided to return to both home and school. The sixth form formal dance was approaching, and I had decided to go, with the help of my Uncle Jim, who offered to drive me there in his pride and joy – a flashy BMW. At thirty-six, Jim was my mother's younger brother, the one member of the family who was always full of fun, and I had seen or spoken to him nearly every day since I was born. He was a constant in my life. Music was his big passion, and he played in various bands for years. He owned a music shop on the Falls Road beside the Republican News Office, though he was afraid of anything to do with republicanism. He rented out and sold equipment, but he was too nice to be a businessman. Any money he made went towards his passions – guitars, CDs and cars. He had also recently bought a motorbike, and when he agreed to take me to the dance, he offered me a chance to try the bike out. I hopped onto the back and held onto him tightly as he drove me up the Andersonstown Road. It was scary, but enjoyable. I haven't been on a motorbike since.

Two days before the formal dance I still had no dress, but had arranged to go into Belfast city centre with a friend to buy one.

On our way, we called into the Sinn Féin youth office. My father's business was based in Conway Mill, with an adjoining door that led into the Sinn Féin offices, and my friend and I were laughing and joking when my dad put his head around the door and asked me to come outside. I knew instantly there was something wrong. I walked out onto the fire escape with him and he told me straight: 'Jim's dead. He was killed on his motorbike an hour ago.' My head started to spin, and his face blurred as tears pricked my eyes and shock kicked in and cushioned me from the reality of what I had just heard. I started to wobble, and my father caught me. A cry of pain lodged in my throat. Tears ran down my cheeks and into my mouth, leaving a salty taste. Sobs racked my body, and I could not catch my breath. My father pulled away, took my face in his hands and told me to get my bag, and we drove to my grandmother's house in Turf Lodge.

I stayed at my granny's that night, alone with her. Jim's body was too badly injured to be put in an open casket and the undertakers needed an extra night to patch him up, so we sat up without the body on the first night of the wake. We tried to hide our feelings for fear of upsetting each other, enveloped in the deathly silence of stopped clocks, broken only by Granny trying to hide her tears as reality came back and assaulted her in waves, slicing through the numbness that shock produced. I held her. We both cried, then returned to our silence. He wasn't coming back. My carefree, fun-loving big eejit of an uncle had driven his motorbike out in the sunshine that day, the sun that blinded his vision and stopped him from seeing the indicator of a bin lorry turning into St Louise's school, and the lorry knocked him off at speed, causing massive internal injuries, killing him outright. A black taxi driver whispered the act of contrition in his ear, which gave my granny some comfort. I hated God. I hated him for Jim, and for Marty Morris. More than anything, I watched my grandmother, who I loved more than life itself, break into pieces that night at the loss of her child, and my heart broke for her. Nothing was going to take away her pain, and I felt completely powerless. All I could do was pass hankies, hug her and sit in the silence and hear Jim's voice in my head, laughing and singing along to one of his favourite bands, Del Amitri. I sat with my grief, and nursed it, and mentally told God to go and fuck himself.

8

Towards the end of August 1999 I started focusing on the fact that I would be starting university in a matter of weeks. Moving on to the next stage of education is daunting enough for any eighteen-year-old – but I was crippled with fear. I came across as confident to most who knew me when I was working in the radio station, but inside I was extremely shy. I did badly in new situations and meeting new people. I didn't think I was likeable, or good enough to be around 'normal people'. I felt like damaged goods.

I was bright enough and should have done well in my A-levels, if my GCSE results were any marker of how I coped with exams. I sat the GCSEs before the abuse and achieved three A*, two As and four Bs. I chose Politics, English Literature and Irish for A-level, and should have come out with straight-A grades. I wanted to study law or journalism. Coping with what Morris was doing to me, a death in the family and other issues meant that I drifted through my last two years of school. I was disconnected from the academic subjects and from my former friends, whom I couldn't relate to any longer. When I should have been sitting in the common room laughing about discovering boys and what the latest fashion trends were, I spent a lot of time reading the broadsheets or sleeping my life away in the library. I lived the last year of school numbed out, addicted to the painkiller Kapake and other codeine-based drugs. My Politics teacher took me aside. He was worried I was being swallowed up by republicanism, and asked me if there was anything wrong.

'You're my best student, and you are going to throw your grade down the toilet,' he said.

And I did. The morning the results came I wouldn't get out of bed. My father brought them up to me in anticipation and tried to get me to open them in front of him. I put them under my pillow unopened and went back to sleep. In the end, I opened and closed them again and felt nothing. Two Bs and a C. I'd passed, but it wasn't good enough.

I enrolled in Politics, Politics and Law, Women's Studies and Psychology modules at Queen's University Belfast, but I was frightened at the prospect of being on the campus. I declined the opportunity from Queen's to be shown around the university because I was too shy to go in a group of people who I didn't know. I did attend the first few lectures and tutorials, but skipped most of them, and sat the first round of exams. Events then took a turn which made me unable to cope with full-time education.

In tandem with university, I was working every spare minute in the Sinn Féin Six County Office. It was a cold, damp cluster of offices stretched out along a corridor behind that steel security door. There were mice for company and at times a few two-legged rats. It was a busy network of offices, and ours was next to the press office where Eoin O'Broin, who later became a TD, was stationed. Ted Howell, an influential adviser, was based with ex-prisoner Sile Darragh down the corridor in the Foreign Affairs office – a nucleus for any negotiations in which Sinn Féin was involved. The Prisoner of War office was next door, which dealt with IRA men and women still in jail, and the late Seando Moore liked to decorate the place with various posters of republican icons.

I shared an office with Martina McIlkenny, Councillors Fra McCann and Sean McKnight, Margaret Adams, and later, Maureen McGuinness, Danny Power, and Tony Catney. Other Sinn Féin Cúige reps would drift in and out. Duties mainly consisted of typing, answering the telephone and attending weekly Cúige meetings. Sinn Féin split their party into Cúigí based on the four provinces of Ireland, though the Ulster Cúige consisted of the Northern Irish six counties only. I combined my work with my role as Ógra Shinn Féin (Sinn Féin Youth) National Secretary and the radio station – all of this voluntary, though I was paid twenty pounds a week from the Sinn Féin coffers for my trouble.

I enjoyed it for the most part, and it was certainly far from dull, a year after the major tensions at Drumcree in Portadown, County Armagh, when members of the Orange Order wanted to march down the largely Catholic and nationalist Garvaghy Road. Other marches were also contentious, and I protested against them with other Sinn Féin members at the Springfield Road in west Belfast and the Lower Ormeau Road. It didn't occur to me to question what I was being told by Sinn Féin, I just drank in all of it without question, largely because I was surrounded by people who were fanatics in varying degrees, and homogenous thinking was normal in this environment. On one occasion we wired up a pirate radio from a house on the Garvaghy Road so that they could broadcast to people in the local area.

That year I was also beaten by the RUC while taking part in a sit-down protest on the Lower Ormeau Road in south Belfast to block an Apprentice Boys march, and I ended up in hospital for a day. I had not intended to go to the protest at all, but had been waitressing in the Felons Club and other staff were travelling over to the demonstration in a taxi. A spontaneous decision to sit out all night with residents led to one of the strangest experiences of my life.

We sat in the dark watching street musicians, meeting and talking with people I hadn't seen since the last protest, eating stew and drinking cups of free tea supplied by the local residents. Someone brought out a projector and showed the film *Braveheart* on the gable wall of a house. At the point when Mel Gibson, face painted blue and white, rode in front of the Scottish army on his horse shouting, 'They may take our lives, but they'll never take our freedom!', the crowd on the street let out an almighty roar of approval. It was at that moment I realised that the protest would probably turn nasty. There was no way out, and the police had sealed off the roads.

The siren sounded in the early hours of the morning to call protesters from where they were mingling on the sides of the road to sit on the road itself. I sat down at what I thought was the back of the protest until we were all told to turn around and I found myself in the front row. The sight of the riot squad, batons drawn and shields at the ready, made me think that Braveheart had an easier time of it with the army of Edward I. They moved in slowly and menacingly as their jeeps advanced. The protesters sang a chorus of 'Always look on the bright side of life' and swayed their heads in unison. The late Mickey Ferguson, a Sinn Féin MLA, sat on the road on one side of me and former Sinn Féin MLA Sue Ramsey on the other.

I was afraid, but I couldn't show it. I sang with the rest of them. One drunken eejit stood up and shouted, 'I'm Spartacus!' Someone shouted for him to be taken out of the crowd when he stood up again and shouted at the waiting media, 'SS BBC, you killed our people's princess!' in reference to the death of Diana, Princess of Wales. The Apprentice Boys parade wasn't due for a few hours, and the police lines picked off protesters one by one while pointing out targets and hitting them with their batons. It took six of them to lift Sue, her trousers falling down as they pulled at her, and one of her trainers was left behind on the road. I got clocked on the head with a baton but managed to avoid being dragged out. I ended up with the last of the protesters, hemmed in from both sides by members of the riot squad. Someone played the song 'Fenians' from a loudspeaker – a song by New York band Seanchaí. Their chorus of 'I will stay an unrepentant Fenian bastard' was swiftly followed by a version of the Labi Siffre song 'Something inside so strong' sung by Belfast IRA man Bik McFarlane and his co-singer 'Cruncher'.

An RUC man with a riot shield shoved it against my back in an attempt to move the last remaining protesters together. Gerard Rice, the spokesperson for the residents, realised we were going to be annihilated if we stayed there any longer and moved the last of the protesters into a side street, where a melee ensued. The road was now clear for the bands to march through, and we could hear the music as the RUC charged people at the end of the street while being pelted with bottles. I was taken off to the Royal Victoria Hospital in an ambulance with a former IRA prisoner,

Rosa, and her boyfriend Barry, who had sustained matching black eyes. I didn't really question at the time why I was protesting. I attended automatically, and I had witnessed some disgraceful, provocative behaviour from the Orange bands previously. On one occasion, I had walked with the Orange bands, microphone recording the music for a news report, when an Orangeman left the march to ask me who I was there on behalf of. When I told him it was Festival Radio, he snarled in my face as they struck up the well-known tune 'The Sash': 'Is the music loud enough for you?' As the band passed, an observer with muscly tattooed arms shouted 'Up the UDA!'*

I was also caught up in the Springfield Road riots. For decades, the Orange Order had marched to their old lodge building on the Springfield Road, past nationalist houses. Local residents wanted this to stop. The rain pelted down, and some residents were completely out of order in the way in which they lifted and hurled anything they had to hand to attack the police lines, particularly because it resulted in the RUC discharging baton rounds. Protestors were angry – the atmosphere was charged with an electrifying intensity of danger and outrage and fear. It was also exciting. Young people sometimes get attracted to anarchy and disorder, and I was no different. I was too afraid of the consequences to lift and throw a stone or a bottle, but I stood in the middle of it all and watched the madness unfurl around me.

The first Orange band I ever saw that didn't display the old triumphalism was outside my house in 2013. My friend was playing in the local band in Derry and I took my daughter out to watch. The Churchill flute band's music was good; they marched in their pristine white shirts playing silver concert flutes to the beat of a large bass drum as the sun shone down upon them. I didn't feel offended. Then again, they weren't playing blood-and-thunder music, nor was I hemmed in my house half the day, as Catholics sometimes had been in the past. I turned on the TV later that

---

* Ulster Defence Association, an Ulster loyalist paramilitary organisation.

day to see riots in Belfast and I remembered my own attendance at similar events. I hated being viewed as inferior because of my religion, and I hated the way songs like 'The Billy Boys' ('Hoorah, hoorah, we are the Billy Boys/Up to our knees in Fenian blood') were played as soon as the louder Belfast bands reached nationalist housing estates. I hated the cat-calls and the waft of hatred from both sides drifting across the air like a potent spell.

Later that night in 2013, I watched online footage of loyalists burning an effigy of a Belfast priest I had known, Father Matt Wallace, on a bonfire, and I was sickened to my stomach. I argued with a Protestant friend that senior loyalists had been calling on people for years to break the law, and that they were probably sitting in the comfort of their armchairs while their minions, young Protestant working-class men, earned criminal records for their drunken venting of anger. To my surprise he agreed with me.

Back in 1999, I hated what I saw as the naked sectarianism of the Orange Order, their traditionalist views and their exclusion of Catholics from membership. It didn't occur to me that it was a useful propaganda vehicle for Sinn Féin to use until I later found archive footage of Gerry Adams speaking at the West Belfast Festival in 1997, stating:

> Once we saw the people of Garvaghy Road were in trouble, the people right across Belfast mobilised. And I was at rallies in north Belfast which were bigger than rallies … even during the hunger strikes. If the Unionist and the Brits want to play the numbers game, let us play that game as well.[5]

In later years, as an SDLP councillor I went from protester to bystander when I was invited to watch a Black Preceptory parade in Tyrone. I took my daughter Saorlaith with me, and she twirled a red, white and blue band-stick as she danced to the beat of the drum. Northern Irish traditional lines are rarely crossed, and as a politician I wanted to honour the invitation by being respectful. Country loyalist bands are markedly different from inner-city Belfast, and the atmosphere is more relaxed. We had great fun walking in the field beforehand and drinking cups of tea with friends. The man in charge left the parade to shake our hands and make us feel welcome. There was only one blip that day when a young person, face contorted with hate, shouted over at me something about being a Fenian disgrace. I shook it off and thought back to when I was younger, and how my views and fixed political positions had mellowed.

In the late 1990s, the Six County office usually buzzed around marching season and Belfast Sinn Féin had watch committees which operated from their local constituency advice centres. I would sit up at night as part of a rota, taking phone calls from people who were at trouble hotspots. Once, we did nothing except log incidents and watch *Jerry Springer* with a man I knew as Marty Fox, but who used the name John as he had been adopted as a child. Marty, who is now dead, ran Sinn Féin's advice centre and was gay. Every time a guest on *Springer* said something contentious, he would shout out 'Ach, thon's a dickhead', or 'Oh mammy!'

Election times were also extremely busy, and I loved being part of them. Maths was never my strong point, but I had a knack for predicting the correct number of seats, quotas and votes. I worked closely with Tony Catney (known as TC), the Sinn Féin director of elections. He was fun to work with, and the only person in Sinn Féin at that time who ever challenged me to have an opinion of my own and not to trust 'the Leadership' for their views. He was also one of the few republican men at the time who didn't 'chance his arm' with me, as my granny would say. TC was controversial, but he was interested in my views and asked me to oversee aspects of election campaigns in Antrim, which helped to give me a bit of confidence and think for myself. We later crossed paths again when he had a public spat with the Sinn Féin leadership and established a rival political organisation, Republican Network for Unity. He was also alleged to be a leading figure in the Real IRA, and separately, a British agent, prior to his death in 2014, both of which he denied when I asked him about it.

It may seem strange to those who have not been brought up steeped in republicanism that someone like me, who was obviously being traumatised by the IRA, would continue to work for their political wing. It is strange for me too, in retrospect. Republicanism is like one large dysfunctional family. When inside it, you belong. Step outside it, and you are isolated, cut off and frequently the target of rumour or innuendo. It was simply easier to remain inside, and it was what I knew. I also enjoyed politics very much and I was living day to day. I didn't have the capacity to see things clearly, or to envisage a life different to the one I had. At that time, it was a bonus to get to the end of the week in one piece.

Northern Ireland was taking fledgling steps toward peace, and there was a concerted effort to move Irish republicans away from violence and to develop a genuine political project. Sinn Féin were resolutely opposed to the RUC and held numerous protests with placards calling for the force to be disbanded. On one occasion, under the leadership of Bik McFarlane, Sinn Féin blocked traffic in and out of the CastleCourt underground car park in Belfast city centre to force the closure of an RUC 'information shop', which had been set up in response to rising crime levels. Sinn Féin's Gerry Kelly hailed the protests at CastleCourt as showing 'what can be achieved by grassroots campaigning … Pickets combined with concerted lobbying can achieve results, and the closure of the CastleCourt barracks is just a small example of the potential which exists.'[6] He didn't happen to mention that as part of the car park protest, a woman with a crying baby was trapped for ages underground, in tears, pleading to be allowed to go home. Perhaps he simply didn't see her.

In November 1999, as the leader of the Ulster Unionist Party David Trimble was trying to convince his party to share power with Sinn Féin, and Martin McGuinness had been nominated as Northern Ireland's Education Minister, sending shockwaves throughout the unionist community, the IRA was still active and showing no signs of retiring. And while the political melodrama played out in Stormont and on the streets, I was being taken to the living rooms of IRA safe houses and repeatedly questioned about my sexual abuse. Unable to continue with my university studies as the IRA investigation dragged on, I dropped out. I had no long-term plans for my future, because at that time, I couldn't see one.

9

Remember O most gracious Virgin Mary that never was it known, that anyone who fled to thy protection, implored thy help, or sought thine intercession, was left unaided.

The Memorare Prayer

Even though I had cut all ties with God after Jim died, I found myself in times of stress reciting the above lines from the Memorare prayer, in a mantra-like way, just in case. It's a Catholic thing. You stop believing and then in the strangest of moments, those words, rote-learned from primary school, pop into your head subconsciously. Suffice to say, Mary never saved me even though I asked her over and over for her help.

I could never accept the fact that I was sitting meeting with *them*. The enormity of accepting that reality was too much. I have no idea how I, as an eighteen-year-old, managed to get through it. So when I found myself talking to the imaginary Mother of God, I was really hoping against hope that the IRA would fuck off to high heaven themselves. I can feel the nervousness I felt at the time rising up now as I write this. I don't think that feeling will ever go away.

I hadn't asked for their investigation, and I was scared of them. I was clearly traumatised from the abuse, and they were meddling in things that made my mental state, and my ability to deal with the most intimate part of my life, so much worse. I wasn't in control, and that feeling of being completely helpless was also a throwback to the abuse and compounded the difficulties I was having. It felt like I was being abused all over again. There was also the fact that their 'meetings' were happening almost daily, and I was rarely given advance notice of when they would happen. They would usually take place in one of the Andersonstown flats or in the Women's Centre, but occasionally the women would come in when I was waitressing, or to the Sinn Féin centre, or telephone the radio station if they were unable to reach me. Sometimes it was as simple as coming out of a building and finding Breige Wright's car there, and she would wave me over.

I was eighteen years old, legally an adult, though not yet free of childhood. Life, for me, was suspended; I swung between wanting to be like other young adults and taking responsibility for my studies, and going out in the world, but instead felt as if I were on a hamster wheel being spun by the IRA. Senior republicans who terrified me because of what they represented were telling me that 'this is the way it's going to be', and that they had an absolute right to probe into the most disturbing and upsetting parts of my life. I was embarrassed and felt constantly ill. I couldn't talk to anyone about it because I was warned not to. I was also wondering whether or not this was ultimately going to lead to my death. People have asked me why I didn't run, why I didn't tell someone, why I didn't tell them to fuck off. I did try on two occasions that I can remember, but I had really nowhere to go, and they sent for me anyway. I tried to tell them it was none of their business, but that didn't work. They were in control of the neighbourhoods that I lived and worked in, and the IRA ruled that entire area of the city with absolute authority. Had it been about anything else, I might have done things differently, but the subject matter of this 'investigation' meant that I was dying inside with embarrassment, and afraid of where the whole thing was going to lead. I had no way out and was completely under their control.

Not knowing in advance when they were coming to get me meant that I was constantly living in a state of hyperarousal. American physiologist Walter Cannon coined the phrase 'fight or flight' to explain the body's physical reaction to stress. At the time, all I knew was that I felt ill and nervous, and I could never make plans because I knew I would have to cancel them if they decided I had to meet the IRA 'investigators'. I lost a lot of weight with sheer worry. I was, in short, conditioned to do what the IRA said I should do, except that I retained a slight degree of autonomy by having a 'fuck you' mentality. I tried to make it mask just how afraid I was, but I'm sure they knew.

Looking back now, I don't understand why it lasted months, though I later heard they blamed the longevity of their 'investigation' on my inability to speak in detail about what Morris had done to me.

And that inability was profound. Think of the worst sexual experience you've ever had. Now, slow it down. Think about where the person put their hands, how many fingers were used, what it felt like, what position you were in. Uncomfortable? Imagine you are sitting in a room with two or more people who you don't like, who scare you. Could you answer questions about that experience as an adult? I doubt it. As an eighteen-year-old who had suffered at the hands of a sexual abuser, it was next to impossible for me.

The IRA barked questions, or at least Maura McCrory did. The other woman was mostly softer, but they were still the same questions, and I still couldn't answer them. Their good cop/scary cop routine was exhausting and beyond anything I can ever describe effectively. And it was having an impact on my life. My mother, concerned at the weight I was losing and the obvious stress I was under, came up one night to my bed where I was lying after a row and asked: 'What's wrong Máiría, has anybody touched you?'

I had been told by the IRA that I couldn't tell anyone, and so petrified was I at the consequences of doing so that I simply rolled away from my mother's touch. If anyone is in doubt about the power that a secretive armed organisation can have over a young person's mind, this moment illustrates it perfectly for me. I couldn't even tell my own parents.

At one point I asked the IRA to allow me to speak to someone outside the movement, as I couldn't deal with the secrecy. I wanted to talk to someone at the Rape Crisis Centre in confidence, and argued with my inquisitors that it was unfair of the IRA to expect me not to be able to talk about the impact events were having on me. They were left in no doubt that raking up my abuse, in the way they were doing it, was causing me great distress. A week or so later they told me that they were going to be very 'good' to me and break with procedure, and they were going to 'allow' me to talk to somebody.

That somebody was Gerry Adams's secretary, my cousin Siobhán O'Hanlon. I was relieved, because I trusted her, stupidly as it turns out. I didn't know at that time that everything I was saying to Siobhán – my fears and feelings and the innermost thoughts in my head – was being relayed straight back to my inquisitors. The IRA, of course, picked Siobhán because she was their volunteer, but also because I had already disclosed my abuse to her about a year before the IRA 'investigation' began. The organisation was not risking anything by telling her, but was instead gaining a valuable asset. She had my trust, which meant that she was invaluable to the IRA as an information source. She was also a member of the Cahill family; her mother Tess was my grandfather's sister. As such, she had a level of access to information within the wider family unit, critical for the organisation if they decided to inform them. For me, she was a woman whom I needed to speak to, to offload my fright, worries and abusive memories to. Like an idiot, I believed that my conversations were confidential.

On one occasion the IRA women had been asking questions and as usual I hadn't been able to answer them. Breige left me in the room on my own with Maura. We sat in silence, save for when she cleared her throat from time to time and stared at me. It was extremely uncomfortable. Maura McCrory was around the same age as my grandmother. I had been brought up to respect my elders, but I had no respect whatsoever for her. Her age was not the problem. Her manner towards me was hostile from the start, and I was acutely aware that she had the weight of an armed group behind her. I was being forced to prove that I was telling the truth to the people that were so terrifying to me. She also had a way of talking to me in a monotone that would have me digging my fingernails into my skin. I had never met, and have never met since, a woman like Maura McCrory. Quiet and controlled, yet aggressive and abrupt when she wanted to be, I felt intensely that she was watching my every move. When the IRA was frustrated that I was unable to speak, it was Maura who communicated that angry impatience forcefully to me.

10

Looking back now at the 'statements' I made to the IRA, they are childish. Written in a scrawl, they contain very little detail. I remember vividly sitting at a table scribbling them down. Forcing myself to remember. Little detail, but enough. I wrote about the first incident, another was distinguished by the memory of drinking Bacardi Breezers beforehand, and one when I had my period. It is uncomfortable reading them over again, but I imagine much more uncomfortable for my mother, who found a copy of the statements some years later hidden in my bedroom and reading them broke her heart.

After I handed those 'statements' to Breige Wright, I spent a long time mortally ashamed that people who I didn't know, never mind like, would know what had happened to me.

I didn't want to write any more, or any more detail, and though they asked I couldn't do it, and I didn't want to remember. I just wanted it and them to go away. Either I was a liar or I was telling the truth. They had to decide that. I didn't know or care about their internal procedures.

But Morris was one of *them*. He was also considerably older than me; a hard man with a reputation not only for toeing the republican line, but also for dishing it out. Inevitably, the feeling that the IRA had the ultimate power over life and death never left my mind. He had himself talked with me about IRA 'justice' during a row one night about so-called punishment beatings, which I argued against. He explained the IRA's position, eyes dancing with excitement. He raped me a few hours later, which pumped the adrenaline out of him.

At no stage did I think they would believe me over him. When he eventually left Ballymurphy in August 2000, the local young people held a bonfire party at Whiterock Leisure Centre to celebrate with lots of drink and chants of 'burn burn burn Marty Morris'. Someone spray painted graffiti on the main wall along the Whiterock Road as word broke that a newspaper article was printing allegations of abuse against him: 'Marty Morris is a bull root.'* I didn't know what 'a bull root' was, but Sinn Féin members were out painting over it in the early hours of the morning. It didn't occur to me during the IRA 'investigation' that he would really be punished. I believed the punishment was destined for me, and I don't remember anyone assuaging that fear.

Around halfway through the 'meetings' I became anxious about my family finding out. My granny was elderly and vulnerable and had already lost her beloved son, and I knew my parents would be devastated if and when they found out. One indication of exactly how outlandish my thinking was at the time is that I believed it would be better for the IRA to kill me than for them to go to my parents. Once my parents found out what had happened, in March 2000, my thinking changed. But that is what the IRA did – they hammered me so much mentally that I almost willed them to put me out of my misery. I was at rock bottom. They put me there, through their constant questions, their aggressive, sceptical manner, and the length of time they took to question me. The constant instructions and implied threats. The confrontations. And through their insistence on becoming involved in the first place.

After I gave them the handwritten notes, the two women nitpicked every line, read them in front of me and made me answer their questions all over again. I was dying of shame. They

---

* The *Urban Dictionary* definition of a bull root is 'a bell end of unimaginable proportions. A complete and utter cunt.'

made it very clear that they had to remain impartial, that Morris was innocent until proven guilty, that it was my word against his, that they were partaking in the first stage of a 'court of inquiry'.

An IRA court of inquiry, according to the organisation's *Green Book* (the name given to the IRA constitution), is 'set up to investigate allegations against any member of the Army'. It is normally held with three members presiding, witnesses are sworn in and 'testimony' is provided. It is modelled on the normal criminal justice system's 'preliminary investigative hearings'. In the latter, a judge presides in a courtroom, but an IRA 'court' is held in someone's living room, with witnesses watched over by an army volunteer in a bedroom. Whereas in a court hearing a magistrate has to decide whether the evidence threshold has been met in order to refer a defendant to crown court for trial, an IRA hearing decides whether to submit the accused volunteer to a court martial. The IRA representatives in my case were tasked with gathering evidence so that it could be heard in a court of inquiry. Their dilemma was that I was refusing to take part.

Their other problem was that it was taking a long time, and they often told me they were under pressure to wrap the whole thing up. The IRA were afraid of word leaking out before they had finished. I kept stalling. At first, as I've said, I sat and said nothing and told them I was too embarrassed to speak. Seamus Finucane was brought in intermittently, but I would only answer in nods or shake my head, and it was clear that he was in charge and trying to hurry the women up. Frequently I asked them why they were insisting on an IRA 'investigation' that I did not want. That usually resulted in a lecture from him about how they had explained that to me over and over. I began to act as if I was stupid. On more than one occasion I felt pressure to withdraw my written account of the 'incidents', which they were now treating as a statement. If I did, I thought, I would be accused of slandering an IRA volunteer. The IRA would then swap the pointed finger at my face for a gun.

Their questions, trying to pick holes in what little I had told them, were unbearable. 'You said you had a few tins of Harp, were you drunk?'

'No, a bit fuzzy.'
'After three tins of Harp, just a bit fuzzy?'
'Did this happen, Máiría?'
I nodded.
'You were sleeping?'
Another nod.
'Then how did you know what he did? How did you know it was him? What did it feel like?'
I exploded. 'Why are you asking me this?'
'We need to hear you telling us, so we know whether you are telling the truth or not. How many fingers? How did you know? Did you see him?'

And on and on and on, for around five months. Sometimes every day, sometimes twice a week. Sometimes for an hour while they clarified something to their own satisfaction, sometimes far longer.

11

After five months, something changed. I had tried to escape the IRA investigation a month before and went to Dublin to stay for a few days with Sinn Féin's National Secretary Lucilita Bhreatnach, who was then a friend. The pressure was indescribable. I felt like I was in a goldfish bowl, the IRA appeared to know my every move and I feared I was constantly being watched. This was probably true – they knew too much about where I had been, which bar I had gone into, who I had visited. At the end of February they began to convey an elevated sense of urgency. The emphasis now was that they had to put Morris's rights as a volunteer to the fore and that I was denying his rights by not cooperating. They said they were nearing the stage for a hearing, which I now know was for their proposed kangaroo court, but they needed to explore all the options first. I was, as you can imagine, scared of going into a hearing, which I suspected would be even more hostile to me than McCrory and Finucane had been.

While I was speaking to Siobhán, after I had been given 'permission' by the IRA, it wasn't enough. It was a confusing relationship. Sometimes she would simply put her arms around me and let me lie on her shoulder, and other times, she told me I just had to get on with it and do what the IRA said. I had defied them and spoken to a woman whom I will call Aoife, who had previously been jailed for spying for the IRA. I explained that there was an IRA inquiry going on, who was involved, and that they had mentioned moving towards a hearing. She explained to me what a court martial was and who was likely to hear the evidence. That allowed me to understand what their likely next move would be.

We were back in the flat in Kenard Avenue in west Belfast, which I now knew belonged to the senior IRA woman Marie Wright. Marie, while she was in jail, had been Officer Commanding (OC) among the prisoners there. She had been released under the Good Friday Agreement two years previously, and immediately involved herself once more in IRA activity.* She provided her home to the IRA for use in their 'investigation'. Breige Wright was her sister.

'You need to start talking, because you are going to have to do it in front of other people,' Maura McCrory said. This induced a new wave of panic in me. It became clear to me that this was going to happen soon. Finucane said that the IRA were going to have to inform Marty Morris of their inquiry. There was another discussion about how it wasn't fair to have Morris kept in the dark, about how he had rights and how they needed to move the process forward quickly.

They said they were going to him that night. I went home, lay in bed and prayed. I wasn't religious by then but I talked to dead people. I talked to my Uncle Jim who had died the year before. To my two grandas. I called up every dead person and saint that I could think of. I asked them to look after me and I prayed that they would get Morris to admit what he had done. I was in the middle of a living nightmare, and I wanted it to be over. I found my old school tie and tied it around my neck. I strapped one end to the pine bannisters in the attic of my parents' house and I tried to lower myself onto my own weight. I dangled for around two seconds then found the nearest stair with my foot. I couldn't do it; I was too afraid. I was afraid of fucking everything. I got back into my single bed, buried my face in my pillow and sobbed.

I spent much of the next day in pure panic, going through the motions but not really making sense to myself. My stomach was

---

* Marie Wright died of leukaemia in 2004.

cramping with nerves, and I tried to keep busy. I had a waitressing shift at a café on the Falls Road near to the Women's Centre which started at 5 p.m., and at 6 p.m. the women walked in, nodded and walked straight up to the middle floor. That was my cue to leave what I was doing and follow them. Looking back now, the others who saw me leave must have known I was meeting the IRA, because a room was made available to them with no questions and no interruptions.

It was a fairly big room with green pot plants. We took our place in a corner of the meeting room. The IRA women sat near the door on standard chairs, and I took the other one which had been pulled over for me and sat facing them.

The previous evening, the IRA had given me several 'options'. I had the sense to write them down when I got home, and I passed that note to the police in 2010. One option was to withdraw my accusations completely; or I could confront Morris with the senior IRA people present; or they could run a court of inquiry with the information they had. I could start talking and give them more detail, or I could allow them to put the rape allegations to him as well as the three incidents I had written down, which didn't include the rapes. It became apparent that the IRA had chosen the option for me, and I circled the one that they were leaning towards. They wanted to put me in a room with my abuser.

It was Maura who told me that the allegations had been put to Morris. I flinched. I had convinced myself that he would admit it since I had given them as little as possible, and that he would think that he was off the hook. All they were putting to him was the digital penetration – and I believed that surely he would be able to see that it would be easier for him to admit those incidents than own up to everything he had done to me?

'Well, did he admit it?' I said, hoping against hope that they would tell me he had.

'He's denying it,' said the other IRA woman.

I completely lost it, one of the few times I let them see me show how upset I was. I flew up off my chair, stomped out of the room and tried to slam the heavy fire door, punched the bannister and hissed 'Bastard!'

I went down through the restaurant trying to hold it together and into the disabled toilet, locked the door, slid down the wall and cried. I couldn't breathe properly. I heard a knock on the door and Aoife, who had been working downstairs in the restaurant and had seen me, asked to be let in. I told her they had put it to him and that he had denied it, and she put her arms around me and I cried onto her shoulder. She cupped my wet face in her hand, asked where the other two women were, and told me to dry my tears and get back up to them.

'Don't let them see you crying,' she said. I dried my eyes and my nose, splashed water on my face and went back to them.

'We know you are upset, was that a surprise to you? We thought he would deny it,' said Breige.

'He should just tell the fucking truth,' I spat back.

'Máiría,' she replied, 'we have decided that we are going to bring the two of you into a room tomorrow. Sometimes in cases like these we can read people's body language to see who is telling the truth.'

It didn't occur to me then that this was a grotesquely damaging idea. I had just been through five months of constant questioning, and I was mentally and physically exhausted. But I didn't feel like I had a choice. If I had, I would never have allowed them to put me in a room with my abuser and three other IRA members.

They picked me up the next evening from the West Belfast Festival office on the Falls Road. I was extremely nervous. I had a carton of Sukie orange juice and I was shaking so much I spilled it over myself in the back seat of the car. I had been sick all day thinking about having to confront Morris, and the comment about reading my body language made me think that I had to be careful of every move. I felt that I was about to be put on trial.

When we got to Marie Wright's flat in Kenard Avenue, I sat down on the right-hand side of the settee near the wall, and Maura McCrory took the chair facing me to the right at the door to the kitchen. The other woman made a cup of tea.

I heard the door open and then the echoing sound of footsteps coming up the linoleum tiled stairs, and the living-room door behind me opened. I stopped shaking, I became completely and weirdly calm, and I sat in silence. I kept my eyes focused on the wall in front of me so that I wouldn't react when he came in. I once again dug my fingernails into my skin, something I had learned to do subconsciously since his abuse had started.

Morris sat down on the chair at the left near the window. Finucane sat on the floor beside him on the edge of the fireplace and proceeded to take his trainers off. He joked a bit with Morris about how he'd better not complain that he had smelly feet. Comrades having a little laugh to break the ice. I was disgusted. I remember seeing out of the corner of my eye McCrory studying me and then looking at him. Breige came back into the room and sat to the left of me with a notebook and pen. Morris, for his part, looked as if he hadn't got a care in the world – as if all of this was a minor inconvenience to him.

After a brief speech from Finucane about what we were here for, he asked Morris if he had anything he wanted to say to me. I don't know what I was expecting, perhaps some devious expression of sympathy and regret, but instead Morris launched into a vitriolic tirade about how much of a fucking sick bastard I was, that my head was wired up to the Black Mountain (a hill that is the backdrop to west Belfast), I was a lying bastard, how the fuck could I say he did this to me, on and on. I sat there and took it. No one stopped him or tried to moderate his language, they simply sat back and observed the show.

Finucane had the three pieces of paper I had written on months before, and he passed them to Morris. Then came the most mentally damaging part of the whole process. He read my notes out loud, which was a fraction of the abuse he subjected me to. Here's an example: '... Again, after it he sat and smoked a cigarette. Nothing different about this except I made more noise and turned as if I was waking up – but again he didn't stop.' Another:

> ... I remember after it that he went into the bathroom and was sick. He then came back and smoked while sitting on the edge of the settee. After he had gone up the stairs, I waited about an

hour and checked for blood on my clothes and settee. I changed my clothes and washed myself and went into my granny's the next morning so I didn't have to face him.

Deeply personal, and deeply upsetting. He was enjoying it, I could see that, but it was painfully obvious that I couldn't bank on the IRA members present doing anything about that. Flecks of spit were flying from his mouth and when he came to one of the lines in the statement that said 'then he went to bed', he read it wrong and thought it said 'we went to bed'. I clarified that the word was 'he'. Finucane took the paper off him and read the sentence aloud once more and confirmed what I'd written. My face was now burning with embarrassment.

When he said, 'You're saying I did this? How could I do that with my wife in the house?'

I snapped back: 'And that's what makes you a bastard.' I hissed the words at him. Breige stopped writing and turned to me with a shocked look on her face.

The two women said very little during this verbal onslaught. Then I asked Finucane if I could say something.

I looked Morris in the eyes and as calmly as I could said: 'This is the point where you throw your hands up and say, "I did this." See, as far as I'm concerned I am not asking for anything else, I'm not even looking for an apology from you – after this you can go back to your fucking life and do whatever you want, but as long as these people know what the truth is, I know and you know what you did and you don't do this to anyone else again.'

He told me that I was a sick fucker. The man was at least consistent in his horrible violence and contempt.

Finucane told me to go into one of the bedrooms and the two women came in. I was nearly eating my knuckles with rage as I sat on the edge of the double bed. I wanted to hit something or someone.

Maura said to me, 'You're very angry.' As if she was surprised.

'Fucking right I'm angry, you'd be angry too if someone was calling you a liar at the other end of the room. I'm not leaving here until he admits this,' I said.

'He's not going to admit it if he hasn't admitted it by now,' Breige said.

They took me back into the room and Finucane said that obviously there had not been a 'resolution' and we were told not to discuss it with anybody until they decided what to do. Morris then left with Finucane. Breige told me to get into her car and asked me where I wanted to be dropped off. I couldn't go back to my parents in the state I was in so I told her to bring me to the Felons Club, a republican drinking club for ex-prisoners, where I could at least go upstairs and collect my thoughts.

Five minutes into the journey, the past few hours in that claustrophobic flat caught up with me. I shouted to her to stop the car, she hit the brake, I opened the door and vomited onto the street until there was nothing left. Then I lit a cigarette and smoked it out of her window. Once at the Felons Club, I leapt out of her car, slammed the door in anger, punched the wall on my way in, went to the bar, ordered a double vodka, drank it straight and rang Siobhán O'Hanlon. I was livid. I told her about the confrontation they'd staged with Morris and she asked me if he had denied it. I told her yes. She told me to come to her flat. I immediately ordered a taxi.

When I arrived, Siobhán was sitting with her baby son on her knee. A friend of hers was also there, so I had to act normally, though my insides were churning. The friend didn't stay long, and when she left, Siobhán asked me what had happened. Words did not come easily. The phone rang and Siobhán handed the baby to me. I concentrated on putting my finger into his tiny hand and watching his fingers curling around it. He had beautiful brown eyes and I calmed down and spoke gently to him.

She returned, took the child and sat on the sofa opposite. She asked me what I thought would happen. I didn't know. I was so angry at the fact that Morris had sat in front of others and denied ever laying a finger on me, that he'd been allowed to rant and swear at me. Had I been discussing this with anyone else, they might rightly have been outraged. In retrospect, I realise that Siobhán's primary loyalty was to the IRA, while trying to keep me onside.

When I got home, I immediately went up to bed, pulled the duvet over my head for comfort and allowed myself to cry again. His harsh, impudent voice was swirling around in my head. The uncertainty about their intentions meant that I was feeling an inordinate amount of fear, and I had no way of easing it. I would just have to wait it out until they came back yet again looking for me.

12

I knew at least that something would happen quickly. The IRA woman telephoned the next day telling me to go back to the now all-too-familiar flat in Kenard Avenue. As usual, I made excuses to my parents and left. When I arrived, the two women and Finucane were waiting for me.

The IRA was having 'discussions', they told me solemnly, and reiterated that Morris had rights. They were very caring about his rights. They had taken the decision to bring a family member in, in order to speak with someone so they would gain a clearer picture of how my family would react. The IRA now had another problem on their hands. It wasn't going to stay quiet forever, and they didn't know my parents or what they would do. Siobhán knew my dad but she didn't know my mother, and so the IRA needed someone else. They said they were going to speak to one of my uncles who they knew, and who they could be confident would adhere to the IRA code of *omerta* until they could stage manage the business of others finding out. I was stunned and said very little. I zoned out and stared at my hands.

The IRA's person of choice was my father's older brother. He had two nicknames, 'Cack' and 'Wee Boots'. The former related to the inability of some people in west Belfast to pronounce our surname properly – 'Cahill' became 'Cackle', and so most of us were called 'Cack' at one time or another. The latter was a nickname usually used by republicans who knew him. Cack had been detained in prison for suspected IRA activity, once on the word of supergrass Robert Lean, who retracted his evidence, which resulted in charges being dropped. Cack left Belfast in the early 1980s to live in Dundalk, returning to Belfast after the birth of his second child. He was a familiar part of my life, as were most of my uncles. He was a small man, well respected in republican circles. I liked him.

After the IRA spoke to me, I was sent to Siobhán's flat in the next street to wait. My leg was shaking, and I wasn't able to control it. Siobhán initially tried to keep me talking, in an effort to stem my nerves, but I wasn't able to control my panic. There was a piece of artwork on the wall, a painting of a prison cell window illuminating a black background. I had looked at it many times, and wondered what Siobhán had thought about in her own prison cell. I felt trapped, and couldn't get my thoughts into any coherent order.

We sat for around an hour, mostly in silence broken every now and again by the coos of her son, who I was now holding. I focused on bringing up his wind. The two IRA women eventually came, and Maura lifted the baby from me and started animatedly talking to him. This was a softer side to her that I had never seen.

Belfast was a harsh place, and most of the republican women I knew were no exception to the hard rule. Any semblance of a gentler femininity was lost as the women of the republican movement tried to be coarser, ballsier and tougher than their male counterparts. There were exceptions, but they were few and far between. Some of this was due to living in rough inner-city areas, some of it to a romanticised notion of everyone having to be self-sacrificing (families included) in the struggle to free Ireland. But most of it was derived from having to prove themselves in a patriarchal army structure where women were publicly espoused as the 'backbone' of the movement, yet privately treated as commodities and domestic servants. They were useful for gathering information, for dealing with the finer details, or for making up the numbers on active service units so as not to arouse the suspicion of the police or British army. They rarely held leadership positions within the structure.

Maura McCrory was a tough woman, and I was scared of her. To see her dandling Siobhán's son on her knee and talking nonsense to him in gentle tones unnerved me more than being on the receiving end of her brash, no-nonsense questioning.

Breige gestured to Siobhán to go with her and left me with Maura and the baby. I stared at the wooden floor, not wanting to make eye contact, but it also helped me to try and concentrate on what was being said between the two women in the kitchen. I could understand little, except a few words here and there. When they returned, I was told that the IRA women were going round to the flat in Kenard and that I was to wait in Siobhán's for a call, and then follow them. The call came around forty minutes later. I stood up to go and Siobhán hugged me and told me to try not to worry. I wanted to stay enveloped in her arms with my head on her shoulder, but knew I had to leave. I went out into the blackness of the night and walked for a few minutes into the next street. I was so unnerved that I went to the wrong house and had to make up the name of a person I was looking for to the pissed-off man who answered the door in his boxer shorts, and apologise further when the fictitious person turned out not to live there.

I retraced my steps. The outer door was slightly ajar and I walked up the dark staircase and pushed open the door. Breige met me in the hall, steered me towards the bedroom on the left and told me to wait there. I sat uncomfortably on the edge of the green and yellow bedspread and stared at the wall. I could hear muffled voices from the living room, and what seemed to be some sort of a civil argument. I could hear my uncle's voice and Finucane answering. He appeared to be trying to explain himself. Ten minutes passed and the door opened. I closed my eyes. Cack walked into the bedroom with a chair. He pulled it up close to my knees and sat down facing me, leaving me no room to avoid his gaze.

'Máiría,' he said, 'this is a really serious situation. If he didn't do this, you need to tell me now. If he did it, he's a scumbag and he deserves to be punished. You need to tell me the truth.'

'He did it,' I said quietly, tears streaming down my face. Every single emotion I had been holding in during questioning by the

IRA came out at that moment, I couldn't stop crying. Cack went to the bathroom and came back with some toilet roll. He gave me a hug and I sobbed hard, then he patted my back and said I needed to get myself together. He then said he would 'sort it', and went back to the IRA people in the living room.

I put my head in my hands with my elbows on my knees and became hysterical, rocking back and forth and crying with a wad of toilet roll stuck into my mouth to muffle the sound. Breige came in with more tissues and asked me to stand up. I did so, but I couldn't bring myself to look at her. She hugged me and I cried, and she tried to make a joke about being glad I wasn't made of stone after all. I could feel the side of my face sticking to the shoulder of her black leather jacket. She pulled back a bit and moved my head with her hand so she was looking straight at me.

'Do you know something, Máiría?' she said, as if she was trying to convince herself of the obvious. 'There is nobody in this world that would let this go on as long as it has if it wasn't true.'

That was the turning point in my feelings towards her. From that night on, I felt some empathy from her, rather than suspicion. I also sensed her guilt, and some sort of a connection was made. In later years, a counsellor I saw for a long time likened this to Stockholm syndrome. I had been holed up with the IRA, sometimes day after day, for around six months, and this was the first time I felt that any of them had shown me any kindness.

I didn't see Cack again that night, he was locked in discussions with Seamus and Maura, and they sent for Siobhán. Breige asked me where I was going. I was too upset to go home and my parents would have immediately known there was something wrong, so I said I was going to stay with Aoife, the friendly woman who had comforted me in the disabled toilet at the café. Breige took me in her car, stopping on the way up at the petrol station on the Andersonstown Road. Aoife lived in Lenadoon. I thumped on the door and collapsed in a heap when I got inside. It was a one-bedroom flat so we both climbed into the double bed, and she stroked my hair until I couldn't cry any more, and I fell asleep.

13

Siobhán collected me at eleven the next morning. I stood on the street to wait for her. She drove up in her usual mode, seat too close to the steering wheel, glasses on, gripping the wheel with two hands together at the top and looking as though she couldn't see out of the windscreen. I got in and we went to her flat and talked. She told me that my family would have to be informed that night. I was still crying, and I knew that my relationship with my parents was never going to be the same again. This news was going to hurt them deeply, and I didn't want to have to see the pain on their face as they were told – but this was exactly what the IRA had decided I would have to do. There was no question of me not being present while someone else told them.

Siobhán stayed with me most of the day, probably to ensure that I didn't run. It didn't cross my mind, I was so conditioned by then to the fact that the IRA was in control that I just accepted I would be where I was told to be, with little ability left to question their orders. She kept trying to get me to eat. I managed to eat half an apple and smoke twenty Benson and Hedges, and around 6 p.m. we made the journey to Cack's house.

He was sitting on his own in his regular armchair in his living room, remote control in his hand. He turned the noise down on the news programme he was watching as we sat down. He explained that both he and Siobhán were taking me to my parents' house, and he got up to phone my dad, who panicked when Cack asked him if he would be in and said he needed to come down to talk to him about something. My father thought his mother had died. I put my head in my hands and almost put my finger in my ears in a childish effort to drown out Cack trying to reassure him there was nothing wrong.

The three of us left his house and got into his car. Cack activated the internal locking system in the car, probably automatically, and it meant I was unable to open the car door until he did. I might not have noticed this except for the sound, but the realisation that the door was locked sparked a fleeting fantasy of opening it and hurling myself onto the road. It was dark outside, and I watched the orange street lamps of the Monagh bypass whizzing into one long line of light as we sped down the dual carriageway.

The memory of events that night in my parents' house is indelibly etched in my mind. Cack walked in first, I was next, and Siobhán behind me. My mother was sitting at the chair near the door, and I smiled nervously at her as I went in. This panicked my mother, and her voice raised an octave.

'What have you done, Máiría, are you pregnant? Have you killed someone? What the hell have you done?' she asked.

Cack answered her. 'She hasn't done anything, Noreen, calm down.'

My daddy was standing up at the fireplace moving from one foot to the other, clearly agitated. We all found places to sit. My parents were crushed by the words that came next.

'We are here,' said Cack, 'because Máiría has said that Morris has abused her.'

He had barely got the last word out when my mother leapt off her chair and flew across the room and over to where I was sitting. 'Jesus Christ! Jesus! Jesus!' She pulled my head into her shoulder and held me tightly, and both of us cried.

I lifted my head and watched the look of wounded pain on my dad's face, an image that has never left me. Amid the chaos of my mother's wailing, Cack was trying to explain the involvement of the IRA.

My dad shouted at him, 'Where is he?'

Cack told him he was not to go near him, and that the IRA had been dealing with it. I remember my mother turning to Siobhán at one point, who was looking pretty guilty, and asking her how long she had known, snapping: 'This is my child, and you should have told us. This is abuse, you should have come to us. God knows the untold damage you have caused to my child!'

Siobhán said nothing. I wanted to escape, so I left my parents' house and went and stayed with a friend, explaining that I was too upset to answer any of their questions and too upset to see them hurt. Siobhán gave me a lift. 'They're raging at me,' she said, adding, 'That was very difficult.'

I said nothing; I was still reeling at what had just happened. I arrived at my friend's flat, got into her bed, curled up in a ball and fell asleep. The secrecy of the previous few years had begun to unravel and I knew that none of our lives would ever be the same again.

14

I was told to be at the Women's Centre the next day. I arrived to see the two IRA women and Seamus Finucane waiting for me. I was kept waiting in the corridor; there were no other staff around.

The front office doors were slightly ajar, and I recognised one of the voices as that of Harry Maguire. Maguire was a prominent republican military figure. Originally from north Belfast, he had been convicted and sentenced to 79 years in prison for an attack which led to the murders of two British corporals, David Howes and Derek Wood, who were beaten by a mob and then shot close to Casement Park after driving into an IRA funeral in Andersonstown in 1988.[7] Although I was young at the time, I remember clearly the week of events that started with the shootings of the other members of Siobhán O'Hanlon's bombing team, the 'Gibraltar Three', on 6 March, and the murder of the corporals, and the preceding attack on Milltown Cemetery during the funerals of the Gibraltar dead by the loyalist Michael Stone. My family home was within five minutes of both attacks, and I remember the chaos and the fear when watching my father frantically trying to locate my mother, who was stuck that day at the Busy Bee, a small area of shops in Andersonstown.

The other man seated in the office was Gerry 'Blute' McDonnell. Blute had spent a combined total of 23 years in jail, and had only been free for around a year at that time. He was always kind and pleasant to me, and I used to have conversations over coffee with him and his wife, Christine. Both men were now involved with Community Restorative Justice. I stood in the hallway and as the men got up to leave and passed me, Blute came over and hugged me and patted me on the shoulder, and left with Maguire, who avoided my gaze and said nothing. In 2014 I spoke with Blute on the phone. He couldn't remember the meeting, though he did not dispute that it had happened. Sadly, his wife Christine passed away in 2022.

The IRA explained to me that they were taking me up to my parents' house. I knew that this was the wrong thing to do; my mother would want nothing to do with them. She wasn't a republican and found their actions abhorrent. I told them as much.

'You're going nowhere near my parents' house!' I shouted, to no effect. I remonstrated with Finucane for a while, but I knew it was no good. I began to take a different tack and lowered my voice. 'Look, it's nothing personal,' I said to him.

He disputed this.

'Okay,' I said. 'It is personal. I think you're a wanker and I don't want you in my parents' house.'

It didn't work. I got into the car with the three of them and we made the journey to my parents. Once inside the house, I felt like an embarrassed thirteen-year-old. I could see the nervousness in my parents and I hated the IRA for doing this to them. They introduced themselves by name first, said they were there on behalf of the IRA, and I sat on the arm of the settee near the door while a heated argument ensued. Finucane was being his usual arrogant self, explaining how the IRA had a right to investigate one of their own volunteers, and my mum was shouting at him.

When my parents learned that the IRA had put me into a room with Morris (and Finucane had told her it was 'important' to put the victim in front of the alleged abuser), they were beside themselves with anger.

'You stupid bastards!' my mother shouted, 'you should never do that to someone who is abused, what in God's name did you think you were doing? We have no idea what damage has been done to Máiría yet, it could take years to get over this! You stupid, stupid bastards!'

I zoned in and out. I snapped back into my body immediately when Breige started to tell my parents the details of my abuse. I stopped her. 'You have no right to tell them what happened to me. I'll tell them in my own time. Stop...' I pleaded.

She mumbled a bit about them needing to know, and I got up to walk out into the kitchen and boil the kettle, for no reason other than it drowned out the sounds in the living room. Finucane made it very clear that Morris had not been found guilty, that he was still a volunteer in the IRA, and no one could accuse him of child abuse. Going to the RUC was not an option; that clearly mattered a great deal to the IRA.

My mother was still shouting at them and my father was also losing his temper. Finucane wasn't doing anything to help matters; his snide, superior attitude and lack of sensitivity were making the situation worse for my parents. I wanted it to end. My mother was in the middle of making a point about how they, the IRA, shouldn't be involving themselves in cases like this, and that she knew what she was talking about because she was trained in child protection, when Breige cut across her.

'We are trained in child protection too,' she said, speaking without irony, and looking to Maura for reassurance and then back to my mum. 'We work in the Women's Centre with cases like this all the time.'

My dad exploded. 'What? You think this is acceptable? Is it acceptable for the IRA to be using a women's centre as a front to investigate cases like this?'

No one answered him and the meeting was over.

The next five months, from March to July, passed like a blur. Things were very difficult, but my stubbornness was not about to let me hide away. I forced myself to continue to go to the Sinn Féin office. My logic was that I wasn't a liar, and if I had stayed away, people (if they heard something about it) would have believed Morris and not me. There was some stubbornness, too. I was not allowing Morris to drive me out of the office where I had made friends, and where I enjoyed being caught up in the politics of the day, so I kept going back – though the stress I was under meant

I was finding it hard to get any sleep and was still losing weight. I asked my dad to make sure I got out of bed on time and to give me a lift down the Falls Road when he was going to his own job.

I confided in a co-worker and asked if it would be okay if I took Monday afternoons off. I had decided, after speaking with my parents, that I would go to counselling. I wanted a counsellor free from republican control, and after asking around, my father found an Englishwoman, Gráinne, who worked in a community centre building in the Lenadoon estate, a centre which was known to resist Sinn Féin attempts to control their work.

My first counselling session was difficult and I tried to give the counsellor a brief synopsis of what had been happening. I watched her eyes widen. It was alien to her, thankfully, and that helped her efforts to get me to see that these types of events didn't happen in 'normal' society, and were completely wrong. Still, I found it hard to speak during those sessions, and what was supposed to be a six-week consultation turned into a year. Mostly I said very little – I couldn't get the words out. But I began to see that this woman was not going to force me to answer any question I didn't want to, and she helped me in practical ways, such as advising me about sleep, reminding me to eat and allowing me to sit in silence, which was soothing, although I found it uncomfortable at first. She explained how trauma manifested itself, and in her assessment I was badly traumatised. She encouraged me to go to the doctor, and I was prescribed sleeping tablets and antidepressants. The sleeping tablets did not help me to sleep, but allowed me to numb out when everything became too much.

In 2010 I obtained some of those counselling notes. It is strange looking back over them. There are plenty of entries like 'looks tired' and remarks about me not sleeping and being run down, and what the IRA made me do. On 10 April 2000, a week after I had started seeing her, the counsellor's notes of my conversation with her read:

> *Didn't want to go to counselling but glad I came last week. Anger – abuser works with victims of trauma – that he can still carry on working. No control over anything that has happened.*

Group (IRA) dictated to me when I could tell my family. Forced to go into a room with him so they could observe who was telling the truth...

One week later, on 17 April:

Very silent. Felt very down after last week. Felt I had to go out and put on a performance for everyone. Family were talking about it non-stop and now suddenly nothing. Anger – contacting social services still not an option. Worried about the consequences...He normalised everything – after it happened he told me to put the kettle on...I began to question whether I was right or not.

We discussed the possibility of my writing a letter to him. My response shows how damaging the IRA investigation had been to me: 'The last time I wrote something down it was used as an allegation. Very distrustful.' In May, the counsellor noted down what I had said: 'Feels claustrophobic like everything is closing in on me. Can remember stupid things and other things too difficult – very difficult for me to put words to feelings. Afraid of how I will cope if I talk.'

On 15 May 2000, she wrote: 'Looking extremely tired. Not sleeping until 3-4 in the morning. Flashbacks – drifting into a daydream at work.' On the same date, I recounted what the IRA had said to me and how I felt about it: 'Everyone has moved on and left me with the mess. ... "We (IRA) fucked up with this one but we need to move on to other cases." Worried about my anger – getting angry at the wrong people.' On 17 July 2000 I described how I felt when bumping into my abuser: 'feel fear – (it) grabs me in my stomach.'

And I was bumping into him frequently. He was always in the company of known IRA men. He would turn up at the radio station and cast menacing looks in my direction. I would either put my head down and turn away or shoot an equally disdainful look back, depending on what mood I was in, but it was very frightening.

His profile was growing and he gave media interviews on, incredibly, the reform of policing and Community Restorative Justice. What Morris said to *An Phoblacht*, Sinn Féin's newspaper, in May 2000 sickened me to my stomach: 'As the concept of CRJ becomes more familiar to people they are more likely to bring their grievances to us. People have asked us to be involved in disputes between neighbours, in assaults and in incidents of domestic violence. We seek resolution to problems ...'

I sent an email under a pseudonym complaining about that article to the editor of the paper, but I didn't get a response. The IRA told me Morris was entitled to give interviews, as he hadn't been proved guilty of anything. I told them that by making him the acceptable face of policing reform they were allowing him even greater access to children and young people. Sadly, I was right. I discovered later that precisely during this period, and also at the same time he was calling me a 'sick fucker' to my face in front of the IRA 'court of enquiry', he was alleged to have committed other serious sexual assaults against young children in my family – something which he has always strongly denied.

My isolation during this period was intense. I couldn't discuss what had happened with anyone except my counsellor. The IRA were trying to find out what I was saying to her, too. I had a row with Siobhán one day when she was giving me a lift home from work. We were having a general chit-chat, and then she asked me how the counselling was going. I told her it was tough, but okay.

She stopped the car outside my house. 'What have you told her?' she asked.

'That's none of your fucking business!' I retorted.

'Why will you not just tell me, Máiría?' she said.

I exploded. 'Because it's the only fucking thing I have to myself!' I screamed, as I got out of the car and slammed the door.

I distanced myself a bit from her after that, because I was becoming even more severely depressed, to the point of being suicidal. As the pressure increased, it felt like a viable escape route, and I didn't want to give any indication to anyone of what I was planning to do. I sank deeper into hopelessness that anyone would ever believe me about Morris, and I didn't want to have to keep looking at him where I lived, and on the news, and in the paper. I began to self-destruct.

Breige was slightly different to Siobhán because I hated her from the start, then began to tolerate her, and then I liked her. I didn't feel empathy from her, as I've said, until the night they brought Cack in, when she hugged me. Once that happened, I began to feel like maybe there was one person in the IRA who might just see that I was telling the truth and speak up for me when the others were privately discussing what to do with me. She also had a different manner to the others; she was less brusque and had a lower, gentler tone of voice. She with the rest of them was still 'the IRA', and as a group they were terrifying, but I began to see her as a person too. Afterwards, when the whole thing was over, I kept a degree of contact with her because of the connection that I felt. I certainly felt that the woman should realise the damage she had done, and I told her on more than one occasion how difficult it was for me to cope with their scepticism and refusal to accept what I was telling them.

When my father's side of the family found out about my abuse, nothing much was said to me by any of my relatives, and I had little contact with them. The embarrassment and shame and guilt I was feeling, coupled with thinking that I was not believed, kept me away from them. My granny still did not know and I found myself unable to visit her, afraid that I would bump into Morris or my aunt, who still lived next door. I found it unfair that Morris could continue a relationship with my granny, yet I could not. I was also acutely aware that the many children in my family were in close proximity to him, and I felt powerless to do anything about it.

During that period, I was invited to attend a play staged in the Theatre on the Rock, a community theatre on the Whiterock road on the outskirts of the Ballymurphy estate. *Des* was a DubbleJoint production, a one-man show based on the life of Des Wilson, a family friend and renowned Catholic priest who had fallen foul of Bishop William Philbin in the 1970s. He had won the respect of the people of Ballymurphy by standing up for their right to be treated fairly, at a time when it seemed to him that those in positions of power were more content to demonise and vilify them. Critics would say that the church had made its opposition to the IRA very clear and that people like Des Wilson were less willing to condemn armed action. In an interview with *Republican News* in 1982, Des Wilson explained his view on those who joined the IRA:

> I have long since made it clear in public that in no circumstances will I condemn any fellow Irish man or woman for using arms. And I don't believe that anybody else has any right to condemn such people, unless they can point to a non-armed alternative which is effective, and not just which is 'nice'.[8]

Des had been instrumental, along with my grandfather Frank, in the setting up of a number of social enterprises in the Whiterock area, and in empowering the community through accessible education in the form of Springhill Community House and later Conway Education Centre. Frank was a well-known republican who leaned more towards community development than his older brother, Joe, who was one of the authors of the IRA's military strategy and became the organisation's Chief of Staff. I grew up with tales about his time in prison and his belief that people should strive to educate themselves, and in doing so strengthen the community as a whole. Granda Frank was a very smart man, and though he was dyslexic, he could turn his hand to any failing project and make a success of it. His character was featured in the play, and I was looking forward to the performance.

Shortly before the play began, I noticed that my granny was sitting in the front row and I wanted more than anything to go up and give her a hug. She still wasn't aware of the IRA 'investigation' and the venue was neutral ground, but just as I was making my way up to her seat, Morris and my aunt took their places beside her. I wanted to leave, but I didn't want to have to explain why to the people I'd come with, one of whom was the singer Frances

Black. During the interval, Morris left to go to the bar and I seized my chance to run over to Granny and hug her. She was delighted to see me, but asked why I hadn't been up to the house for so long. I told her I had been busy but that I would see her soon, and I returned to my seat, my stomach churning.

A few days later I came out of the Sinn Féin Centre, which had now moved from Conway Mill to Sevastopol Street on the Falls Road and sported a brand new Bobby Sands mural on the outer wall. As I turned, I saw two of my young relatives walking towards me. We had always been close as children, running around the streets of Ballymurphy or sneaking off to the fields at Dermot Hill to have a 'loose' (a cigarette) together, though I hadn't seen much of them that year. We stopped and had a normal conversation about where they were going and what they had bought in the shop, but I detected a heavy feeling as we talked. There was something unsaid in the air, and the conversation stalled. I said I had to go because I was late for a meeting, and I hugged the two girls. The elder one, who was fifteen, clung to me a little longer than normal. It was out of character for her, and it was only for a split second, but as we pulled away from that embrace and I looked into her eyes, I knew she had been abused too. I cannot, even to this day, explain how I knew. I skipped the meeting and went home to lie in bed, staring at the ceiling and praying to God that she and I would be okay. I also prayed that she would tell someone what had happened to her.

Some time after this, it was said that a young woman in Ballymurphy had told her mother she had seen Morris carry a drunk teenager into his home in the early hours of the morning. A quick check revealed that he had indeed been with this young person in a shebeen nicknamed *The Pink Pussy/Ballroom of Romance* on the night in question. The club was a drinking den which only sold tins of beer, shots of vodka or large bottles of cider (called 'barrack busters'), and was full of underage girls and older republican men. At the start of the evening (it opened after other bars in west Belfast had shut), a woman dressed in white shirt and black trousers would stand to attention with the Irish flag, and the club would play the Irish national anthem. Everyone swayed to attention with the flagholder, and woe betide anyone who spoke while the anthem was played or who failed to stand. The club was a dive, and rivulets of urine snaked out of the male toilets onto the dingy dancefloor, while the female toilets had two lumps of wood that didn't quite meet in the middle for doors. No one went to the *Pink Pussy* sober, and they wiped their feet on the way out.

15

On 23 July 2000, I set off early to the only place I felt safe, the radio station. I was leaning out the window smoking with the manager when I saw a maroon car, which I recognised as Siobhán O'Hanlon's, pull into the car park opposite. There had been considerable tension between us, and I didn't want another row. I had quarrelled with her previously when she told me I should just chalk up to experience what the IRA had done. I thought I had been treated very badly, and told her so.

'You're not the only person to go through this, you know!' she shouted at me, and she continued to shout at me while I walked out to her balcony to get away from her.

I ran up the stairs to the recording studio, and I hid under the table. I don't know what I was thinking, it seems ridiculous now, but it was automatic and instinctive. I couldn't leave the studio because I would have run straight into her, so this was the next best option.

It took her a few minutes to find me. She came in with her hand on the strap of the large bag over her shoulder, and smiled to herself when she saw me under the table. 'Are you hiding from me?' she asked.

'No,' I said. 'I'm trying to fix a plug' – sarcastically, yet sheepishly at the same time. 'I don't want to talk to you,' I added, before standing up and trying to brush past her.

She put her hand on my shoulder and said, 'I need to talk to you, stop.'

I knew there was something wrong and I froze.

'Someone else has said Morris abused her,' she said.

I was stunned, then thought of the intuitive feeling I had had at the earlier encounter with my young relatives at Sevastopol Street. I told her I knew about one of them and mentioned her name. She drew in her breath sharply, and lowered her voice and said, 'It's not her, it's…' She mentioned the name of another young relative. I was very fond of the girl. I felt faint. I stood and looked at Siobhán blankly.

'I need you to come with me now,' she said.

I didn't need her to tell me twice. I ran down the stairs of the radio and walked over to her car. She stalled the clutch, muttered 'Fuck sake!', and drove up Slievegallion Drive onto the Glen Road.

'Don't be angry with me, Máiría, please don't be angry with me,' she said.

'I'm not angry at you, I'm angry at him,' I replied.

She started crying. I was too numb to cry, and I still hadn't quite worked out what was going on. I can relive it now, that journey, and I can feel the complete numbness enveloping me.

'Where are we going?' I asked.

'We're going to Seany's,' she said. 'Your ma and da's on their way up from Donegal.'

She stopped the car in Ballymurphy, outside my father's brother's house. I was scared to go in, and when I did, I walked into an atmosphere reminiscent of a wake. A few of my uncles' wives were sitting in the living room talking amongst themselves, though they stopped dead when I came in. Their children had all been shooed out into the street. Seany was sitting out in the back garden and I was told to go out to him. Siobhán left the house and told me she would be back soon. I walked out into the garden and sat down on the plastic white patio chair opposite him. Seany had daughters of his own, and while none of them had been abused by Morris, he could empathise with the child who was now alleging abuse. He wanted to help, hence allowing us all to congregate at his house, and he thought I should speak to her to comfort her, which I agreed to do.

He was crying. I wasn't really sure what to say, but he told me that the wider Cahill family were devastated. We went upstairs. I took a cigarette and lit it, blowing smoke out the window, and asked Seany when my parents would be arriving. I was worried about being caught smoking. Seany laughed and ruffled my hair and said: 'For God's sake, Máiría, I think under the circumstances that being caught smoking will not register in the grand scheme of things!'

Seany's house phone rang, and I was called out. It was Breige Wright. It was three months since I had seen her. I said hello and was stunned by her opening remark. 'Do you want to say I told you so?' she said, adding: 'I'll be over in a half an hour.' I was given no choice in the matter. I put the phone down and wanted to get out of the house for a while. When I got back downstairs my mum and dad had arrived. I was too upset to have a conversation with them, so I told them I was going to the shops.

When I returned to Seany's house, Siobhán's car was outside. Breige was sitting in the front seat. Siobhán was in the house talking to Seany and my father. My mother hadn't forgiven her for not telling her about my abuse, and was ignoring her. They stopped talking when I went in and Siobhán lifted her handbag and asked me if I was ready. I nodded, and my mother called me over.

'Where are you going?' she said.

'I'm going out just for a while with Siobhán, I'll see you later.'

I will never forget the hurt look in her eyes as I left the house that day; she couldn't understand why I was leaving them to go with the woman who they felt had betrayed them. I couldn't tell them without having to explain that I was being taken to an IRA meeting – though everyone else knew who I was going with. I lowered my eyes and walked out and into the car.

There wasn't much said during the car journey. Siobhán left us at Breige's flat in Glassmullin Gardens and said she would come back for me. Breige explained the IRA position. 'Don't be worrying about Morris at the minute,' she said.

I hadn't even thought about where Morris might be. It wasn't until later that day I found out he was under supposed 'house arrest'. She went on to tell me that they had taken a decision that they could not speak to the girl, as she was a minor. But they were 'reinitiating' their 'investigation'. She asked me to speak to the child who was now alleging abuse and come back to them with details.

And she said, 'We also need more detail from you about yours.' I was revolted. I couldn't believe that after everything that had happened, and just when I had begun to think that I was free from IRA questioning, she was telling me that I was going to have to go through it again.

'No way,' I said, and the words caught in my throat. 'I'm not doing go-between for the IRA. And I'm not forcing her to tell me anything. You want details?' Something broke within me, and I poured out further details of my own abuse.

16

The other young person I had hugged that day outside the Sinn Féin Centre on Sevastopol Street was travelling abroad and due home the next day. The IRA were awaiting her return – they wanted to question her to see if she too was a victim of Morris. She was, so now three people – two young teenagers, and myself – were alleging that we'd been abused by him. This gave the IRA a headache. They had successfully managed to stifle me with their first 'investigation'. It was now next to impossible, since word was out all around Ballymurphy about the other two girls, to control the consequences as they liked to do.

The IRA had told me that they waited so long to question me after they learned of my allegations through a third party because 'morally' they had to wait until a person was eighteen. This pious rule had obviously gone by the wayside. Now they decided to come back to question me. I had started counselling to try and keep myself sane, and I did not want them turning my life upside down again. But the IRA decided unilaterally that they were inviting themselves to my house to meet with my father, and at the time he felt powerless not to meet them.

I was not letting any of my family meet the IRA on their own and I insisted to my father I would be there for the encounter. My mum was in Donegal at the time. He cautioned me against it, and said that I was clearly unwell. I had developed a viral infection through stress, but I was resolute that I was not budging. I wanted my dad to have a witness.

Breige and Seamus Finucane turned up, like bad pennies, and sat in my parents' living room. My father sat on the settee alongside Breige, I took the chair near the window and Seamus sat on the chair near the door. He told me to leave and I told him I was going nowhere. He remonstrated with my father that they had been under the impression I wouldn't be there, and my dad replied that as they wanted to talk about me I had a right to sit in my own living room and hear what they had to say. Finucane muttered something about possibly not continuing with the meeting and I replied that that was his choice. They stayed.

My dad mentioned that he was urging me to go to the RUC. That appeared to panic the two IRA personnel, and they glanced at one another. Finucane explained that they were there to tell us that Morris was under house arrest, but that they needed to decide what the IRA were going to do with him. 'No decision has been taken and he is still presumed innocent, until we have evidence otherwise,' he added.

Their respect for their own judicial process for a man who was alleged to have abused children, and who people alleged had maimed dozens of teenagers by shooting them in the kneecaps, was surreal. My dad shouted at him that there were now three known victims and no room for a shadow of a doubt, and lashed into our uninvited guests for involving themselves in the first place. Finucane said they had to wrap up things quickly, before the RUC got wind that Morris was being held, and I added that I had already been through one of their 'investigations' and didn't see why they were telling me to go through another one. Finucane became aggressive towards me, and my father then raised his voice and told him not to speak that way to me. I could see the whole thing was becoming dangerous, and I asked if I could speak to the IRA and then my father on his own – I wanted him to cool off.

I spoke to our two unwanted visitors first. I explained that I wanted to make a criminal complaint, and Finucane replied: 'Okay, Máiría, want to go to the RUC? Remember this – at the minute we have him under house arrest. The minute you say the police are becoming involved in this, I will let him go, and I can't guarantee you won't bump into him later, in an hour's time, or sometime tomorrow or when you're doing your shopping.'

I bristled at this bald threat. If I went to the RUC, the IRA would cut Morris loose and he would come after me. Finucane then said they needed a court martial to convict Morris, something which they had decided not to do the first time round, and that they wanted me to give them more evidence. I asked for a break to speak to my father.

I went into the front room and said to my dad, 'They won't let me go to the RUC. I don't have an option but to let them go ahead with whatever they want to do. But I'm not giving them any more statements.'

He cried. I could see he was almost at breaking point – he felt utterly and totally powerless to advise, never mind protect his daughter, and he knew better than to tell the IRA people sitting in his living room to 'fuck off'. They had the person who had abused his daughter out of the way, and we had to choose whether to go to the RUC and risk being harmed by either the organisation or Morris, or to bide our time. We went back into the living room and I told Finucane I would reserve my position on contacting the RUC for a week, but in the meantime I would not be giving them any more evidence.

I was a few years older than the other two victims, and so I felt responsible that even though I had gone back to that house to try and stop it happening to anyone else, it hadn't worked. I felt very guilty, and in fact felt guilty for decades because I believed that I was the first of the three to have been abused. As it transpired, though I didn't find out until 2014, the other two had been abused before me. At a counselling session later that week, on 31 July 2000, my counsellor noted that I had told her:

> *Nightmare. Two other girls have reported abuse by the same man. One of them gave me details and it was like going back there again. I feel sick, cannot eat, sleep, not coping. IRA told me they cannot do anything unless I'm prepared to give further*

evidence. Blamed me the last time for not giving enough detail. Feel angry. He is still denying everything. I want everyone to know what he is but don't want him to flee the country, that would be worse. Feel I'm being forced to make all the decisions again. Afraid that they'll kill him and I couldn't cope with that on my hands. Cannot go to RUC, cannot take the risk that he will walk free from them …Feeling suicidal. Cannot cope.

The same night I had gone to a friend's house in Hawthorn Street to escape the world. I was close to having a nervous breakdown – the stress and the pressure were becoming too much to handle. My wider family was split. Some of my uncles and their wives were still finding it very difficult to believe that Morris had abused children. Everyone was concerned about the effect on my aunt, who was having an even harder time accepting that the IRA man she married had turned out to be not quite the perfect husband. My own parents also felt isolated – few people contacted them, probably because they didn't know what to say. Everyone was in avoidance mode, and I felt responsible.

Looking back now, I was so concerned about the way in which everyone else was handling the abuse revelations that I didn't have any capacity left to be concerned about myself. I wanted to fix the family. I wanted to rewind to a time before Morris landed in it like a ticking bomb, when everyone was easy in each other's company. I wanted the loving, caring family that I thought I knew.

That family, I have come to realise, was a myth. They may have loved each other, and some of them may have been close to each other, but at the one major time of adversity – at the most horrific time for us collectively – they failed the basic test of collective compassion. While that may be forgivable, it is also a significant indicator of how revelations of abuse, and people's reactions to it, can irrevocably affect the binding nucleus of a family. Initial reactions of shock and disbelief I expected, but, as time went on, the complete burial and denial of the abuse and the fracturing of relations as a result only served to reinforce the message that I was somehow different, disturbed, not worth listening to, and not worth caring about. I don't think it was the conscious intention of anyone involved, but that is how their responses made me feel: like damaged goods.

17

It is very strange to be sitting in the office of one of the most powerful men in Ireland and be asked to give your opinion on whether a man should live or die. We were in Gerry Adams's office, Breige and I. Siobhán O'Hanlon had let us in while Gerry was out. She pushed a yellow Post-it note across the circular meeting table to me. It read: 'What do you want to happen to him?'

I knew she was asking me whether I wanted Morris killed. She put her finger to her lips so I wouldn't answer her out loud, and pointed to the light on the ceiling in case there were British listening devices in the room. The potential political ramifications were huge. It was 2000 and there was supposed to be a peace process under way. This type of scenario was what an aide to the British Secretary of State Mo Mowlam had referred to when they talked of 'internal housekeeping', and people were expected to turn a blind eye to the brutal murder of people like Charlie Bennett, the young taxi driver whose mutilated body was unceremoniously dumped in the grounds of St Gall's GAA club in west Belfast in 1999. But the IRA took flak over his murder. Having the Morris case explode in the summer of 2000 would have faced them with a similar or worse predicament.

I very much doubt that if I had said 'kill him' they would simply have obliged. I didn't want it on my conscience and didn't want to take the risk. I was nineteen in 2000, articulate but frightened. I had been through abuse, lost a family member, and been put through a forced IRA investigation during which I had to face my rapist – all in the space of three years. I was a mess. 'Like something out of the famine', someone described me, looking at the weight I had lost. I weighed around six stone, if that.

But Morris was still under 'house arrest' and they had to decide what to do with him. I pushed the note back in disgust and pointed my finger at my head like the barrel of a gun. 'See that?' I said. 'That's too easy an option. I don't want this on my conscience. How dare you try and place the responsibility for this onto me. Youse fucked up. You forced me into this investigation and you took the decisions. This one is not mine.'

Stupidly I thought that if the IRA stood Morris at the top of the Whiterock Road and tied him to a lamp-post with a placard round his neck admitting the rapes, that would be some kind of justice. People would all know he was a liar and a rapist and that I had been telling the truth. I thought that he could then go back to living in Ballymurphy, where people would know exactly what he was doing and could keep an eye on him to make sure children did not go near him. Naïve, perhaps, but not so far-fetched; the IRA did this regularly to burglars and other 'anti-social elements'; that was 'justice', republican style. 'No going to the RUC. If you do, we will let him loose and walk away.' I didn't realise that Morris staying in Ballymurphy or even in Belfast wasn't an option.

Siobhán O'Hanlon was also very direct with my father and asked him if *he* wanted to have Morris shot. He told the IRA that he wanted him handed over to the RUC, but that it was their problem, as they had created the mess.

I sometimes wonder if I should have pulled the imaginary trigger I was holding up to my head in Adams's office that day. I wonder if I would have been able to live with that. I do know that I'm often tormented by the fact that he is still alive. But hypotheticals don't help. Neither does rough justice. The most bizarre thing for me is that one of the self-styled 'most sophisticated guerrilla armies in the world' let a nineteen-year-old girl think she was making the decision for them, causing a huge amount of pain as a result.

18

Festival week was starting on 4 August, and I volunteered to help with a multitude of events. My heart wasn't in it, but I thought that if I could keep busy, it was better than having too much time to think. I had to go to the marquee on Saturday to help with collecting tickets on the door for the Kilfenora Céilí Band concert, though I ended up getting hammered drunk with some of the radio staff.

I left around 2 a.m. to go home, and received a call from my Uncle Sean around an hour later to tell me that the *Sunday World*, an Irish tabloid newspaper, had printed an article about Morris and the abuse of girls related to Joe Cahill. My heart thumped in my chest. I was on my way. I called a taxi, which took me to the garage at the top of St James' estate in west Belfast, where I bought the paper for myself, and then dropped me off at Sean's house in Ballymurphy. I didn't know what to say. I had so many questions: How had Sean found out? Who leaked the details (albeit not completely accurate ones) to the paper? What was I going to do? My head was a bit fuzzy from the alcohol I'd consumed, and that probably cushioned me from the full impact.

Siobhán arrived shortly after I did and walked in, efficient as ever. She picked up Sean's copy of the paper and threw it in the unlit grate. She explained that she had prior knowledge of the article, and that she had gone to my Uncle Joe to warn him. He was celebrating his daughter's wedding when she broke the news. I shouted at her, asking why she had not thought that telling me would have also been the right thing to do. She asked how I had found out, accusingly, insinuating that I had leaked the story to the newspaper.

I was disgusted. 'Sean's only after phoning me and telling me, I never went to any newspapers about this.' Sean confirmed this to her and Siobhán and I glowered at each other. Sean explained that the local youths who hated Morris were having a bonfire in his honour at Whiterock leisure centre. It was all happening too quickly for my head to process. I heard Siobhán and Sean discussing something at the door in low voices, and then she was gone. I told Sean I was going to go to the carnival parade the next day. He cautioned me against it, but I explained I didn't want people to be talking behind my back – that I wasn't going to hide away because if I hid away now, I would find it difficult to ever come outside my front door again.

Sean gave up trying to dissuade me, and I set the alarm on my phone for 6 a.m. I arrived at the Festival Office, where the rest of the security staff were gathered, and walked in to the smell of a fry cooking for the workers – and complete silence as I came through the door. Someone said hello to me nervously, and I forced myself to act normally. I walked into the kitchen and lifted a sausage sandwich, and saw another worker hiding the *Sunday World* behind the desk. It was obvious that everyone had been talking about the article. I said nothing. I wasn't starting that conversation with anyone, and no one dared to start it with me. Some of them were still trying to work out who the abuse victims were, although most had obviously made the connection to me.

My allocated position was to stay with the start of the parade, which was being led by black taxis at Conway Mill. Children in colourful costumes had started to gather with their community groups. It was raining as I met my colleague Maureen and we took refuge in the back of one of the taxis. She was starting to mention the newspaper article to me when my father called me from Donegal. I was going to ask him if he had heard about the newspaper article when he stopped me in my tracks. 'Máiría,' he said. 'Marty Morris has disappeared.'

'What?' I was stunned. 'Say that again?'

'Morris has disappeared; he's been gone since Tuesday. I just took a call from Seany.' His voice faltered. He was clearly angry – and I was cold with rage.

'The fucking bastards, Da,' I shouted.

Maureen's eyes narrowed inquisitively at me as she mouthed, 'What's wrong?' I batted her query away with my hand.

'Máiría, don't be doing anything stupid, I'm on my way home,' my father said.

'Daddy,' I shouted, 'they've let him fucking go, and people knew, and all that time no one thought to say anything to me? Where is he? Where did he go?'

'I don't know,' said my father. 'The details are pretty sketchy, but I'm going to find out.'

'I'm going to find out for myself!' I shouted, and I hung up the phone.

I immediately phoned my friend, former IRA member Aoife. 'I want you to meet me at the corner of the Springfield Road now.' She knew by the tone of my voice that there was clearly something wrong, and she agreed to meet me in ten minutes. I ran up to the corner of the Springfield, and I put my hands on her shoulders, told her that Marty had gone and screamed in her face. 'You go and tell Bobby Storey, and Seamy Finucane, and whoever else you can get your fucking hands on that they're a pack of bastards!' As she was an ex-prisoner and someone who was in regular contact with Storey (then the head of IRA intelligence), I didn't think it an unreasonable request, and nor did I stop to ponder the fact that I had insulted the IRA. I was beyond fright. The news had unleashed all of the emotion that had been bubbling under the surface, and I was past consequential thinking. Later, she told me that my eyes were dancing with rage. I didn't want to control the anger and I didn't want to believe that Morris had simply vanished. Been allowed to vanish, in fact.

I left Aoife and ran back down towards Conway Street. I didn't even know what I was going back for, I wasn't thinking straight and I needed to calm down a bit. I passed senior republican Marie

Moore and another woman called Elsie, who nudged each other as I approached.

'Seen the paper?' she asked.

'Yes I did,' I replied curtly and walked on.

I met Maureen close to Conway Street, and she was standing beside another elderly republican. They were talking about the article. Maureen looked uncomfortable when I approached, but the man was in full flow and obviously hadn't made the connection between me and the subject of the news.

'Yeah, what age were the girls, 14 going on 28?' he said sarcastically, implying that it was the abuse victims who had enticed the abuser.

I was raging at this crass comment, which effectively blamed us and not Morris, and wanted to shout back 'Actually thirteen, fourteen and sixteen', but I said nothing. I left him standing there, and caught up with the parade as it moved off. There were a few more nudges and looks, which I ignored. As I passed Siobhán's new house I saw her standing outside it with her son and her friends Sue Ramsey and Bridie McMahon. One of them waved at me, and I threw a look that could have killed dead things and looked away again.

It had started raining heavily, big sheets of water that soaked everyone right through and matched my dismal mood, and I decided to stop fronting it out and go home. I ran the whole way, trying to lose some of my angry energy. I arrived at the house wet through, tears streaming down my face, and called Siobhán. She said hello, and I ignored the pleasantries and cut to the chase: 'You get me somebody to speak to now,' I ranted.

She sounded a bit taken aback, but clearly expected the call. She answered me calmly, if a little sheepishly: 'I can't, Máiría, it's festival week, they'll probably all be on the drink.'

'I don't care,' I countered. 'You fucking get me somebody to speak to!' I suddenly didn't care whether Siobhán lost her cool with me or not. She told me she would come back to me, but that a meeting with anybody would most likely take place the next day. I put the phone down and sat in my wet clothes and dug my fingernails into my skin in frustration.

19

If there was any doubt as to who Marty Morris had abused, one man put an end to the speculation in the west Belfast community later that evening. That man was the Sinn Féin president Gerry Adams. The arrival of Adams at any event during Féile always caused a stir, not least in the Féile marquee, where the festival was hosting a concert by a group called the Afro-Cuban All Stars. It had been a blow learning that Morris had gone from Belfast, and I was in a state of anger and shock, but I wasn't about to be conspicuous by my absence. I was working as a member of the security team that night. If people were going to talk, I was damned if they were going to do it behind my back. I wanted to show my face and to remind people of what they had done.

I knew that senior IRA figures would be there that night, and I wanted to make it as difficult as possible for them. So I positioned myself at the entrance door, checking handbags as people came in. I ignored the likes of senior IRA men Bobby Storey and Martin 'Duckster' Lynch as they came through, but I made eye contact with them and then looked away in disgust. I was dead inside and I didn't care if they took issue with that. I was past fear.

I was also tired from being up the previous evening, and I was getting sick. I knew I needed to see a doctor. I was suffering recurrent heart palpitations and had broken out in a rash. I also had a stinking cold that I couldn't shift. I hadn't eaten in days, and couldn't keep anything down. I adopted a 'fuck you' attitude with the IRA that night and I think it took them by surprise. Some of them made an effort to engage me in conversation, but I told them all I was too busy. I hadn't the energy to stand the whole night, and when the bulk of the revellers were seated, I also sat down for a bit.

Then I saw Moke, one of Adams's security guards, and another, wee Roy. These men were well known in west Belfast, and I knew many of them personally. Where Adams went, they went. I hoped that Adams wouldn't come my way. I knew that all eyes would be on him, and as he was the figurehead of the republican movement I wanted to slap his face. I sat on my hands. He walked past me and then backtracked after about five steps. He came back over to me, put his two hands on either side of my face, and kissed me on the head. The Judas kiss, I remember thinking at the time. I could feel two thousand pairs of eyes focused on me, and it was as if they were burning my skin. Any anonymity I had was gone at that moment. I know that because of the people who came up to me afterwards to be nosy, or commiserate with me over the *Sunday World* article, or genuinely to express concern. It was as if Adams had given them public permission to do so. Adams asked me quietly after that greeting if I wanted to come and see him and I told him no. He came back a few minutes later with his friendly adviser Richard McAuley, and I then agreed to a meeting.

I was curious as to what he wanted and although he had become an international celebrity during the peace process, to me all my life he had been 'Gerry' and I think I felt that it might even be helpful to meet, despite my anger at him and the people he led. I might even find out where Morris was. McAuley said Adams would be free at 11 a.m. in two days' time. Adams returned to me a few times that night and tried to joke with me, but to say the least I wasn't in the mood. Siobhán O'Hanlon came in shortly before last orders and took me out to her car. She told me that the IRA could meet with me the next day at 3 p.m. but that she wanted to see me the next morning in Sevastopol Street. I left the marquee shortly afterwards and went home, and spent the night retching bile and the half pint of Tennent's I had drunk.

If Siobhán thought my reaction the previous day was angry, she was not prepared for the meltdown I had on the upper floor of the Sinn Féin offices in Sevastopol Street. She was photocopying a book on abuse – in case, she said, it might be of help to me. It was a tiny room, like a broom cupboard, stuck between the press office and the media briefing room. She closed the door and shut us in when she saw my face.

'What's wrong?' she said. 'What's fucking wrong?'

I told her I had just received a phone call to say that my Aunt Ellen had possibly known for some time that Morris had left the city. I told her I was going up to Ballymurphy to confront her.

'Wise up and calm down,' she said, adding: 'You're going nowhere in that state.'

She tried to reach for me and I shrugged her off. I phoned my granny's house from my mobile. My aunt answered. 'I'm on my way up there,' I shouted, 'and you better be there by the time I get up.'

'What's wrong?' she said, sounding worried. I exploded again.

'What the fuck do you think is wrong? You tell me, what do you think is wrong?'

I hung up. Siobhán looked worried. 'Please, Máiría, you need to calm down, you're not well.'

'Fuck you and fuck her and fuck the IRA, fuck the lot of youse,' I said, and I walked out.

I arrived at that house in Ballymurphy just as my great-Uncle Joe and my Aunt Annie were walking into Granny's house. Joe had obviously been called by Siobhán to calm me down. If anyone was going to be able to do that it was him. I was his favourite, and we had a good relationship that transcended age. We talked to each other about life in a way that put us on an equal playing field. Not that day, though I hugged and kissed him, my grandmother and Annie.

My mobile rang repeatedly. Siobhán. Then my aunt came out of the kitchen. I couldn't contain myself any longer. I unleashed on her all the emotions that had been building up inside me. She was the target of my anger for the abuse, for the IRA, for the whole wider family who had dealt with it so abysmally. For the girls, for my parents, and for Morris leaving Belfast.

My father arrived soon afterwards. I went into the kitchen still ranting and raving and my aunt followed me in. I had a few more choice words to say to her, then I told her to fuck off out of my face. I went back into the living room and sat down beside my dad, who was trying to talk to my granny, who wasn't saying very much. She didn't know what to say, but thought I should try and pull myself together.

'For fuck's sake, Ma,' my da shouted. 'This was not some sort of hanky panky, this was serious sexual abuse!' Everyone looked stunned. My father is normally the quiet, gentle one of the family and he rarely raises his voice.

The house phone rang. Siobhán for me. Joe spoke to her and passed the phone to me. 'You're late, you're supposed to be seeing these people!' she shouted.

I had forgotten about the IRA meeting. Joe offered to drive me. He left Annie in Ballymurphy and took me to Glassmullin Gardens to meet the IRA. On the way, driving like the half-blind cartoon character Mr Magoo, he told me he was concerned. 'I never want to see you that angry again, Máiría,' he said. 'It will make you worse. Stay focused.'

Outside, I buried my head in his shoulder, inhaling the familiar mix of washing powder and fustiness. Just Joe. 'Come and see me later,' he said softly. I said that I would.

I got out of the car, took a deep breath and walked into my meeting with the IRA Army Council.

20

As usual with the IRA, as I was discovering, this meeting of senior figures in an illegal military organisation was taking place in yet another ordinary Belfast suburban house, like the one in Kenard Avenue. The house in Glassmullin Gardens was divided into flats. I heard the echo of my footsteps as I made my way up the short flight of stairs to the first floor, this time to Breige Wright's flat, though she was not there. My footsteps didn't mask the beating of my heart, pounding from the confrontation at my grandmother's house. I didn't know who I would be meeting.

I knocked on the door, which was opened by a thin, attractive, blonde-haired woman who smiled at me and ushered me into the living room. She pointed towards a sofa against the wall near the door I had just come through and motioned to me to sit down. There was an ashtray, and I thought that Breige must have told them I smoked. She sat on the chair to the right of me and a man who I instantly recognised as Padraic Wilson sat on the chair to the left of the settee. Behind him was a window, through which I could see Glassmullin Pitches – a large green manicured field surrounded by terraced houses, at the end of which in the distance was a row of shops with flats above them. It was strange to see a few kids playing football on the pitch and going about their daily lives. I wondered what the neighbours were doing, and if they had any idea the flat I was sitting in was hosting an IRA meeting.

I waited for one of them to speak. Padraic introduced himself, and the other girl as 'Marie'. I had a vague recollection of where I had seen her before, and it clicked at the moment of her introduction. She was Marie Wright – the one who, during her second term of imprisonment in Maghaberry Prison, had been Officer Commanding (OC) over the other female prisoners. I had been at her welcome home party in the Felons Club with Siobhán and her partner Pat in October 1998, when she and Rosie McCorley, another ex-prisoner, had celebrated their early release under the terms of the Good Friday Agreement. Both Siobhán and Pat had a connection with Marie, as Siobhán had been arrested with her in a 'bomb factory' in 1983, and Pat had been arrested with her in 1989. She had been released only two years before her second arrest and as a consequence had spent much of her adult life in jail. I knew the flat in Kenard that the IRA had used for their first 'investigation' was hers. I knew she held a senior position in the IRA, though I wasn't entirely sure what that position was.

Padraic Wilson was a small thin man, with hair shaved close to his head and a nose that curved up in a point at the tip. He was wearing a blue checked shirt with a white T-shirt underneath it, and a pair of faded blue jeans. His eyes were cold, but he smiled as he made the introductions. He needed no introduction to me – I knew his background well. He had held the position of OC of the prisoners in Long Kesh until his early release in 1999, when he had served a third of a twenty-four year sentence for possession of a car bomb. Unlike Marie, I had often seen Padraic around, mostly in the company of IRA head of intelligence, Bobby Storey, and it was clear from the people he kept company with that he was also in a senior position within the IRA. If there was any doubt, he dispelled it with chilling clarity.

'Máiría,' Padraic said, 'I want to make it clear that we are here, that I am here, from the Leadership. Not Belfast or the northern leadership, but the Leadership.'

By now, so much had happened that I didn't think it unusual to be sitting with this man, nor did I give a thought to what he may have done during his lifetime to warrant such a position

– I was on a merry-go-round of jarring shocks, and the more often they happened the less impact they had, as the machine spun faster. And, like the playground rides of my youth, it still produced a sick feeling, but as time went on things became so much of a blur that they blended into each other. Nothing seemed real any more. I didn't feel fear, which seems strange now: the IRA wasn't an organisation known for its benevolance. It felt almost normal to be sitting there with 'the Leadership' discussing Morris's disappearance. After all, who else was I going to be able to get answers from?

He got up and moved closer to where Marie was sitting, so that he was directly facing me, and hunkered down at the fireplace, clasping his hands together over one of his knees. I was starting to lose the rattled feeling of adrenaline that I had after my encounter with Ellen, and I calmed myself and lit a cigarette.

Marie informed me that Breige had been away and had been telephoned by another IRA woman, Mary, once the newspaper article appeared, and asked to come home. 'She never gets a minute's peace. She's really feeling it over this, you know,' she said.

I let her words hang in the air. All these IRA people feeling for me. She had an easy-going manner and a nice smile, and I identified more with her than the more serious and intimidating Wilson.

I spoke next: 'Look, there's no point in me being here for a guddying* session,' I said, having resigned myself to the fact that it was fruitless to have an antagonistic meeting. I didn't see the point in that, if I was going to get any answers as to where Morris was. And I needed answers. For peace of mind and to reassure myself that he was not going to come after me in the immediate future.

'I need youse to understand,' I continued, 'that I do not believe Morris has disappeared; I believe you have let this guy go.'

Padraic looked me straight in the eye and told me they were still trying to piece together what had happened. 'No, no no,' he

---

* 'Guddying' is Belfast slang for 'gutting'.

said. 'We haven't, like. This is a really unfortunate chain of events, and Morris has done a runner, he's disappeared.'

I snapped: 'Well, you [meaning the IRA] had him under house arrest from 23rd July. It's now the 7th of August, and are you seriously telling me from a period of Tuesday to Sunday of this week you didn't know he was gone until it appeared in the newspaper?' Wilson was after all a man who it was rumoured had kept suspected informers locked up and made people disappear; the notion that he couldn't keep Morris under surveillance for more than a week was farcical.

He looked disgruntled at the fact that I was effectively criticising the IRA, and he also appeared to be struggling to control his temper. 'I've been instructed to issue an apology to you on behalf of Óglaigh na hÉireann,' he said. 'We're really sorry. We don't know what has gone wrong, but rest assured we'll get to the bottom of it.'

I ignored the apology. 'Well, are you going to go and find him?' I enquired.

'Well,' he said, 'you know we're not really sure... you'd be as well just concentrating on your health and sorting yourself out...'

'Do you want to explain to me what happened?' I said in an exasperated tone. Wilson told me again that they weren't really sure what had happened, but that they were making enquiries. I was chain-smoking in an effort to keep my own temper, and I could see the clouds of smoke encircling his head as he spoke, like the metaphorical smoke he was blowing at me. Every time he moved, he disturbed it, and every time he spoke, he disturbed the thought process in my head.

I still needed answers to my questions. 'Where was he being held – in Ardoyne?' I asked. I had been told by an uncle that Morris was in his relatives' house in Ardoyne at one point, but I wasn't sure what to believe.

'Yeah,' Padraic confirmed, looking embarrassed. Pink spots were starting to appear on his cheeks, flushing the grey pallor of his face. Until that point no one would confirm to me where Morris had been hidden. Had I known at the time, it might have been easier for me to involve the police, because I would have had some knowledge of where they could find him. Padraic continued: 'He was under strict instructions not to leave.' As if he was a good boy told to come home on time!

I exhaled sharply and let his words hang in the air. Marie lowered her head. All three of us, I have no doubt, realised how stupid that statement sounded, and I wanted to hammer that point home with them. 'Did you have someone watching him?' I asked sarcastically.

'We can't go into that, that's internal operations stuff!' he exclaimed. I knew he was beginning to become frustrated with the unspoken assertion that the IRA couldn't organise a piss-up in a brewery, and that in this case they hadn't wanted to.

Marie tried to calm things down. 'Look, love,' she said, 'we appreciate that this has been very traumatic for you, and in hindsight we have traumatised you. Breige wants you to know that she has taken this to heart, and she thought she was doing the right thing.'

I didn't respond. What could I say? No answer would have really been appropriate at that moment. I could have wailed about the unfairness of it all, about the fact that the IRA had traumatised me to the point where I wanted to be dead, but that would have taken the focus away from Morris and trying to find out where he had gone. I wanted to keep my head as far as possible.

Padraic began a monologue about how it was important that I didn't speak to anyone about meeting them, and that they needed to protect their positions, that they had families too.

'I'm fucking talking to nobody about this,' I said. 'I just want… you know, this guy just needs to face up to what he's done. He's out there, God knows where, doing God knows what…'

It was Marie's turn to look uncomfortable again, as she clearly understood exactly what I was saying. I think she felt that concern, though I can't be sure, except for a look that passed between us as Padraic wrapped the meeting up. He told me they would come back to me with some answers to my questions, and I left and walked to my parents' house.

I didn't know what to think. I was due to meet the Sinn Féin president the following day. I needed to prepare myself mentally for that. I tried, at least, but discovered that you can't really ready yourself mentally for a meeting with Gerry Adams.

21

The meeting with Adams was a little less hostile than my encounter with the Army Council pair on the previous day. It did however start badly. He was lounging back on his seat, feet up on the desk. He had a pair of Moses sandals on with the hairs on his toes poking through the gaps in the leather. I didn't know whether to laugh or cry at the sight of him. He had his hands clasped across his stomach, fingers entwined, almost priest-like. He motioned for me to sit down. I sat on the other side of the desk and waited for him to speak.

He took his time, looking at me and smiling before he said in his measured way: 'Well so, have you questions for me?'

'No, it's okay, I got all the answers to the questions I needed yesterday,' I said drily, meaning that I believed the IRA had moved Morris on. He swung his feet off the desk and his eyes flashed briefly. I felt the burn. He tapped his fingers but recovered his outward serenity just as quickly as his mask had slipped. I was surprised at the flash; I had never experienced that side of him before and it scared me a bit. I had known Gerry Adams since I was a child and was used to seeing him in the company of my relatives. I saw him frequently in the radio station, the Festival office and in west Belfast at events where he would always offer me a hug. Later I worked in an office two down from his. I was used to his fun side, his childish antics – like the time he hopped all over pages I was photocopying or confiscated my Down GAA colours that I had hung in the office to taunt his support of Antrim. Of course I had also seen him in serious mode on the television, but I was not used to an angry Gerry up close and personal.

'Look, I'm under pressure here and I can't understand for the life of me why youse waded in to do this. I want a guarantee that this is not going to happen to anyone again,' I said to him.

'You need to take your time, Máiría. This was a unique situation and the resolution has not been great for anybody,' he said.

I exhaled in frustration: 'Look, Gerry, what has all this been about, you're not getting this, why have youse put me through all of this – and there certainly has been *no* resolution for me.' I wasn't about to play the game of making a distinction about who had what position within the republican movement. I spoke about him and the 'Army' as one and the same entity, and he didn't correct me. He smiled and tapped his fingers on his beard, then said he didn't know Morris.

It was my turn to get angry: 'You don't know Marty Morris, Gerry, do ya not? He's been sitting on the Festival management committee with you for the last three years, he's been a member of the IRA in the Murph for the last twenty or so, he's an ex-prisoner, he works in the resource centre, you were invited to his wedding, and he's the public face of CRJ, and you don't know him? Do you think I'm simple?'

He smiled again and shifted slightly in his seat. 'What I meant is I don't know him very well, he's not a personal friend. I want to say I'm sorry on behalf of the republican family for what happened to you. I know from my own experiences of talking to people who have been abused like you that it is very damaging, and I know that your abuse has been traumatic. I believe *you*.'

That emphasis on the 'you', I took to mean that either he wanted me to think that he didn't believe the IRA about their thoughts on my abuse, or he wanted me to think that the IRA didn't believe me. I let him continue. He talked about me being bright and having a future ahead of me, and about Morris escaping. He said that the 'Army' had told him that it was a mistake and he said that he didn't know Breige Wright well but he had heard she was a good girl.

I retorted, 'You want to be slapping the head of Seamy Finucane well, for he's a fucking arsehole.'

He grimaced a bit and told me that some people would say Seamy was a respected volunteer. I told him I didn't respect him, and that the IRA should never have become involved in things like this. He said he had been told that the whole thing had stalled the first time because I couldn't give enough detail about the abuse. I asked him to put himself in the head of an eighteen-year-old who had been through what I had, and then try to talk out loud in front of three IRA people, one of them male, about what had happened.

He said that the republican movement was not always equipped to deal with 'cases like this'. He never mentioned social services, or the police. He told me that I needed to concentrate on healing myself and that if I thought I needed any help he would try his best. He told me that some people thought of suicide when they were abused but it wasn't the answer. He asked me if I wanted him to ask the IRA any questions.

I said I wanted to know why they had let Morris go where he would have access to other children, and were they going to try and find him? He replied that his understanding was they hadn't let him go but he was not sure about the second question.

He got up from where he was sitting and came round and sat beside me, the window behind him. I was tired and looked out of the window. A tourist bus went by with people taking photos just outside the window on the top deck. It was a strange feeling. I began to watch the traffic; it was a good distraction for me so that I wouldn't cry. We spoke about the impact the rapes and abuse had had on me. He was going on about abusers and about how they could manipulate their victims. He talked about how they made them afraid, and how they groomed them. 'You know, Máiría, sometimes abusers are so manipulative that the people who are abused actually enjoy it.'

That brought me back to my senses and I snapped: 'Well I didn't fucking enjoy it! And another thing, Gerry, yes, I do have a question for you. Do you really expect me to believe that you have known nothing of this when Siobhán has known about it for years? Do you expect me to believe that she didn't come in and tell you at any stage that this could potentially blow? Do you think that I'm that stupid? I don't believe you.'

Siobhán was Adams's adviser and secretary; it was inconceivable that she had not forewarned him of the potential damage this could do to the republican movement if it leaked. I believed he had known about it from the initial stages of the investigation at least.

He took a breath and stroked his beard again. He put his hand on my knee, saying, 'I love you and we love you.'

I looked at him but said nothing. There was a short silence which began to grow uncomfortable. He asked me to give him a hug. I did and he kissed my cheek. My head started to spin. 'You know I'm here if you need me, we're here.' There was no point in continuing.

I looked at him again. 'I just want Morris back so that he can admit what he has done and so that no wee child ever goes through that again.' Then I coldly thanked him for his time and walked out.

22

When my Uncle Joe died in 2004, I wrote a piece about him in *An Phoblacht*. Although I was long out of Sinn Féin by that stage, the family tie to republicanism meant that I was reluctant to break from what I knew, from the mentality of the 'sons of Róisín' that had unconsciously seeped into me as I grew up.

I signed off at the end with: 'We are winning Joe, and you made a lot of that possible.' It was a reference to something he would say to me to check if I was feeling okay: 'Are we winning?', and I would smile and say yes, though most took it to mean that the 'republican family' was succeeding. Adams congratulated me on the piece at a tribute concert that Christy Moore played after Joe's death in the Beechmount Leisure Centre, and told me to keep writing. '*Dáiríre*,' he said, using the Irish word for 'seriously'. It is doubtful that he would give me the same encouragement now.

I only saw Joe really lose his temper once, in the West Belfast Festival marquee, then situated in an industrial estate in Kennedy Way. A music group called Seanchaí & the Unity Squad was playing, and Joe and Annie had come to see them, sitting down at my table. They were in great form, though slightly bemused at the group's fusion of hip-hop and reggae beats. The band, fronted by Chris Byrne, were based in Manhattan but were popular in west Belfast due to a 'mistake' for which I was in part responsible, when on the last night of the Festival Radio station we caused uproar (and international headlines) by pressing the repeat button on their song 'Fenians' and played the song over 140 times, all that night.

Joe knew they were popular and was enjoying the reels they were playing, tapping his foot along in time to the beat. All of that changed, when the drum-beat started up again and the group launched into a rap song, 'Thirty Years On', which was infused with verses from songs about Kevin Barry (the young IRA man executed in 1920) and Joe McDonnell (the Wolfe Tones' song about the hunger striker who died in 1981). Joe went nuts. He was old school, and while the song was very popular with the crowd, Joe did not appreciate the fusion of rap and republican lyrics. He got up and told Annie they were going, and I walked with them outside to try and calm him down. Siobhán O'Hanlon, who was Joe's niece, was inside the entrance hut counting up the night's takings. She knew immediately something was wrong and came out to see what it was.

'That's a fucking disgrace in there,' Joe shouted at her. She tried to get to the bottom of exactly what his objection was, but he was apoplectic. He wanted to know who had booked the group and told her whoever it was should be ashamed of themselves. Siobhán, uncharacteristically, said nothing and took the tongue-lashing. As he was leaving, he threw his arms around me and told me he wasn't angry at me, but 'at that effin monstrosity in there'. As they left, Siobhán, embarrassed by the dressing-down, looked at me, sarcastically said, 'Well, he wasn't shouting at the golden child anyway,' and went back to counting the money.

Other occasions with him were more enjoyable. One night in the Devenish bar, at the Bobby Sands memorial lecture, music from the Wolfe Tones was blaring out over a speaker as we sat and talked. 'The Boys of the Old Brigade' started playing, and Joe laughed and shouted in my ear over the music: 'Where are the boys from the old brigade?' As I turned to him with my eyebrow raised, he looked at me and smiled. 'I'm the bloody last one standing.'

He had views, too, on a very different brigade: those who fought in the Spanish Civil War, particularly those from the Lower Falls and Shankill roads who fought side by side in the International Brigade:

They were very courageous people, they went out there because they believed it was the right thing to do. But I have a personal opinion on that and whilst I appreciate their thoughts on going out there, and whilst I recognise their cause was just, we had a bigger cause in Ireland and I think they should have stayed in Ireland and fought here.[9]

Even in his seventies, he was haunted by what had happened to Tom Williams in 1942: 'I think Tom's name is synonymous with the struggle for freedom in this country and in my day, he was our Kevin Barry. To me it is just as if it happened yesterday, it's something that I have had to live with all my life and Tom is still very close to me.' He reflected on what Tom would say to him now and what his thoughts would be:

They are no different today as what they were when he and I talked in the condemned cell. And I have happy memories of those conversations I had with Tom. His hope for the future, what he'd like to see in Ireland and the great love he had for Ireland and its people, he would talk about for those who carried on after we were gone, what he would like to see for them, and he had always one great saying – 'if we were left alone there would be no problems in Ireland', and by that he meant if there was no British influence in this country then the people of Ireland could live in harmony. And I think that message would ring throughout Ireland today, he would say: 'without a British influence in this country we could solve whatever differences there are between all the people of Ireland, and that the people of this whole island could live in true freedom, justice and equality. And I know that Tom is looking down on us tonight, and me saying those words, I am echoing his words. And if he were sitting at this microphone tonight he would reiterate the message that he wrote the night before he went to the scaffold: 'Carry on my comrades until that certain day.' I believe that in spite of what doesn't seem to be going right today, in spite of all the obstacles that are in our road, that prophecy of Tom Williams is coming to pass, that certain day is approaching. And Tom, you will be able to rest in peace. The people of this island will enjoy true friendship, freedom, justice and equality.[10]

Joe firmly believed those words, but he also knew that it was useful propaganda. Republicans often invoke the ghosts of their dead to sell their ideals. In March 2017, Gerry Kelly MLA tweeted: 'In all negotiations our patriot dead are there with us in the room…' It's always useful to have a few spirits around.

I was at Tom Williams's formal funeral in January 2000, 58 years after he was executed. For decades, the republican movement had campaigned to have his body released from Crumlin Road Gaol, where he was interred in an unmarked grave, so they could bury him at Milltown Cemetery. The night before the funeral, there was a mass in St Paul's chapel, and I attended with Joe and Annie. I sat between them and Gerry Adams, who knelt and said prayers with the rest. The next day, crowds surrounded the church and lined the route to the cemetery, nestled between the Black Mountain and the M1 motorway. Shortly before Tom was hanged, he wrote a letter to his Uncle Charlie: 'If it comes to the worst, as I'm sure it will, I will face my enemies with courage and spirit, which many gallant Irishmen have done this last 700 years … I am writing this letter to let you know that my heart was in the IRA.'

Joe had come a long way on his own journey by the time his comrade Williams was buried. No longer an active IRA man, but honorary vice president of Sinn Féin, he had endorsed the Good Friday Agreement two years earlier. He had no regrets about his role in the armed conflict, except that he didn't get to spend more time with his wife and children.

By the time I became close to him, Joe was a bespeckled elderly man with a kindly face and a twinkle in his eye. He never lost his temper with me, and provided comfort at difficult periods of my life. He would wear numerous vests under his two jumpers to keep warm, and this meant that hugs were like snuggling up to a blanket. At the launch of Brendan Anderson's book about Joe's life, he signed a copy for me: 'To cheeky face, my favourite niece, love Uncle Joe.' He looked at me and said: 'You are my favourite, you know.' I cannot reconcile the man I knew with the one who I now see on video clips as a younger man.

In one Associated Press pool interview, recorded in August 1971, the interviewer asked: 'Brian Faulkner, the prime minister of Northern Ireland, describes you and your colleagues as subhuman murderers. How would you describe you and your friends?'

Joe sat back nonchalantly and said: 'Men inspired with the highest of ideals, that's something that Brian Faulkner can't claim to have. He is a man without a country, without an ideal.' He went on to say that IRA recruits were 'flowing in' and talked about 'a revolutionary army' needing bigger weapons to fight the British army. To anyone who didn't know Joe, the clip would be chilling. I did know him, and it was still chilling to see that side of him – though I know he wasn't exactly an angel. A psychotherapist might analyse the clip and see someone who had desensitised themselves, who instead of seeing the tragedy of taking individual human life, saw the battle instead as one of wits – of one army taking on another, in a David and Goliath fight.

In September 1971, Joe was deported from the United States. In a press conference the reporter held up a newspaper for him to look at. 'Mr Cahill, I've got here a picture of an eighteen-month-old baby in a coffin, killed, it says here … by a sniper's bullet fired by the IRA. What's your comment about that?'

Joe looked at the newspaper, held a few inches away from his face, took a breath and said: 'Both wings of the IRA have emphatically denied responsibility for this or any involvement in it. I accept their word on it.' There were no words of condemnation for the death of baby Angela Gallagher, who, according to the book *Lost Lives*, 'died in the arms of her young sister after a bullet fired by an IRA man ricocheted and hit her'.

Joe Cahill was taking a risk in allowing himself to be interviewed – though it proved a propaganda necessity in the campaign to win support for the IRA in the United States. In 1971, the IRA were responsible for 107 violent deaths out of 180 that year in Northern Ireland. Sixty-four of them were soldiers, RUC, or UDR, and the rest civilians – what the IRA later callously termed 'collateral damage'.

Yet when I was a child he was just Uncle Joe, and when I learned that Morris had disappeared I wrote a letter to McCrory and Wright, telling them how they had affected me during the first IRA 'investigation' and saying that I was going to speak to my uncle. I thought this might worry them because of his previous seniority in the IRA and the respect in which he was held by the wider movement, and give them pause for thought. I met the two women outside the Sinn Féin office and grunted at Maura McCrory while handing the letter to Breige. She read it and said she didn't have a problem with me speaking with Joe, though I didn't need a green light from her now that he already knew.

As it happened, he was at the Sinn Féin office himself that day and we went out to his car to talk. I told him I wasn't coping very well, and he asked me how the IRA meeting had gone. I told him, and he said angrily: 'There's been a fuck up of the highest order in the movement.' He told me about another young person who he knew had been abused, and that they had gone to the RUC, who were 'decent' in their dealings with her family.

But he then explained the problem, as he saw it: because the IRA had involved themselves in holding an inquiry into my abuse at the hands of an IRA volunteer, going to the RUC was not an option for me. We discussed this – he was of the opinion that the police would seek information on the IRA, and that I would be placed in a vulnerable position. I had met with Gerry Adams and senior IRA representatives. I knew too much, in other words. Joe was a seasoned republican. He looked at me sadly and said: 'If I had known [before the IRA investigation], I would have told you to go to the RUC.' He left me in no doubt that that option was no longer on the table. I hugged him, and he held me for a while, and he said he would be there for me and told me to dry my eyes.

In November 2003, Sinn Féin organised a testimonial dinner for Joe in the Citywest Hotel in Dublin. It was a big event for the party, hundreds of people buying tickets at 100 euros each, and it was a far cry from other events that week, such as housing protests outside Tánaiste Mary Harney's constituency office organised by Ballyfermot Sinn Féin.

I went to see Joe in his room. Both of us were in wheelchairs; I had dislocated my kneecap and was in plaster from my ankle to my hip, and I offered to race him up and down the corridor, which amused him greatly. Many people had bought tickets to the dinner, though few knew just how sick Joe was, or that he had just been released from hospital a week before. He was on oxygen in the hotel room before the event and afterwards, and his health soon began to fail further. He gave a speech that night, and I looked at him, marvelling at the difference between the man I had watched struggle for breath a few hours before and the one in front of the microphone. The republican movement was his life-blood: his entire existence had been inextricably linked with the IRA. I saw a man who was tired, but who signed every last book put in front of him later that evening in spidery handwriting. I also saw a political party that knew how ill he was, and did not urge him to take a break. I resolved never to allow republicanism to suck the life-blood out of me.

Still, it was an enjoyable evening. Joe had insisted I sit at his table, and I spent the night being wheeled around the place by various relatives and friends. The next morning, as my friends Julie and Carol and I were waiting for our lift back to the bus station, Gerry Adams came over to me, lifted a pen out of his pocket and signed my plaster cast.

My last encounter with Joe was on his deathbed when my father and I called to see him. He was struggling to breathe. The asbestos dust he had inhaled decades earlier while working at the Harland and Wolff shipyard had ravaged his lungs, and he sounded as if he was sucking in water when he took a breath. I held his hand, and he was conscious as I spoke to him. I was making small talk with him, and he stopped me to whisper that he would look after me.

I said to him: 'Hey boy, you better look after me, I need it,' and a few tears came out of his eyes as he lifted his hand slightly and squeezed mine. I cried with him in silence as I stroked his hand with my thumb. I kissed his cheek, and left the room walking backwards, holding his gaze until I got to the doorframe. 'I'll see you soon,' I said quietly and blew him a kiss, knowing the next time I would see him would be in his coffin.

Thousands attended his wake in the small house he had lived in, which meant there was an almost continuous single file of people for days to see Joe's body laid out in the living room. People filed in through the front door and snaked into the room on the right. Six IRA members stood guard at the coffin. People shook the family's hands and then filed through the hall and out through the back door of the house. A gazebo had been erected in the garden, and I spent a lot of my time over those few days sitting with Colette and Gerry Adams or with my cousins. The weather was good, and there were lots of people milling about: old republicans like then Sinn Féin councillor Christy Burke with his dark glasses who stood outside the door with other Sinn Féin leadership figures; the very large Cahill clan of cousins; and people from all over Ireland who came to pay their respects. Marie Wright, who was dying of leukaemia, came in a wheelchair; her sister Breige was one of the people standing guard at the coffin.

They took it in shifts, the IRA guard, some of them resting in the front bedroom upstairs while the others were on coffin duty. When it was time to change, the house was cleared, except for the family. At one stage, I found myself sitting on the stairs in the middle of the shift change, thinking to myself: 'What in the name of God…?' A man called them to attention in Irish and they marched into the room where the coffin was, while the other members of the guard only relaxed when they were relieved of their positions. They would then go and take their place in the bedroom. No one was allowed to speak during this shift change. An official republican photographer was sent in to photograph Joe lying in his coffin, and his funeral was also filmed, a DVD which Sinn Féin later sold for £5 a copy.

One man came with his caravan and parked it outside on the street. No one knew who he was, though he caught everyone's attention. At the funeral, he somehow ended up in the cordoned-off area of the cemetery reserved for the family, though he was eventually asked to move. Years later his face appeared on the television news and I recognised him. He was Ted Cunningham, one of the few people convicted of laundering the money from the £26m Northern Bank robbery in Belfast, the largest in the history of the two islands, which took place a few months after Joe's funeral and is widely believed to have been organised by the late Bobby Storey on behalf of the IRA. Chris Ward, the bank worker kidnapped and taken hostage who was later charged and found not guilty of involvement in the robbery, was a friend of mine, and we later had a brief relationship. The Northern Bank was a big coup for the IRA, and Chris Ward's parents, ordinary decent people who were also held hostage by people from their own community, were treated despicably.

The funeral was held on a sweltering hot day in July. Former IRA members flanked the hearse, while other republicans marched in two lines on either side, in black and white attire. It was a piece of political-military theatre, to demonstrate the strength of the republican movement rather than to provide any measure of real respect. Senior leadership figures such as Adams and McGuinness walked with the cortège, and I found myself at one point walking between Mary Lou McDonald, the current leader of Sinn Féin, and Lucilita Bhreatnach, the former general secretary of the party, with whom I was friendly. I was devastated by Joe's death and it was hard to conduct small talk in that situation, so I have very little memory of anything anyone said to me that day.

Adams gave the oration at Milltown Cemetery, making a joke about how Joe would have seen his funeral as a missed opportunity for a republican collection bucket, and singer Frances Black sang 'The Bold Fenian Men'. We threw our roses and mud into the space where his coffin lay, and went to the Felons Club afterwards, where my cousins and I bought a Jameson's whiskey and left it untouched on the table in his memory, and drank other glasses of alcohol to numb the grief.

23

Towards the end of the first week in August 2000 Siobhán O'Hanlon came into the office where I was working. I was on the telephone, so she wrote a note: 'I'll talk to you tomorrow. His national insurance number was passed on to social services so they could check where he is and to ensure he doesn't have contact with kids. Also, I have asked about your meeting with Padraic.'

I motioned for her to wait until I could finish the call. She wouldn't tell me who had spoken with social services or how she knew.* I was finding it difficult to remain calm, so she drove to her

---

* The 'tip off' to social services named a relative who had not been abused, but did name the correct perpetrator. In October 2018, the Police Ombudsman for Northern Ireland wrote in a closure letter to me that: 'The Police Ombudsman became aware that in September 2000 the North and West Belfast Health and Social Services Trust recorded an initial referral and assessment following anonymous concerns and a newspaper article suggesting that two young children may have been sexually abused . . . at the end of November 2000 the N&WBHSST Child Protection team closed the case . . . The child protection team were in contact with a Grosvenor Road CARE Unit Detective Constable and a Detective Sergeant and kept them updated throughout the case. This investigation has not identified evidence of corresponding police enquiries. Instead, and consistent with practice at the time, police performed a passive role, awaiting developments from social services...' In October 2018, I complained to the Belfast Trust and urged them to conduct a review. They found a number of 'key areas of learning' but refused to release their report to me. The Department of Health commissioned an external review in 2019, which at the time of writing, has not begun.

friend's house with me and returned with a tranquilliser. Women in west Belfast were used to living on their nerves and used to sharing valium, and it was normal to hear the phrase 'Have you a wee Roche?' casually inserted into female conversation. I took it, and for a while I felt settled.

I still couldn't eat, and was surviving on half an apple a day and bottles of Coke. I was put on the rota to work outside the Féile marquee for the West Belfast Festival, which took place every August, but I couldn't stop shaking. Siobhán went to the man who was running the security and asked him to move me inside. My heart was thumping in my chest and I couldn't make it to the end of the night, so I went home to try and sleep.

The next evening, the IRA, in the form of Marie Wright and Padraic Wilson, arranged a meeting with my father at my parents' house. My mum refused to see them and drove to Donegal with my younger sister. I had developed a lump on my neck and it was stiff and sore. I was present for the first few minutes of the meeting but, feeling increasingly unwell, I went up to my parents' room, lay on their bed and listened to raised voices in the room below. My father complained about the IRA forcing me into an investigation, and the fact that as soon as he had said to Siobhán O'Hanlon that he wanted Morris handed over to RUC custody, he had disappeared. He was effectively accusing the IRA of moving Morris out of the jurisdiction so he couldn't be reported to the police. The IRA told my father they would be disciplining the people involved in the first IRA investigation. My father told him he didn't want to know the IRA's business.

When it was over and the IRA had left, I ventured downstairs again and noticed that Marie Wright had left a knitted woollen child's hat on our sofa. Assuming it had fallen out of her handbag, we drove in my dad's car and caught up with them at the top of Stockmans Lane, and as I handed the hat back to her Marie Wright looked at me and said, 'You don't look very well, Máiría.'

'I don't feel very well either,' I replied, and when my father and I got home a few minutes later, I asked him to phone the out-of-hours doctor, who came to the house and after examining me advised my father to get me to the Royal Victoria Hospital. I was wheeled to a bed in the old part of the hospital, a large magnolia-coloured room with an outside balcony. Once in bed, the enormity of what had happened over those weeks overwhelmed me. I cried uncontrollably, and the ward nurse sent for a doctor who sedated me. I couldn't speak or open my eyes the next morning when they came to take my blood pressure, and the night nurse who was leaving to go home kept rubbing my cheek with her thumb to tell me it was going to be okay. They at first suspected I had meningitis, but ruled that out and sent a psychiatric nurse to my bedside instead.

The nurse tried to talk to me but I could only communicate by nodding or shaking my head, which I couldn't properly lift off the pillow. She asked me if there was something wrong and I nodded. Was it boyfriend trouble? I shook my head. She sat with me for a while and told me she was there if I wanted to talk. How could I possibly tell this well-meaning nurse about being abused, put through a botched IRA 'investigation' and then having tense meetings with the IRA leadership and Gerry Adams?

It was a concern of Siobhán's too, though in a different way, when I telephoned from the hospital later to explain what had happened.

'Don't be saying anything,' she said, alarmed that I might start talking – the IRA obsession with silence and keeping it in 'the family' overruled all other considerations. There was an RUC man stationed at the end of the next ward and when I discussed this with her, she sent people over to visit me, presumably to give me less opportunity to speak to anyone, above all the police. She also visited me, and telephoned Breige from the hospital and put her on the phone to me. 'I'll see you when you get out,' she said.

I had been seeing her regularly since Morris had disappeared, mainly because I wanted her to know the damage the IRA had done to me. This may seem strange, but I felt a connection with her since she had hugged me and shown me some human warmth. As an entity, the IRA had scared the wits out of me, but being around someone for the duration of that endless investigation, and because I had been hugged – the only act of kindness any of them had shown in a very disturbing and threatening situation – meant that I couldn't let the contact with her go. I never wanted to see any of the rest of them again, but Breige had shown a morsel of what I perceived to be regret for her part in events. I think I needed to speak about why the whole grotesque process was so damaging to me, with someone who was there. So I agreed to meet with her when I got out of the hospital.

Over the next few days, I tried to eat the hospital food and get some strength back. Walking was difficult and Siobhán, who was smaller than me, encouraged me to try and walk a few steps to the balcony with her arm around my waist. I was dehydrated too, and the nurses told me they were going to put me on a drip. Both of my arms were bandaged because of an infected cannula. I couldn't take a shower, so a nurse ran a bath, undressed me and helped me into it while she sat at the door, which was unlocked because I couldn't be left unsupervised. It was embarrassing, and I resolved to drink as much fluid as I could so I wouldn't have to be bathed by anyone else again.

My father visited every day, and once Uncle Joe and Aunt Annie came. It was a risk for him to do so – this was, after all, just two years after he had returned from being on the run; republicans were always wary of being targeted by loyalists and security was not exactly tight in the Royal. I was glad to see them. We joked about my bandaged wrists, and I realised he thought I had tried to kill myself. 'Don't worry, Joe, if I'm going to do myself in, you'll be the first to know,' I said, smiling.

The hospital let me go after a week or so. I was never told what was wrong with me, though my hospital notes indicated I had tonsillitis, which I doubted, as I'd never had problems with my tonsils. Whatever the cause, the lump on my neck persisted for a few years. The body reacts to extreme stress in surprising ways.

I knew I needed to do something to ease the acute anxiety I was feeling. Above all, I needed to get answers from the IRA.

24

The world outside was still turning. It was a new millennium. Robbie Williams's 'Rock DJ' was top of the charts, and the RUC was kept busy defusing pipe bombs left in various parts of Northern Ireland by loyalist paramilitaries. There was a vicious feud between a faction of the Ulster Defence Association led by Johnny Adair, and the Ulster Volunteer Force. Two UDA men, Jackie Coulter and Bobby Mahood, were shot dead by the UVF. Sinn Féin's Martin Meehan was fighting a by-election in South Antrim, and Gerry Adams, writing in *An Phoblacht*, denounced the Northern Ireland Secretary Peter Mandelson's proposed policing bill, stating that Sinn Féin would 'not settle for something less' than an entirely new force.[11]

Sinn Féin was also campaigning for the release of the Castlerea Five, IRA prisoners who were serving time in the Republic of Ireland for the murder of Garda Jerry McCabe. Sinn Féin's Gerry Kelly stated: 'There was a Good Friday negotiation and prisoners were part of that. These men belonged to the IRA ... You cannot have a two-tier system.'[12]

I was struck that Sinn Féin also issued a press statement at the end of August in the name of Vincent Wood, an Ard Chomhairle (national governing body) member, about support services for women experiencing abuse: '... up to a quarter of Mayo women in relationships are experiencing domestic violence or abuse of one kind or another,' he said. 'This is a disturbing statistic, but what is additionally worrying is that but for the existence of women's support groups, abuse of this kind would go unreported[13].'

Meanwhile, in west Belfast, in the same month, the IRA had actively prevented our family reporting my abuse to the police and still had no answers about where my abuser was. In September 2000, frustrated at the fact that the IRA had forced its way into my life uninvited, turned my world upside down and had now gone to ground when it came to answering simple questions, I wrote a letter to the IRA Army Council.

> I first asked for a meeting six weeks ago with yourselves. I do appreciate that people are busy, but given the urgency – which I feel should and needs to be applied to this case, I expected at least a reply.
>
> The fact that I have been waiting on this cruinniú [meeting] for so long leads me to believe that the Army are deliberately delaying the meeting.
>
> I don't believe that my request was unreasonable, given the fact that I have been messed about since the moment when the other allegations surfaced.
>
> The lapse in time has given me the space to think a little with regards to the Army's role in all of this. I now wish to make a formal complaint about, and am asking for clarification on exactly how Marty Morris was able to disappear. Although it pains me to say this, as it contradicts my beliefs and feelings towards the republican movement as a whole – I have come to the conclusion that it was easier for the republican movement to let Marty Morris go, rather than deal with the situation. It is now my view that the Army was not equipped to deal with the situation, and if this is the case, then why bother putting me through the first investigation and also give me the option of re-initiating this investigation, once it became clear that other children were involved.
>
> I also want to make it clear that I believe the Army's intentions were honourable (with regards to the two women

who dealt with me) and one in particular has been of great comfort and has given me support throughout the last year.

However, I have a great personal difficulty with the people who's [sic] responsibility it was to make decisions. I cannot conceive how, when two allegations surface on top of one already made, that an abuser, particularly a member of the movement, can be allowed freedom and how he can disappear. I also do not understand how, from Tuesday night to Sunday afternoon, a period of five days, no-one noticed his disappearance – unless it put the army in a more convenient position not to notice it. Why did no-one check his whereabouts, particularly if he was held on the Tuesday night? How can the army not have the resources in the middle of Ardoyne to make sure he stayed put? Why was no-one aware of his payment from CRJ?

My life has been destroyed – not only by Marty Morris, but also by the people who messed this whole situation up. I can't accept the fact that he is free to live somewhere else, with access to other children. The responsibility for this again lies with the Army. It doesn't lie with me or my family. In my view, if someone is a member of the Army, brings the movement into disrepute, then regardless of the family wishes – the Army should have pressed ahead with the matter. No revolutionary organisation can afford to have paedophiles or suspected paedophiles in its ranks – especially one with a profile in restorative justice. It doesn't make good PR sense, good internal and external relationships, and it certainly doesn't bring republicanism further on in its goals, aims and objectives. By letting Marty Morris go, you collectively planted the seed that it was okay for him to do what he did – it didn't matter that I lost part of my childhood and it was pointless in me going through the investigation. You also changed my opinion with regards to how the Army deals with things…How can I advise anyone in a similar situation to myself to go to you to try and right the wrongs? I could have went [sic] to the RUC and got the same result – at least he might have stayed in the country. Is the message then that it's alright for a volunteer to abuse children, because that's what it seems like at the moment.

I'm asking you to take the above points on board, although I don't hold out much hope of a reply, as I have waited over a month on the last one.

Is mise [yours] Máiría.*

Years later, a policeman asked me how I delivered this letter to the elusive Army Council, and I dryly told him that I put it in the postbox, before explaining that I simply gave it to Siobhán O'Hanlon, who delivered it onwards. I expect it is the only letter the IRA Army Council ever received from a nineteen-year-old upstart, but by then I had had enough. I photocopied the letter and kept the copy so that I would remember what I had said to them.

At the first meeting, Padraic Wilson and Marie Wright had implied that the RUC had helped Morris to go. I now believed that the IRA itself had moved him. My line about going to the RUC was a retort and an implied threat to them, and should be read through the eyes of a young woman who had believed for her whole life that the RUC was the enemy of her community and that the IRA was the real authority in the area in which she lived. It was a two-finger salute to the people in charge of the IRA who had put me through the wringer of their 'investigation': I was saying to them that they couldn't organise a piss-up in a brewery and that the RUC couldn't have made a worse job of it — the insult of insult to republicans.

I was also clearly trying to ensure that the two women involved in the second IRA 'investigation', Breige and my cousin Siobhán O'Hanlon, came to no harm. My father and I had been told by the IRA that the people involved would be disciplined. Maura McCrory was not involved in dealing with me in the second IRA episode, and I was deliberately giving the other two a lifeline so

---

* The normal way of signing off a letter in Irish is 'Is mise le meas', meaning, 'yours, respectfully'. I couldn't bring myself to sign off with respect, so I just wrote the equivalent of 'yours'.

that they wouldn't be hurt – though looking back now, I can see the IRA had no intention of disciplining any of its members.

In a world where an entity which you believed could easily kill you had effective control over your body and mind, those few moments of kindness – like when Breige hugged me – were akin to Hansel and Gretel taking crumbs gratefully from the witch who was holding them captive. What is also clear from the letter is that while radicalised by the republican movement – a fairly predictable outcome for a young woman who came from a respected republican family – by September 2000 I was also hugely distrustful of them, and it was unheard of for someone to put this distrust into writing. By effectively telling them that I wouldn't advise any abuse victim to speak to them, I was making it clear that if any further disclosures were made within my wider family, the IRA would not be dealing with them. God knows what the IRA leadership thought when reading it – but the letter had the effect I wanted, and another meeting was arranged with Wilson and Wright as representatives of the Army Council.

It was antagonistic, and the atmosphere could have been cut with a knife. Padraic Wilson was clearly annoyed, and he was bouncing on his heels as he walked across the floor of the living room of the flat in Glassmullin Gardens. Marie Wright sat on the sofa to my right and I sat facing the fireplace, where I had a view of the green pitch outside. Children were playing football again and I could hear the excited shouts from the young players running on the grass. I lit a cigarette and noticed aloud that my pack was nearly empty. Marie went downstairs and summoned one of the young footballers to go to the shop for more.

Padraic meanwhile claimed that he was being contacted by people who had seen Morris in different places, and I couldn't expect them to have the resources to find out where Morris was.

I said that this was bullshit. This was the organisation that had been able to track down and murder supposed informers and elusive loyalist paramilitaries. The year before, Eamon Collins had been murdered for testifying against Thomas 'Slab' Murphy, the

Armagh IRA commander, during a libel trial in a Dublin court. Now Padraic Wilson offered yet another apology on behalf of the IRA and, in the next breath, complained about it, insinuating that all of this was inconveniencing him. He explained once again that he also had a family and that my accusation that the IRA thought what Morris had done was in some way excusable was wrong, and he insisted he had already made his position clear. What else did I want them to do? I started crying.

The young boy who had gone for the cigarettes rang the buzzer of the flat, and Marie went down and told him to keep the change of the £20 note she had given him. I lit another cigarette and tried to pull myself together as I blew the silvery smoke out towards the ceiling of the flat. It hung suspended in the air as I said that it was a two-and-a-half-hour drive to Donegal, and could Padraic not just get in the car and go and see if Morris was there? He knew very well where men on the run were likely to hide.

'Do you think that I am going to be running around after you?' he said in an exasperated tone.

At that moment I realised that as far as the IRA were concerned, the matter was closed. But I tried explaining to them my fear of suddenly bumping into Morris, and my fear that he could potentially have access to other children. One of them said impatiently that they had to move on to other cases. Padraic said that he frequently walked past a known child abuser and felt like digging his head in, but he had to swallow it and get on with it.

Throughout, the attitude was that the IRA were the victims of this situation, that I was accusing them of siding with Morris and they didn't like it. There was a discussion about informers, similar to the one I had had with McCrory and Wright, and I was told again that the IRA leadership were keen to stress that the RUC would use 'touts' for their own ends.* The more or less overt threat, that if I spoke to the police I would join the ranks of despised informers, was obvious. The *Sunday World* report on our case had quoted a police officer stating that nothing had been reported to

---

* Belfast slang for informers.

them about an IRA member abusing girls in Ballymurphy, and saying that if a victim came forward they would be treated with care. Wilson made it clear to me that he believed the RUC had planted the story in the newspaper. It was also clear that there was still no option for me of using the criminal justice system – had there been, the IRA Army Council wouldn't have met me in the first place. It seemed that the organisation's highest priority was to protect its members.

The meeting was going round in circles, and when it was clear there was not going to be any resolution to anyone's satisfaction, Wilson let his frustration get the better of him and stormed out. Marie Wright followed him to the door, where I heard him tell her that he didn't mean to lose his temper and to go back in and apologise to me on his behalf, which she did. I shrugged my shoulders, and she offered to call me a taxi.

A while after this meeting I met Breige on her own. She laughed when she explained that after years in jail, Marie Wright didn't know the value of money, and she had been horrified when she realised she had given a young boy around fifteen pounds in change to keep for himself. It was a lucky day for him, and an appalling one for me.

I met with Adams for the second time shortly after this bleak and hostile meeting. He stroked his beard as he told me he had heard I was unhappy with my treatment. I asked him sarcastically what gave him that impression. He smiled in that inscrutable way he has, all kindness and goodwill, the smile never reaching the eyes. He told me that I needed to look after myself and that if I needed to talk to him I wouldn't need an appointment in future, and he reiterated the apology on behalf of the republican movement. It meant less than nothing to me.

Throughout the month of September, I continued to visit my counsellor. On 4 September, the counselling notes read:

Nervous big ball at the bottom of my stomach that won't go away. Constant. Still printing stories in the newspaper. Feel I'm being lied to. They've [IRA] told me that everything is under control but still haven't found him. Feel sure now that they've let him go, because they don't know how to handle it. Feel like ending it all – don't want to deal with it anymore. Don't feel anything, would like to get in touch with feelings but cannot. Would like to be able to talk about it -feel frightened – think I feel frightened of myself.

On 11 September 2000, the entry reads:

Looking very tired, run down, been to GP and prescribed antidepressants. Feeling sick and unable to sleep, afraid of becoming dependent on them. Bad day yesterday, too much time to think. Know where he is, they know where he is but don't have the resources to bring him back. What to do with him. "Permanent solution is too easy an option." [IRA] certain that RUC are protecting him, 100% that RUC are behind newspaper articles.

On 25 September, the scale of the trauma I was experiencing was clear: 'Would take someone to force me to go to the tip of a mountain and hit me over the head with a breeze block to get me to feel anything.' I was on a downward spiral and had no idea how to process the events of the past few years. Yet things were soon to become even more complicated.

25

I was walking in the dark a few streets from my parents' house one night when my mobile phone rang. It was one of my distant relatives, who I'll call Louise here to protect her identity, wondering how I was. I rarely heard from her, and instinctively knew that something was wrong. She informed me that social services had been in contact with her and wanted to speak to her about Martin Morris and whether he had had any contact with her children. I remembered Siobhán's note about social services being informed, though why had they contacted Louise? Neither of the two other victims who had come forward were her children. I asked for more information, and Louise said she was meeting the officials the next morning and we could speak afterwards. I agreed to call her at a pre-arranged time.

In the Felons Club that evening, an IRA member and a close friend of Siobhán's who had recently come back to live in Belfast after being on the run came over to me and asked me what was wrong. Drunk and maudlin, I explained to her that social services were asking about Marty Morris. She looked panicked and asked me if I had told the IRA. I hadn't even thought of informing them, and realised that now I had told her they would find out.

I arrived at Sinn Féin's offices in Sevastopol Street the next day, and saw Padraic Wilson and another former prisoner, Mary McArdle, sitting in reception. McArdle had been convicted for her part in the murder of Mary Travers, a teacher at my primary school, who was the daughter of Judge Tom Travers, a Catholic magistrate. As Tom and his family were walking out of St Brigid's church in south Belfast on a sunny Sunday in April 1984, two IRA gunmen stepped forward and shot him six times. His wife was also shot, and twenty-two-year-old Mary was fatally shot in the back. Tom Travers miraculously survived and in an open letter in 1994 to the *Irish Times*, he wrote:

> At that time Mary lay dying on her mum's breast, her gentle heart pouring its pure blood onto a dusty street in Belfast. The murderer's gun, which was pointed at my wife's head, misfired twice. Another gunman shot me six times. As he prepared to fire the first shot I saw the look of hatred on his face, a face I will never forget.[14]

Mary McArdle was caught by police shortly after the attack with two handguns and a wig strapped to her leg. At nineteen years of age, she was given a life sentence plus eighteen years for her role in the killing. She was later released under the terms of the Good Friday Agreement.

It wasn't unusual for such people to be in the Sinn Féin building, though Padraic was the last person I wanted to see. I lowered my head and walked upstairs to the office where I worked, and was startled to see Breige and Maura McCrory on the landing. My stomach rolled. They motioned to a small room in between my office and the Sinn Féin International Department's office, and I sat down at a table equipped with a telephone and four green office chairs. I sat on the chair closest to the door with my back to it, and the two women sat on the other side of the table. They asked what I knew about social services and I said I knew very little, as I'd only found they had been in contact with Louise the previous evening. Maura looked at me as though I was lying and asked me to telephone Louise in front of them. I called her and she confirmed that she had indeed met with social services. I repeated what she was saying back to her, to try and let her know that other people were listening to the call. I watched Maura McCrory's eyes widen a bit, telegraphing that the IRA were not exactly happy with these developments.

Breige and McCrory left for a few minutes. When Breige returned, I told her I was also thinking of speaking with social services, and she suggested that she take me to a solicitor she knew to give me information about what social services did in cases like this. Free legal advice, arranged at short notice. I was too tired to argue and said I would go. While this was happening, McCrory and McArdle were dispatched to another of the wider Cahill family, the mother of the two victims who, in July, had stated they had also been abused, to see if they had been contacted by social services. For the IRA, information was power, and they were scrambling.

I was taken to the offices of Belfast solicitor Pádraigín Drinan, where Breige did the talking. I was embarrassed. Breige described the abuse without naming the man, and said that social services were asking questions. She asked the solicitor to explain to me what would be likely to happen. Pádraigín told me that social services would have to speak to the RUC, and if the man was a member of the IRA, the RUC would be very interested in this aspect of his activity and less so in the abuse. The small bit of hope that I had inside was dimming. She also informed me that as I was over eighteen, I was 'not obligated' to speak with them.

Breige also told the solicitor that I was from a very republican family, and there was a discussion about how the authorities would also be interested in information about them. I felt crushed, but it wasn't the solicitor's fault. She was giving advice based on what she knew and was being told. Looking back, it was a clever move to take me there, because it planted a seed of doubt. I asked to go to the toilet, and as I walked back to her office, I saw a leaflet for the Grosvenor Road police station care unit. It was light green and pink and I lifted and folded it and put it in my back pocket before anyone saw me.

Later that day, I walked to the police station, a fortified barracks in a red-brick rectangular building encased by a high wall with iron stanchions and thick wire on top to thwart bomb attacks, and tried to psych myself up to go inside. I paced up and down a few times, but became nervous. What if I was seen going in? What would happen if I did? Some time later Siobhán telephoned and I told her I had almost gone into the station. She was in a carpet shop trying to choose fabric for her house, but left immediately and picked me up.

'What did you do that for?' she asked, in a tone that sounded as though she wanted to slap my face. I told her I felt like I wanted to kill myself.

I wasn't any better the next day, and my eyes were red from crying. I needed to get out of the house and be around people, where I wasn't alone with my thoughts, so I went to the Sinn Féin office where I could have a cup of tea with someone I knew. Looking back, I realise how trapped I was. The only life I knew was now surrounded with republicanism, and the fact that I could see going to the Sinn Féin office as an 'escape' says much about my state of mind. The receptionist, Sinéad, asked me if I could cover for her for a few minutes and I agreed. While sitting at her desk, Martin McGuinness came in with his security man and came over to me. He put his hands on both sides of my face and kissed my head, saying nothing. He didn't need to. With that simple action, he simply confirmed to me that he knew. I was growing used to the sympathetic Judas kisses of the movement's highest leaders.

Breige also knew I was there, because she showed up ten minutes later and asked me to go with her. She enquired how I was and I told her frankly that I felt suicidal. I really did not care what happened to me by now. She said she would meet with me regularly so that I could talk about Morris and the botched IRA enquiry. She was a different person from the woman who had faced me as part of the 'investigation' team. She was being nice to me and telling me that she knew it had caused me harm, and I believed that she was trying to make up for that. She told me they thought they had been doing the right thing.

I was too vulnerable to see that I should have cut all contact with her. Because it had become almost normal to have this woman picking me up and taking me to safe-house rooms so that they could interrogate me about deeply personal things, my mind misappropriated that perverse normality and skewed my feelings. Every conversation I had with her after that seemed like permission to speak about what was wrong with me in a way that I felt I was not really allowed to do with anyone else, precisely because the IRA was an illegal organisation. I had internalised their obsession with secrecy.

I also had to navigate the deep pain these people had caused me while continuing to work for Sinn Féin and living in a community that was like one huge dysfunctional family: interconnected, insular and ingrained in my psyche. It was similar to living in a cult, where one becomes so conditioned to living in a group-think bubble that a person cannot see a life beyond it. I was surrounded by older adults who, by dint of their IRA membership, had lived for most of their lives knowing they could be put in jail or in a coffin after a violent death. Every part of life was fundamentally different in west Belfast than if I had lived just a mile away in the leafy middle-class Malone Road area, and I knew I needed to get out of it if I was to have any chance of survival. Now the greatest danger to me was not the IRA or my abuser, but my own mind.

26

The time of the 1981 hunger strikes was one of the darkest periods of the Northern Irish conflict, and also one of the most contested aspects of its history. Republicans see ten freedom fighters who starved to death for political status after the failure of the blanket protest to move British prime minister Margaret Thatcher from her approach that all crimes are equally immoral and that IRA men were simply criminals. Others see killers manipulated by the republican movement outside the prison, who saw that they could use the ultimate weapon – the bodies of young men – to evoke sympathy for a wider cause than the no-wash protest, where prisoners smeared their own faeces on walls and refused to wear a prison uniform. There are numerous books and films that are sympathetic to the prisoners' perspective, and tales of beatings from 'screws' (prison officers) are well documented. The story of prison officers' families who were placed under threat, and the murders of those whose job it was to enforce the prison regime, are not so well known. Of one thing there is no doubt: the 1981 hunger strikes catapulted Sinn Féin into electoral politics.

The legacy of the hunger strikes has been used to spin retrospective theories to explain Sinn Féin's rise in support. Mary Lou McDonald is typical of those who would wish to connect the hunger strikers and the peace process. Speaking to the *Irish Times* in 2021, she said:

I certainly would regard it as a turning point in the republican movement, in the republican struggle, the development of electoral politics, and I think you could fairly say that the election of Bobby Sands laid the groundwork for not just the development of Sinn Féin as a political and electoral force but certainly planted the seeds for what would become the peace initiative and the peace process and everything that flowed from that.[15]

Similar talk has angered friends and family members of Bobby Sands. Speaking to the *Irish Observer* in 2001, a friend of the Sands family told Henry McDonald of the *Observer*: 'Bobby was many things, but he was not a dove.'[16]

Senator Fintan Warfield outdid McDonald. At a commemoration on 14 August 2016, he said:

Eight years ago, I became involved with our movement aged sixteen, inspired and informed by our songs, poems and music, and politicised by my sexuality. As in 1916, the ten men who made the ultimate sacrifice in 1981 were cultural as much as political activists. As in 1916, amongst our comrades, and before and after, were prisoners who ensured queer representation from the cells of Long Kesh.

This hyperbolic phrase sparked a round of headlines, notably from the *Belfast Telegraph*, which stated: 'Hunger Strikers died for gay rights, claims Sinn Féin senator Fintan Warfield.'[17]

I sometimes played with Bobby Sands' niece as a child, though she was a few years younger than me. Her mother Marcella was always kind to me and the other children who flitted around the streets of our area. My great-uncle Tom was imprisoned in the cages of Long Kesh with Sands. A photograph taken with a smuggled camera captures a group of them together on a sunny day inside the prison. Tom is sitting in the front row, shirtless. Also in the front row is Gerry Adams, and standing beside him with flowing locks, clad in denim, is Sands. Leaning over Adams's shoulder is his then friend, and OC of the first hunger strike, Brendan Hughes.

I was involved in the twentieth anniversary commemoration of the hunger strikes and worked as the administrator of the 80/81 Hunger Strike office in Turf Lodge, which organised the national commemoration. At the tail end of the 1990s, republican commemorations were becoming smaller and people like Sinn Féin press officer Jim Gibney had voiced concern that this could be read as lack of support for the party. The twentieth anniversary commemoration in Casement Park needed to be a huge affair – secured by booking singers such as Christy Moore and bussing people from all over Ireland to attend. Pageantry was the order of the day, and for some reason Sinn Féin felt that having hundreds of ex-prisoners take to the pitch dressed in blankets would be suitably atmospheric. The result instead was lots of overweight men and women, soggy wet in the rain, fists raised aloft, looking tired and foolish.

An effort was made to have respectful commemoration for the families of those who died on hunger strike, and a mass was held in Clonard Monastery for relatives. No thought was given to any victims of the same men, something for which Sinn Féin will forever have a blind spot. Twenty years later, the party found itself in hot water on this very issue, when the party tweeted out a video tribute to Thomas McElwee. The narrator's voice told the audience:

> He came from a close knit family in Bellaghy and was admired by all his comrades as someone who instilled confidence and belief in all around him ... Tom was a typical young County Derry man, kind and good natured, full of life, and with a craze for cars ... [18]

There was no mention of twenty-six-year-old Yvonne Dunlop, burned to death in her father's shop Alley Katz, as a result of a firebomb planted by Thomas McElwee's IRA cell in 1976. Other Northern Irish political parties accused Sinn Féin of airbrushing history, of selectively editing the past. Fine Gael TD Jennifer Carroll MacNeill accused them of continuing to 'glorify and commemorate murder instead of apologising to victims'.[19]

Sinn Féin's tweet accompanying the video stated that McElwee died 'unbowed and unbroken', but later, a tweet from Ógra Shinn Féin caught my eye, which posted McElwee's last words:

> My Last Wish: I ask for forgiveness from everyone. I would rather live than die but if I have to die I would like to let the people know that I bear no animosity, no ill feeling towards anybody. I would like to live among the people as a social worker and promote peace and harmony among Catholics and Protestants and also with the British.[20]

Clearly, this shone a different light on the notion that McElwee was unrepentant to the last. The *Belfast News Letter* asked me to comment. I responded:

> I think it's sad that he clearly had come to some sort of thinking about what he wanted to do with his future … and it is clear from his note that he also wanted to live rather than die. Of course, he was sacrificed in pursuit of the republican movement's aims, and he was a young man only in his mid-20s. It's a far cry from the 'unbowed and unbroken' narrative that Sinn Féin put out on Twitter about him this week. Everybody deserves a second chance at life. Tom McElwee was instead allowed to die a lingering death by a movement who put their struggle before his. Plenty of senior republicans had a second chance at life – some of whom were involved in the IRA just like Tom McElwee – and some did quite well financially and politically from the memory of McElwee and the other hunger strikers for decades. Unfortunately, for people like Yvonne Dunlop's family, a peace settlement like that mentioned in Tom McElwee's 'final wish', came far too late.[21]

Sinn Féin did not respond to my comments, and has never adequately addressed the conundrum of how to commemorate its dead without offending those damaged or killed by their 'armed struggle'. Such glorification of the ghosts of its past may arouse those who are radicalised by romantic revisionism, but as Sinn Féin inches closer to power in Dublin, it has two choices: to brass-neck it and continue to promote its 'patriot dead', or to quietly keep them in the background.

One hint that the party may be inching towards the latter option came at the 2022 Easter Commemoration at Milltown Cemetery, addressed by party president Mary Lou McDonald. Easter, traditionally the biggest date in the republican calendar, is normally full of tributes to the IRA fallen, and the party makes a big deal of families of former Óglaigh (IRA members). Easter 2022 fell in April, in the middle of an election campaign to the Stormont Assembly, and families of the dead were invited to walk in the parade with pictures of their loved ones. Noticeably absent was the word 'Óglach' beside their names. Getting the vote out clearly took priority.

Over the years, Sinn Féin has also toned down the contents of its souvenir shops significantly, perhaps stung by criticism, though more likely because any prospect of government is not enhanced by selling IRA memorabilia. It's been a good few years since you could buy a calendar with pictures of a volunteer posing with an AK47, or a 'Spirit of Resistance' calendar featuring various balaclava-clad posers. In 2018, the party withdrew items such as a T-shirt with the words 'IRA – Undefeated Army', after the charge of glorifying terrorism was levelled at them.[22]

Dixie Elliott, a man who spent time in a cell with Bobby Sands, is clear in his mind about Sinn Féin's relationship with 1981: 'They use the names of the hunger strikers, particularly Bobby Sands, for political gain.'[23]

The Sinn Féin online shop sells a number of items in the 'Bobby Sands/Hunger Strikers' section. At the time of writing, one could buy a black T-shirt with Sands's face on it, accompanied by the words 'Bobby Sands, Óglach', at €19.99, or various badges.

One of the most expensive items is a limited signed print by the artist Robert Ballagh depicting a smashed concrete H-block, out of which ten doves are flying. One of the more bizarre offerings is a fridge magnet of the famous image of the 1922 IRA patrol on Dublin's Grafton Street.

For Sands's family, the loss is deeply personal and they have no control over how his image is used; and apart from his sister Bernadette, they have rarely spoken to the media. In 2021 a video went viral showing Bobby Sands's granddaughter Erin singing the song 'Grace'. As the young blonde-haired girl sang the haunting air with her eyes shut in a bar in County Down, it was clear that Bobby Sands's musical ability had passed through the generations. To his friends, his loss is keenly felt. But to Sinn Féin he remains one of the republican movement's greatest assets, a cash cow to be milked, a revolutionary to be revered. The man who once wrote 'our revenge will be the laughter of our children' has in death, and at the hands of the Sinn Féin party, become a romanticised figure, used to inspire and radicalise thousands of young republicans.

27

I spent the remainder of 2000 attending counselling and taking antidepressants. I survived on two hours of sleep, couldn't sleep with the light off, and frequently spent the night lying in my parents' living room with the television on to stop the silence in the dark hours engulfing me. Sinn Féin had asked me if I would work in Gerry Adams's old constituency office in Turf Lodge through 2001, which was the twentieth anniversary of the hunger strike. I agreed. My wage was increased to £50 a week, and it would take me out of Sevastopol Street where I was frequently bumping into Seamus Finucane and others. The office had security measures, and although I was mostly on my own, I worked upstairs. Unusually, there was a trapdoor in the floor which enabled a person to drop down into the kitchen, from which they could run out the back door in the event of an attack.

Sinn Féin *cumainn* were supposed to send me any artefacts or memories of the 1981 hunger strike that they had in their possession. I found the work interesting, and enjoyed looking at documents that were not in the public domain. Some people sent me 'comms': tiny pieces of cigarette paper that prisoners had written on and smuggled out of jail during prison visits, wrapped in cellophane and secreted in mouths or back passages. It was an effective communication system between prisoners and their families and the IRA outside the prison. I was also in charge of booking an exhibition on the strikes, put together by

Belfast man Seando Moore, into venues around Ireland, and sat on the commemorative committee in charge of events for that year. I took minutes of the planning meetings and for a short time kept the show on the road on behalf of Sinn Féin's Mairead Keane, who was in charge of the party's commemorative year. I liked Mairead – she was affable and wasn't afraid to speak her own mind. She was too soft on me though, as I rarely made it into the office for 9 a.m., frequently fell asleep at my desk because I hadn't slept the night before, and took Monday afternoons off to go to counselling. To make up for it, I worked late nights and weekends.

I was completely and utterly immersed in the republican narrative of the hunger strikes. To us, Thatcher was cruel and the dead men were simply heroes. It didn't occur to me to explore why the men were in prison, or whether they themselves had victims. As far as I was concerned, they were like members of my extended family, imprisoned because they were fighting the British, who had no right to be in Ireland. It was a binary view, but not entirely surprising, given my father's family history and the fact that I had spent almost every waking moment outside of school from the age of sixteen around Sinn Féin members and IRA volunteers. In those formative years, most teenagers rebel at some stage. Add child abuse into the mix, and I was ripe for radicalisation. I rebelled into my family's orthodoxy. This is clearly evident from a piece I wrote for the Sinn Féin paper in March 2000: 'You only have to walk out on the street in west Belfast to see that the sectarian RUC are still around, the Saracens are still there, as are the barracks and the hatred that this force has for our people.'

Although I had experienced antagonism from the RUC, I had also been on school trips with RUC officers in 1998, when we walked up the Mourne mountains and dived into a freshwater pool off the side of its largest peak, Sliabh Donard. On another occasion I was taken for the weekend to the Cultra area, where we had pizza and were later driven to Dundonald to go ice skating, which I enjoyed. A stop was put to the next trip when Siobhán

O'Hanlon asked me what I was doing that week in school and I casually mentioned we were being taken away by the RUC. She was livid and shouted at me, then organised a Sinn Féin picket of the school without my knowledge. I turned up to school in my ordinary clothes, excited about getting out of its confines with my classmates, only to find a bunch of protestors standing with placards at the school gate. The outing was cancelled, and the picket made the pages of the *Irish News*.

My parents had given me permission to go on those trips, believing it would broaden my outlook on life, and it did. The officers in their plain clothes were good fun to be around. One of them, Phil, after I had raised the issue of sectarianism in the force and the experience of my wider family members, took me aside at lunchtime and told me a story about how an officer, before shooting a plastic bullet in Lenadoon, had put a sticker on the gun which said 'Mind how you go'. He agreed that the force needed to change.

It was officers of Phil's kind that I had in mind to speak to when I walked to the Grosvenor Road police station when I was contemplating reporting my abuse. But after the IRA told me that the RUC were protecting Morris, my mind swung like a pendulum between the friendliness of the officer I had met on that outing and the force with its riot shields and batons that had injured me on the Ormeau Road. The RUC was indeed a heavily militarised force. I didn't stop to think that this might have been the case because the IRA were trying to kill them.

'Turn on the TV', I continued in my *Republican News* piece:

> and you can guarantee that some Unionist or British politician will reinforce the age-old message that republicans are scum, inferior and should be treated as such. It was this harsh treatment of our people that sparked off the Hunger Strike in the first place, and the fight to achieve political status for the prisoners is still continuing in many different forms today – the fight for equal treatment of our mandate is still continuing, the right of our children and people to live free

from sectarian harassment, and the fight to continue the struggle for a 32-County socialist republic.[24]

Ironically, I also wrote: 'I just don't know if my make up as a human being would have withstood the torture in the jails.'

Here I was, almost twenty years old, and for the last four years I had withstood sexual abuse, my uncle dying, two IRA 'investigations' and severe mental health difficulties, and I was wondering if I was strong enough to have lived through the hunger strike. I was swamped in the cult of republican folklore, and I couldn't even see it.

But I was changing. By May that year, life in west Belfast was too claustrophobic for me to continue living there. I needed to get away from everything that was familiar, and from the republican movement. My former next-door neighbour and friend Pamela, who had no truck with politics, now lived in Los Angeles. She threw me a lifeline and asked if I wanted to come over. She had no idea what had happened to me, but knew that I wanted to get out of Belfast. I asked my parents for the fare, resigned my membership of Sinn Féin and was in LA a week later.

I weaned myself off antidepressants. Everything about Los Angeles was the antithesis of west Belfast. No one cared what religion you were, and political discussions were all about American politics. It was hot and the Van Nuys streets were clean, though it was inadvisable to step outside with no shoes if you didn't want to burn the soles of your feet. I lived in an area with a lot of Mexican immigrants and learned how to make cactus soup with my friend Gloria. We had a pool and I loved swimming, and Pamela took me to parties around her friends' pools, where people threw large blow-up balls and drank cold beer.

Everything seemed to be built on a huge scale, cars, cinema seats, food portions. I marvelled at the Hollywood stars on the Walk of Fame. I flew to Burbank and saw singer Shawn Colvin live at the Fillmore theatre in San Francisco. I also saw my first openly lesbian couple – an elderly pair wearing shellsuits and holding hands. The only reminder of Irish republicanism was in a bar in San Francisco, which had framed Sinn Féin posters and front pages of republican newspapers lauding the IRA.

The initial plan was for me to stay for a year, and although I enjoyed the different culture and the endless sunshine, I was hugely homesick, particularly for my granny Nora, and I decided to return a few months later. Once home, I enrolled in a counselling course in technical college, got a job stacking shelves in a supermarket and concentrated on trying to make a life for myself that didn't involve Sinn Féin. I had had enough of them and didn't want to see people like Siobhán. I still had friends who were republicans, and I met them for drinks, but I began to cut myself off from the republican family. The feeling of isolation was intense. I wasn't used to not thinking and working politically in every waking moment.

Sometimes I helped out when I was asked, though it was rare. I worked on an election campaign in 2003 for Caitriona Ruane, as I had known her personally. I also agreed to take my Aunt Annie, Joe's wife, to an Ard Fheis* when my cousin broke her ankle and couldn't accompany her mother. I also took along an elderly Ballymurphy woman called Lily Hall, a legendary IRA supporter, who was very good to me, and I was close to her family. Panic ensued when I lost her in the hall and found the diminutive octogenarian outside rowing with protestor and loyalist Willie Frazer, pointing her finger at him and shouting, 'You're nothing but a bloody Orangeman!'

But I did not want to get sucked back into that world, and the time in America had given me space to think about how wrongly I had been treated by the IRA. My teenage self had been republican by osmosis. I now had to carve out a life for myself financially and emotionally, make efforts to heal the hurt I felt, and try to live as normally as I could in an utterly abnormal environment.

For the next two years I existed from one day to the next, working, drinking at night with friends and playing my guitar at music sessions. I still had contact with republicans – I couldn't

---

* Irish for party conference.

live in west Belfast without being around them – but I increased my community work and mostly stayed clear of politics. I helped to launch a stress clinic in north Belfast with Gerry Adams's sister-in-law Irene, and I enjoyed the craic in the Ashton centre in the hugely deprived New Lodge area. I met Joe Baker, a socialist and historian who was very funny and extremely knowledgeable about Belfast history. He conducted entertaining walks around Clifton Street Cemetery, regaling people with stories of the United Irishwoman Mary Ann McCracken and her brother Henry Joy, and the Edinburgh murderers and graverobbers Burke and Hare, who were brought up in Northern Ireland.

In 2003, I became pregnant and subsequently lost the baby. I was back in contact with Breige after that, and we found ourselves on a counselling course together for a short period of time until I gave it up.

In 2004, when my Uncle Joe died, I dipped again. He was a steadying force for me, and I was devastated he had gone. I wrote the tribute piece I've already mentioned when I received the news in the early hours of the morning and was inadvertently locked into the radio station at Conway Mill. I sent it to the *Republican News*. I wanted to write the piece and send it off out into space, and maybe he would know wherever he was that he had helped me by being there.

28

In 2005, a year after Joe's death, I couldn't see a way out. I unravelled very quickly. Another article had run in the *Sunday World* about my abuser and, although I knew about it, I didn't buy the paper. But someone slipped it anonymously through the door of the run-down house I was renting in Beechmount. I was smoking dope, feeling depressed, and the article brought things rushing up to the surface. I began to cut myself, the tops of my legs at first with a knife, then I used needles or anything with a sharp point to repeatedly scrape my arms until they stung and bled. I wasn't seeking attention, but attempting to get rid of my overwhelming frustration and gain some control over my feelings. I was suffering badly from flashbacks in which I would relive everything. Cutting helped me to regain some sense of reality.

I was still managing to hold down a job, until one night I came home and collapsed. I phoned in sick the next morning. The General Secretary of Sinn Féin, Lucilita Bhreatnach, who had remained a friend after I left the party, had telephoned and could tell I was not in a good state. I don't think I was even coherent. I told her I wanted to die.

I was lying on my sofa in Beechmount trying to escape the world when Breige came to my door. I let her in. We talked over the IRA 'investigation' and she said they had had to investigate because Morris was a member of 'the Army'. I started crying, which I rarely do. She remarked that she was glad to see me crying because I had sat through months of them firing questions at me like a robot without breaking down. She said she felt guilty because it was clear they had traumatised me all over again. I told her that they obviously didn't believe me and that they should never have become involved. She insisted they did believe me. I said that was worse, because despite that they had forced me to talk to them and submit to their endless questioning.

Then I lay on the settee in a trance. I had a dreadful headache and begged her to kill me. I wanted her to get someone to shoot me, or take me out the front and run me over with her car. She phoned the emergency out-of-hours doctor and took me to the Crumlin Road surgery.

The lights were hurting my eyes in the small room where I sat at the side of the doctor's table. I had pyjama bottoms on and a black padded jumper with a pocket at the front and a hood, and I put the arm of my jumper over my eyes and sat like that through the entirety of the doctor's examination. Because Breige was with me, I couldn't tell the doctor exactly why I was there. Instead, Breige rolled up the sleeve of my jumper to show the doctor the cuts on my arms. The on-call psychiatrist was summoned.

I was taken to another small room and I asked the young male psychiatric doctor to dim the harsh lights. Thank God he asked Breige to leave. I told him he had to put me in the hospital, as I had been brought over by an IRA woman who a few years earlier had forced me to take part in an investigation about my sexual abuse and brought me into a room with my rapist. He put down his pen, looked closely at me and became nervous. I knew by looking at him that he didn't believe my story. He said he thought I needed emergency care, but he wasn't sure if there was a bed.

It is no wonder that his notes contain the words 'persecutory/reference delusions'. I suppose it wasn't exactly a story that a young doctor would hear every day. Other notes record that I had cut my arms twice, and that these cuts were *'not tendon injury but more than superficial'*; and that I had rope in my house with which I planned to kill myself, and tablets saved, though the self-harm in itself was not an attempt to end my life. Another line reads:

'could not guarantee safety and no family/friends she could stay with.' The 'history of presenting complaint' reads: *states flashback of sexual abuse that occurred when 16–18yo. By in-law who was in paramilitaries. Was in paper in 2000 and again two weeks ago. Has nightmares re abuse …. feels guilty, hopeless, pessimistic.* The differential diagnosis is recorded as *'PTSD, situational crisis (due to recent newspaper article) and mild to moderate depression.'*

I took my hands away from my eyes, looked him in the eye and said in a low but direct voice: 'Unfortunately for you it is like this. You either find me a bed or you can sit up all night and listen to me but I am not going home.' He found one shortly afterwards and I was admitted as an acute psychiatric emergency to the Mater Hospital in north Belfast.

It was a horrible place. It smelled of urine, almost like a geriatric ward, and was constantly noisy because some of the patients cried all night. The unit was in the shape of a square, where you could walk around the four wards on a loop, with the showers in the middle and some private rooms off to the side. There was a TV room too, and at that time a small smoking room, and the suicidal patients were put near the observation desk. I had a bed there.

Once I lay down and reality began to sink in, my face burned with shame. A nurse came to take all my belongings and to fill in a questionnaire. She asked me why I was in hospital and I showed her my arm. She cleaned it and bandaged the cuts. I was sent to two psychiatrists to 'talk'. I have never seen the movie *One Flew Over the Cuckoo's Nest*, but I know of the 'medication time!' line. That's what it was like. They got the patients up at 6 a.m., and those that couldn't be bothered were allowed to just lie in their beds. They made us go to the canteen, gave us plastic forks or spoons for our food, and tea, then the same ritual again at 11 a.m., then at 1 p.m., 4 p.m. and 6 p.m. There seemed to be shredded tinned lamb for dinner every day – though that could be just the way I remember it. I hate lamb. When I first went in, nobody spoke to each other in the canteen; we were a line of zombies who sat, tried to force food into our mouths when the nurses walked round, and then filed out again back to our beds.

A woman from Ballymurphy occupied the bed to my left. She heard voices and she kept screeching out to her imaginary husband Jack and laughing and fighting with him. 'I've won the lotto,' she shouted one day. 'Sixty thousand pounds and you've drank the heap on me you bastard!' She would wet and soil the bed, and she was left to lie in her mess for ages.

I texted my family the day after admission and told them where I was. I also told them I didn't want to see anyone for a day or two. The two women who had conducted that IRA investigation years before came down the next day with toiletries for me. Maura never spoke. I think in hindsight they might have been feeling guilty, but the implied message to me was also that I shouldn't open my mouth.

I started to talk to people in the smoking room a day or two after I was admitted, but quickly learned to watch who I spoke to. A tall girl came into the room. She didn't smoke, but she was clutching a picture of a rainbow. I said it was a nice rainbow. She started squealing at me: 'It's not a fucking rainbow, it's a house and don't you fucking forget it!' You start to think you are a nutcase in a place like that, but you quickly learn to grade the level of nuttiness. I had her close to the top of the scale, with me a good bit below her at that time.

She scared me. Later that night I heard squealing about 2 a.m. or 3 a.m. that continued for about fifteen minutes. She was in the bathroom banging her head on the wall. There was a smash. I later learned she had somehow got hold of a mirror and tried to stab herself with shards of the glass. She was sedated for the rest of the time I was there, a few beds away from me.

An elderly woman would walk the block, round and round, shouting: 'You stole my St Anthony medal, what about my St Anthony medal?' to no one in particular. It passed the time watching her. She eventually lost the plot one day and started shouting about hearing voices on the imaginary tannoy, and went into a rant: 'My St Anthony medal youse stole, and my knickers, give them back you fucking bawstards.' Over and over and over. I saw that wee woman in a chippy in west Belfast a few years later, nice and quiet and normal. I'm glad she didn't remember me.

On the third day, a woman was admitted to the bed next to me crying and continued to do so for hours. I pulled the curtain back, frustrated that none of the nurses had spent any time with her. I put my arm around her and let her cry. She was about forty and she was there because her husband had had an affair and she had tried to kill herself by slitting her throat. She was nice. It was funny because after a few hours of talking she suddenly stopped and said: 'You seem normal, what are you here for?' I showed her my arm sheepishly by way of explanation and tried to justify my place on the ward. I told her I had been abused years ago and couldn't deal with it.

The doctor had put me on some antidepressant or other, and twice a day the patients lined up while two nurses wheeled a brown dispenser box into the ward, called our names and dispensed the tablets. We had to swallow in front of them. It was humiliating. I began to become angry at the way the patients were being treated, and I started a mini-revolution by continuing to talk to people. There was a girl from Ballymurphy who was really funny. She had a radio player the day she was brought in and played Luther Vandross over and over. She caught my attention because she was shouting about the 'fucking peelers'. 'Get me Paisley on the phone, has anyone got Ian Paisley's number? He'll help me. No point in ringing Adams, he does fuck all.'

I spoke to her in the smoking room, and it transpired that she had been sectioned because of a row in a caravan site the night before. When police were called, she had resisted arrest and tried to boot the window of the police car in. She said they'd stolen her money and she wanted it back. That was the reason for ringing Paisley. She asked me if I could do French plaits and I confirmed I could, so she came twice a day to my bed. 'Hey Frenchy!' she shouted. I obliged.

I had about five people then in the mornings who would come to me to get their hair plaited. One was a really quiet woman who asked me apologetically if I would do hers. She was crocheting and said it calmed her. I asked if she would teach me, and this quiet woman who had the worries of the world on her shoulders sat on the edge of my bed and patiently taught me how to make a slip-knot, and the double-crochet stitches required for a granny square. I borrowed a hook from her and tried over and over to get the stitches right. The woman was brilliant at both encouraging me and fixing my many mistakes. I liked the methodical movement of the needle, and watching a string of wool turning into something shapely before my eyes. I also found that it replaced the urge to cut myself when I was frustrated. I still have the blanket that I made in that ward, and when I get stressed I take up the hook again and use the time to push everything out of my head.

The nurses moved that funny Ballymurphy woman into a side room because her constant talking annoyed them. I used to lie back and watch the show and laugh to myself. She often tried to escape, and they couldn't tell her when she would be released, which increased her frustration. Her teenage son visited every day and she was clearly proud of him. When they moved her into the side room, the other patient in there asked to be moved out because of her talking. I don't think she should have been in hospital at all. I sat her down and told her to play the game. I told her she had a better chance of getting out if she calmed down a bit. She said she missed home.

'Give me your son's number,' I said. I rang him and asked him to bring up a few things from home for her. He arrived that evening with a small rug, pictures and fairy lights. She stole a six-foot plant from the smoking room and all I could see was this disembodied pot plant walking down the corridor. It was hysterically funny to watch the nurses just give up as we set about making that room hers. The fairy lights went on the plant, the pictures went on the bedside cabinet and we got an A4 piece of paper and a pen from the observation desk and wrote her name on it, and secured it to the door. She was very proud, and the nurses eventually got in on the act and helped her to decorate it. She called it the penthouse.

The day after admission my notes record the following in relation to my abuser: 'this man "disappeared" after being dealt with by the Republican Movement – Máiría thinks he is still alive.'

It also noted: 'feels "safe" in the hospital at present.' It continued: 'Máiría has spent most of the day in bed but did attend the dining room at tea time and ate some dinner. Spent individual time with Máiría this afternoon and she was very reactive. Initially eye contact was poor but same improved throughout interaction.'

I began to relax there and fell into the routine; I didn't want to leave. I locked horns with a junior psychiatric doctor who came to see me a few days after my arrival. She spoke to me for five minutes, asked me stupid questions and then looked at her wristwatch and left. The next day I was called to see her and a male doctor. He was holding up a clipboard that almost covered his face, and I let him have it.

'If you want me to talk then have the decency to treat me like a human being and stop talking to me through your clipboard,' I said. 'And as for you, if your level of patient care to me yesterday is indicative of the way you treat all the patients in here then God help them. You looked at your watch yesterday after five minutes and made me feel like I wasn't worth your time. God help everybody else in here.'

She looked at me in a slightly puzzled way, and the man lowered his clipboard and tried to stop a smile.

'She's a good doctor,' he said. 'Why don't you tell me what's going on for you?'

So I did. I told him about my abuse, and about the IRA and their investigation. I told him I was self-harming and suicidal and that I couldn't cope with the flashbacks, that they were so real I remembered the smells. That interested him. He took notes. I think I wanted to convince him that I was nuts so he would keep me in hospital, but I failed. He told me I was articulate and that he was off for the weekend but would see me after he came back. I got a weekend pass and a lift with the husband of another lovely patient who was in there for depression to the house of a woman I knew, but I couldn't settle. My medical notes state that I returned early, agitated.

That doctor must have recommended that I be sent home because I was called to a meeting after the weekend. I was brought into the TV room, where five or six medical professionals sat in a semi-circle facing me. It was very daunting. They told me I was going home that day. I was devastated. I told them that as far as I was concerned, they were sending me home to die. I cried in front of them, which embarrassed me even more. One of them made the remark that a hospital was not meant to be a safe haven from the IRA. There was no point speaking to them after that.

The hospital may not have been a haven, but after just six days it felt safer than being alone. I was given a psychiatric appointment for the following week as an outpatient. I failed to turn up because I was so angry at being discharged from the hospital where, at the age of twenty-four, I had enjoyed the best sleep I'd had since I was sixteen, even if it was induced by sleeping tablets.

29

Once out of hospital, I knew I needed help. Someone I knew recommended a woman I shall call Mena, a support worker based off the Falls Road in west Belfast. She was not under Sinn Féin control, but I knew she would understand the intricacies of the republican movement. Over the next four years, I saw her twice a week and spoke about my abuse, the IRA 'investigation' and the myriad problems I was having in my life. She was direct and stood no nonsense, and I needed that approach. At a time when I saw no reason to live, she helped me to regain some self-respect, and also helped me to fully appreciate how wrong the IRA were in the way in which they had dealt with me. She encouraged me to think for myself and to trust my instincts, and I will always be grateful to her for that, and for keeping me alive.

Slowly but surely, I began to improve. I completed a diploma, and then a degree, for which I studied at night. I secured a part-time job which I loved, training adults with learning disabilities.

Shortly after my release from the Mater hospital, Mena received a call from Gerry Adams's office saying that they knew she was working with me and asking if I wanted to see Adams. When she relayed this news to me, I was incensed and I worked through with her what my response would be. I telephoned Adams's secretary Paula, and told her that I didn't appreciate Mena being contacted. She told me that 'Gerry was concerned', to which I retorted that I would see him in my own time and if he was really that concerned, he could lift the telephone and punch in my mobile number. I was worried that Adams was on a 'fishing exercise', to see what I had disclosed in the hospital.

I bumped into Paula a few months later, in January 2006, in the car park of Conway Mill. Christmas was generally a very difficult time for me, because memories of the abuse were very strong at that time of year. I had spent that Christmas trying to get thoughts of suicide out of my head and sleeping through much of the festive period. The doctors had upped my intake of antidepressants to the highest dosage of Zispin, a soluble tablet that made my lips go numb in the first few hours of taking it, and which also made me extremely sleepy, though I was doing well at my job.

It was a time of change for me, and I began to think once more about how angry I was at my treatment at the hands of the IRA. I decided I would confront Adams and tell him this. 'I'm ready to see Gerry now,' I told her. A meeting was confirmed for 3.30 p.m. the following day.

I spent the next day trying to work out exactly what it was I wanted to say to Adams, but I couldn't get it straight in my head. I walked from the Springfield Road, where I was working, to Sevastopol Street, and sat down in the waiting area just as Adams was walking down the stairs. To the right of me, Jock Davison was sitting. I remember thinking this was odd, because at that time Davison was supposed to be suspended from the republican movement, suspected of giving the order to IRA men in a Belfast bar to murder Robert McCartney the previous year, a grotesque murder that had caused huge controversy. Sinn Féin had been under huge pressure as a result of it. I thought Jock Davison shouldn't be sitting in the Sinn Féin centre, much less meeting anyone there. I was curious who he could be seeing.

Jock stood up as Adams reached the last stair, and I walked towards the Sinn Féin president, who put his hand up to halt Jock, nodded towards me and said to him, 'No, hang on a second, this won't take long.'

'It'll take as long as I want it to take,' I replied, with a smile.

Davison nodded and sat back down, and Adams ushered me through to the right, into the advice centre building. This was unusual because my other meetings with Adams had taken place in his own office. This office, in his constituency clinic, was smaller but there was a desk and a few chairs. I sat on one and he sat to the side of the desk and crossed his legs and put his feet up. No Moses sandals this time, I noticed.

'Are you still writing?' he asked me with a smile, referring to the piece I had written a few years earlier about my Uncle Joe. I was fuming. I thought of things I had wanted to say to him, and his careless, casual tone caught me off guard. I had to concentrate to not lose my temper and keep control.

I told Gerry Adams that my treatment at the hands of the IRA had been disgraceful. 'Youse are a geg.* Youse walked in, turned my life upside down, my head apart, and then youse were able to fuck everything up and walk away and left me with absolutely no support.'

I spoke about the fact that I had transferred the blame for the IRA investigation onto myself, that I thought the IRA actions were abusive just as Morris had been abusive, and I accused the IRA of letting him go. I told him forcefully that I did not believe Morris had 'disappeared' of his own accord.

Adams leaned back on the chair, smiled a bit, put the tips of his fingers together, a gesture which reminded me of a priest, and said, 'I'm sorry.'

'You're sorry? I'm not asking you to apologise, Gerry, an apology means nothing to me. What are you sorry for anyway?' I asked.

'I'm sorry on behalf of the republican movement for what happened,' he uttered. 'I'm sorry and we're sorry.'

I reiterated that I had received an apology years ago, and that it meant nothing then and it meant nothing now. 'What I want,' I said, 'is to hear from you that this has never happened

---

* *Geg* is sarcastic Belfast slang for laugh.

to anyone else, and never will again. Youse can't just go around taking it upon yourselves to "investigate" cases of abuse, youse aren't qualified to do so. Youse completely retraumatised me, youse forced yourselves into this situation, left me suicidal for years because of what happened, and you had absolutely no right whatsoever to do that.'

By 'youse', I meant the republican movement. I wasn't making any distinction, and he wasn't either.

He mumbled something about people not being equipped to deal with cases of abuse, and he was sorry if I had been retraumatised. And then he gave me a guarantee that a) it had never happened to anyone else, and b) it wouldn't happen again. I stupidly took him at his word, although I know now, from speaking to both other victims of abuse and former IRA members, that this was far from the truth.

Once I had calmed down a little, I tried to impress upon him that as MP for the area, he had a responsibility to ensure that mental health provision was not failing people. I told him that half the women of Ballymurphy, the area he grew up in, had been in the Mater psychiatric unit, that they were being neglected by everybody outside and that he should get his finger out and do something about it with the health services. He said that the party was working on a mental health report and that he had raised the issue in the past.

I was still holding it together, just about, and then there was a bit of awkward chit-chat about abuse, Adams again stating that he knew how difficult it could be for abuse victims, but essentially I was going to have to concentrate on my life. I had a habit of trying to tune him out when he talked like this, because I had heard it all before from him, and I didn't believe he was sincere. I think I wanted this meeting simply to record my feelings about what had happened, and I had done that. There was nothing else for me to say and I knew it was the last time I would talk about it with Gerry Adams.

At the end of the meeting, I did something that Adams must have thought unusual. When he got up to give me a hug, as he always did whenever I saw him, I sidestepped him and walked out, and left him to his meeting with the supposedly disgraced but clearly still very welcome Jock Davison. As I left his office, I thought that I had finally taken some control back over my life. Adams had not managed to cloud my head during this meeting with glib sympathy. Although I had been very obviously angry, I had not showed any signs of weakness and had not left the door open for any further manipulation by Adams or his party and shadow 'army'. I could finally feel I was in control of my own emotions.

30

In 2006, I received a phone call to say that one of Morris's other victims had been in Donegal and thought she had seen him in a branch of McDonald's in Letterkenny. She was so frightened that she locked herself in the toilet and called her parents in Belfast. Someone else had seen him in a bar drinking in the vicinity, and in the same week, I thought I saw him driving in Belfast, panicked, and phoned Breige to see if they, the IRA, knew he was back. She assured me that he wasn't back, and I surmised that there must be some level of contact between Morris and the IRA in Belfast.

I was very angry and told Breige I wanted to report Morris and go public so that people could make an informed decision to keep their children away from him. She told me to think of my granny, who by that stage was battling bowel cancer, and that she thought I should meet Adams again. I said in no uncertain terms I wouldn't be doing the latter, though another relative of mine did meet him, and said when she told Adams that Morris was drinking in Donegal, he said to her: 'What do you want me to do, bar him from every bar in Ireland?'

Siobhán died in 2006, and I took it badly. We had been estranged because of her unwavering support for the IRA and her acceptance without question of the organisation's handling of my abuse. My feelings about her were confused – and they still are. I loved her, but at times she treated me despicably. She would come and hug me one minute, and walk past me without acknowledging me the next. She could be kind, and also nasty, when she wanted to be. She had her own adverse experiences in life, and I have a little more understanding these days of what she went through.

I went to her wake and funeral and, as I stood at the coffin looking at her perfectly made-up face, a man came and put his arm around my shoulders. I put my head into Gerry Adams's chest and cried. At the funeral, as I was walking into the church with family, his arm went around my shoulder again and I found myself swept along, and sitting in a pew between Adams and Martin McGuinness. Perhaps it was kindness, but after everything I know now, I cannot help thinking that it was a pathetic and deliberate effort to keep me onside.

My grandmother Tess died in 2007, and Adams came to the wake. He again put his arms around me and said in Irish: 'Tá ár gcroíthe briste' ('our hearts are broken'). Six months after her death, once more in a very bad state, I swallowed a month's supply of antidepressants. I was hospitalised overnight and placed on oxygen to keep me awake while the tablets ran through my system. As I was being brought in the ambulance to hospital, my low blood pressure was causing the monitor to beep, and even though I was semi-conscious, when the ambulance staff asked me if there was anything I was allergic to, I dryly answered: 'Men.'

After that attempt at self-destruction I went on working. It was a dark period, but I threw myself into campaigning on behalf of local residents, setting up a committee that was not under Sinn Féin control. Little happens in west Belfast without the Shinners knowing, and I received a call from Sue Ramsey, then a Sinn Féin MLA, asking if I would consider joining the party again. I very politely and firmly told her that I was too busy and smiled to myself as I put the phone down. We were doing good work in the area and had had some success. It was organic community development, and although there were republicans of all shades on the committees, there were also many people who were apolitical, and no group or political party had control. In fact, despite my treatment by Sinn Féin, I believed that they should do the job they were elected to do, and did not stand in the way of the committee when they invited their local Sinn Féin and SDLP political representatives to meet with them. The apartment block had lots of young families, and lots of party animals. It was akin to living in a youth hostel at times, but I met good friends and am proud of the work that we did.

In December 2009, I finally thought I had pieced my life back together. I was physically well, in better shape than I had ever been, and continued to work full time. But life has a way of coming at you fast. It was a Friday evening and, unusually for me, I was not out with friends socialising. Instead, I had my feet up on the sofa and was channel hopping, when I turned on Ulster Television's *Insight* programme. The programme featured Áine Tyrell, niece of Gerry Adams, alleging abuse by her father, Gerry's brother Liam, when she was aged just four. I felt sick. She described how on one occasion she was taken to meet her father, with Gerry Adams present, and how she remembered a packet of Mikado biscuits on the table.

That detail, so trivial in the grand scheme of things, those ridiculous pink marshmallow biscuits with their central vein of jam, yet important enough for Aine to remember, was a trigger for me, and I was back in a room facing Morris with Seamus Finucane joking about his feet as he took his trainers off. I spiralled almost instantaneously. A few years earlier I had asked Adams for a guarantee that my case was a one-off. At the very moment I was meeting him, he was not only aware of allegations of child abuse against his own brother, but also that the victim had, like me, been taken to meet her abuser. I decided that I must finally do something about my abuse – drag it out of the twilight world of IRA inquiries, half-meant patronising apologies and the 'concern' of people who'd put me through hell.

I met my parents over the weekend and told them I wanted to report what had happened to the police. In order to do that, I felt I needed a level of public protection. Even in late 2009, people from my community rarely made statements against the IRA.

And I had no way of talking about my abuse, and how my abuser was allowed to leave Belfast, without also talking about the IRA. I needed to speak with a journalist and describe my experience, in order to make it possible for me to speak with the PSNI* without fear of being killed. That fear was real – I had no way of knowing how the IRA would react, and my parents were worried not only about the impact on my physical safety, but also about whether I would be able to cope with the psychological pressures. I, on the other hand, had this huge ball of upset bubbling inside, and I knew I needed to speak frankly and openly about the details, if I was ever to get any semblance of closure.

Choosing a journalist to speak to was easier said than done. I did not want to speak to a TV reporter. I also didn't want to waive my anonymity fully. I was happy for my surname to be used, and some identifying features to distinguish me from the other victims, but I also had my maternal grandmother Nora to think of. I hadn't wanted my family to tell her about any of my experiences; I was extremely close to her and I had watched my relationship with my paternal grandmother change once she learned of my abuse. I didn't want to do that to Nora, or to hurt her, and stupidly thought I could put my story in a newspaper and that she still wouldn't find out. It is a measure, I think, of just how naïve I was about the interest my story would generate. I needn't have worried. When she did discover, because one of my uncles put the newspaper in front of her, she called Morris and the IRA and Gerry Adams all the bastards of the day, and our close relationship continued.

The Irish *Sunday Tribune* journalist Suzanne Breen had covered the Liam Adams story extensively, and had unearthed evidence that he still had roles within Sinn Féin *after* his brother Gerry became aware of allegations against him. I decided to make contact with her and see if she would be interested in covering my story. I met her at her house and spent hours describing what had happened to me in detail. It was tough, but I also found it cathartic

---

* Police Service of Northern Ireland.

to explain what my life had been like. Like all journalists, her ears pricked up at the mention of Adams, and I knew his name would feature in any story the paper published. I was not interested in attacking Adams, but very focused on the fact that I wanted people to know what had happened, and I believed that there must be other cases like mine and that the story might provoke other republicans to come forward with information.

My story appeared in print on 17 January 2010. There was a photograph of the back of my head on the front page, and the title of the piece read: 'Grand-niece of Provo legend endured horrific sexual abuse.'

> It's 10 years since that night in Andersonstown and Cahill sits in her own flat in west Belfast. She's an attractive, intelligent and confident young woman who now holds a good job in the criminal justice system. Yet it takes her five hours, interspersed with countless tea breaks, because she becomes so emotional, to tell the story of how M raped her dozens of time when she was 16 and how the Provisional IRA and Sinn Féin engaged in a massive cover-up. Speaking out isn't easy, she says, because loyalty to the movement is ingrained in her.[25]

As ever in my life, nothing was straightforward and I discovered the evening before the article appeared that I was in the early stages of pregnancy. I shoved this knowledge to the back of my head until I could get proper space to think about what I was going to do.

I was aware that copies of the *Tribune* were scarce in west Belfast, and there were rumours circulating online that known Sinn Féin personnel were buying them up in the local shops. Certainly, I had trouble obtaining a copy. My friend Julie Ann and I decided that it would be too risky for me to go into a shop, so I waited in the car while she tried to buy the paper. We had to drive to four shops before we had any success. I made some wisecrack to deflect the tension about how awful the back of my head looked. Then I drove up to my parents' house.

It was evident to us as soon as we walked in that my parents had already read the article. My mother was so upset that she had gone to bed, and my father looked as though he had been crying. I was conscious that it was the first time I had ever really disclosed to them any of the intimate details of what Morris had done to me. I didn't think about how awful it must have been for them to read what had happened to their daughter in the pages of a national newspaper. I also chose to ignore the fact that other people would also read it, and the effect that would have on me and my family. Had I realised this, I would never have gone through with it. I had a few hours' prior warning that my story had hit the front page when someone posted a photograph on the internet in the early hours of the morning, yet looking at it online and holding it physically in print were very different things.

Julie was bemused. We joked between ourselves to take some of the seriousness out of the situation, and looking back, her willingness to be seen with me in public in west Belfast the day the article went to print was remarkable. Julie has been a friend from childhood, and has no interest in politics. Yet she knew I was telling the truth, and made a point of staying with me on the day that I most needed people around me. The same could not be said for most of my father's side of the family.

I received a call from my uncle Sean first. 'Jesus, Máiría, I just wanted to say I'm really really sorry,' he said, voice cracking with emotion. 'I had no idea about you wanting to protect the family, and I'm really ashamed. We failed you.'

I told him not to worry about it and thanked him. It was the only call I received from any of the Cahills that day. It hurt that some people in the family claimed not to have even read the article yet criticised me for speaking out.

Julie and I took ourselves off for a walk to the Bog Meadows, the nature reserve near Milltown Cemetery, and joked about what we would do if we bumped into Gerry Adams. Adams had written a blog about walking his dog there a week or two previously. Julie put a brave face on it when I said I would say hello to him if we came across him. She told me later she was hoping to high heaven that Gerry was having a lie-in that day. The beauty of the natural bogland was wonderful, Monet-like brown and wheat-coloured reeds swaying in the wind which whipped my face until it burned, and walking around the mud-coloured lake reflecting glints of winter sun on that January day brought me such great calm. Even though we were still in west Belfast, it felt like a hundred miles away from the IRA and Sinn Féin.

Word came to us that someone had painted graffiti on the Falls Road saying 'Adams, you're a disgrace'. Some of the wall messages were cruder. Another night-painter had called him a wanker. I couldn't believe it. I had never seen a situation before where Adams had been criticised rather than lauded on the walls of west Belfast. Walls were used like message boards, often to reflect the mood of the community at the time – or to tell them how to think. I began to think that, maybe for the first time, people would break ranks and speak about the republican cover-up of abuse. I hoped that Adams would just come out and tell the truth; I didn't think he had any other option. I was wrong.

Other media picked up on my story and there was another shocking piece about the abuse of a woman by Sinn Féin councillor Briege Meehan, and I spent most of the next week listening and watching in the hope that Sinn Féin would admit what the party had done. I also fielded calls from journalists who were looking for me to elaborate on what I had already said. I hadn't foreseen that, and had no intention at the time of speaking to anyone else. I had no desire to become a household name. I just wanted my story on the record.

Marian Finucane's Raidió Teilifís Éireann (RTÉ) show featured the story, which became a topic for a panel discussion, and she sounded horrified at my recollection of Seamus Finucane joking about his smelly feet as he sat in the room preparing for the 'confrontation'. It was strange sitting in my flat listening to people discussing a part of my life, but I was glad it was happening, and it was also showing other people like me that they were not on their own. Marian was one of the first people to make a comparison between Sinn Féin and the Catholic church, and the programme touched on the tribal loyalty amongst republican supporters.

The Week in Politics also covered the story, and I laughed out loud when Sinn Féin MLA Gerry Kelly claimed with a straight face that he hadn't read the *Tribune*. It got him off the hook of answering any probing questions. Sinn Féin was clearly rattled. Other newspapers covered it, and the morning I went to the doctor to have my pregnancy confirmed, I read the *Irish News* and the *Daily Mirror* in the waiting room. I slunk behind the newspapers, embarrassed that I was reading about myself with other people sitting nearby. The internet also went into overdrive, and some republicans were fiercely critical, while others were supportive. The ex-IRA man and critic of Sinn Féin Anthony McIntyre wrote a piece for his website 'The Pensive Quill', entitled 'Ballymurphy Rape', which touched me:

> For long enough I thought I was the republican facing the most problems in Ballymurphy for having the temerity to suggest that Sinn Féin would end up just about where they are now. On my side I had the benefit of experience and was prepared to mix it with my detractors in public. I could always draw public attention to my situation. Here was a teenage girl whose torment went on in the shadows; who because of the anonymous pressure of the group coupled with a sense of loyalty to the movement which her family had given so much to, was forced to undergo much more than I ever had to put up with. Unlike me she felt unable to speak out. A teenager being repeatedly raped by a prominent local IRA member and she had to suffer in silence, alone, in order to maintain the pretence demanded by 'the Movement' that it was without blemish. There was nothing in my experience that comes close to the pain and misery that this young woman was put through.[26]

It was an important piece that started a discussion amongst republicans about other cases of abuse by IRA members. A well-known former IRA woman sent word through a journalist that she thought I was brave, and another two female IRA ex-prisoners I did not know very well sent a bouquet of flowers to my home with a lovely card saying simply 'Just to let you know, we believe you'. I was so touched by that gesture, particularly because the silence from other people, including family members who I'd have expected to contact me, was deafening. Nothing. People didn't want to break ranks. Even people who knew the story was true had severe difficulty with me putting the details into the public domain. I told myself they didn't matter, but was also disturbed by the fact that those who I thought might have had some backbone and would stand up for what was right obviously felt they could not risk speaking to me, let alone criticising the movement.

A few days later two of the IRA men involved in my case released statements. Both men admitted that they had had contact with me, but their version of events was far removed from my experience of them. Seamus Finucane's statement read:

> I want to confirm that I did have a role to play in trying to resolve the complaint of sexual abuse made by Ms Cahill. This was a very sensitive issue and very traumatic for her. Ms Cahill did not wish to involve the RUC in the investigation of this complaint due to the fact that the alleged perpetrator's partner was a relative of Ms Cahill. At that time our view was that complaints of this nature should be referred to the social services whose staff were expertly trained to deal with sexual abuse. I am sorry that she felt that I was dismissive of her complaint but this was far from the case. I want to make it clear that I did my best to resolve this serious matter.[27]

I had of course never made a complaint to him; the IRA had come to me and forced an inept investigation on me. I was never given the option by the IRA of going to the RUC. And nowhere in his statement was the acronym IRA mentioned, nor did he stipulate on whose behalf he was acting.

Padraic Wilson's statement read:

The Sunday Tribune in its edition of January 17th carried a series of articles concerning allegations of sexual abuse. Two women who were the victims outlined traumatic abuse to which they had been subjected. They should be commended for that.

On the front page and in an article on page 11 reference was made to myself in relation to one of the cases. Quotes from the victim attributed to me are inaccurate. I did speak with the victim and another member of her family. At all times I emphasised that the only way that the situation could be dealt with was by bringing it directly to the attention of social services. This was not a route that the victim or her family were, at that time, prepared to take. That very point is made by the victim herself in the Sunday Tribune. I had no dealings with the person alleged to be responsible for the abuse. My only involvement was to try and give constructive advice in a very sensitive and traumatic situation. It was not within my gift to deliver the outcome demanded by the victim. As no charges have been brought at this stage in relation to this case, I have been advised by my legal representative to make no further comment about this matter so as not to interfere with any potential future legal proceedings. The Sunday Tribune also described me as the 'go between' with the International Independent Commission on Decommissioning (IICD). This is also inaccurate. I have never met or been involved with anyone from the IICD.[28]

Note the language. I was a victim who 'demanded'. Wilson, according to him, was being 'constructive' with 'advice'. He had in fact never mentioned social services to me, and like his comrade Finucane he never mentioned the IRA in his statement. It was at least useful to have an admission on record that both men had met with me. That admission was very helpful to me over the next few years, and I had an additional advantage – anyone who knew anything about the way the republican movement operated in west Belfast, or these two men, knew who was telling the truth.

My story was not in question in the streets and the houses of the area I came from. I just needed to convince the rest of Ireland: no mean feat when the movement had clamped down to defend its conduct.

Adams gave an interview to ITV's Conor Macauley, and he was clearly annoyed. I felt like he had slapped me in the face when he was asked about Finucane's and Wilson's roles in my case, and replied that he felt the men had been 'grievously wronged'. He also piously told the media that the focus should be on the victims. My father was very angry after watching that interview, and I felt an urge to throw my TV out the window.

I decided to hit back. I visited the Rape Crisis Centre, introduced myself to its founder Eileen Calder, explained the situation and asked if I could issue a joint press release through their centre. I didn't give her a chance to refuse. I sat down at their computer and typed frantically. I knew Sinn Féin would read the statement and I used it as an opportunity to send a message. I was not going to allow myself to be portrayed as a victim who had been used by the media. I noted that Adams and Sinn Féin had said they were considering suing the newspaper, and I got great satisfaction out of writing: 'Sinn Féin say they are considering suing the *Sunday Tribune*. If Sinn Féin is challenging the truth of my story, let them sue me.'

Eileen Calder laughed and murmured out loud: 'In my thirty years of working in this field, I've never met a victim like you.' I joked that I wasn't sure how to take that statement, and then we set her room up as a mini press office, as she rang around all the newspapers, secured email addresses and mail-shotted the press release. The *Sunday Tribune* printed my statement in full the following Sunday.

I returned home exhausted. Pregnancy wasn't agreeing with me, and the combination of that and the stress of being thrust into the public gaze meant that I was unable to keep any food down.

The *Daily Mirror* ran a good counterattack to Wilson and Finucane's statement the next day. Under the headline 'It's the truth', they carried parts of my statement released after Wilson and Finucane's. Martin McGuinness was asked for a quote and came out in defence of Adams. I wasn't surprised, but felt a bit sick that the photograph used was of him standing alongside some of the Bloody Sunday families – people who had been fighting a campaign for justice for years – and the irony of McGuinness supporting them, while ignoring my right to justice from the republican movement, was not lost on me.

And yet complete strangers offered kindness. Aside from my immediate family, I was feeling abandoned by people who up until a week before had assured me they were on my side. One supportive message came through to my Facebook account on 20 January 2010 from one such stranger:

> As a lifelong Republican I'm totally appalled by what has happened to you. I can honestly say that nothing could have prepared me for the appalling way in which you have been treated, including by those whom you approached for help. Although it pales into insignificance alongside what you have been through, all of us who struggled during the dark days for justice, have been betrayed as well. I think your courage is remarkable and if there is anything at all any of us can do to support you please do not hesitate to ask.

I was very touched that people like this man, who I didn't know, had taken the trouble to write, and moments like that helped to keep me focused.

By Wednesday of that week I was running on empty. The stress was making me bleed, and I went to the maternity hospital. The midwife was less than helpful and told me there was very little they could do. I left in a very bad state, and drove myself back to the flat. The bleeding stopped after I went to bed for an hour, but it served as a reminder that I had to look after myself in order to protect the life that was growing inside me. It was impossible to avoid the stress completely, or to sleep, but I made myself turn my phone off for a few hours and tried to both relax and escape.

On Thursday, predictably, the *Andersonstown News* and the *Republican News* gave ample coverage to Sinn Féin's denial of any cover-up of abuse. The *Tribune* was harshly criticised, but my surname was replaced by xxxxxx in both papers. Anonymity made it easier to marginalise me. Wilson and Finucane's statements were given serious attention, as was a statement from their solicitors. Equally predictably, I was not given a right of reply. I took the breadth of the coverage as a signal that Sinn Féin was under pressure, and I focused my attention on the weekend coverage. I released my own statement referring to Seamus Finucane as 'Y', stating: 'Y has…asserted that he did his best in this very serious matter. If that translates into leaving a victim severely traumatised and suicidal, after a year of enforced IRA contact with her, I would hate to see his worst efforts.' I believed that if I could ride the weekend out, the media attention would die down, and I could get back to some sort of normality. I couldn't have been more wrong.

The internet coverage of the story was increasing and it was hard to avoid. The online comments were mostly positive, though some of the comments in defence of the republican movement were vitriolic. Those who had a problem with the *Sunday Tribune*'s coverage of Liam Adams, and now my case, wrote things like: 'The Cahill story has been churned out yet again to add fuel to the attack on Gerry Adams.'[29]

It was hard not to take those comments personally. I was also still trying to get used to the fact that people were talking about what happened to me. Mick Fealty's 'Slugger O'Toole' website (sluggerotoole.com) ran some good pieces, and gave me the opportunity to set the record straight and to counteract some of the Sinn Féin propaganda. On Saturday night, one poster on an internet site falsely reported that a van carrying all copies of the next day's *Tribune* had been set alight in Newry, and that there were no papers left. I contacted Suzanne Breen, offering to drive to the distribution centre and pick up the copies and distribute them myself. I laugh now when I think of that and of how panicked I was. Someone else wrote underneath the post about burning all the books, and suddenly, the satirical intention became clear – it was a dig at Sinn Féin members buying up copies of the paper the previous Sunday, and a reference to extreme forms of censorship used most notably by the Nazis.

The papers made it safely to the shops. The tabloids had also covered the story in their typical sensationalist way, though the *Sunday Independent*'s Eilis O'Hanlon also wrote an opinion piece. I didn't know Eilis, but of course I knew her sister Siobhán well. They were polar opposites politically: Eilis was well known for her critical writing about Sinn Féin and Siobhán was Adams's secretary. They were estranged in the latter part of Siobhán's life. I had thought about contacting her before going to the *Tribune*, but I wasn't sure if she would want to hear from me.

I had a strong reaction on reading her column that week. I saw the headline first: 'Ultimate love is reserved for the revolution itself'. She began by writing about her mother, my great-Aunt Tess, with whom I had had a good relationship. I had been at Tess's wake, and it was there I had met Eilis briefly for the first time. 'Among the visitors during that awful week,' she wrote, 'was the woman who has now gone public with her claims of having been raped in her teens by an IRA member, and then being badly treated in response by Sinn Féin, who effectively, she says, shielded her rapist from justice.'

I closed the newspaper, closed my eyes, opened them again, and read further. My face was burning. It was embarrassing not because she had written about me being at the wake, but the fact that she had known who I was. Reading about myself in a newspaper piece written by a member of my extended family was strange. The article also described the IRA version of justice, and how people knew about it, but chose to turn a blind eye for the 'greater good'. I agreed with her on that; I had been making the same point repeatedly for years. However, what came next was a shock: 'Including the woman who has now spoken so painfully of what happened to her, who has been keen to stress her continuing loyalty to the republican movement.'

That sentence had the effect of making me feel angry, sad and relieved at the same time. Eilis O'Hanlon had obviously understood some of the hurt that Morris had caused. I took that as a good thing. But in fact I didn't associate myself any longer with Sinn Féin and hadn't done so for years. I was sensitive to that republican label, and I had wanted to make the point in the original Breen article that while I identified in general with the republican ideology, I didn't want to blame all non-violent republicans for the ones who had perpetrated violence or abuse.

Eilis quoted Sergey Nechayev, a Russian revolutionary terrorist who believed in sacrificing every personal scruple for the sake of the cause, and deftly made the link between Adams and the republican family, and how the larger struggle meant that all personal considerations, or acts which people knew to be wrong, were pushed to the side in pursuit of the revolution. I agreed with all this, and with her insistence that there was a link between sexual and terrorist violence. I had been making that very point to anyone who would listen to me, based on my own experiences. Here was a woman who had removed herself, long before. I was envious of that, and annoyed at myself that I was too scared to cut the remaining threads that linked me to republicanism. And I was still living in west Belfast, an IRA stronghold.

I needed out. But it would take another year, and the birth of my daughter, before I actually made the move.

Part Two

31

The atmosphere was tense in the days and weeks after the *Sunday Tribune* article appeared. I spent some time in the Belfast Rape Crisis Centre, trying to work out what I should do next. Women there, especially Eileen Calder, who had helped me with my response to the IRA men's statements, had worked for years to ease the pain of rape victims, while challenging authorities to hold perpetrators to account. It wasn't easy, and neither was fighting for funding to keep the centre afloat. Their office, now closed, was located in Belfast city centre to enable victims on both sides of the religious divide to seek help. Their quarters were spartan, there was paper everywhere, and the large windows let in a good deal of light. Smoke clouds always hung over Eileen, a small woman with dyed red hair and a raspy laugh. She was charismatic and easy to trust, and seemed to live on nervous energy, taking calls twenty-four hours a day from rape victims.

I asked Eileen to use her influence to get me a meeting with the Victims Commissioner, Mike Nesbitt, and I said that I wanted to make a formal police complaint. I needed someone that she thought would 'take no shit', given the sensitivities of the case. She recommended an officer called Stephen, and called him. He was at the centre within the hour. I was unnerved, pregnant and running on empty. When he arrived he dramatically sniffed his nose at the cigarette smoke and smiled, ignoring the obvious breach of the law. My initial impression of him was someone who was cheeky, likeable and committed to the work he was doing. I told him briefly that I wanted to make a statement and asked about the process. He explained that I could do it via video in Garnerville station in east Belfast, in a suite specifically designed for the purpose, and that whenever I was ready, I should contact him. He asked if there were any other victims, and I confirmed there were and that I would speak to them. I left him with my number, and went off to talk to them.

One of the young women agreed that she would give a statement, but the other victim wanted time to think about it. Meanwhile I arranged to meet with the PSNI. I hadn't yet told my family I was pregnant. I became very sick with hyperemesis, which necessitated the cancellation of my first police interview. Had it not been for Stephen ringing me repeatedly for weeks, I might not have gone through with it at all, but I am thankful he took his job seriously. It is doubtful if other officers would have had the same persistence.

I agonised, of course, over giving a statement to the PSNI. Most rape victims do. I had an additional difficulty – I knew the evidence I had to give was politically sensitive, to put it mildly. I was afraid that either my evidence would be buried and that nothing would come of it in order to protect certain individuals in Sinn Féin, or the police would be far more interested in finding out more about the republican movement than in arresting a child abuser. I also assumed that I would be at risk by naming known IRA members. I gambled that my interview with the *Sunday Tribune* would give me a level of protection that I would otherwise not have had; and that the public attention would prevent me from coming to any harm.

I also knew that I couldn't speak to police about the abuse without also speaking about the IRA 'investigation', because the minute they had involved themselves in 1999 they intertwined themselves with my life, and they had information that would obviously be important to a criminal prosecution. In addition, their involvement allowed Morris to leave the jurisdiction, they had traumatised me, and they were referred to in my counselling notes. They had also put me in the same room with Morris, and they had taken it upon themselves to visit my family.

Aside from the fact that some of these actions could and probably should be seen as criminal, it also meant that if my statement resulted in charges against Morris, any barrister worth their salt would ask me in court about the people I had disclosed information to, and what happened after this disclosure. Deciding to speak to the police meant that I had to divorce myself psychologically from the community I came from, risk losing my extended family and friends, and potentially put my life in danger. That isn't an exaggeration: these were very real concerns at the time which each had to be carefully weighed up. In the end, I decided that I couldn't torture myself with 'what ifs' any longer, and I wanted to put on record what had happened to me as a teenager. What the police decided to do with that information after that, I thought, was entirely outside of my control.

Garnerville was not an area of Belfast with which I was familiar. It lies to the northeast of the city, not far from the airport. The police station housed a training college for new recruits, and a suite specifically to deal with abuse cases. Rather than a complainant sitting in uncomfortable chairs in a regular interview room, there are soft furnishings and low lighting. A police officer sits on one chair, while another officer sits separately to operate and monitor the camera, which records the interview. The video is then sent off to be transcribed and this forms the basis of the criminal statement.

I had no idea what to expect the first time I arrived. Policing in Northern Ireland is different from that in other countries, and no matter how soft the chairs were in the abuse suite, the station was still encased in a compound behind green corrugated iron walls – a reminder to me that what I was doing was still potentially dangerous. I drove to the yellow checkpoint just inside the gate, and the security man directed me to a space inside the corrugated iron fencing, where I parked. The police were late, and I felt awkward and vulnerable waiting for them to arrive. I contemplated leaving, but knew that if I did, I would never come back. I needed to unburden myself by telling someone in a position of authority outside the republican community about what had happened to me.

In the interview room, one interviewer sat facing me and the other sat behind a screen, recording and occasionally talking into the other's earpiece to prompt a question. It was a far cry from the IRA's approach to such matters. We started recording the interview, which the police refer to as 'achieving best evidence' (ABE), around 2 p.m. and dealt with the abuse first. I found this the most difficult part of the interview, due to the sheer embarrassment and the level of detail in the questions, but it was totally different from the way the IRA had extracted information. The policewoman was trained, and her voice was soft. She asked about general things first, hobbies and what I liked doing for fun, to ease me into the questioning, but it was still difficult – it is hard to answer things like how many fingers he used, or where his penis went, even as an adult. My answers were stilted. I needed to take lots of breaks, which the police were good about, and they made endless cups of tea.

Normally the police break up interviews over a number of days, but I feared that I would be harmed once the IRA found out that I had been giving evidence, so we recorded until the early hours of the morning. During one of these tea breaks, I overheard the policewoman expressing nervousness about her own safety, being involved in a case like this. I hadn't thought about that. I was too worried about my own survival. The policewoman took her time going through each incident in detail, prompted by Stephen in her earpiece if he thought she had left anything out. The pregnancy sickness entwined with the nervous tension, and I frequently felt uncomfortable. At one point, the police officer was concerned, remarked that I looked 'green', and we took a longer break while she went off to get sandwiches from the canteen.

Once I had discussed the abuse, it was time to recount what had happened to me at the hands of the IRA. For this, the police officers swapped roles and Stephen became the lead interviewer. The PSNI go through rigorous training in order not to react when horrific details are being relayed to them, but at one point as I described what the IRA had done, I looked across at Stephen, who was angrily gripping the sides of the chair he was sitting in. He was a skilled interviewer, and through open questions and checking details for clarification, he got most of my testimony on tape. We only stopped and agreed to reconvene because the fifth tape they had brought with them had run out.

As I was leaving and the PSNI officers were making sure I was okay to drive back home again, I said to them, very seriously, that I was at that moment in no way suicidal, and that if they found me dead in the near future, they had better investigate the IRA. Stephen later told me that when he left the police station that evening, he was incensed that any victim of abuse could be put through that bizarre process. He went home and drank a few beers to try and get it out of his system. I just crawled into bed and pulled the duvet over my head to shut out the world.

32

Naïvely, I wasn't really expecting Morris to be found by the police, but in a matter of weeks they had him. The houses and trees I was looking at through my car window swam before my eyes as I pulled in when Stephen called to explain that Morris had been arrested at his workplace in London, and flown to Belfast by the PSNI.

'Where is he now?' I asked.

'He is in the custody suite on a holding charge,' he said, adding: 'I expect, once charged, he will go to Maghaberry Prison.' Morris had denied any allegation of sexual abuse put to him, and responded 'no comment' when any of the IRA-related activity was put to him.

I exhaled and put both shaking hands on the steering wheel to steady myself. I thanked Stephen for informing me. I then called my parents, fearful of them hearing first from someone else. I drove back to my flat, opened the door and, once inside, slid to the floor with my back against the door, replaying the conversation in my head.

My family was angry and anxious. Everyone had a different expectation. I hoped that Morris would finally admit what he had done, though I knew that was highly unlikely. I also thought it would probably come to court and be dealt with that year, which posed a problem for me, due to my pregnancy. How was I going to avoid damaging the baby if I went through with this? What would

I do when it was born? I was also holding down a full-time job. To their credit, my employers were understanding and allowed me time off for police interviews, and later for court appearances. Without that, it would have been impossible to continue.

The police, worried also about protecting the evidence, spoke to me about witness protection. I wanted to know what it would entail. I thought that they could put up some CCTV cameras around my flat, which would give me an extra level of protection. A man called John telephoned and explained the process to me. Cameras were not an option as I was renting the flat I was staying in. He explained the witness protection programme, which is offered by the police if someone giving evidence is judged to be at risk. I had just given lengthy statements on the IRA and described my contact with senior Sinn Féin figures such as Gerry Adams. It was probably the first time the police had had a witness of this kind, who was prepared to speak freely and on record about senior republicans.

Had I agreed to the witness protection programme, I would have had to leave the country, change my identity and cut ties with everyone I knew, including my family. I refused, for this reason, and because I was not an informer in any sense. I was simply giving evidence of what had happened to me in order to present the strongest case possible, both about my abuse and its aftermath, and I was going to hold my head high. If that took a year or so to get through, then so be it.

In fact, it took four. Had I known this before I gave the statement, and that the process would disrupt every aspect of my life, all while I was raising a new baby, I would never have done it. Each day brought its own difficulties, and I was living with a constant ball of stress in the pit of my stomach. I was also living in fear from another man, who was controlling and put me through hell. The fear was justified; at the time of writing this man has been in custody for several years, and has racked up numerous charges for harassing and threatening behaviour against a range of individuals.

Somehow I coped, and my daughter Saorlaith was born in September 2010, a lovely, healthy baby with big blue eyes and blonde curly hair. My waters broke while I was sitting on the wooden floor of my flat typing on Facebook. Typical New Age mother. Four hours later, as I snuggled into this tiny infant to breastfeed her, I could hardly believe that, despite a difficult birth which necessitated the midwife hitting the emergency button, she had made it into the world in one piece. All of the worries of the previous few months disappeared, and as her little wrinkled fingers gripped around my thumb, I stroked her cheek with my other hand and my protective instinct kicked in. Until that point, I had only had to think of my own safety. Now I resolved to move away from west Belfast as soon as we could.

I had been involved briefly with Republican Network for Unity (RNU), a republican pressure group composed of a small number of individuals, most of whom had previously been members of Sinn Féin. I had been asked to join by Tony Catney, a man I've mentioned earlier in this story, who I had known since the early 2000s and who had previously been the Sinn Féin director of elections. I liked TC; he was intelligent, and encouraged me to think for myself. I left RNU a few months after I became involved, in 2010, and as the pregnancy progressed, I was convinced I had made the correct decision for me and my child. I drifted to them because it was what I knew – I was always interested in politics, and I had grown up with republicans all my life.

It may seem bizarre that after everything that had happened to me I would take part in a dissident republican group, but that was the only political ideology I knew, and I had a naïve idea that there could be a republicanism cleansed of corruption, that we could start again. When you've grown up in a community and a family as fiercely insular and tribal as mine, breaking with it is never straightforward. The RNU was formed after Sinn Féin decided to recognise the PSNI as a legitimate force. Most members of the group were against the Good Friday Agreement and felt that it had betrayed republican values, but I wasn't. I was, however, hostile to Sinn Féin and I identified with that aspect of the group's discussions. I suspected there were people involved who had what was euphemistically known as 'outside involvement' – a role in other armed organisations – and that was no different to Sinn Féin, which also had many members who were in the IRA, albeit Sinn Féin were now publicly professing support for peaceful solutions.

A year after I left RNU, it aligned itself with a small dissident IRA splinter group called Óglaigh na hÉireann. But my involvement with RNU was purely political, and I believed that if enough people like me argued for political action it would insulate us from militarism. Instead, I saw people who seemed to be involved in some type of turf war with each other, and while they never admitted involvement in anything nefarious, they still wanted to run things as if they were in some nationalist version of Dad's Army. I once emailed the chair of the group and called those people 'criminals and gangsters', which was probably not wise. But I was past caring.

I also argued in writing that no republican group should take it upon themselves to investigate child abuse, something which, thankfully, they agreed with. Paranoia was constantly rife within the group, largely due to the fact that most of the small membership were ex-prisoners who were used to looking over their shoulder, or had experience of working alongside people who later transpired to be police informers. I found this aspect frustrating because most of the discussions were childish, full of distrust, and personal rather than political. I used to speak to a writer friend at the time and fill her in on what was happening, regularly ripping the back out of other members or calling them 'a bunch of eejits'. We joked that if you wrote down what went on at the meetings, and how amateurish they were, no one would believe it.

On one occasion – no laughing matter – a few members of the group suspected that another member had previously been a British agent, and those who were suspicious wanted to hold a meeting in order to dismiss him from RNU. The man, who happened to be a friend of TC, strongly denied the association. TC came to me privately and said that both sides should be heard and he was going to put my name forward to sit on an RNU panel

– but urged me not to worry because the proposed review hearing would never take place. I was to tie the process up in knots by arguing with the person in charge weeks before it was due to start. I was then to resign from the panel, which I did.

The hearing, as TC had predicted, never happened. Had it looked like it was going ahead, I wouldn't have been there anyway, and I was glad it never took place. Later, the man left the group of his own accord. I met him shortly after I went public, and he thanked me.

Some months after I joined, I realised that I was in over my head and wanted nothing more to do with the group. It was small, with little influence, and I was at a vulnerable point in my life, with a pregnancy to deal with. Looking back, it was yet another way for me to self-destruct. Gravitating towards people I had known and liked from my time in Sinn Féin, but who were now opposed to them, was probably natural, irrespective of what their views were. In the end, I knew that my views did not align with theirs, and left the group. In 2010 it split, as all Republican groups do, and a year later those who had remained aligned themselves with ONH. Unlike other republican groups, the row which cemented the split happened in a room next to a pole-dancing studio.

When my daughter Saorlaith arrived in September 2010, I knew I had made the right decision and I concentrated on raising her instead. When she was born, the police came to visit with clothes for the baby. I appreciated it at the time, and I understood they put themselves at risk to do this in the middle of west Belfast. I still have the card they gave me for my daughter. I still saw TC from time to time until I moved house in 2011, as he lived in the next street, but I cut contact with all RNU republicans.

33

In any historic abuse case, a victim will always be asked three questions:

1. Who did you tell?
2. When did you disclose?
3. Why did you only report it x years after the abuse?

I knew a good defence barrister would ask me these questions, and I needed the totality of my evidence introduced to court to be able to answer them. This was a problem, because although a decision to charge Morris had been made, no decision had been taken on whether or not to charge him with IRA membership, or the individuals involved in the IRA 'investigations' into my abuse. It was impossible for me to answer the question about who I had told about my abuse without mentioning the salient fact that quite a few adults who should have known better had – uninvited – questioned me about that abuse.

The 'confrontation' with Morris was important evidence, but imagine not being able to talk about it in court because I was gagged from speaking about the IRA if no charges were brought on that account. There was no question of the IRA individuals being approached as witnesses for the prosecution – because they would have then had to admit their roles in order to give evidence regarding Morris. It was a headache for the PSNI and the Public Prosecution Service (PPS), because they had a victim whose abuse evidence was intrinsically linked with what the IRA did afterwards – and the IRA's decision to involve themselves meant that I couldn't report my abuse to the PSNI until thirteen years after it happened. Imagine me being asked in court why I didn't report earlier and *not* being able to say: 'Well, your honour, there was a small matter of the IRA frightening the wits out of me, coupled with being told by others I would be used for information by the police if I did report the abuse...'

I needed a decision on charges to be made in respect of the entirety of the evidence, something that the police hadn't quite grasped. Other witnesses were frightened of mentioning the IRA in court, for obvious reasons, and so some bright spark came up with the idea of editing the statements to take references to the IRA out – which, in my view, was weakening any prospect of my being able to speak freely in court to secure a conviction. The IRA had tainted my evidence.

Sir Keir Starmer in 2015 was asked to compile a report into my court cases, and he wrote:

> The facts and issues in the sexual abuse case and membership case were entwined. The questions of (a) why the complainants had endured the alleged abuse for so long and (b) why they had not reported their allegations to police earlier were live issues from the beginning of the sexual abuse prosecution. The issue of the '10 year gap' in reporting was mentioned by defence counsel at a bail hearing on 11 May 2010 as a point they intended to take. Leading Counsel, in his first written advice in the sexual abuse case on 13 December 2010, 'was prepared to accept that references to the defendant being a member of the 'punishment squad' within the PIRA might conceivably be relevant to issues such as why the complainant did not speak sooner – and references to the 'investigation' equally so'. Explaining these issues was not possible unless evidence relevant to the membership case was admitted in the sexual abuse case.[30]

In April 2010, Morris was charged with six counts of abuse against myself and my two relatives, whom I will refer to, as Sir

Keir Starmer later did, as AA and BB. The charges brought were rape, gross indecency and indecent assault in relation to me; gross indecency and indecent assault in relation to AA; and indecent assault in relation to BB. By September 2010, these charges had been expanded to twenty-two counts of varying degress of abuse, as the PPS reviewed the evidence. He further added that it was 'probably the first case of its kind to reach the PPS'.

In June 2010, Morris was again arrested, this time in relation to the IRA aspect of my allegations. In July the *Sunday Life* reported after a court hearing:

> A woman who claims she was abused by a top republican cowered in a toilet at a McDonald's to phone for help after spotting him in the street.

The court report also stated:

> 'The [man] admitted during police interview to being a member of the group and that he left Northern Ireland fearing that the organisation would target him.'

The judge refused bail according to the newspaper report 'due to the potential risk of interference with witnesses'.[31]

Morris secured High Court bail in the weeks following and returned to England, where he was then living.

In October 2010, a few weeks after I had given birth to Saorlaith, Justyn Galloway, the officer in charge of the PSNI Major Investigations Team (MIT),* informed me that they had arrested those I had named in my statement whom I had alleged had run the IRA 'investigation'. That weekend, the *Sunday World* reported: 'The IRA's leader in Belfast was arrested this week in Belfast by detectives probing "historical terrorist activity".'[32] The paper was referring to the arrest of Seamus Finucane. There was no mention of what such activity related to, leading to speculation on the internet. The four people arrested – Finucane, Padraic

---

* The PSNI unit which deals with terrorism and serious crime.

Wilson, Agnes 'Maura' McCrory and Breige Wright – were not formally charged until December 2011.

In December of the previous year, the first cracks in the court case began to appear. I received word from the police dealing with the abuse case that they had been instructed by the PPS to have edited statements signed, which would effectively remove any reference to the IRA from them. Concerned, I asked for a consultation. I met the prosecutor, the barristers and the police in the court building with my solicitor Joe Rice, and outlined my objections. No decision had yet been made in respect of whether or not to charge Morris with IRA membership, and given that my evidence recalled him asking me to move guns shortly before he started abusing me, it was a highly relevant piece of evidence. It was now ten months since I had given my statement. I was concerned about what would happen if the PPS decided to charge Morris and statements had already been edited. Where would it leave me when I was asked, as I most certainly would be by a defence lawyer, why I hadn't disclosed my abuse earlier? How would I explain the fright at being abused by a member of the IRA, if I couldn't say in court that he was an IRA member? It seemed preposterous to me, and I told the lawyers that if they went ahead they would be weakening my evidence. A decision was taken to leave the editing of the statements until the court case was imminent, and that the matter would be assessed then.

Others in my family were understandably not happy. They were still living in west Belfast and felt at risk of having to give evidence against the IRA, something which I understood. But I also had to try and ensure that my evidence was the strongest it could possibly be in order to try and secure a conviction. That remained my focus for the duration of the court process.

A 'mixed committal', as it's known, was looming in July 2011. In Northern Ireland, defendants have a right to test the evidence in such cases, like a mini-trial, where they also have the right to have their teams cross-examine witnesses. All three complainants, myself, AA and BB, were told to attend.

I was scheduled last, and the younger two complainants were called first. Both were shaken and upset by their experience, not helped by the court's video equipment breaking down several times on the first day. When it came to my turn, the defence team decided they were not going to cross-examine me, so my evidence went forward in statement form only. The judge ruled that in the Morris case there was a prima facie case to answer, and it would proceed to trial in the crown court.

I moved out of Lenadoon in June 2011 and into a room in a house with a then friend and her children in south Belfast. She needed a lodger, and I needed somewhere to stay. We were both victims of the IRA – they had stabbed her brother to death – and I stayed there for around a year. I went to work, came home to her house, put the baby to bed at 7 p.m., and then I read, watched TV or tried to deal with emails about my case. In the entire year that I stayed there, I socialised with other people on only three occasions. I cut contact with most of the people I had known, save my immediate family and two or three close friends.

Sixteen months after Morris's arraignment on the initial abuse charges, no decision had been made on whether to charge the people who had conducted the IRA 'investigation' into my abuse. On 10 August 2011, in desperation about developments, I called Pamela Atchison, the deputy director of the PPS. In the course of the conversation I became aware for the first time that the PPS were applying to have a 'non-jury trial' – essentially a Diplock court, where a judge sitting without a jury would hear the evidence. Cases like these were normally only held if there were concerns about the safety of juries and witnesses, and it worried me that it was being applied in a sexual abuse case.

Two days later, I followed up with an email. I complained about the amount of time the case was taking to get to court. I argued that I felt the evidence threshold had been passed against those who participated in the IRA inquiry. There were other concerns, too. I wanted a hearing in open court. I complained about the previous preliminary inquiry, and set out my misgivings:

There was no information from PPS regarding what I as a victim could expect in terms of length of PI, potential of adjournment, attendance of defendant, cross examination, and other matters. As a consequence I suffered from panic attacks and severe stress in the run up to the hearing and was prescribed anti-anxiety medication. There was also an absolute failure by PPS to communicate in adequate time that the defendant would not be attending – I found out at 5pm the previous day, after steeling myself to give evidence […] I later learned that the defendant's flight had been cancelled one week previously. That is a disgrace, and only served to exacerbate my stress, which was resultant (with separate forms of confrontation and ostracisation because of my involvement in this case) in my having to leave home suddenly and permanently with my ten month old daughter and move across Belfast to be safe both mentally and physically, shortly after,' I wrote.

I also asked for a meeting, which was granted.[33] When we met, I outlined my concern that the PPS would come under pressure from the Northern Ireland Office not to bring charges for IRA membership. Atcheson assured me that the PPS was an independent body and would come under pressure from no one. Nevertheless, I still couldn't shake the feeling that something catastrophic would happen. In December 2011, the PPS did eventually charge five people in connection with the investigation: Martin Morris, Breige Wright, Maura McCrory, Seamus Finucane and Padraic Wilson. The Starmer report outlines the charges as follows:

1. Wilson, Wright, Finucane and McCrory with one charge of belonging or professing to belong to a proscribed organisation;

2. Wilson with two charges of arranging or managing a meeting to support a proscribed organisation;

3. Wright, Finucane and McCrory jointly with one charge of intimidation and one charge of arranging or managing a meeting to support a proscribed organisation;

4. Wright and Finucane jointly with one charge of arranging or managing a meeting to support a proscribed organisation;

5. Wright and McCrory jointly with one charge of arranging or managing a meeting to support a proscribed organisation;

6. Finucane with one further charge of arranging or managing a meeting to support a proscribed organisation.

Morris was also charged with belonging or professing to belong to a proscribed organisation.

In August 2012, I had a strange phone call from one of the police officers who was working in the Major Investigations Team. My case, by this stage, had been split into two – the abuse side of things was dealt with by the Care Unit, and the MIT team/Serious Crime Unit assumed responsibility for the IRA 'investigation' into my abuse. A reporting restriction had been put in place which stopped the media from naming the defendants when they appeared in court. I was not happy with this and had communicated my concern to the police officer. He agreed and suggested signing a statement asking for it to be lifted, as I felt the secrecy surrounding the case would put me at risk. I was not an informer and had nothing to hide, and I wanted the case to be as open as possible. A reporting restriction was fuelling speculation within the community. Being restricted also meant that if I wanted to waïve my anonymity at any stage in the future, I would be hampered from doing so, and I would not be able to name those who had done such harm to me. I resolved to fight the secretive nature of the proceedings. I thought this would be a formality, and was not prepared for the mammoth battle it became.

34

I can only describe the proceedings in court on 30 August 2011 as 'a shitshow'. I arrived already feeling unwell. I had had a blinding headache for days and my left eye was frozen open, meaning that water was running out of my eye and down my cheek. Had I been in a better frame of mind, I would have gone to a doctor much sooner, but I was so focused on the restriction row that I was determined not to miss court, come hell or high water.

The SDLP councillor Tim Attwood, who had been extremely helpful to me along with his MLA brother Alex, had come to court to support me, as had Pearl Sagar and Eileen Calder from the rape crisis centre. The prosecutor was on leave, and the PSNI were not aware of this. As a result, the statement I had signed waiving the reporting restriction had not been given any consideration. A police officer explained to me in court that the PPS would not be applying to lift the reporting restriction. I exploded, and told him he had better get me someone from the PPS to speak to before the judge appeared, or I was walking out of the courtroom. They took me to meet the PPS disclosure lawyer, and I explained my concerns, forcefully. He agreed to put it before the judge, which he did, and the case was put back to 17 September 2011 for the PPS to make an application.

I requested a meeting with counsel, and was informed that the PPS wanted to get the two other complainants' views on the issue. While I understood they would have to be informed, I couldn't see why they would have a say in the reporting restriction on the IRA membership case, given that they were not witnesses in that particular trial. They didn't want their evidence heard in anything other than the case against Morris, and they were afforded legal protection in the form of a lifetime right to anonymity. The PPS were concerned about the potential for 'overlap', and whether this would lead to the jigsaw identification of the other victims. I understood this, but sought to surmount that hurdle by proving how it would be legally impossible to argue that they could be identified.

There was some reporting after the case, with the *Irish News* noting: 'Five people have been charged with Provisional IRA membership dating back to 1999 but cannot be named because of highly unusual reporting restrictions.'[34] After the court case, it became clear to me that I was going to have to contact the media if I was to have any hope of a trial coming to court. I needed extra scrutiny on the decisions the PPS was taking.

I drove to Derry and stayed with Marie Brown, a family friend who also happened to be the director of Foyle Women's Aid. When I reached Dungiven, one of the police officers telephoned me and said that he would personally go to the judge to ensure the reporting restriction was kept in place. The whole farcical and brutal IRA inquiry into my abuse would not be judged in an open court. I was incensed, and that phone call cemented my decision to contact the media. As I sat in Marie's living room the next day with a laptop on my knee, hitting the send button on a press statement, I inhaled and knew I had crossed a Rubicon. There was no way back.

The *Belfast News Letter* had already reported on the proceedings. No byline was attributed to the journalist, but the piece read:

> Earlier this month a judge imposed a ban on publishing the names of the five defendants. The prohibition was put in place to protect the identity of the alleged victim. However, at a further procedural hearing yesterday, it was revealed that she does not want the reporting restrictions. As the woman sat in

the public gallery a Public Prosecution Service Lawyer said: 'She has asked for that to be lifted. I'm to make that application today.' None of the five accused were present in court. But a lawyer for one of them, John Finucane, stressed that he was given no prior notice of the application. Mr Finucane argued that there was more than one alleged victim in the case. He also told District Judge Mervyn Bates that when he originally sought anonymity orders it was not done 'on a whim'. The solicitor said: 'Not only was there no objection from the PPS, but the PPS instructed on that date that if I hadn't made the application, they would have.'[35]

The 2015 review into the cases by Sir Keir Starmer and Katie O'Byrne uncovered a police log from 31 August that indicated the other witnesses did not know that their evidence could be used in the IRA membership case. It reads:

> Police log recorded that AA and BB wanted reporting restrictions to stay in place but MC* wanted them lifted. It became clear that up until this point, AA, BB and other witnesses had apparently been unaware that their evidence was intended to be used to support the membership case as well as the sexual abuse case.[36]

Journalists made contact with me soon after my press statement was mailed. The freelance journalist Susan McKay was in Derry at the time, and called at Marie's house. I sat in the conservatory and recounted what had happened to me in detail. She offered to contact the BBC to see if they would be interested in doing a documentary about the case. I agreed, thinking that the legal situation would probably prevent anything like that happening soon.

When I returned from Derry that weekend, I felt increasingly unwell and visited my GP, who suspected I had had what he called 'a neurological insult'. I was sent to the emergency department

---

* Máiría Cahill.

of the local hospital, where I was admitted and discharged a few days later with medication that made me woozy. I immediately began contacting my lawyers, the police and journalists ahead of the forthcoming hearing on reporting restrictions. The *Irish News* asked if they could send a photographer out to take my picture. I agreed, on the condition that my face was blacked out. I presumed it would be a small piece on the inside pages. The next morning, I went to the shop to pick up the paper and was stunned when I saw a huge photo of my head on the front page. 'Police do not want to lift IRA veil of secrecy', the headline read.

Once home, I took the newspaper out of my bag and read it. 'Well, the shit has hit the fan now,' I thought to myself. The report stated:

> A prosecution witness in a Provisional IRA membership case claims police are opposing attempts to have the defendants named in open court. The West Belfast woman, who says she was forced into cooperating with an IRA investigation more than a decade ago, has argued that the reporting restriction potentially puts her life at risk by 'fuelling speculation within the community'. The highly unusual order, granted using Contempt of Court legislation, bans identification of three men and two women charged with belonging to a proscribed organisation between 1999 and 2000. During a short hearing last month the prosecution said the alleged victim wants the restriction to be lifted. However, she claims police have since told her they intend to challenge her request. Yesterday police said: 'As with any court case the final decision whether to lift reporting restrictions lies with the court and is based on the wishes of all of the victims involved in a case.' All involved have to be in agreement before a court could lift the reporting restrictions on any case.[37]

Not all of the victims were in agreement, but the police were wrong in their assertion. We didn't have to be unanimous. I was under the impression that the other two alleged victims were not participating in the second case that I was involved in, and as such, I needed to be able to make a decision about what was right for me.

I met with Justyn Galloway in the Antrim Road police station later that afternoon. He was not happy about the *Irish News* article, and we argued over the issue. I was intrigued with the fact he had a pitch-and-putt golf mat on the floor of his office, presumably to practise his swing in frustrating moments like these. I explained that the restriction was causing harm. He brought another police officer called Stevie in, and I explained that my extended family were having difficulty with the IRA evidence. This was confirmed to me when I left the meeting and drove to see some of my relatives. It was the last time I set foot in their house. They were worried about the IRA case, had concerns about being called touts, and said they would be withdrawing their statements from the IRA case. I couldn't stop them, and I told them if that was what they were thinking of doing, they would be better to do it sooner rather than later.

I met with counsel, the police and the prosecutor on 17 September 2012 and took Marie Brown along with me. I was extremely distressed. I argued with the lead counsel Philip Mateer, and explained to the PPS that there was little risk of jigsaw identification of the other two complainants, as I saw it. My extended family had well over a hundred people in it. I told the PPS that I was so stressed that I was on the verge of withdrawing from both cases, but would be more likely to do so if the reporting restriction stayed in place.

On 19 September, an email arrived from the prosecutor, informing me that the PPS position was that they would not seek the lifting of any restrictions in court. Their reasoning was risk of jigsaw identification, and also the views of the other victims. There was also the matter that the PPS had not applied to impose the restriction in the first place. I explained that I was disappointed, but not surprised. My reply read:

> Regarding the safety concerns, I have already been

homeless for the last year and have just found temporary accommodation as a result of having to leave West Belfast. I had informed (the detective) I do not wish to avail of a witness protection programme, and J Galloway's team have informed me that if they receive any information regarding safety concerns they will let me know. Unfortunately the mental stress caused by the imposition of a reporting restriction and the subsequent speculation it caused is outweighing the potential physical threat at present.

On 27 September 2012, disaster struck. In a move that a policeman described to me in an email as 'shocking', one of the defence counsel put forward a written application to have the membership case heard *prior* to the sexual abuse case. This was a key moment in the prosecution, because it meant further delay in the sexual abuse case, which had already been in the court system for two years. The defence were perfectly entitled to argue what they thought would be their best strategy, but word reached me that the other two complainants were understandably upset and informed the PPS that if that happened, due to further delay and because they had fears around the membership case, they would pull their evidence from the sexual abuse case. If they withdrew, I would be the only complainant. The judge granted the defence application on 8 October. There was another difficulty in hearing the membership case first – if a Diplock court, sitting without a jury, found the defendants not guilty, then the evidence about all the IRA activity surrounding my abuse would not be able to be used in the abuse case, meaning that it would be very difficult to secure a conviction.

Two days later, on the morning of the challenge to the reporting restriction, I met with my solicitor Michael Sinclair in Joe Rice's office. He was fresh-faced, schoolboy-like and hopping about on his heels, and I could see he was anticipating a fight. I asked him if he was nervous and he replied that he was excited. This was a big case for him, and he had worked hard on it – and I had confidence that we would get a fair hearing. My gut was calm and it rarely let me down. However, we both knew that we could not be certain of even getting into chambers to ask the magistrate to hear us. We had spent so much time sending through points for the barrister; it was hours of daily work. Not getting in would be a major blow. Michael believed that if we passed this hurdle we would have a good chance of getting the restriction lifted 'in some shape or form'.

I was nervous and Michael's enthusiasm was making me worse. Belfast city centre was bustling, with crowds of tourists mingling with office workers around the City Hall; it was a clear crisp day and there was a big queue for the bus. I looked at the throngs of people and wondered wryly if their lives were as complicated as mine. As I people-watched, I silently rehearsed the argument I would make if I was called in front of the magistrate. I walked with a still hopping Michael up Chichester Street towards Laganside Courts, and as we went through the revolving door and the security screening machine towards the lift I began to relax a bit. I was here on my terms and because I felt the PPS were not representing my best interests. It was almost unprecedented for a witness to hire their own counsel. Game on.

I seated myself in the public gallery of Court Number 10 beside the two MIT police officers, Denis and Stephen. Stephen called things as he saw them – including police failings. I anxiously awaited my barrister Leona Askin's arrival.

Denis leaned across and said in a conspiratorial tone, 'So, what's your action plan then?'

I laughed and retorted: 'Now Denis, do you honestly expect me to tell you that after all that's happened?'

Stephen guffawed and Denis slunk into his seat. I felt a bit bad, so I smiled at him. I wanted them to think we had it in the bag, even though I wasn't even sure if we would be allowed to speak with the judge.

The court announcement system summoned Michael to the judge's chambers. We were in – a huge achievement when no one had actually decided if I was even entitled to my own representation yet. Leona breezed calmly into court, her black robe flapping behind her. Her hair was swept up into a bun and she had a mound of papers under her arms. She looked like she meant business. She floated over to Morris's solicitor John Finucane, and handed him a copy of our submission to the magistrate. He didn't appear to be pleased, though it is always hard to tell with John, as he has a permanently wooden demeanour. She also served a copy of the submission to a BBC lawyer. I had no idea they would be there, but now know it is routine for a media corporation such as the BBC to fight a reporting restriction on behalf of all media and to highlight the open justice principle. I was glad they were in the court. Peter Madden, the lawyer for the other four accused, strode into the court and all of the lawyers walked together into chambers for the audience with Judge Fiona Bagnall.

They emerged around thirty minutes later. The court staff were frustrated that the normal procedures were being delayed and I could hear them complaining as Michael and Leona came to tell me what had happened. They had explained to the magistrate that they wished to make submissions on my behalf, and the BBC barrister had also indicated that he wished to challenge the reporting restriction on behalf of the media. The magistrate agreed to hear our representation in open court, and we went back to sitting in the public gallery until the normal defendant court list was dealt with before the magistrate could get around to hearing ours. Scores of young men were produced, most in tracksuits or T-shirts, shoulders hunched, and either remanded until the next hearing or bailed.

Leona was excellent in her summary of what I wanted. In essence, she argued that the restrictions were harming me and that in order to adhere to the principle of open justice these should be lifted and the defendants should be named. Morris's lawyer argued that the restrictions should be retained. The most dramatic speech came from the solicitor for the other four defendants, Peter Madden, who stated that his clients never asked for or would be asking for a reporting restriction, and that while no one wanted their names in the public domain for 'an offence like this', that this was his clients' 'stated position'. That was news to me and the rest of the court, and I remarked sarcastically to the PSNI that the only people now apparently in favour of a reporting restriction were Morris's legal team and the PPS.

Judge Bagnall took time to consider the arguments, and ultimately agreed to lift the reporting restriction.

35

I was so disturbed by the way in which the court process was developing, and concerned about the potential for political interference, that I reached out to politicians from across the political spectrum. I spoke to unionist politicians like Jim Allister, and met with SDLP politician Mark Durkan, former Deputy First Minister of Northern Ireland, who informed me he had been approached by senior British politician and former Secretary of State, Shaun Woodward, who, he said, had called Padraic Wilson 'poor Padraic'. When this revelation eventually made it into the public domain in 2014, Woodward denied he had said Poor Padraic. Mark, a lovely man, was genuine in all of his dealings with me, and he cried at times when I was meeting him.

I also met with the leader of the then-dominant southern Irish party Fianna Fáil, Micheál Martin, in Dublin, along with his political adviser Pat McPartland. Micheál, a quiet, reflective man, was horrified when I explained to him what had happened to me at the hands of the IRA. He drank green tea at the meeting in his offices in Leinster House, gently asked questions, and enquired about how the court process was going. I told him that I thought the cases were being weakened, and at some point, I wanted the republican movement held accountable, not just for my treatment, but for that of others. I wanted him as a politician to keep a watching brief. I believed that the more people in political life knew that my court case was happening, the better. I figured that the PPS would be more careful and less likely to make a mistake. And if they did, then politicians on both sides of the border would be able to hold people accountable and raise the wider issues that my case represented.

On 3 December, the PPS emailed to say that they were considering severing the indictment, effectively splitting the other two complainants from my case. There was a logic to this, as the PPS had conceded a defence request that the membership case should go first. If that collapsed, it would weaken the evidence in the abuse trial, and they thought they might have a stronger chance in running the other complainants' abuse case first. However, I had serious concerns, which I communicated via email:

> My case and prospect of conviction on my evidence alone would I imagine be severely weakened as a result of splitting the complainants. I do not wish to see this happen, and did not put myself through this process to have my abuser acquitted due to weakened evidence. I believe that to proceed with my charges separately would severely weaken the case. Not to proceed with it at all after three years of a stressful experience within the criminal justice process waiting on trial is worse and is an abuse of process for me as a victim.
>
> There are IRA references in all three complaints, I can't reasonably see how the same argument the defence used with reference to the recent crown court hearing would not be used again – and if Morris is acquitted of membership, how does that affect my evidence in the abuse trial if heard afterward? I would have thought if there was a conviction in the abuse case, it would have made the IRA case stronger if heard afterward?

I also wanted to know whether it would weaken the other two complainants' abuse cases if the charges were severed, as I believed that would be 'disastrous' for them, and for my case, which would then run behind it. On 14 December, the PPS wrote back:

> I agree that the strongest abuse case is one where the allegations of all three complainants is heard. The PPS has to make an application for your evidence to be found to be 'cross-admissible' with (the other victims) allegations and the same application is made with regard to their evidence. I agree that it is impossible to imagine the case proceeding without some reference to the belief that Morris was a member of PIRA and that he used this position as a means of control and to instil fear. Similarly it is likely that some reference to the PIRA investigation will be made, as evidence of recent complaints will be lead in support of the allegations.

However, at this stage the PPS were in a tricky position, as they were dealing with a conundrum, not least that the other two complainants were reluctant to mention the IRA in their evidence. Editing it out would weaken my prospect of securing a conviction against Morris.

It became apparent to me that this case was probably going nowhere. I was frustrated by the fact that I felt I was fighting my own case, and although I had a good relationship with the police whose responsibility it was to gather evidence, I was angry that, in my opinion, things were being overlooked. No one had yet taken a statement from the counsellor I had seen in 2000, and whose notes had been supplied to the police three years earlier. I was worried the police had no real strategy for finding information that any of the accused had actually been members of the IRA.

I emailed the policeman Stevie with information that was already in the public domain about Morris. The evidence of MI5 agent Martin McGartland was one such example. He had been an IRA member while working as a British agent. When suspicion was aroused, he was kidnapped by the IRA and held in a flat in Twinbrook on the outskirts of west Belfast. He escaped by hurling himself out a window several storeys high, and was rushed to hospital in an ambulance. From there he was relocated and given a new identity in England. He was originally from Ballymurphy and wrote a book about his experiences, *Fifty Dead Men Walking*, later made into a film starring Ben Kingsley. In his book, he wrote about Morris: 'They came to my mother's house at around 3:00pm one day during the winter of 1985. The two men were in their 20s – one was generally known by the nickname 'Andy' and the other was called Martin Morris.' He wrote about how the men told his mother they wanted to talk to him because they had been told he was selling blocks of cheese. He continued: 'Instinctively, my mother knew that they were IRA and also that if she did hand me over then I would be punished.' In another chapter, he wrote: 'Two Republicans ordered to police the estate and crack down on the joy-riders were Johnny [...] and an IRA sympathiser, Marty Morris.'[38]

I met with the BBC NI *Spotlight* team, explained how the cases were going and discussed making a documentary. I wanted people to know what had happened to me, and I wanted Morris named so that people could make an informed choice whether to have their children around him. I also wanted to ensure that no other abuse victim was treated by the republican movement the way I had been, and to do that, I needed to expose it. The then head of current affairs, Jeremy Adams, outlined the risks to me, and I was of the opinion that if not-guilty verdicts were returned, it would be extremely difficult to air any documentary. And after I spoke about concerns regarding my safety with my solicitor, I moved to Derry to escape Belfast for the remainder of the trials. Saorlaith was two and adapted quickly, and the move allowed us some breathing space. We were lucky to find a good landlord and nursery and were both happy, though I knew the move would only be for a year or two. In May 2013, the PPS applied to the court to sever the cases and have the evidence of AA and BB heard first. The court recorder refused. AA and BB formally withdrew from the case on 7 June 2013. This was devastating, as it left me as the only complainant.

In August 2013, I flew to Glasgow to film the BBC documentary with Susan McKay. I had another dislocated kneecap and was hobbling around on crutches. We filmed over three days and the producer, Chris Thornton, and cameraman, Bill Browne, were meticulous about getting the right shots, and both had an easy-going manner.

On the last day of filming, they needed filler shots, so we found a square, and I hopped to a bench and sat. Chris took my crutches off camera and Bill started the camera rolling. Some nosy people came along to see what was happening, and asked if it was for *Eastenders*. I was thankful that the BBC had had the presence of mind to film in another city, not in Belfast, where word would have instantly leaked. I returned to Derry glad that I had got most of my story on camera, but thinking it was probable that if my court cases collapsed, they would never be able to use the footage.

On 1 October 2013, Gerry Adams's brother Liam Adams was found guilty of abusing his daughter Aine, and although it was an entirely separate case to mine, it left me with some hope that I might get a guilty verdict after all. I was still hanging onto the criminal justice process by my fingernails, and the verdict helped me to lift myself up onto the ledge a little. The media parsed the result, along with information which had come out during the second trial. The first trial had been vacated in April 2013, and Liam was convicted at the second. His brother Gerry had been called as a witness in the first, where he was excoriated under cross-examination by barrister Eilis McDermott, but he wasn't called in the second. The verdict, however, allowed details from the first trial to be made public for the first time.

The Irish *Sunday Independent* wrote the following account:

> Gerry Adams reported his sister-in-law to social services, accusing her of having a 'dirty' house and poor 'hygiene' but he failed to tell a social worker assigned to the family that his brother had sexually abused his niece. Official records show that the family first came to the attention of social services in

January 1986, when Gerry Adams reported that the children were 'dirty and had lice in their hair.' These records reveal that Gerry Adams had said that 'poor home-management standards had, in some way, contributed to the marital difficulties of his brother Liam, and his then wife [...].'

The confrontation with his brother Liam was in March 1987 in Buncrana. The next day, Adams bumped into the social worker in Aine Adams's home – but failed to tell her of the allegations. He stated that his brother Liam had confessed to him during a walk in the rain in 2000. He only reported the abuse in 2009.[39]

It was a startling revelation, as was the fact that after the trial, Gerry Adams released a statement stating it had been a 'difficult and distressing ordeal for all of my family, and for my niece, Aine', and called on the media to respect 'our right to space and privacy'. Adams was a public figure, and the contradictions in his cross-examination should have been placed under scrutiny. The transcript of what he said had been uploaded to the BBC's website, and was easily available. The journalist Eilis O'Hanlon addressed this point specifically in her column in relation to the wider republican movement in the *Sunday Independent*, writing: 'Nor do family considerations excuse instances where other Sinn Féin members apart from Adams treated victims appallingly. No one who bothers to delve beneath the surface of Sinn Féin's family-friendly facade can be in any doubt that the republican movement has been covering up sexual crimes for decades.'[40]

The Liam Adams trial renewed interest in other cases of abuse. The various press organisations were aware of my case, but were unable to report on it as it was still before the courts. On 16 October, the wider issue was raised by the Democratic Unionist Party (DUP) MP Gregory Campbell, who had received a document from a whistleblower alleging that the republican movement had internally investigated cases of abuse rather than reporting them to the police or social services, and he asked a question in the House of Commons:

Campbell: Will the Secretary of State comment on information I have received about a fixed committee that existed within the republican movement in 2000, which dealt with almost 100 sex abuse victims and in which some very prominent republicans were involved, and will she join me in calling for those people to come forward and help those many innocent victims deal with the nightmare they are still dealing with 13 years on?

Mrs Villiers [Secretary of State for Northern Ireland]: The hon. Gentleman raises some very grave matters, and I would certainly encourage anyone who has been the victim of abuse to approach the police with that information, and anyone who has knowledge of such cases to do so too. It is obviously crucial that this scourge of society is eliminated and that the voluntary sector, the police and the Government give all the support possible to victims of abuse.[41]

I was blindsided by the Westminster question, and I was also nervous. I believed that I would, wrongly, be blamed for being the source of Campbell's information, and I was concerned that the reporting of it would fuel more social media speculation. I didn't want my trials affected as a result of the report encouraging comments that could have affected the continuation of the cases.

Victims of sexual abuse are often badly affected psychologically if they are not in control of events around them. This was certainly outside of my control, and it unsettled me greatly. I called Gregory Campbell's office and explained who I was. He returned my call, and I outlined my concerns. He wasn't aware of my case, apologised, and agreed not to speculate further in case it might impact on my court cases. The media, of course, reported on Campbell's comments, which were made under privilege.

Sinn Féin simply denied that there was any pattern of covering up abuses. This angered me, and I contacted Micheál Martin's office to say that I was happy for him to refer to the wider issue without going into the details of my case. He did so, saying at a press conference that he knew the IRA had investigated cases of abuse: 'From information that we have picked up, and we have talked to other people, this may have been a broader trend within the republican movement,' he said, continuing: 'Just like the church, the republican movement says the institution of the republican movement is more important than individual victims.' Sinn Féin's Donegal TD Pearse Doherty, one of their rising young stars, countered in his trademark angry voice that the claims by Michael Martin were 'unfounded and untrue, and they're disgraceful'.[42]

I didn't have to pretend to feel anger. I wrote an anonymous piece for the *Sunday Independent*. It was my first proper piece in a newspaper. I warned Sinn Féin that they needed to admit the problem. I knew they would know who was writing, whether I was anonymous or not.

> I have for the last significant number of years watched denial of this issue with both sadness and incredulity. I have been absolutely devastated at the fact that people I know personally – including some in senior positions within Sinn Féin who I can categorically say they have heard cases such as mine directly from my own mouth – have repeatedly deflected responsibility. Devastated because I know exactly how traumatic it is to be at the receiving end of sexual violence as a child. I know how difficult it is, the shame that you feel the minute the first finger is laid on you in the act of exercising power and control for sexual gratification […] I also know what it is like to be on the receiving end of a republican movement interrogation. Because that's what it was. Repeated and systemic and forced questioning of the details of what had happened to me.[43]

I ended the piece with a pointed reminder of what Sinn Féin needed to do: 'They need to apologise publicly to all of those people who they have continued to treat disgracefully by minimising and denying their experiences; effectively insinuating they are liars in the process. They simply need to tell the truth.'[44]

I knew my article would leave the party in no doubt that I was prepared to speak if they made another attempt at public denial. It was risky when the trials had yet to conclude, but I was prepared to stand by what I said; and writing in this way allowed me to have a voice at a time when I felt mine was being suffocated by the anonymity given to me as a rape victim.

Two days after the article appeared, the four people charged in connection with the IRA 'investigation' were arraigned, as was Morris, on membership charges. I was advised by the police that I didn't have to be there, but if I wanted to attend, two officers would accompany me to court. I needed to be there, if only to have a level of control. My only way of doing that was to listen to the legal arguments in the courtroom. I went to almost all of the court hearings during the four years that the case ran. Eilis O'Hanlon offered to come with me, and I was very grateful for that. I watched the first four being arraigned, but Morris was arraigned separately that afternoon.

At lunch, I noticed him go through the court doors while we were standing outside. He was with his daughter, who was pushing a pram, and I couldn't tell whether he had seen me or not. My stomach lurched. I expected to see him in the dock, but hadn't thought that I might see him anywhere else. Mindful that he was probably going up in the elevator, I held back for a while before making my way to court 11. When we eventually went inside, we met Stevie from the PSNI, checked our belongings onto the security belt and went through the scanner. I noticed Stevie had a holstered gun and thought how strange it was that I hadn't noticed it before. He had an easy manner and we were talking about things in general as we entered the elevator. As the doors opened at our destination, I could see Morris standing on the other side of them. Stevie was to my right and Morris leaned across him, almost in my face, and said 'hiya' directly to me. I dug my fingernails into my skin. It took effort to keep my face blank as if I hadn't seen him. I walked away from him and quietly said to Stevie, 'I can't believe he just said that to me,' and shook my head to try and shake the memory off.

When we got into court and sat down in the public gallery, the confrontation got worse. Morris came in and sat down a few seats away. I could see him in the reflection of the glass dock, which was around ten feet in front of me, and it was obvious that he was looking straight at me. The prosecution barrister came to check that I was okay, and asked how I felt about Morris sitting so close. I was telling her what had happened at the elevator, when his solicitor came in and he moved away from me.

Morris was placed in the dock for the arrival of the judge, and he sat with his arms stretched out like an aggressive animal, claiming it as his own. As the judge ordered him to stand for the charges to be put, he rose slowly and very deliberately turned his back on the judge and faced me. His eyes locked with mine. I panicked, but refused to let my eyes drop. It was a considerable amount of time, time enough for those sitting near me to not only notice but to turn to me to see my reaction. When the judge was finished putting the charges and Morris was leaving the dock, he took two quick steps in my direction instead of moving towards the court door. The rapid reactions of both police officers ensured that I didn't need to move a muscle – they shepherded him out of the court, and one of them told the person with him that if Morris did anything like that again they would arrest him. I wanted to be sick and I wanted out of the claustrophobia of the courtroom. I was trying to control my breathing, and Stevie asked me to hang on a while, to give Morris time to go. Eventually I couldn't wait any longer and went to the toilet, where I started heaving. I couldn't shake that image of him staring at me. We made witness statements to the PPS about it, and CCTV clearly showed the interaction at the elevator, but little could be done about it.

I drove back to Derry in a haze. Even now, I have no memory of the journey home, yet I can remember the court incident clearly. I was sent home from work early the next day by my boss Nicola, who could see the impact events were having on me. It was probably the worst moment of the entire four years at court. In November 2013, No Bill applications (effectively an attempt to argue that there is no case to answer) were heard in respect of

Padraic Wilson, Seamus Finucane and Martin Morris. This was granted in relation to one charge against Wilson, leaving the remaining charges against him and the other two.

I needed to keep Saorlaith's life as normal as possible while all this was going on. To clear my head I drove up past Quigley's Point outside Derry, a spectacular view where the sealine seems to blend into the road, up through Redcastle and onto An tSrúibh, a small beach on the coast of the Inishowen peninsula. I would take Saorlaith there rain, hail or shine – stick on a pair of wellies and delight in her as she tried to jump tiny waves or screamed and ran away, scared by the seaweed. The clean sea air was good for getting her to sleep at bedtime, allowing me to write in the evening. I would type out what had happened to me, and also send emails to the PPS if something had come up that I felt would have an impact on the case.

Marie Brown, who lived nearby, started bringing me out into society again. When the trials started, I had been afraid even to enter shops in Belfast in case I bumped into anyone who would be hostile to me. Most of my shopping was done online and apart from taking Saorlaith to the beach, I didn't really go out anywhere. Marie began to take me shopping for groceries, and then to Foyleside in Derry's centre, and I slowly got used to the noise and the presence of people again.

In January 2014 – four years after I had given my original statement – I was told that the cases had been severed yet again. There were now three. The first case would deal with the charges of IRA membership against Morris, which were needed to strengthen the evidence in the second and third cases. The second case would deal with the abuse charges against Morris, and the third would judge the four individuals accused of IRA membership and other charges connected to the IRA 'investigation'. To add insult to injury, I also received the proposed edited evidence statement. It was substantially reduced from the original one I had given three years earlier, given that lots of references to the IRA had been taken out of it. It was a crushing blow, and on 29 January 2014, I wrote to the Public Prosecution Service about how I felt:

> It is my view that the cases have been weakened to such an extent now that proceeding with them is ... ludicrous. Expecting me to go ahead and give evidence in trials where the outcome is by default pre-determined due to the weakness in the prosecution case and test for membership required, before it has begun is in my view, scandalous.

On 13 April, I met with two police officers from the MIT team. I was concerned that Joe McCullough, one of the people named in my evidence as a friend of Morris, and who I had repeatedly asked about, had never been spoken to by police to elicit his version of events.

Joe McCullough's parents' home was a few doors away from my grandparents in Ballymurphy. His late mother Kitty was my Grandmother Tess's best friend, and both families knew each other well. He had been a remand prisoner on an IRA wing at one point in the 1990s, his name once appearing on a list of IRA prisoners in An Phoblacht. McCullough was arrested on more than one occasion, but he was acquitted each time. He later worked as Gerry Adams's head of security for seven years.

A meeting between Morris and myself in 1997 was contained in my evidence file against Morris on the charge of IRA membership. I had named McCullough as also being present. McCullough, for his part, to this day strenuously denies the meeting took place.

I informed the police that I was concerned that McCullough would be called as a defence witness, and I wanted the PSNI to speak with him.

In a later statement to BBC NI Spotlight, McCullough said my allegations about him were 'nonsense and a fabrication'. After I appeared on the programme, the Irish News carried a story in November 2014 which included some coverage of a press statement from him, which stated:

> 'I had no option but to attend Belfast Crown Court at an IRA membership trial and only at this specific IRA membership trial, both to challenge the initial statement she (Ms Cahill)

made directly implicating me in the matter and also on legal advice,' he said.

'The BBC programme in question portrayed the image that I had turned up in support of Martin Morris. This is not the case. I turned up to protect my own name and also on the foot of advice that a summons would be issued against me. […] 'It should be noted that all of this arose because Máiría Cahill implicated me in the IRA membership trial. I should say that if Martin Morris had made a statement pulling me into the matter I would have had no hesitation in turning up for the prosecution.'

[…] 'I have no idea why Máiría Cahill would involve me in the matter between her and Martin Morris,' he said.

'I cannot understand why my appearance in court as a witness has caused such a stir.' [45]

I was due in court the next day for the membership case. I was so annoyed at the response from the police and worn down by the whole arduous process, four long years of it, that I handed them a statement withdrawing my support for the prosecutions. I was, instead, cajoled to go to court and see how things progressed.

The next morning I met with the barristers, who persuaded me to go ahead with the case. It was my word against Morris, but they believed that I was a strong and credible witness. There was a hurdle, though. It is almost impossible to get a charge of membership of an illegal organisation over the line in a Northern Irish court on the word of a witness alone, without forensic evidence or being caught in the act. We were relying on my word alone, so it was a gamble but one that the PPS was prepared to take. They went into court to argue for special measures so that I would be allowed to give evidence by video link rather than in the courtroom, pointing out that Morris had previously waylaid me in the court precinct. The defence team stated that they would have to seek CCTV of this event. I wasn't worried about this, as the PSNI already had the CCTV and it could be produced to the judge. Proceedings were adjourned until after lunch, and as we left to get coffee, the elevator doors opened. 'That's Joe McCullough,' I said. I now had two witnesses who would testify against my evidence. It was now going to be even harder to get a result.

At lunch, as I was playing about with the food on my plate rather than eating it, my barrister was informed that McCullough was indeed being called as a defence witness by Morris's team. That changed the stakes in the case. A prosecution barrister had previously ruled out introducing character evidence, which would have meant that Morris's previous history with the criminal justice system would have been likely inadmissable, and therefore the case was reduced to the word of the accused and his witness against mine.

My barrister informed me that a conviction was now much less likely. I told Eilis O'Hanlon and the barrister that the case was over. I handed the lawyers a lengthy withdrawal statement and asked them to give it to the judge. In that statement I criticised the PPS, the police and the court service, and reiterated my allegations. Without a witness there was no case, and not-guilty verdicts were returned, as is the process, without hearing any evidence.

Within a fortnight, I had also withdrawn from the other two cases. My sexual abuse case had needed a successful prosecution of Morris for IRA membership. When that prospect vanished, it had a domino effect on the other two cases, which had been weakened beyond repair. In my withdrawal statement, I said:

> I believe that the evidence that the Prosecution was relying on to secure a conviction initially was strong. However, due to various factors, this evidence has been weakened to such an extent that I am of the opinion that the prosecution would no longer be able to secure a conviction based on the evidence they now intend to rely on in this case. This is the worst possible outcome and is extremely distressing.

In May 2014, all five defendants had not-guilty verdicts returned because no prosecution evidence was offered against them. The 9 May *Irish News* report on the dismal proceedings was concise:

> Kate McKay, prosecuting, asked Judge McFarland that the charges 'be left on the books and not be proceeded without the leave of the Crown Court of the Court of Appeal.' But Mark Mulholland QC, defending, said in the case last month of his client Martin Morris, of Wellbeck Road London, the prosecution offered no evidence against him on a charge of membership of the Provisional IRA. Ms McKay told the court that the prosecution was now 'not offering evidence' against the four accused. 'In light of that decision, we say that the prosecution in this case should offer no evidence in the same terms.' [...] As a result the Belfast Recorder said he would enter "not guilty verdict" [sic].[46]

In 2015, Jim Allister of the Traditional Unionist Voice party (TUV), himself a former barrister, in the wake of Sir Keir Starmer's review into my court cases, stated: 'The failure to even interview Joe McCullough was an elementary blunder, which to me speaks of a lack of official enthusiasm for the prosecutions. The PSNI role and handling of this issue is not investigated in this report, but still needs [to be] explored and explained.'[47]

After four years in court, my cases had collapsed like a set of cards. I felt badly let down by the legal system. I still do.

36

My attention now turned to the BBC NI *Spotlight* programme. The not-guilty verdicts were a disaster, but the BBC did not think that this was insurmountable. We decided to continue to record, and they could gather as much information as possible; then, if it was legally viable, the programme would be aired.

The BBC brought in one of their most talented reporters, Jennifer O'Leary, and I was immediately impressed at the background research she had done. Susan McKay's previous interview would still be used as footage, and Jennifer would film more interviews with me, work on pulling together the information, and present it. It was a colossal task to pull it all together.

I had no control over what the BBC would decide to broadcast, and I needed to be able to trust that they would make a first-class programme and not screw me over. I met with Chris Thornton and Jennifer, handed over whatever documentation I had and answered their questions. Our meeting place was usually a hotel on the outskirts of Ballyclare, which was unlikely to be frequented by IRA supporters. At other times we met in rented rooms, or simply in a car.

In July I took Saorlaith to Disney World in Florida along with my friend Julie and her daughter. We had been saving for the trip, but when we got there I couldn't relax. The kids loved it, and I enjoyed the time away, but I couldn't completely escape the stress and adrenaline levels I had become accustomed to over the previous four years.

When I returned I met with Jennifer and Chris again and agreed to a further interview in August. The BBC found a large remote house on a rural road near Newry, with a tree-lined driveway. There was no danger of being seen or disturbed. In Glasgow, the interview had stretched over four days and allowed me to tell my story with few interruptions. This interview was different, because the BBC needed to test my story and ensure they had covered all of the legal angles.

It was tense at times. Jennifer O'Leary was a formidable interviewer, and I found the going tough. I later joked with her that she was like a rottweiler once the cameras started rolling, which surprised me, because her default persona is that of a kind, gentle-natured woman. We filmed for hours on the first day, and I had a few hours' sleep. We avoided speaking about my situation unless the cameras were on. The team looked after me well and I could take breaks when I needed, which prolonged filming for them but ensured that I was able to do it with a minimal level of distress. I didn't refuse to answer any question put to me, though I remember bristling when asked questions that cut close to the bone. I explained, for example, why I had gone back to the house I had been abused in after the first time, and how victims often take on all of the responsibility for their situation.

I was taking a big chance in waiving my anonymity, a protection the courts had offered me for life irrespective of the verdicts, but my instinct was that the BBC would treat my case responsibly. And they did. The documentary was titled *A Woman Alone with the IRA* and in October 2014, it catapulted me into the public domain.

*

The documentary was due to be broadcast in a few days. I was nervous, not only because once I waived anonymity there would be no going back, but also because I couldn't predict what the reaction from the republican movement and the community around it was going to be. The BBC were worried about safety and suggested putting me up in a hotel. The Culloden in Cultra, a prosperous suburb on Belfast Lough, was a world away from the inner-city streets of Belfast.

Sinn Féin had been offered a right of reply, and the party had been sent a detailed list of questions a few weeks previously. Wholly unconnected to this, Sue Ramsey, a Sinn Féin MLA in whom I had confided about my abuse in the late 1990s, announced her resignation from her position due to ill health a week before the programme aired. Paying tribute to her, Gerry Adams, who referred to her as his friend, stated: 'Across a distinguished political career, Sue has made a huge impression on all of those she met and worked with…She has a good heart and I hope her health is restored as quickly as possible.'[48] In 2015, given I had disclosed in confidence to her, Siobhan and another woman, I had publicly called on Sue Ramsey to clarify if she knew who had reported my abuse to the IRA all those years earlier. No response was forthcoming. Ramsey was subsequently made a trustee of the Sinn Féin party.

The programme would air on budget night in the Irish Republic, and I was worried that it would get lost in the coverage of rows over tax policies. I contacted the SDLP's Tim Attwood and asked if he could arrange meetings for me with Micheál Martin and someone in the Irish Labour Party after the programme was shown. Initially, Labour offered a meeting with one of their TDs, Alex White. I asked Tim to go back and check if Joan Burton, party leader and Tánaiste (deputy prime minister), was available.

I had taken a few days leave from work and fully expected to be back at my desk the following Monday. Naively, I hoped that I could get back to my life quickly. I asked *Spotlight NI*'s producer Chris Thornton if he thought that the programme would have an impact. 'I think it'll cause a shitshow,' he said. I trusted him, and he had treated me well, but for all that I wasn't sure how the documentary would be received. I had no idea of the drama that would drag out in its wake. Holed up in the Culloden, I felt removed from it all, as if the impending programme had nothing to do with me. My room was bright and airy, with two beds and a

At home in Belfast, aged one-and-a-half.

On holiday near Ardara in County Donegal, around 1986.

With my parents, aged nine.

With Gerry Adams, summer 1997.

With Aunt Annie and Uncle Joe in west Belfast, 1998.

With Saorlaith at Seaforde Gardens and Tropical Butterfly House, 26 April 2011.

With Granny Nora, Christmas Day, Belfast, 2011.

Filming BBC NI *Spotlight*'s, *A Woman Alone with the IRA*.

Meeting with First Minister Peter Robinson, Stormont, October 2014.

Speaking to media after the meeting with First Minister
Peter Robinson, October 2014.

Hugging Taoiseach Enda Kenny outside government buildings, Dublin, October 2014.

Former Tánaiste Joan Burton and Saorlaith, February 2016.

Graffiti on the wall, Springfield Road, Belfast, December 2014.

Niall O'Loughlin's powerful image for the
Irish Independent, October 2014.

Winning the Seanad election, November 2015.

Taking a break during the General Election count, Dublin, 2016.

Last Day of Seanad, with fellow Senators Michael Mullins (left) and the late Terry Brennan (right). Leinster House, February 2016.

Saorlaith practising her photography skills and taking a portrait shot of her Mammy, 2022.

writing desk, and I could see the sea from my window, so I spent a lot of time trying to ground myself. I also sat in the car park, smoking. I spent the next two days on edge, taking calls from Jennifer and Chris, who were having their own battle to ensure that the programme was ready in time. They kept this from me to keep me calm, and listened to my concerns. I needed a lot of reassurance.

People who had seen the trailer for the documentary were already texting and calling. I couldn't concentrate on the calls, and posted on Facebook asking friends not to contact me until the programme was over. One friend, Ann Travers, whose twenty-three-year-old sister Mary had been murdered by the IRA as she came out of Mass in south Belfast, offered to write an online blog in advance of the programme. I was touched, and wept when I saw what she had written.

> Máiría Cahill is my friend. We make an unlikely pairing, considering our diverse backgrounds, her great Uncle was once the chief of staff of an organisation which murdered my sister, and tried to murder my father. We also have diverse views…I am fully behind her in her tough decision to waive her anonymity […] My friend has always told me that the truth is the most powerful thing a person can have. And she will tell it. And it's never easy for her to do so because like any abuse victim, speaking brings everything back. Yesterday when I tweeted about tomorrow night's BBCNI *Spotlight* programme the usual disgusting tweets came back. It happens every time I tweet about anything to do with republicanism. There was no concern for how this alleged abuse was handled, or for the young woman – who was a 16 year old child when it started – but a full on further abuse of the victim from people who claim to be republican. I don't know why I was surprised. What else would they do, only try to deflect from their collective shameful behaviour on this issue […]. As I say, I consider Máiría Cahill a friend. For the past number of years I have listened to her and supported her on her journey where

she desperately tried to achieve justice in order to hold people accountable for what happened to her. I have also witnessed her supporting many others, including myself. She is a kind hearted and courageous young woman, and I have no doubt when people see tomorrow night's Spotlight documentary, they will be horrified at what she was put through.[49]

It was a shot across the bow for those who were already putting up disparaging comments online. Ann was well known, and had succeeded on getting the law changed in Northern Ireland through a bill proposed by TUV politician Jim Allister in 2012 to bar anyone with a conviction of more than five years for terrorist offences from working as a SPAD (special adviser) to any politician in government. I had supported the proposal, and attended the debate in the Assembly with her. All parties in Northern Ireland supported the law, except Sinn Féin.

I woke up and turned on the television that morning and saw a clip of myself on the breakfast news. Jennifer was also on the BBCs *Good Morning Ulster* radio programme discussing the documentary. I didn't know at the time that an attempt had been made at the High Court to obtain an injunction preventing the programme from being aired. Tim Attwood of the SDLP texted: 'Good luck today your courage to reveal the truth is an inspiration.' I deeply appreciated that. I went out for a drive to calm myself down, and bought the newspapers. The *Irish Independent, Belfast Telegraph, Belfast News Letter* and *Irish Times* all mentioned the programme. The *Irish Independent* had a quote from my relative Eilis O'Hanlon saying that I was 'feisty and determined'. I didn't feel it at that moment.

Eilis was driving up to stay in the hotel and to watch the programme with me. I rang the Dublin Rape Crisis centre to alert them that the programme was coming out and to ask them if they would tweet out their support number later in the evening, mindful that other people might be upset when they watched it. My father texted, prompting tears: 'Just in case it gets lost in the madness I just want to tell you I love you and

I'm very proud of you.' The Ulster Unionist leader Mike Nesbitt, whom I had first met when he was Northern Ireland's Victims Commissioner, issued a statement which was both welcome and helpful. He had contacted the Chief Constable George Hamilton and asked for his assurance 'that the police will investigate fully and appropriately the extremely serious allegation in tonight's programme. I recognise Máiría comes from a family at the heart of Irish republicanism but this transcends political allegiances and strikes at the heart of what sort of society we want to build.' He also said that I had an 'unfailing determination to put the interests of the abused ahead of her own personal safety'.[50] I appreciated that, because it alerted people to the pressure I was under. It also helped to gain unionist support.

I collected Eilis, and we ate dinner in the hotel. My dad brought Saorlaith over to see me, and soon after she arrived the trail appeared on the television. I turned the sound down so she wouldn't hear it, but she saw my face appear on the screen. My three-year-old daughter scratched her head, looked from the television to me and back again, then pointed at it, shouting: 'Mammy, how did you get into the TV?' We laughed and I scooped her up, buried her blonde curls in my neck and hugged her tightly. She left with my father to see her granny, and reality loomed large again.

Eilis and I sat in our beds and watched the programme together. It was an incredibly strange experience, but it was also an excellent documentary. The programme broadcast my allegations of abuse, and the fact that Morris denied he had raped me. The public could make up their own minds. It did not deal with the second IRA investigation or mention the other two victims, who had not waïved their anonymity. Instead it concentrated on the first IRA investigation, and told the story as it happened. It was stunning and shocking to see, even for me.

On 14 October 2014, reaction was swift, and my Twitter account, which had all of 22 followers prior to the programme going out, was growing by the thousand. Notifications were pinging incessantly, and because I couldn't work out how to turn it off, my phone kept whistling at me.

I was glad the programme had gone out, though I still had the feeling that it was happening to someone else. I was also frustrated that Sinn Féin had chosen not to answer any of the questions put to them, instead cynically advising the programme makers to take any information they might have to the police.

My mother rang to offer support, and a former IRA man wrote: 'We congratulate you on ur strength and integrity.' This was a good sign, as it meant that some republicans knew the truth and might be prepared to speak out against the movement. Seamus McKendry, the son-in-law of Jean McConville, the mother of ten shot by the IRA – one of the first IRA 'disappeared' victims – texted me: 'Have to say we've just seen Spotlight. Notwithstanding the horrors you've endured, you are a very brave and articulate young Lady.' A friend, whose ninety-year-old mother had supported the IRA all her life, wrote: 'Very brave love. My wee ma said as soon as it was over "I believe her," that says it all.' Those were the messages that meant the most, the ones from within the republican family who knew without a shadow of a doubt I was telling the truth. I was disappointed that others were not courageous enough to challenge their own blind faith in Sinn Féin and the IRA.

The internet exploded, and both my name and Jennifer O'Leary's Twitter handle were trending. The programme had the effect of seriously damaging Sinn Féin, causing outrage which led to parliamentary debates on both sides of the border, and exposing the IRA on the issue of child sexual abuse and the way they had covered it up. Sinn Féin supporters' Twitter accounts were engaged in a vociferous online campaign, complaining about 'trial by media' and always pointing to the formal not-guilty court verdicts in the cases of Morris and the others. I ignored them and instead replied to as many positive responses as I could, though I did tweet to Gerry Adams, angry at his party's lack of proper response to the programme:

> I have spoken to other victims over last number of years of Republican cover up of sexual abuse. @GerryAdamsSF should now acknowledge them.[51]

I wanted them to know that I was aware of other cases apart from mine. I knew this because I had spent considerable time speaking to former IRA men, one of whom I had met just a few months earlier.

I met him in a house in west Belfast, alone, having arranged the meeting with a person who was once close to the Belfast IRA. I had asked if there was anyone who could speak to me who might know of other abuse cases like mine. Within days, I had an address to go to and an assurance that the man had information that might be useful to me. I thought long and hard about meeting him, but I needed to know if others apart from me and my relatives had had their abuse investigated by the IRA. I didn't think it was a set-up, but I told someone I trusted where I was going and asked them to raise the alarm if I wasn't out by a certain time.

I was scared, nonetheless. I had left my phone in the car, and the man told me that he didn't want me taking notes. I put my notebook away and listened to what he had to say. He had piercing eyes, and was incredibly direct. As I got to know him better, he was kind and scrupulous in his recall of detail. I had no doubt he was telling the truth, but what he told me shocked me to my core. He reeled off names and incidents in which the IRA had known about suspected paedophiles and had simply moved them on, mimicking the worst behaviour of the Catholic Church. In some cases, the perpetrators were dead. In others, they were very much alive. He told me about a senior IRA man suspected of abuse who had further access to other children. In another case, an IRA man was moved to the south of Ireland after abusing a young child. He was again accused of abuse in a safe house in Dublin. Another man, a senior figure in the movement, had been given help to flee the country and had set up home somewhere in America. Some of the people mentioned were household names.

I operated on the basis of trust with this man, who had personal knowledge of a small number of cases and who had made an effort to find others. He had also known Gerry Adams well, and claimed that Adams had direct knowledge of at least one other case. It was sickening to listen to, and I told the man that I would be passing the names of the living suspected abusers to the authorities and, separately, trying to find out more information. I was very conscious that for a case to stand up like mine, the victims would need to confirm what had happened.

I met the man a few times, and on the second occasion, my heart leapt in my mouth when there was a knock on his door while I was sitting there. My relief was palpable when the man who walked through the door was a former IRA member whom I had known all my life. He hugged me, and I relaxed. Neither man was now involved with the republican movement, and both were angry at how the IRA had covered up abuse. I was grateful that they spoke to me. Irrespective of their political beliefs, when it came to matters of child abuse they wanted to do the right thing.

I also met with another two individuals in a different part of inner-city Belfast. The arrangements for this meeting were more cloak-and-dagger, and arranged through a third party. I was told to park on a certain street, but not given any details about who I would be meeting. In hindsight, I was mad to agree, but I was driven to get as much information on suspected abusers as I could, in order to pass these details to the Gardaí (the Irish police service). I had struck up a good relationship with a detective inspector called Declan Daly and I knew he would work hard to provide information to Tusla, the Irish Child and Family Agency, in order to ensure that any abusers still alive could be risk assessed in terms of their access to children.

I parked the car and waited about ten minutes before I saw a man carrying a pint of milk walk up the street. He crossed the road before walking past my car and tapping its boot. This was my signal to get out and follow him. I waited a few seconds and then did so. I had no idea what this man's name was or where he was from, but I walked behind him and he led me to a dingy house with brown walls. Inside was a dreary room with a brown sofa. It didn't look lived in. The man said hello and sat down. He told me he wouldn't be giving me his name so that he could protect himself, and that he had debated blindfolding me and taking me to the house through a connected network of alleyways. He then spent hours giving me very useful information on republican investigations into sexual abuse, before another man arrived. Both agreed to speak to a journalist along with me, and I was relieved to be able to go and collect Jennifer and still be in one piece. The information has never aired, though it was given to the Gardaí, who shared it with the PSNI. I hope someday the victims come forward to get help. All of the detail was beyond disturbing and concerned abuse by former members of the IRA.

37

Spotlight NI was a separate entity within the BBC, with its own legal advice, and Jennifer O'Leary was taking calls from other journalists within the BBC trying to work out how they could broadcast my testimony while not overstepping any legal line. *Talkback*, the lunchtime current affairs radio programme, hadn't asked me for an interview, presumably because they were afraid of me revealing anything in a live interview situation that had not been first cleared by the corporation, but Eilis O'Hanlon agreed to appear and to speak about my case.

I sat in the bar of the Culloden Hotel and tried to listen to the programme as it went out. I still hadn't worked out how to turn the notifications on my phone off, with the result that every time I got a tweet or message (which were then coming every few seconds), my phone made a whistling sound. The waitress was clearly frustrated, and diplomatically offered me a pair of headphones to stop me torturing the other guests. Gerry Adams then followed me on Twitter before, presumably thinking better of it, unfollowing me again. I texted Mark Durkan to thank him for appearing in the programme. He recalled that the former Northern Ireland Secretary Shaun Woodward had spoken to him about my case:

> He asked me if I was concerned about what was happening to 'Poor Padraic', and he referred to the issues and the difficulties and the concerns that he was aware that Sinn Féin had and

this all had to be very worrying for the process. And I asked him if he was aware of what was fully involved. I referred to the prevailing mood and the attitude that was in the air of the back of the Jimmy Savile situation and he just simply said that we couldn't go pursuing people around these sorts of issues. [52]

It was an explosive revelation. Woodward was asked to respond by the BBC, and denied that this was what he had said to Durkan. Jennifer O'Leary's voice-over told viewers that Woodward had told them:

> It is inaccurate and misleading to say he referred to Padraic Wilson as 'poor Padraic', and stated that Woodward 'said he was 'unaware of any political lobbying.' He said he has always been consistent in believing no one is above the law and he has always supported police investigations in Northern Ireland.

The DUP MLA Paul Givan telephoned me to see if there was anything his party could do. I asked him to arrange a meeting for me with the First Minister Peter Robinson so that I could raise the issue, and he agreed. Here I was, a member of a republican family, asking to see a Democratic Unionist First Minister. But I didn't care now about the political views of individuals – I needed the issue front and centre to put as much pressure as I could on Sinn Féin and the IRA, in the hope that they would just admit the truth.

I went out to do some shopping. Browsing my phone, I noticed that on the Sinn Féin website a statement had appeared in Adams's name:

> In the Spotlight programme, broadcast last night, Máiría Cahill made an accusation relating to a meeting with myself. I totally refute the allegations Máiría made about our conversation. I met Máiría in good faith, at the behest of her cousin and my late friend Siobhán O'Hanlon who was

concerned for Máiría's welfare following an episode of self-harming. When I learned of the allegation of abuse from Siobhán, she told me that Máiría was refusing to go to the RUC. Siobhán and I met with Joe Cahill who was Máiría's uncle. We told Joe of the allegation and asked him to speak to Máiría about reporting this to the RUC. He did so. Máiría did not want to do this at that time. I have contacted my solicitor with regard to the allegations made against me in the Spotlight programme.[53]

Enraged, I hit back while walking up the bakery aisle of the local Tesco. I sent out a series of tweets, which together read:

First proof of Gerry Adams lies [...] He says he met me at behest [sic] of Siobhán O'Hanlon. Only Adams arranged the meeting himself with me. He says he was asked to meet me by Siobhán following a period of 'self harming'. Only problem for Gerry. My medical notes will confirm that I never self harmed in 2000. Gerry Adams is a liar who has just released a very personal inaccurate detail to the media. Disgusting. Should Gerry Adams wish to test the strength of my allegations, he should sue me. I welcome it. Because I have irrefutable evidence.[54]

'Might as well be hung for a sheep as a lamb,' I thought. I allowed myself a smile, but I was also nervous at what Adams and Sinn Féin would do next.

I had a foggy, dissociative feeling while standing in Tesco, tweeting about the party president of one of the most powerful movements on the island of Ireland, and telling him to sue me. 'Fuck him, the lying bastard,' I thought. I believed that he should have just answered the questions raised by *Spotlight NI*. By ignoring some of the queries put to the party, Sinn Féin had drawn a line in the sand, and it was going to be very difficult for them to vault over it without looking like liars. It felt good to be able to metaphorically punch Gerry Adams in the nose, and let him know I was not going away quietly.

When I returned to the hotel, I tweeted again:

> Read Gerry Adams statement. Interesting [sic] he uses two dead people. I entirely stand over my account and absolutely reject his. I will in due course be providing more information on my meetings with Gerry. He clearly has trouble with some aspects of his memory.[55]

These tweets generated some interest, and journalist Paddy McDonnell from Newstalk, a radio station in the Republic of Ireland, contacted me privately on Twitter with the following message: 'Hi Máiría, hope you're well. Saw your extraordinary story. Are you available for a phone interview tomorrow morning?'

Because I had grown up listening to the BBC, I was less nervous with their journalists, but southern Ireland was a whole different ball game – I had no idea what angle a station like Newstalk would take, but it was important to me to reach people there. I requested to do the interview early, as I would be meeting Micheál Martin the next day. And so Newstalk became the first station to broadcast my story south of the border, thanks to Paddy's initiative. The station remained in contact with me, and they were very active in chasing the story in its initial stages. RTÉ were infinitely slower and more cautious.

Nolan Live featured my case on television that night. Stephen Nolan is the most listened to and watched broadcaster in Northern Ireland, and once his show picked up the story north of the border, I knew other journalists would follow suit. They played clips from the *Spotlight NI* programme. All three guests were Assembly MLAs – Alliance Party leader Naomi Long, Dolores Kelly of the SDLP and Jim Allister. They were asked to respond. 'I believe Máiría,' said Long, and the other two echoed her. That was a huge relief to me. I had met with both Jim and Naomi, and the SDLP had been supportive of me for years, but to hear those politicians say it on television gave me a lift, and also a level of public protection from what I now felt certain would be further Sinn Féin attacks on my credibility.

The original *Spotlight NI* programme was also airing across the UK on BBC2, which meant more Twitter notifications from people who were only just catching up with the story and had missed it the previous evening. I spent the night again responding to messages and trying to get a few hours' sleep.

Sinn Féin's Jennifer McCann, an ex-prisoner and junior minister in the Stormont Assembly, appeared on BBC Radio's *The Nolan Show* the next morning confirming that I had previously spoken to her about my abuse. I tweeted that she didn't give a statement to the police confirming this, although she would presumably make the point that she was never asked to do so. Still, it could have been useful corroborating evidence that I had disclosed abuse to her.

I then did the Newstalk interview, pre-recording it from the hotel room. Broadcasters were still wary of legal trouble, but it suited me to pre-record because I knew if I talked too much, that they could simply edit out anything that worried them. Still, I was nervous. I went out for a walk around the hotel grounds to calm down. I did the interview looking out of the window onto the patch I had walked around, to give me something to focus on. Jonathan Healy, the presenter, quoted some of the Adams statement to me, and I walked him through it and made points similar to my tweets. I also gave him some details that weren't in the *Spotlight NI* programme, such as the fact that social services knew as early as 2000 about my abuse. I accused Gerry Adams of being 'more than economical with the truth'. I thought the interview went well, and it was due to air at 1 p.m. later that day. I had time to get changed and into the car for the drive to Dublin, where we would hear it go live around the time we were arriving.

Just after 9 a.m., I checked in to read my Twitter account and found more abusive tweets. I retweeted one of them from an account @check20629080 which said: 'Compulsive liar. Shame on you. You take our leader down, you'll take our country down. Lying tramp. Your [sic] a vicious fantasist.' I couldn't believe some people could be so cruel, but I filed the hurt to the back of my head and kept on going.

Eilis and I arrived in Dublin just as the Newstalk interview was airing, and pulled up outside the multi-storey car park in case we lost the signal. I had been forceful about Adams. I smiled as it finished, exhaled and said 'fuck'. I knew Adams wouldn't be able to keep quiet. Sinn Féin were used to being criticised north of the border, but in the South few living victims of the IRA openly challenged them in the way I was doing. The horse had bolted. From here on, it was going to be a war of words between me and the Sinn Féin president. I had a good memory. I didn't believe he had, and that gave me an advantage in interviews. Their advantage was that there was only one of me, and they had a team of press officers behind them. Still, there is nothing worse from the point of view of a political party than an angry, hurt, articulate woman with a forensic memory. I resolved to keep going.

We arrived at the Irish parliament and were met by Fianna Fáil's Kevin Dillon and brought to Micheál Martin's office. It was good to see the leader of Fianna Fáil, who had always been decent towards me, and he had a calming manner. Micheál had seen the *Spotlight NI* programme, and we talked about the fact that Sinn Féin had effectively called him a liar when he had stated in 2013 that republicans had internally investigated cases of abuse. 'Unfounded and untrue', Pearse Doherty had said – and added: 'The claims by Micheál Martin are a new low.' I told Micheál he should seek an apology. An aide told us Adams was live with RTÉ's Richard Crowley and someone switched the radio on so we could listen to it. I asked for paper and a pen so I could jot down what Adams was saying, but I didn't take too many notes because as soon as I heard Adams's angry tone I exploded and tried to bite my own anger down, repeatedly shaking my head.

Adams admitted knowing me; he could hardly do otherwise.

> I knew Máiría Cahill. I didn't know her terribly well but I knew her well enough. She was a young, friendly, young woman. She was from a republican family. She was in the Sinn

Féin structures for a while and active in the community. Her cousin – my at that time, personal assistant and friend, the late Siobhán O'Hanlon, who was very concerned at Máiría's behaviour at a particular point. [...] when it later transpired around the allegations of abuse, that this was at the core of Máiría's, you know, behaviour at this time, Siobhán O'Hanlon and I went to her uncle Joe. Joe Cahill. Because Siobhán told me that Máiría would not go to the RUC. And it was I who said to Joe Cahill, 'would you go and talk to Máiría and tell her to go to the RUC about this issue.' And Joe did that. And Máiría, at that point, which is understandable in the time that was in, but Máiría at that point would not go to the RUC.[56]

Adams was telling the Irish public that my behaviour was 'concerning', as if I was at fault. The innuendo was unbearable. Nor did he mention that it wasn't Siobhán who arranged my first meeting with him. It was Adams himself, after he kissed the top of my head in the Féile marquee just after the *Sunday World* article appeared in August 2000. But the main and glaring untruth was that his friend and loyal personal assistant Siobhán, and indeed my Uncle Joe, had wanted me to go to the RUC, and that Adams had been supportive of this. I knew that republicans listening would know very well that Siobhán would never have allowed me to go to the RUC to discuss an IRA investigation – of which she herself had been a part. Uncle Joe had told me that *if* he had known, he would have told me to go to the RUC, but then went on to say that this wasn't now an option as the IRA had involved themselves.

Adams blandly asserted that I had never discussed the rape allegation with him. We listened as Adams said:

> I met her specifically at the request of her cousin Siobhán after there was some, either she, I can't remember the exact detail but either she had been taken into hospital or she was ill overnight or she had some row or something. And at this point I don't think that Siobhán O'Hanlon was aware what was at the source of all of this.[57]

Even the mere suggestion that Adams, the leader of Sinn Féin, would meet me because I had had 'some row with someone' would have been laughable if it wasn't so serious. But the assertion that Siobhán may not have been aware of the 'source of all this' was particularly grotesque. Siobhán had not only known of my abuse from 1997 onwards, but I had stayed with her for a time after it had taken place. She was then later involved in the IRA investigation – and she had been in my parents' house, in fact had driven me there with my uncle Cack at the IRA's behest to tell them about it. I didn't meet with Adams until five months after this. The lies flowed effortlessly out of him, and I was becoming more angry by the second.

He then contradicted himself quickly.

> This is a very crucial point. When it did transpire, I think on the back of a newspaper article, which might not have been specifically about Máiría, Siobhán came to me and gave me the newspaper article and said to me 'that's our Máiría who is a victim of this but she won't go to the RUC.'[58]

The idea that Siobhán O Hanlon could give Adams a newspaper article about Morris being investigated by the IRA for child abuse, identify me as a victim of it and not know the 'source of all this' was risible. But Adams insisted live on air that he was not aware and that I never discussed it with him. However, I had met him on 8 August 2000, two days after the *Sunday World* article appeared. That article contained the following claim:

> Veteran republican Joe Cahill is to be asked to probe serious sex abuse allegations which are shaking the IRA to its foundations [...] it is claimed Sinn Féin chiefs in the west of the city have been fully briefed of the details surrounding the alleged rapes. But as yet, no action has been taken and the alleged perpetrator is still free to walk the streets [...]. Last year, an IRA volunteer broke ranks to tell the *Sunday World* the full shocking facts of the saga which is threatening to

tear the republican movement apart. He said: 'Gerry Adams should realise this is not going to go away.'[59]

If the paper was correct, the journalist Hugh Jordan had been told the facts by an IRA volunteer a year previously. This was significant, because it was before the disclosure of the two other alleged victims, and during the first IRA 'investigation' into my abuse.

The article continued with a quote from an IRA man:

> It is clear from the facts available at present that there is a case to answer. But the way the leadership has dealt with it so far, has only spread dissent and anger among volunteers. Some of these men in the past have been ordered to shoot and kill paedophiles, but it now appears, we are operating a policy of double standards because it's one of our own involved.[60]

Adams's timeline was also highly dubious. According to him, Siobhán O'Hanlon approached him and did not know what the issue was. This suggests that she must have gone to him before my disclosure to her in 1997, and then again when the *Sunday World* article was published in 2000. Is it credible that she, his secretary and friend, would not have also told him once she found out the 'source of all this' in 1997, and then again throughout the first IRA 'investigation', and again when the other two victims emerged? It is for the reader to decide, but certainly Adams's statement raised more questions than answers, and infuriated me.

The interview concluded by Adams saying that republicans had tried to help me. He didn't say the IRA investigation had not happened, but he didn't confirm it either. Someone in Micheál Martin's office got up to turn off the radio, and I let rip. I told Micheál that Adams was a lying bastard and that I had been asked to do a media interview with Ursula Halligan of the Irish station TV3 after the meeting. I asked him to come with me, because I was now so angry I was terrified of doing it on my own.

Poor Micheál couldn't get a word in. I just kept talking and talking. I said I was going to go for a smoke, so we agreed to meet at the smoking area at Leinster House. I sat with Kevin Dillon, and Eilis spoke to Ursula Halligan to tell her I would do the interview shortly after I had spoken to the press and other media at the Dáil. The parliamentary sketch writer for the *Irish Times*, Miriam Lord, was also there, and she said there were a few other journalists in the AV room, the modern building just off the side of the Dáil. A few journalists had turned into a lot of journalists and I was taken aback at the number of cameras. I was shaking and, ridiculous as it sounds, I wanted to hold Micheál's hand for reassurance. I managed not to do so.

I did, however, go off like a rocket. As soon as the first question came, the words came flying out, and because I was angry, there was a staccato tone to my voice.

'I am appalled,' I said. 'Gerry knows the truth. He knows I know the truth. I have been forced into the position where I have had to waive my anonymity because of his previous denials on that issue and I think that is reprehensible.' I added that Adams owed Micheál Martin an apology. 'And his party colleague Pearse Doherty came out and said those claims [of the IRA investigating abuse] were unfounded and untrue. And I think at this point Sinn Féin needs to come out and say that the IRA internally investigated sex abuse cases that Sinn Féin members were involved in.'[61]

I also referred to Adams's claims about Joe Cahill and Siobhán O'Hanlon.

> Gerry has chosen two dead people and I think that is absolutely reprehensible given his close relationship with those two people. That he has told lies about them and he has lied about me and he clearly has trouble with some aspects of his memory and it is not just on this issue but on other issues in the past, just like he denies his membership of the IRA which I also know not to be true.[62]

I could see the journalists' eyes widen as they realised they had their soundbites.

Micheál was asked a few questions, and it was strange hearing him talking about me when I was standing beside him. His response was:

> [Máiría's] fear was that it would never see the light of day or get through [...]. Unfortunately it has come to pass in that way and what is very clear from my perspective, I did make a public statement, some time back in relation to how Sinn Féin/IRA dealt generally with victims of sexual abuse very similar to the Catholic Church. The institution came first [...] today both Máiría and I listened to Gerry Adams on RTÉ1 and I just watched the reaction of Máiría to it. Disbelief in terms of his comment that he didn't know her [...] you don't in a very underhand way try to undermine the credibility or the character of the person involved and I think that was absolutely despicable that that happened today on the *News at One*. [...] There clearly was an internal kangaroo court operated by the IRA to keep Máiría quiet and silent.[63]

It was an emotionally charged press conference.

I was scheduled to meet Joan Burton, then the Labour leader, but the cameraman Gerry Mooney had asked if I could go to a park around the corner to have my picture taken. I hadn't even thought properly about what I was wearing; I wish I had now, because the red lace crocheted top I had on looked like something I had borrowed from my great-grandmother. The Labour party's chief of staff, Ronan Farren, then took us to meet Joan Burton.

Joan was easy to speak to. She hadn't seen the programme – it had come out just after the budget – but I explained to her what had happened to me. She looked at me and said three words, which caused my eyes to burn with tears: 'I believe you.' The meeting ran over time, and we had to rush to get to the *Sunday Independent* offices to meet the paper's editor, Anne Harris. On the way I tweeted:

Met the Tánaiste this evening. Thanks to her, and Micheál Martin for listening sensitively.

I then tweeted Mary Lou McDonald, and tagged her in:

Mary Lou Mc Donald blindly defending Gerry Adams in media apparently. Said she hasn't even watched Spotlight. Watch it @maryloumcdonald.

38

In 2014, Mary Lou McDonald was Sinn Féin's vice president. I had first met her around ten years earlier in Belfast. She was attractive, with short glossy brown hair, and smartly dressed in black slacks and a figure-hugging top. I listened as local Sinn Féin people complained about her and said she was pushy, with no background in a party that prizes republican family connections (like mine), which always aroused curiosity and suspicion. I defended her at the time, on the basis that many people who came from a similar background were now members of the party. None of us thought then that she would be leading the party two decades later.

Privately educated at Dublin's Notre Dame school, articulate and clever, she grew up in the leafy suburb of Rathgar, a world away from the hard men in west Belfast whose 'struggle' she subsequently adopted. She joined Fianna Fáil in the late 1990s, before jumping ship to Sinn Féin. In 2022, the *Irish Independent*'s Fionnan Sheehan quoted a Fianna Fáil source explaining why she left the party: 'The lads were talking about the Snugborough Road extension, which was a big deal locally. She was more interested in the Garvaghy Road,' he wrote, referring to the conflict over the controversial Orange march through a Catholic area near Portadown.[64]

Inside jokes in Leinster House claimed she put on a 'posh accent' – typical south Dublin rounded vowel sounds – when meeting with former Taoiseach Leo Varadkar, but that it changed to a Dublin drawl when meeting with locals in her Cabra constituency office. Whatever the truth of her accent, McDonald certainly has a history of adapting her language to meet particular situations in agile and interesting ways.

At Sinn Féin meetings, she would make a beeline for people who had republican pedigrees, such as Adams or McGuinness; the running joke was 'if she got any closer to Adams she'd be "up his hole"' – crass, but typical Belfast humour. She certainly stood out in terms of her self-assuredness and willingness to contribute her point of view. Belfast and Derry republicanism is tight and nepotistic, and was then mainly a collective of families who could boast of participation in the pre-war movement, the border campaign of the 1950s and the early years of the Troubles. The Adams and Hannaway families in Belfast, the Keenans in Derry and Belfast, and the Cahill and O'Hanlon families all had bloodlines which ran, in my family anyway, back to the Fenian movement. Perhaps it is not surprising that I was described by the BBC as coming from 'republican royalty', though I hated that phrase.

It is also unsurprising, therefore, that McDonald would reach for an example within her own family tree to justify her adherence to republicanism, once stating: 'My family's association with the IRA goes back to the 1920s.'[65] Her grandmother's brother was shot dead in the wave of Irish state executions carried out in 1922, though she 'never really spoke about it'. So we can assume that her family's historical association with one executed IRA member did not play a formative role in Ms McDonald's life. By her own admission, she only became interested in the Northern Irish conflict when she saw news footage of the 1981 hunger strikes on television. 'For me it was the precise moment that I, as a Dublin girl, realised how seriously wrong something was. I completely understood and understand why people volunteered for the IRA. I support and recognise the right to meet force with force.'

The woman who many credit with attracting new votes for the party, precisely because she lacks IRA baggage, appears to capitalise on former IRA volunteers when the circumstances seem right. On 13 November 2016, she stood on a podium in Derry on which was draped a picture of two crossed rifles in front of an oak leaf and the words 'Derry Brigade, Óglaigh na hÉireann'. Attired in a formal black leopard-print dress, hair swept up and wearing a sparkly necklace, McDonald was the main speaker and guest of honour. She was so happy to be there that she later tweeted: 'Delighted to speak at Derry Volunteers Dance. Very moving occasion for all the families. Honoured to be honoured.' She must have had a good time, as she returned – albeit remotely due to the pandemic – as the main speaker for those dead Derry IRA volunteers in 2021.

I don't know what I expected from McDonald. Perhaps I naïvely believed that I would be treated better by Sinn Féin women when I went public. As it turned out, the opposite was the case. She had form when it came to her defence of Gerry Adams on kindred issues, and I should have expected a similar reaction when it came to mine. On the day of the sentencing of Gerry Adams's brother Liam for the abuse of his daughter Aine, Micheál Martin was asked by reporters to give a response: 'In the cases we have become aware of, he (Gerry Adams) would have been aware of as well [...] and an attempt was made to deal with those internally.'[66] He went further, and the *Irish Times* reported:

> Sinn Féin president Gerry Adams was allegedly aware of at least two other cases of sexual abuse dealt with internally by republicans, the Fianna Fáil leader has claimed. Micheál Martin made the allegation as he revealed two victims contacted him with concerns over investigations into their cases. Sinn Féin said the claims were disgraceful and totally untrue.[67]

On RTÉ's *Morning Ireland*,[68] broadcaster Rachel English asked McDonald about Martin's statements:

> If I can give you a quote from what he said yesterday, 'I have to say from information we have picked up, and we have talked to other people, this may have been a broader trend within the Republican movement.' If he has those concerns is it not his right to raise them?

McDonald replied:

Well, Rachel, if he has those concerns and he has any information in respect of any child in danger or anything pertaining to the abuse, maltreatment or neglect of a child then the correct place for Micheál Martin to go to is the social services or to An Garda Siochana.

Rachel English then asked: 'Just to be clear on this, then, are you aware of any other case where a republican may have questions to answer about how they treated abuse allegations?'

'Well, I'm not, Rachel. But that is not to say that there might not be a case like that.'

English pressed her again: 'You are not aware of any other case where concerns have been raised?'

Again McDonald stated that she was not aware: 'No. I have seen speculation in the media. I have seen other people raise these issues ...'

It was a pretty clear answer. To my keen ears, it was an incredible one, because, by that stage, my court case was in its third year. And Mary Lou McDonald actually took part in a radio interview with Pat Kenny in 2010 on the *Sunday Tribune*'s coverage of my case and one other case, in which she pointed out that both victims were easily identifiable: 'not alone is what they carried last Sunday vicious, and deeply malicious and perhaps even politically motivated, but it is also grossly inaccurate,' she said.[69]

The journalist Suzanne Breen in the same programme defended her paper's coverage:

Absolutely not, if there has been any smearing and manipulating going on this week, it has been by SF and not the *Sunday Tribune* [...] the *Sunday Tribune* is a paper of integrity. What we do is put secret information into the public domain that people in power would rather keep hidden.[70]

Knowing that the media wished to interview Adams about his brother Liam, during that Rachel English interview McDonald pleaded for space for the Sinn Féin leader: 'Could I just ask Micheál Martin and others to just have a level of concern, for the family, for the victim [...] and even for 24 or 48 hours to give a respectful space to that family to come to terms [...] with everything that has unfolded.'[71]

'He was as you know a witness against his brother in this case,' she added. In fact he wasn't, as Adams, though called to give evidence for the prosecution in the first trial against his brother, which collapsed, wasn't called at the second trial. In the first case, lawyer Eilis McDermott made mincemeat of him, as she forensically walked Gerry Adams through facts, contrasting them with statements Adams had made publicly.[72] For example, he had claimed in a television documentary: '...Now some time after that Liam left where he was living and went out of the country.'

McDermott had spotted an anomaly, stating in court: 'I suggest to you that it is a lie to say that your brother went out of the country at that time or at any time thereafter apart from the odd two-week holiday to Spain.'

Adams answered: 'Well, I take exception to you saying it's a lie.'

The barrister answered: 'Well I am suggesting to you just so that it is plain Mr Adams, that it is a lie and he never went out of the country?'

Adams retorted: 'Well he did go out of the country.'

He was asked by McDermott: 'And where did he go?' Adams told her he had gone to Canada.

McDermott filleted him: 'Mr Adams, your brother went to America for about six or eight months and also to Canada, but that was in 1983 long before the meeting in Buncrana?' The 1983 date was significant, because Aine Adams had stated that she and Gerry Adams had met with her father Liam in Buncrana in 1987 to discuss her abuse allegations against him.

The lawyer spotted another inaccuracy in what Adams had told Ulster Television's Chris Moore in the documentary about the Aine Adams case: 'Well, let's see what your recollection is about the next part of what you told the journalist: "And basically he was out of my life more or less for about the next 15 years." Now that's another lie, I suggest to you?'

Adams again denied that he had lied. McDermott then showed him a series of photographs showing Gerry Adams and his brother, taken in 1991 in Dublin, in 1996 at Liam Adams's wedding, standing with their arms around each other, in 1997 at Liam's child's christening, and in 1997 at an election campaign, along with another from 1998.

Even then, McDermott wasn't finished with him: 'You wrote an autobiography Mr Adams called *Before the Dawn*, isn't that right? You thank various people at the end of your foreword, do you remember that?'

Adams answered: 'Yes I do, yes.'

McDermott continued: 'And you thank your publisher and people in the publisher's office and then you say, "I want also to thank Colette, our Paddy, my father, brothers and sisters, especially Liam".'

This detail had horrified those following the case, the idea that anyone knowing that his niece had accused her father of abuse would thank his brother publicly in the acknowledgments of a book. Worse still, Aine alleged that Gerry Adams had sent her a copy to read.

Hardly less disturbing was the following exchange:

McDermott: Now, you say, Mr Adams, that your brother made an admission to you when you were walking around Dundalk in the rain in the year 2000, is that right?

Adams: Yes.

McDermott: And if that – I should make it clear to you that I am suggesting to you that no such admission was ever made, do you understand?

Adams: I do understand. I don't accept it, but I understand.

McDermott: If what you say is true, then you can have been in no doubt whatsoever in 2000 and onwards, but that your brother had sexually assaulted your niece, is that right?

Adams: That's true, yes.

McDermott: Did you know that he was working in youth clubs?

Adams: I did, yes.

McDermott: Which youth clubs did you know that he was working in?

Adams: Well he was working in Clonard Youth Club.

McDermott: And also in a youth club in Beechmount known as the Blackie Centre, is that right?

Adams: That's right, yes.

It emerged that Liam Adams had also worked for a time with young people in Dundalk, and the questioning continued:

McDermott: [...] the youth club that your brother went to work in was the Clonard Monastery youth club, isn't that right?

Adams: That's right, yes

McDermott: And he went to work there, Mr Adams, I suggest, in 1998.

Adams: He may well have, yes.

McDermott: I'm suggesting to you that you know that he went to work there in 1998 because he was living with you at that time for a period of six weeks.

Adams: Where was he living with me?

McDermott: In your house ...

Adams told the court he had no recollection of this, and, when asked why he didn't inform the police, he stated that Aine was an adult and 'I was trying my best to resolve these matters in a way which helped Aine, but also, if I may say so, in a way which allowed Liam to get rid of these demons'.

There were other moments in court, too, which exposed Adams's need to be in control, and his childish petulance when challenged.

'Now, Mr Adams,' Judge Philpott said, 'I noticed you're taking notes.'

Adams replied: 'Well, I'm doodling.'

The judge replied: 'Well, it would be better if you don't.'

Adams, seemingly keen to get the last word, said: 'All right, your Honour. When I say I'm doodling, I have written down one or two bits, yeah.'

The judge told him: 'Don't…'

Another bizarre episode from that case was the matter of missing exhibits from the trial – photographs that had been shown to Adams by the barrister earlier in the proceedings. Just before the court rose for lunch, Adams asked the judge specifically about documents in the witness box that didn't belong to him. The judge told him to leave them there. When court resumed in the afternoon, the judge turned to Liam Adams's defence barrister: 'Ms McDermott, there were photographs put in the dock. Were they taken out by anyone?'

McDermott replied: 'The witness box, your Honour?'

The judge, realising her mistake, said: 'Yes. Did I say dock?' Then the barrister suggested that the judge ask Gerry Adams, who was sitting in the court, about them. This was the exchange:

Judge: I just want to confirm, you didn't take these photographs out?

Adams: Yeah, I have them in my briefcase here.

Judge: You have them?

Adams: Yeah, yeah.

Judge: Well could you get them back?

Adams: I will surely, yes.... They are family photographs, some of them, but I will get them back, yeah.[73]

The idea that any witness would remove exhibits from the court, after being told not to, was strange enough. But Adams, a public figure, was making a point – and in the process revealing a side to himself that the public rarely see. Not in control, and just having been made mincemeat of on the witness stand, he disregarded the authority of the court, took away photographs of his family and was ready to walk off with them.

During that trial, it emerged that Liam Adams had confessed to abusing his daughter to Gerry Adams during a walk in the rain in the year 2000. It took nine years for Gerry Adams to let the police know of this fact, during which time Liam Adams spent time working with children and canvassing for the Sinn Féin party. Yet Mary Lou McDonald went on the radio after the second trial and Liam Adams's conviction, pleading for space for the family, when instead her party president should have been placed under much closer scrutiny.

Yet, although I believed that McDonald's response to the Liam Adams case had been inadequate, I was not prepared for her reaction to mine. There have been few issues which have tested her mettle in the same way, or which have damaged her so publicly, before or since. When I urged her to watch the *Spotlight NI* programme, I meant it. I wanted her to see and understand my account of my experience, and then tailor her own response accordingly rather than blindly defend Gerry Adams. She fell at the first hurdle.

39

We made it to Talbot Street, albeit late, and as I turned the corner into the busy newsroom of the *Independent*, and to the glass-fronted editor's office, I drew in my breath. Anne Harris's office was full of people, and a hush fell over the newsroom while journalists craned their necks to get a look. I liked Anne immediately. She was stylish, with long blonde hair, and smelled of Angel perfume. She also had a kind and maternal manner, and it was clear she was appalled by what had happened to me. Eilis and I sat down and Anne asked questions and I answered them directly. We spoke about how the paper might cover the case that weekend.

Meanwhile, people were noticing that RTÉ had been slow to pick up on the story. Labour TD Joanna Tuffy issued a statement, which included the following:

> It is staggering, that while Ms Cahill's story is covered prominently in every national newspaper today, including on the front pages, it somehow did not even merit a mention on Morning Ireland's *It Says in the Papers*. As a politician it is not my job to second-guess the decisions of producers and editors on what issues they cover. But as a public representative it is my duty to ask why our national broadcaster has taken a distinctly hands-off approach to an issue that is so clearly in the public interest.[74]

Micheál Martin had also expressed concern about the RTÉ coverage. I had been asked to do *Prime Time* and another RTÉ radio show, and had agreed, but both had cancelled me. *Prime Time* had asked if I would sit in a studio and debate with Adams. I said I didn't think that it was acceptable to suggest putting a rape victim on the same level as a politician like Adams, given the subject matter and his and his party's treatment of me. I hadn't refused outright to go on the programme, but in any event my appearance was pulled.

Other people were now tackling Mary Lou McDonald online. On 16 October, Regina Doherty TD tweeted:

> Your silence of treatment of @mairiac31 by republicans is deafening_@MaryLouMcDonald – show some leadership – women of Ireland are waiting.

The *Irish Independent* carried Joan Burton's comments after our meeting. She said: 'Máiría's story is deeply disturbing, both in the incidents she describes, and in the frustrations she has experienced in seeking justice, and it raises serious questions for all of those involved.'

Sinn Féin was under pressure, and it was growing. I was also under pressure, but I felt good that I was at least able to use my voice. The worse it was for them, the better it was for me. I was staying in County Wicklow while attending meetings and doing media interviews in Dublin. I didn't know my way around Dublin, or its political personalities, but I had to learn quickly. Meanwhile, my mother looked after my daughter.

I was interviewed on TV3's *Tonight with Vincent Browne* programme later that evening. It was scheduled to be broadcast after 11 p.m., but was recorded 'as live' an hour before. Browne is a formidable Irish journalist with a reputation for being cantankerous in interviews. I enjoyed watching him on television, and had no qualms about doing the interview. All I had to do was tell the truth. I explained what life was like during the first IRA 'investigation', and told him it was hard, and I couldn't 'plan my day', because I never really knew when the IRA wanted to speak to me until the last minute. I described watching the kettle boil during the first IRA meeting and being relieved when the woman made a cup of tea with the hot water. He let me talk, with minimal interjection. It brought my story to a wider audience in Ireland who would not have seen the original BBC programme.

On Friday, I got a call from a journalist with an English accent called Nick Sommerlad. It was a call that remains burned into my memory, because it upset and shocked me so much. Nick only got the first sentence out before I started crying. He claimed that British intelligence services had recruited my Uncle Joe in the 1970s as an agent, after photographing him abusing a fourteen-year-old girl in a car. Tears rolled down my face. My gut instinct was that the story was horseshit, but I wanted to see what details he was going to print, as he said he was intending to run it come what may. He claimed two separate intelligence sources stated that Joe Cahill had an agent reference number and that there was a photograph. I asked him if he had seen a photograph. He said no. I asked him what the reference number was. He didn't know. I asked if there was a victim on record. Negative. I put the obvious point to him that he was going to run a story with no evidence, against a dead man who was not here to defend himself.

Annoyed at myself for crying on the telephone, I tried to converse with him as coherently as possible. I told him that if there was a victim, I would have to accept the allegation, but there wasn't, and that I believed from the information I had just heard that Joe was either in jail, or on the run, when the photo was allegedly taken. He didn't even have time to see his own children, let alone anyone else's. Added to that my own experiences with him as a loving grandfather-like figure, who was so supportive of me, and I felt that this story must be a fantasy. Joe's elderly wife Annie was still alive, and my main concern was the upset it would cause her. I tried to get word to the family to prepare them, and then there was nothing more I could do.

I was respectful of the journalist – he was, after all doing his job – but I nevertheless suspected that someone planting that story with him was using it to try and embarrass me into silence, to nobble a victim's ability to speak in the public domain, shaming them by outing a close relative as a paedophile. I was damned if I was going to be silenced by it, but I felt, and still do, that whoever saw fit to give that story to Sommerlad had a sordid agenda. I came off the call upset and disturbed, and with a sick feeling in my stomach.

I had to speak to RTÉ's *News at One* in order to respond to Adams's previous comments. The presenter, Richard Crowley, allowed me the space to speak. He referred to the fact that Adams had denied we ever discussed my rape allegations or the IRA 'investigation' and asked for my response. I said I was 'completely appalled' and then asked: 'Do people think that I was discussing the weather with Gerry Adams? I mean what do they think that we were discussing?' The frustration in my voice was evident, and I continued: 'Of course we were discussing the abuse. Of course we were discussing the IRA internal investigation into that abuse.'[75]

I challenged Adams to meet me in a public forum so we could discuss the issues. The radio presenter put it to the party while we were on air. Sinn Féin responded, saying that both Gerry Adams and Mary Lou McDonald had stated that they would have no problem in meeting with me. But, as the presenter noted, when RTÉ asked the party specifically if Gerry Adams would do it in a public forum, the party replied: 'We would need to find out what she wants.' I responded, angrily:

> What I want is for Sinn Féin to tell the truth, it's as simple as that. Sinn Féin are completely re-traumatising me again and again and again, and I actually think that is quite disgusting as someone who has suffered severe trauma at the hands of the republican movement. I want them to tell the truth. I want Gerry Adams to stand up and say 'yes, she is telling the truth.' And I think what Sinn Féin have done, and I think they think they have done it in a very clever way, is that they have tried to attack my credibility […] what Sinn Féin need to remember is that I have witnesses to this, who were prepared to go to court and give evidence.[76]

It was my way of telling the party to back off, and to stop attacking me online and through the media. I also mentioned a very awkward fact, which I hoped would give the party pause for thought. 'Most of those meetings (with Adams) took place in Gerry Adams's office.' I pointed out that at the time senior Sinn Féin officials had complained of being bugged by the British government. 'If some section of British intelligence has a record of those meetings taking place in Gerry Adams's office, I would very much like them to put them into the public domain, because they would categorically prove my account.'

Richard Crowley asked me if I wanted to add anything and I said yes, that Gerry Adams wanted people to believe that I was told to go to the RUC.

> I'm sitting with a statement that Gerry Adams made in July 2000, about the RUC and what he said was: 'Sinn Féin's position on the disbandment of the RUC has not changed. We believe that the RUC have no place in the future of this island. They are a partisan, quasi-military armed wing of unionism.' Is Gerry Adams seriously expecting people to believe that one month later, he was urging me, or other people [in his party] were urging me, to go to the RUC? I find that completely ludicrous and I think his credibility is completely shot to shreds on this issue.[77]

In another interview that afternoon on Newstalk, I said that other abused people seeing Sinn Féin's treatment of me would be afraid to come forward. In response, Gerry Adams issued a statement, saying: 'No one should be living in fear and no child should be at risk. Anyone who has any information whatsoever about any child abuse should come forward to the authorities North or South and they will have the full support of Sinn Féin in so doing.'[78]

I also appeared on *Six One News*, on 17 October, and decided to widen the issue out from my own case. I knew that if I told people there were other victims like me, that Sinn Féin would be under further pressure. I also knew that other victims would be likely to come forward, although I didn't envy them, watching the way in which I was being treated by the party. The presenter, Brian Dobson, put it to me that Mary Lou McDonald had stated that day that if anyone had been found to have covered up abuse, they should be brought before the law, but that she had also said that there was no evidence that anyone in Sinn Féin had concealed abuse. I asked how Mary Lou knew that there was no evidence. She had also said that she hadn't even bothered watching the *Spotlight NI* programme, and I urged her to do that. I pointed out that Sinn Féin didn't actually answer any of the questions asked of them by the BBC. Then I made a statement which shocked the Irish political establishment and allowed them to push further in trying to hold Sinn Féin to account.

> I think this is a huge issue for the South, because it is quite apparent now that there was a pattern of behaviour on behalf of the IRA and Sinn Féin, because what I am seeing, and what journalists are seeing, because they are contacting me today to say that victims have been in contact with them and that they are now corroborating stories across the board. Perpetrators in the North were accused of abuse, and the IRA clamped down. And they moved the perpetrators out of the jurisdiction so that they couldn't face the full rigours of the law. And victims had no idea where these people were moved to, and in some cases, they were shot, which was wrong, the IRA had no business involving themselves, but I think the crucial point about it is that at the minute, in Ireland north and south, there are people who have been alleged to have committed serious crimes of sexual abuse who potentially have access to other children, and those children are at great risk. And Sinn Féin knows this information, they have refused to cooperate with the police on it and they haven't brought the information forward. And I am appealing to members of Sinn Féin who know without a shadow of a doubt that this has happened, to soul search, to come forward, to say that this has happened, to bring the information forward, because

that is the only way that we are going to be able to protect children on this island.[79]

I watched that interview as it went out from the offices of the *Sunday Independent*, when someone turned up the newsroom television. You could have heard a pin drop in the room, which was full of journalists writing copy. The only noise came from the clicks of photographer David Conaghy's camera as he snapped me watching the screen. I knew I had put the cat among the pigeons. Up until now, the media had been focused on a single IRA investigation into abuse. Now they were making a mental connection between how the IRA dealt with sex abuse and how the Catholic church had moved perpetrators around the country. I imagined that somewhere in a Sinn Féin press office, a spin doctor was sitting with their head in their hands.

Later that evening, I was on the Dart back to Greystones with Eilis and Anne Harris joined us for part of the journey. As we were talking, a Twitter DM came from Mary Lou McDonald:

> Máiría please forward me an email or telephone contact so I can get in touch. All the best. Mary Lou.

A second DM had been sent two minutes later providing me with two email addresses for her. I read it out to Eilis and Anne and then replied:

> Mary Lou, I received your Twitter DM. I see no point in receiving contact from you, or answering further until you are ready to say that I am telling the truth on all matters and admit that Sinn Féin and the IRA internally investigated sexual abuse perpetrated by republicans, moved perpetrators round the country, and put children at risk. And admit that your party President and close friend Gerry Adams had knowledge of some of these cases. Your behaviour has been disgraceful on this matter in the wake of the Spotlight programme, and as a

female, as someone who you know, and as a victim of sexual abuse, I find that reprehensible. [80]

'She can put that in her pipe and smoke it,' I thought. McDonald didn't reply.

40

Media coverage intensified the next day. It was a sunny Saturday afternoon, though bitingly cold, and I was exhausted after the intense interviews and frustrations of the week. McDonald reiterated in the *Irish Times* her assertion that no one from Sinn Féin had 'been shown to have covered up abuse'. The party, which presumably had thought that their denials at the start of the week would be enough to bury my story, now found itself in the position of putting its deputy leader, Mary Lou McDonald, on RTÉ's *Saturday with Brian Dowling* show – a panel discussion, which also involved the Labour Party's Alex White and the veteran political commentator and barrister, the late Noel Whelan.

It wasn't a comfortable discussion for McDonald, or for me as I listened to it. What was particularly interesting was an apparent slip of the tongue by McDonald. Until then, Sinn Féin had refused to confirm whether I had been made to take part in an IRA kangaroo court, yet McDonald said, on air: 'I've spoken to one of the named individuals who was part of this kangaroo court. She tells a very, very different story and she contends that in fact she was very supportive to Máiría Cahill.'

It is a pity that those present did not seize on this slip at the time. Noel Whelan, forensic as ever, picked up on the theme later in the broadcast, asking: 'Because the question is do they accept these meetings happened? Or are they disputing how she is characterising them? That's an important distinction. Do they accept they put her in a room with the person she says abused her?'

McDonald replied: 'What I do know is that there has been an acceptance, I think by two of them, yes they met with Máiría, but they absolutely dispute the fact that it happened in the manner or for the purpose that she describes, Noel.'

Whelan countered: 'That hasn't answered the question.' He skewered McDonald, leaving little wriggle room. McDonald did state that she believed I had been abused, but also tried to rely on the fact that not-guilty verdicts had been returned:

> Your listeners may or may not be aware that there was an investigation into the two aspects of Máiría's story – on the one hand her allegation of rape and on the other hand, the involvement of named individuals in what you have called an interrogation [...]. Your listeners may or may not know that in both cases, no convictions were found.[81]

She was legalistic to a fault, stressing the formal verdicts of courts that not so long ago republicans had refused to recognise.

The following exchange from the programme was also interesting:

> *Noel Whelan*: Here's the gaping hole in the situation you advanced this morning, Mary Lou, because I watched the *Spotlight* programme. I watched the *Vincent Browne* interview. I listened back to Richard Crowley's interview with her yesterday. And I can't decide whether she was abused or not. I can't decide whether she was abused. I can only decide what view I take as to her credibility. And like you, I found her to be extraordinarily credible in her description of the events and I've sat in many courts and taken many witnesses through the type of abuse she described. But she was equally as credible – she was equally as credible when she came to describe these nights she was brought to a house and cross-examined by heavies in Sinn F ... IRA frankly, heavies in

the IRA about what was the truth about what she was saying. And she was very credible when she described the trauma of being exposed to her abuser, or her alleged abuser, for two hours. And there was no conviction in respect of the abuse upon her, yet you are accepting her credibility on that, and here on national radio are prepared effectively to call him an abuser. You accept her credibility on that but you change your mind when she comes to make allegations that touch on your current responsibilities. And I say you do that out of instinct. You do that out of instinct to defend…

Mary Lou McDonald: No, no. As a matter of fact I don't.

Brian Dowling: Allow Mary Lou McDonald to reply to that.

Mary Lou McDonald: As a matter of fact, I don't because I think it's entirely wrong for any institution to pull down the shutters in the way that you describe. And you say that I've responsibilities and you're absolutely right, Noel. One of the responsibilities I have is to make it absolutely crystal clear, as a matter of fact, that Sinn Féin is not in possession of information as regards child abuse. Sinn Féin is not sitting on that information and Sinn Féin is most certainly not refusing to cooperate with any Garda investigation. Those are the assertions that were made on the *Six One News* and I am putting the record straight on that.[82]

I found all this interesting because I knew well that some members of Sinn Féin indeed had information about abuse by republicans and had *not* brought it to the authorities. I had spoken to former IRA members since 2010 and pieced together information about almost fifty cases. Some of those abusers were now dead, but some were alive. In an attempt to force the party to put more information into the public domain I tweeted the initials of some IRA personnel suspected of being abusers, before almost instantly deleting them. I knew there was a great deal of interest in my Twitter account, and I knew Sinn Féin were watching. I expected them to move on the issue, and I waited to see what the Sunday papers would bring.

I met Jennifer O'Leary, who had offered to give me a lift back to Belfast, the next morning outside the Ballsbridge Hotel. I had no idea whether or not I would be safe, but I had to see my daughter and I was supposed to be meeting then First Minister Peter Robinson, the following day. Jennifer and I didn't get much of an opportunity to speak, because my mobile phone was ringing relentlessly. I then listened to RTÉ radio's *This Week*, for which Sinn Féin put up Pearse Doherty, who said:

> Yeah well, I've known, and I've said this and just for clarity, I've known Máiría Cahill for quite a lengthy period of time. We served on the national executive around this period and I'm absolutely horrified to learn that during this period she was suffering the type of trauma and abuse that she went through. You have to remember, and your listeners have to remember that in relation to the alleged IRA investigation, this was dealt with before the courts.[83]

It was true that I had known Doherty. I was the first elected National Secretary of Sinn Féin Youth, and he was also on the national executive. He was articulate and passionate about his politics, but I wondered, given that he had known me, how he could allow himself to be put on the airwaves to discuss an issue which wasn't of his making. Sinn Féin were still relying on not-guilty verdicts which had been handed down because I had been forced, in effect, to withdraw my case. Pressed on whether he would condemn an IRA kangaroo court into my abuse, the furthest that Doherty would go was to say 'if it happened it was wrong'. I felt like banging my head against the dashboard of the car in frustration.

The *Sunday Independent* had questioned female representatives in the Irish parliament about whether they believed me or not. Sinn Féin's women TDs unanimously failed to respond. In another report, journalist John Drennan revealed that Sinn Féin had sent a letter of complaint to RTÉ after I was interviewed on the *Six One News* programme. I also wrote my first piece for the *Sunday Independent* under my own byline. I wanted directly to address the Sinn Féin party.

> Repeated questioning for months of anyone, over any issue, is mental torture. But when it comes to a young victim of sexual abuse, it is much more than that. I was slowly dying inside. And when you go from a position of thinking you are going to be killed, to a position of internally willing them to do it to put you out of the misery they are causing you, you have a serious problem. They turned me into a complete shell of a person, and the republican movement should take responsibility for the damage they caused me...[84]

I also referred to what I saw as Mary Lou McDonald's blind defence of Adams on the case:

> 'I am absolutely satisfied Gerry Adams is telling the truth' said Mary Lou McDonald. How can you say so, Mary Lou? When you also publicly confirmed the same day that you hadn't even bothered to watch the BBC NI Spotlight programme where I recounted my painful experiences in an effort to finally use my voice to do the right thing. Absolutely satisfied? Here's what I am absolutely satisfied with. I am satisfied that you have listened to Gerry Adams – and taken his word for it without actually listening to me. By your own definition, if you haven't seen the programme, you don't know what you are talking about.[85]

The journalist Eoghan Harris referred to the republican online campaign against me: 'For a moment, Máiría Cahill silenced the Sinn Féin trolls. But after a short intermission, IRA apologists were soon back on the internet. As usual, the facts had made no impression on their closed minds.'[86] The abuse had indeed been rampant, and I had been called everything from a 'tramp' and a 'bitch', to a 'liar' and a 'fantasist'.

There was a more insidious side, too, where I was falsely accused, by anonymous accounts which appeared to be set up solely for that purpose, of being an MI5 agent. I laughed about it with Jennifer in the car. In truth, I was broke and had to borrow the money from my mother to pay for that week's daycare for Saorlaith, while I used the last of the money in my account to finance food and travel around Dublin. I refused to take any payment from the *Sunday Independent* for my article, as I didn't want to be accused of making money from my abuse. 'More like an MFI agent,' I joked online.

Una Heaton, who I later learned was the sister-in-law of Garda Jerry McCabe, murdered by the IRA during a robbery in 1996, wrote:

> When are we really going to get honesty and the truth from Mr Gerry Adams? I feel so sorry for Máiría Cahill [...]. Are they a mafia/terrorist/untouchable organisation, above the law? What a shame that they can get away with this. Shame on the people who protect such evil. Is this the Ireland of the future – lie down, keep quiet, accept the status quo?[87]

I appreciated the support. I was tired, but I had also agreed to write a column for the Slugger O'Toole website addressing part of the Sinn Féin smear campaign against me. My late friend Olive Buckley, who lived in Skegoneill in north Belfast, had offered to answer my phone for me and let me use a laptop at her kitchen table. Her partner Gary would upload the blog to Slugger. I knew it would only take an hour or so, if I could get enough peace to do it. And Olive made good tea and gave great hugs. It was important for me at the time to remember that people were on my side.

While I was at Olive's house, I discovered that the story on my Uncle Joe had appeared on Twitter, in a preview of the next day's *Daily Mirror* front page. 'EXCLUSIVE: British spies recruited paedo IRA chief: Spooks used pictures of Joe Cahill to "turn him",' it said.[88] Papers have a habit of putting up the worst photos of people with such stories, and the one of Joe was not flattering.

I was upset again, and thought about putting a photo of Joe and myself on Twitter as a subtle way of hitting back. I found one from the early 2000s of me leaning on his knee, both of us smiling for the camera. It was a small act of solidarity for a dead relative I had loved greatly, but enough for people to see that I thought the story was a load of crap. Anthony McIntyre, the former IRA prisoner, telephoned me to say that he thought the planting of the story was a smear campaign, and was very much of the mind that it was designed to distract attention from the Sinn Féin leadership.

I smoked far too many cigarettes, before finishing the Slugger blog in a hazy rage. I was scathing of Sinn Féin and Adams in particular, and wanted republicans to think about what he was saying. Adams's comments on Siobhán O'Hanlon in particular were nonsense, and I bargained on republicans realising this if I explained precisely how they were untrue.

> Equally, anyone who knew Siobhán O'Hanlon absolutely knows that she would never have suggested involving the RUC a matter of days after the second IRA investigation ended […]. The proof of that however is this. Siobhán O'Hanlon learned of my allegations in 1997. She learned of the IRA investigation in 1999. She participated in it. Do you think she would have seriously exposed herself to being named in an RUC complaint? Gerry Adams has reprehensibly used his deceased friend and loyal colleague – and everyone who knew Siobhán knows it.[89]

It was a factually correct takedown of the Sinn Féin president. I had one advantage on my side. Adams kept tripping himself up on detail that he had not mastered, whereas my memory was extremely good, partly because trauma had seared these events into my mind.

As I was writing my own blog, another by Gerry Adams was appearing online, uploaded at 7.06 p.m. In it, Adams essentially admitted that the IRA dealt internally with sexual abuse victims and perpetrators:

Despite the high standards and decency of the vast majority of IRA volunteers, IRA personnel were singularly ill-equipped to deal with these matters. This included very sensitive areas such as responding to demands to take action against rapists and child abusers. The IRA on occasion shot alleged sex offenders or expelled them. While this may have been expedient at the time it was not appropriate. Victims were left without the necessary social service support and abusers without supervision. It ultimately failed victims and the community alike. That is a matter of profound regret for me, and many other republicans. But these actions were of their time and reflected not only a community at war but also an attitude within Ireland which did not then understand or know as we now do, how deeply embedded abuse is in our society.[90]

When I read these lines at the time, there was no sense of relief that the then leader of Sinn Féin was finally admitting to catastrophic mistakes, but rather annoyance that he was offering self-serving reassurances that the majority of IRA personnel were decent. This was being tone deaf to the many victims the IRA had damaged over the years, as was his assertion that they were essentially only doing a job reluctantly, one that the RUC would not do. The blog went on:

The reality of course is that a professional, accountable and impartial policing service was absent and unattainable in a society that was manifestly unjust. In many republican areas the community put pressure on the IRA – which sprang from and was sustained by the community – to fill this policing vacuum. The IRA itself often viewed this role as a major distraction from its central function.[91]

Reading this, I thought, 'Sorry, what?' The poor old IRA were distracted from bombing and shooting people, by having to deal with bombers and shooters from within its own ranks who were also abusing children. I thought that perhaps someone should have proofread what Adams was writing.

Adams was admitting that the IRA were effectively policing their own communities in an alternative justice system, but of course the admission didn't go far enough. Not only did Adams not acknowledge that the IRA had dealt with me disgracefully, but he threw a metaphorical hand-grenade into the mix, something which at the time got lost in the melee. There was, it seems, no 'corporate way' of verifying my account because the IRA had disbanded:

> The recent publicity surrounding the case of Máiría Cahill has brought this particular issue to the fore in public consciousness. Máiría alleges she was raped, and that the IRA conducted an investigation into this. The IRA has long since left the scene so there is no corporate way of verifying this but it must be pointed out that this allegation was subject to a police investigation, charges were brought against some republicans who strenuously denied Máiría's allegations. They insist they tried to help her. They were all acquitted by the court.[92]

An alert reader would have to conclude that this would mean that any victim of the IRA would never get answers or accountability, as the responsible entity could just claim it no longer existed to answer for what its members had done, as if they were a company that had gone bankrupt. It was a stunning line that deserved a whole analysis on its own, and it was this that really incensed me, because I had just spent four years in court taking part in a case where people charged with offences connected to the IRA had simply denied them. Adams's assertion that these individuals were trying to help me would, I thought, be laughable if it wasn't so serious. It was this admission that the IRA *did* deal with sex offenders that probably damaged Sinn Féin the most. I was not about to let it go without comment, if only to claim vindication for what I had been saying publicly all week since the *Spotlight NI* programme had aired.

'There are many dirty tricks employed when anyone speaks out about Sinn Féin,' I wrote on Slugger.

> And those decent Sinn Féin members – and most of the rest of the people on this island – will see through them. Because they know that I am telling the truth. And they know that, just like what happened to me, the IRA internally investigated cases of abuse and covered it up. Tonight is the first time Gerry Adams has admitted it – after years of my assertions that it happened. They have now vindicated those assertions they have been denying for years. It is now time for them to apologise to me, and to every other victim of abuse out there that they have shamefully, disgustingly, and disgracefully treated on this issue.[93]

I also wrote about my complicated relationship with Breige, and how even if someone could be initially terrifying as part of the IRA, it was still possible to develop a personal connection with her. What I said was angry, perhaps confused, but it was my passionate attempt to explain the complexity of that relationship:

> Spotlight broadcast that I had told them that one of the IRA women who dealt with me was 'sensitive' to me at the time. Sinn Féin have in the last two days tried to discredit my story by saying that I was lying about being frightened during the IRA investigation. Think about that too. I was very frightened of the IRA as an entity. They were, after all, repeatedly questioning an 18 year old about very intimate details of her abuse. Who wouldn't be frightened? But to do what they did – to bring me into a room with my abuser, sent me off the scale in terms of fright. And I hated that IRA woman, and the rest of the IRA members for doing that to me, and for turning me into a shell of a person. But there was a point – six months in – when the IRA brought in a family relative who was also an IRA member [...] to inform him of my abuse. And that IRA woman came to me and told me out

of earshot of the other two that she believed me. And for the first time, after six full months I felt that one of those IRA people maybe had a degree of empathy. And I told Spotlight this. I didn't hide anything, unlike Sinn Féin. And later when I attended counselling (and records of that counselling exist dealing with aspects of the IRA investigation and the abuse), that counsellor told me that she thought I was suffering from Stockholm Syndrome in relation to that woman. All I know is that she had opened up a Pandora's box in my head. But I also knew she felt guilty, and I knew that a senior IRA person told my father that those two women, and the other IRA man would be internally disciplined. And, just as I blamed myself for my sexual abuse, I blamed myself for this woman maybe facing a kangaroo court of her own. And she had also suffered tragedy. Her brother had been killed by the IRA, her father had died, she had other relatives jailed for most of their lives, other relatives had died tragically, and crucially, Gerry Adams told me she was a 'good girl'. And, the odd time, at Christmas time, I used to send her a card. I knew that her mother was dying and her sister was dying, and I felt sorry for her. It was twofold, and I was confused. That woman put me through absolute hell – but she also apologised in later years and told me that she and the other IRA people had 'completely retraumatised' me. And so she should. Her involvement in repeated questioning of myself was beyond disgusting. But to allow people to deny that she and others did that is worse.[94]

I knew the issue of my complex relationship with Breige would be used by Sinn Féin in some way. They are relentlessly creative in finding the weaknesses of anyone who opposes them, and I wanted to set the record straight before they exploited my necessarily tortured interactions with her. Blog uploaded, I went home around 3 a.m. and tried to sleep.

41

After a restless night, I woke up in the spare bedroom of my mother's house. I was utterly exhausted, but I had to do more interviews that morning. One of them, with RTÉ, I never want to hear again. In it, I exploded at the ludicrous idea that my Uncle Joe, as Adams claimed, had told me to go the RUC. As I've explained, this was inconceivable.

After this RTÉ disaster, I realised I had not given any thought to what I was going to wear to Stormont to meet the first minister. I was living out of a suitcase, and started digging through a pile of clothes I had dumped on the floor a week before. I regretted that morning not doing more ironing. I found a black suit jacket and a pair of leggings, decided to pair it with a pair of blue leather boots, and finished it with a white scarf. I had no time to wash and straighten my hair, so I swept it back, pinned it up and hoped for the best.

Robinson had issued a statement in which he called me a source of encouragement for others in similar circumstances. I didn't feel it. My stomach was churning and I was panicking in case I ran into any Shinners. 'Whilst I could never fully imagine the trauma Máiría has had to endure, I will be listening to her story, supporting her campaign for truth and justice and providing any help I can,' the Robinson statement continued. But I was so worn out that I was treating the Robinson meeting like I was going to meet Joe Bloggs for a coffee. The enormity of the situation meant that I couldn't process it properly, so I was just going through the motions and reacting mechanically to what was happening. One interview followed another. That very afternoon I talked to the journalist Matt Cooper, who threw me a curveball and asked me if I had ever been a member of the IRA. I could only answer honestly, but it was a question I hadn't been expecting. I told him I hadn't, adding that 'unlike Gerry Adams, when I tell you I was not in the IRA, I am telling the truth'. I felt aggrieved that I had even been asked the question, but tried to reason with myself that Matt did not know my history, and some would think it was fair.

Then it was on to Stormont, and I joked that I should get a picture taken in front of the looming statue of Sir Edward Carson. So, blue boots and all, I posed in front of Carson and his bronze hand raised to the blue skies of Ulster. I laughed at the thought of it – and of what the extended family would say. It was a big thing for a Cahill to meet Peter Robinson, a protégé of Ian Paisley, an intransigent unionist. I knew he was also due later that day to meet the Ballymurphy massacre families (ten of whose relatives had been killed by the Parachute Regiment in August 1971 during the imposition of internment without trial), and I resolved to say that I wished them well in their campaign for justice. I wondered how many people in Ballymurphy were currently standing behind mine.

The DUP MLA Paul Givan had arranged to meet me at the side of the enormous Stormont building, and he told me there were some members of the press waiting. 'Some' turned out to be a crowd of around twenty journalists, photographers and camera operatives, some of whom were following me to get shots of me walking. I dumped my handbag and my ever-present bottle of Coke off to the side and stood in front of a pre-arranged microphone stand. The reporters kneeled or stood in front of me at a respectful distance. The sun was shining in my eyes, but it was windy, and because of this, I felt I was straining to be heard. Givan stood beside me, presumably to get in the shot, but I had no thoughts about that either way. I didn't really care who stood there, what mattered was answering the questions.

I spoke about how I wanted Robinson to put in place more resources for rape victims. I was asked if I was prepared to meet Sinn Féin. I said I didn't mind meeting them as long as the meeting was recorded because I didn't trust them. 'I will be asking the First Minister to put in place an emergency response or to make available counselling for those victims who are contacting me in absolute turmoil,' I said. 'They need to be listened to, they need to be believed, but more importantly, they need help.' I also called on 'ordinary decent members of Sinn Féin to stand up and be counted on this issue'. I wanted them to know that they should put their own party under pressure to tell the truth and to stop leaving a question mark over my credibility.

> And I am saying to those victims, if you want to go and report your sexual abuse, I certainly will offer you my support, and walk into a police station or a Gardaí station with you to be able to do so. All I am trying to do is tell my story to enable to bring the issue up so that we can deal with it and move on from it and so that people can get help. And I do note that there has been a shift in position from Sinn Féin last night, which actually vindicates my account and they are now admitting that it [the IRA investigations] happened to other people, but yet they are still denying that it happened to me and I think that is reprehensible.[95]

Impromptu press conference over, it was time to meet Robinson, and I walked up the large marble stone staircase and into the members' room for a cup of tea ahead of the meeting. DUP stalwart Gregory Campbell was there and kissed me on the cheek. 'If my Uncle Joe could see this ...' I thought. They were all very friendly and we made small talk until it was time to go to the first minister's office.

We sat down on brown leather sofas, and I had a brief look around the room. It was spacious, with a luxurious red carpet. There was a small coffee table in front of the sofas, and trinket cabinets around the yellow walls. I sat to Robinson's right and we had an informal chat. He was pleasant and used what I described to him jokingly as his 'soft voice'. I had grown up with him on my home television and radio, mostly complaining angrily as politicians do, and he can be forceful when he wants to be, but that day he was measured, compassionate and practical. We spoke about Sinn Féin and he mentioned that he was going to have a private word with Martin McGuinness, then his Deputy First Minister.

'You tell him from me that he knows his party is lying on this issue, and he would do well to admit it,' I said.

We spoke about victims being comfortable enough to come forward and the creation of a climate where that could happen. Robinson mentioned people with mental health difficulties and how he knew that abuse stayed with people through their lives. I don't remember everything I said to Robinson, though I remember insignificant details, like the fact that there was a book about Croatia on the table.

The First Minister told the media after our meeting: 'No-one could fail to be moved by what happened to Máiría. It is incredibly courageous for someone in Máiría's position to step forward so publicly.'

While our Stormont meeting was under way, the Taoiseach Enda Kenny had been doorstepped in Belmullet, County Mayo on the issue of my treatment by Sinn Féin. His TD Regina Doherty had contacted me after I had tweeted the previous week that I was 'seeking an urgent meeting with the Taoiseach', and she told me she would arrange it. Kenny told the media he was 'looking forward' to meeting me and that there had been 'utterly despicable conduct by Sinn Féin to discredit Máiría Cahill over the last period'. He also said he had seen me on the TV: 'I've found her to be articulate and a person of great confidence.' I felt that I was on another planet, hearing the Taoiseach speak like this. If I were to stand any chance of forcing Sinn Féin to come clean I had to get politicians behind me, and no one was more important for this than the Irish prime minister.

Stormont's Sinn Féin junior minister Jennifer McCann was also appearing in the media. I had worked with her in a community project in Poleglass and found her to be very pleasant. A former IRA prisoner, she had been close to Bobby Sands and was well respected within the republican movement. She could have corroborated my story, as I had discussed it with her over drinks. In fact, I was once in such a bad way that she took me home with her and I stayed in her house. This was someone I had liked and trusted. What she said now was: 'I think that anyone that I have been speaking to even over recent days now, you know, are trying to reach out and help Máiría.' (This was news to me, as I hadn't heard directly from any member of Sinn Féin, apart from the private Twitter message from Mary Lou McDonald.) 'So, I would hope that she would take up the offer of a meeting, even with myself, and to come and talk to us about that,' she continued.[96]

All very soothing and plausible. But I had no intention of meeting Sinn Féin after the statements their various talking heads had made, particularly south of the border, and these public offers of meetings were a transparent damage-limitation exercise. My credibility had been called into question. I had no intention of giving them the chance to stage a photo opportunity with one of their representatives oozing sympathy and uttering platitudes.

Publicly, other members of the party were stating that they knew I had been abused, but refused to admit that there had been an internal IRA investigation, while privately others were briefing the media that my account was actually untrue. I was also being tormented online by their supporters. That wasn't going to stop anytime soon.

I still had to meet Enda Kenny. I thought I probably had another week or so before the story fell off the media's agenda, and I wanted to use that time constructively. Adams, for his part, was not happy with Kenny's intervention, calling it 'mischievous and clearly politically motivated'.[97] Meanwhile many people were contacting me to say that they were appalled by the sheer level of vitriol on the issue that was emanating from republican politicians and their supporters online.

I knew the next day was likely to be hectic but again I failed to sleep, choosing to respond to trolls instead to try at least to counteract some of the more ridiculous rumours floating around the internet. Adams's inept blog was now a real headache for Sinn Féin. Mary Lou McDonald appeared on Newstalk's *Ivan Yates* programme and was asked about what she knew. She floundered into this deliriously weird exchange:

> *MLMD*: I was aware obviously of the background as Gerry has set it out. I was aware – I have to say not having lived through it myself but knowing people who did in areas where there was really a breakdown of democratic structures [...]
>
> *Yates*: I just want to ask you something. No, no, I just want to ask you a specific – because this is all new stuff to me. What Gerry Adams is saying is the IRA shot sex offenders?
>
> *MLMD*: Yeah.
>
> *Yates*: Like, here we have, I mean, a control-and-fear regime, the modus operandi was that there was no jury, no defence, no trial, no appeal. That looks terribly like fascism to me.
>
> *MLMD*: What it looks like, Ivan, is a society in crisis and communities that had nowhere else to turn. And it's not right, you see, to say either and I think Gerry makes this clear in his blog, that the IRA were sort of controlling with fear in their communities. Very often what happened would be that there would be anti-social behaviour, drug-dealing, all of this stuff that I've outlined and people, naturally enough, wanted a response to it. They wanted it to stop because these are the communities where people live and try to raise their children, in what were incredibly difficult circumstances anyhow. So in the absence of a police service, a bona fide police service, inevitably, I suppose there were other responses. Was that an ideal ...

Yates: ... You talk a lot about human rights. In such a system how can you protect someone's human rights?

MLMD: Oh no. Ivan, Ivan, I'm not pretending for a moment that this was a good situation. It clearly wasn't.[98]

It was an incredible conversation, with Mary Lou McDonald denying that the IRA had controlled their communities. I lived in one, and they most certainly were in control. Yes, some people had gone to Sinn Féin advice centres over the years to complain about anti-social behaviour which the IRA then acted on, but this was not the case in my experience. I hadn't reported my abuse to the IRA, they had come to me and forced me to take part in an investigative charade. They could do this because they were very much in control, and we all knew the consequences of not acknowledging that.

Towards the end of the interview, Mary Lou McDonald took off her gloves:

A number of assertions have been made about the IRA – that's one thing – but specific assertions have been made by Máiría in respect of Sinn Féin. She has accused us of covering up abuse. She has asserted that we refused to cooperate with the police – An Garda Siochana and the PSNI presumably – on matters pertaining to abuse. I want to say again, categorically, that that is not true. That is a falsehood. And it's most unfair. It's most unjust to cast a slur such as that against Sinn Féin, against those of us that are members of Sinn Féin and elected representatives of Sinn Féin. On the issue of…

Yates interjected: 'Just on what you just said there, Mary Lou. Methinks, you're demonising Máiría Cahill.'

McDonald replied: 'Listen, I'm not. And let me say if that in asserting our position…'

Yates again cut across her: 'But you're calling her a liar.'

McDonald's voice rose an octave: 'I'm not calling her a liar. I am telling you…'

Yates was not letting the issue go: 'On the Gerry Adams issue you are.'

This left McDonald with nowhere to go, so she doubled down: 'Ivan, Máiría Cahill has made, has told her story, which is her – which is brave of her, I don't underestimate for a second how difficult it is to do that. She's come out and told her story and in the course of telling that story…'

Yates chipped in: 'But you've said you don't believe her entire story.'

McDonald, exasperated, let out a sigh and said:

No, no, no. She has made assertions against Sinn Féin which are untrue. That's it. That's the position. You will also be aware, Ivan, in the course of the telling of this story, that the issue of the abuse and rape itself and the issue of the IRA involvement was the subject of a police investigation and those that were named and implicated were investigated and indeed cooperated fully with the investigation. The matters went to court. There were no convictions. There were, in fact, acquittals – verdicts of not guilty returned.

Yates allowed her to waffle for a while, but as a former politician himself, he saw trouble on the horizon for McDonald and backed her into a corner:

I'm not putting it to Sinn Féin, I'm putting it to you personally, that you have huge credibility, huge growth in Sinn Féin support. But when it comes to Gerry Adams on every issue, including this issue of Máiría Cahill, you have a blind faith in accepting his word on everything. Do you still, I mean, here he gives insights into how the IRA policing worked. Do you believe he could know that and not be a member of the IRA?

McDonald could sense the danger:

Well, I think lots of people who come from communities like west Belfast know all this and have never any hand, act or erm, were never a member of the IRA. And in fairness, I think even people looking at this from some distance could look at it – and not to approve of it, just to be clear. Not to give this the green light or to say this is how things should be. But I think most of us can imagine a set of circumstances where there is, essentially chaos around you, where society is in crisis, conflict is raging. You have no access to the Garda Siochana as I would have in the neighbourhood that I grew up in in Dublin. Things happen and people want a response to it and they go to others. And just to say to you that, some people listening to this programme might actually say, might actually recognise that sense of wanting direct action or a direct response. But it doesn't make it right, it's entirely wrong.

Yates was not letting up: 'But Mary Lou, the question – the question I asked you [was] not about policing. It was the truthfulness of Gerry Adams. Do you not have a blind spot in relation to, it's generally acknowledged he was a commander of the IRA.'

McDonald tried her best to deflect:

... I have discussed this matter very thoroughly with Gerry and I've had the conversation with him about Máiría, about the circumstances pertaining to that specific case. More to the point, we have discussed all of it, and are committed to a situation where in the here and now anybody with information of abuse needs to bring it forward and most particularly Ivan, if there is any chance that currently any child is at risk, that information needs to be brought directly to the relevant authorities.

Ivan Yates then went in for the killer question: 'Okay, no, I got all that. But finally – yes or no answer. Do you, Mary Lou McDonald, believe Gerry Adams was not a member of the IRA?'

McDonald's answer pulled her credibility on every explanation she had offered about conflict and the IRA down around her: 'That's – Gerry has stated that position out time and again and I accept his word on that. Yes I do, Ivan.'

It was now no longer a case about my credibility, but Sinn Féin's, and not for the first time McDonald had been dragged into a northern saga not of her making. If I couldn't believe what I was hearing, I suspect it truly shocked some of those who had looked up to her in the past. Referring to the Adams blog, she had described a community with no effective policing who went to the IRA to sort out issues for them, and the IRA kindly but reluctantly responding. 'What happened was a form of very rough justice in circumstances where there were allegations of sexual violence or abuse. It's not a case of them being moved,' she said. 'They were told to leave.' She also made the following statement about the IRA in general which I suspected many people would find hard to swallow: 'I believe that the people who volunteered to the IRA were decent people.'[99]

Former IRA man turned Sinn Féin TD Dessie Ellis went on *Morning Ireland* to state that while he wasn't aware of specific cases, the IRA had investigated abuse, agreeing that some of those were 'well-standing'.[100] He explained this peculiar phrase in the following way:

> I'm just saying, what I said was, that the IRA did carry out, if any member was accused of anything, and it was across the board, that they would deal with that internally, they would investigate it and that's what I said. I didn't specifically mention anything to do with child abuse, but that is a well-known fact.

His interviewer, Gavin Jennings, attempted to get clarity for the public, most of whom were trying to understand all this for the first time: 'So, if a member, if it was alleged against a member of the IRA, or a republican, that they had raped or abused somebody, how would that have been investigated?'

Ellis responded: 'Well, I wouldn't have been part, so I wouldn't know. But all I would say is that if there was an allegation made against any member of the IRA, it would be investigated, and…'

Jennings tried again, asking: 'How?'

Ellis answered: 'There would be a team set up to investigate it and that team would be chosen by republicans that would have a good standing.'

Jennings asked: 'And how would they do that investigation?'

Ellis countered: 'Well, I honestly don't know because I wouldn't have been involved in it, you know.'

Later in the interview Jennings addressed the glaring contradiction between what Sinn Féin representatives had said previously, and what Adams and Ellis were saying now: 'Last week, when Máiría Cahill made her claims through *Spotlight NI* that the IRA had investigated allegations of abuse themselves internally, several members of Sinn Féin denied that this had happened. Is Máiría Cahill now vindicated?'

Ellis, the first Sinn Féin member to come close to stating the IRA 'investigation' into my abuse had happened (although was still saying he didn't know in other parts of the interview), said: 'No, well I made it clear, when, I said myself, you know, that there was investigations, and when an allegation was made against someone there would have been an investigation, and if in Máiría Cahill's case there was an allegation, that would have been investigated.'

Jennings then referred to what Pearse Doherty had said in 2013: 'But several members of your own party, including Pearse Doherty, when asked if the IRA and Sinn Féin had dealt internally with cases of abuse said no, that was 'unfounded and untrue', to quote him.'

Ellis did his best to extricate himself: 'Well I'd say that they probably didn't know. Likewise, I wouldn't know about cases being investigated. I just think that that's the case that a lot of people wouldn't have known.'[101] He did not address the obvious question: why, if people like that famous non-IRA member Adams knew enough to write a blog about IRA courts of inquiry, he didn't correct Doherty's public denials at the time, particularly when Doherty's assertion was in response to a public charge that Micheál Martin had made, stating that the IRA had internally investigated cases of abuse. Now Sinn Féin representatives were tying themselves up in knots on the airwaves.

42

Monday 20 October

I picked up a copy of my interview the previous day with Brian Campbell of the *Irish News*, after the Robinson meeting, and I was glad that I had evoked the image of the Catholic church to illustrate how I felt the republican movement had dealt with abuse:

> The Catholic church behaved in the wrong way towards victims, but I don't remember a time when someone from the Church went on the airwaves and called a victim a liar and that has happened with me in the past week…Swop the crozier for a gun and you have a very different situation. Not only do you have the weight of a political party coming down on you but you have the threat of an armed organisation which may well have decommissioned; but it hasn't decommissioned the fear surrounding those victims.[102]

Tuesday 21 October

I woke up the next day to discover my story had reached America. The *New York Times* headline stated baldly: 'Sinn Féin leader is accused of covering up rape.'

Foyle Women's Aid CEO Marie Brown did a Newstalk interview confirming that there were indeed other sexual abuse victims of IRA members. This was important, not only putting

Sinn Féin under more pressure but shoring up my account of what had happened. At 11.13 a.m., the Taoiseach tweeted unexpectedly:

> I am very much looking forward to meeting Máiría Cahill at 10 a.m. tomorrow here in Gov buildings #bravewoman.

Enda Kenny was not a prolific user of Twitter, and apart from one tweet the previous day about a mental health initiative, his account had been silent for three years. Regina Doherty had been instrumental in getting Fine Gael to support me and I was also looking forward to meeting her.

Gerry Moriarty of the *Irish Times* interviewed Anthony McIntyre, who had spent eighteen years in Long Kesh for killing a man. McIntyre said that while he was unaware of a culture of sex abuse within the IRA, he also had knowledge of other abuse cases. He cited the example of a former IRA man who was 'deemed to have sexually assaulted the children of his girlfriend', who was sent to the Republic for psychological counselling, though McIntryre noted 'as far as I'm aware that never happened'.[103]

Anthony, or 'Mackers' as he is known, has been a political opponent of the republican movement for decades, and faced rough justice himself when republicans picketed his home when his wife Carrie was heavily pregnant, after he publicly accused the IRA of murdering twenty-six-year-old Jo Jo O'Connor in the early 2000s. He knew the internal workings of the IRA, and likened the 'beyond fright' I felt during my IRA interrogations to what people would have felt when facing the IRA 'nutting squad', their internal security unit that interrogated (and shot) suspected informers.

Later that afternoon, I learned that the Public Prosecution Service had agreed to be independently reviewed in respect of my cases. Jim Allister, who was a QC as well as leader of the Traditional Unionist Voice party in Northern Ireland, had pressed former PPS director Barra McGrory to do so. The person leading the review had yet to be announced, but I welcomed it anyway – I was confident that if it was truly independent it would find I had been failed as a victim. Northern Ireland Justice Minister David Ford publicly stated that the decision by the PPS 'takes this particular issue further than what has been established practice of the PPS in recent years', adding that it also took it 'to a higher level'.[104]

That afternoon, I had been planning to take a break. I was completely exhausted, and I had constant pain on the upper quadrant of my right-hand side. A text arrived from a Newstalk journalist saying that a victim of abuse by an IRA man and a subsequent kangaroo court had contacted them asking to put him in touch with me. I took his number and called him. The man was very upset and took me through the detail of his abuse and the fact that he had been put through a dreadful ordeal by the IRA in his family home after he disclosed his abuse. I found it hard to listen to, and I was angry on his behalf, but I was also conscious that I didn't want to upset him further so I tried to stay as calm as possible and let him speak. He was nervous and scared, and he explained how watching what was playing out in the public domain with me had both terrified and angered him. I apologised to him if my case had triggered him and asked him if I could do anything to help. We agreed to keep in touch.

After I put the phone down, I looked at my relative and broke down. Crying is not something that comes naturally to me, but I heaved huge sobs that racked my whole rib cage, and I put my head on her kitchen table. I felt so helpless and guilty, because this man had gone through IRA kangaroo courts after mine, and I couldn't help thinking that if I had said something publicly at the time, then he might have been spared it. This was irrational, but a deeply troubling feeling nonetheless.

After that, I went for a short walk and picked up the papers. The *Irish Times* excoriated Sinn Féin in its editorial:

> What we know now [...] of the way the brave and utterly plausible Máiría Cahill was treated by the IRA following her rape and abuse by one of its members has uncanny echoes of the church's response to abuse. The methodology, the denial, the internal secret inquiries, the arrogance of those who did not believe that the law should apply to them. And then the

pleading of ignorance – Gerry Adams in his blog yesterday insisting that 'these actions were of their time and reflected not only a community at war but also an attitude within Ireland which did not then understand or know as we do now, how deeply embedded abuse is within our society'.

Yet this was not the 1950s – by the time in 2000 that Mr Adams met Ms Cahill about the issue, child abuse and responses to it were widely discussed. His regret that 'the IRA on occasion shot alleged sex offenders or expelled them', is mealy-mouthed. 'While this may have been expedient at the time it was not appropriate ....' Not appropriate. Not to mention brutal, illegal, and immoral [...]. Mr Adams's claim that there was 'absolutely no cover up by Sinn Féin at any level' is worthy of the most cynical bishop. It appears to be based on the fact that the IRA came to accept that she had been abused. But its response was not to assist in bringing the culprit to some external forum of justice, or to counsel and assist the victim, but to offer to shoot him. That way the organisation wouldn't have to face the opprobrium of guilt by public association or suggestions of tacit complicity. No cover up? [...] being willing to ask tough questions of your own leader, demonstrating that you are not just dupes of the Sinn Féin machine, may be as important in making the party a credible force for government as any airbrushing of a paramilitary past.[105]

It was a brilliant filleting of the party, and I thought their leaders would be very nervous reading it. There was now no question of my story going away, and the Taoiseach meeting with me would keep it on the agenda for another day. My problem was that I was utterly exhausted and emotionally spent.

Some of the letters in the *Irish Times* that day also got to the heart of the matter. Pat Burke-Walsh, from Wexford, wrote:

In the past few years we have been accustomed to seeing Mary Lou Mc Donald's terrier-like stance on the Public Accounts Committee. She has been to the fore as an inquisitor. She has left no stone unturned to get to the truth. I believe Ms McDonald needs to use these skills to question her party leader on the Máiría Cahill allegations.[106]

Later that evening the journalist Gavan Reilly, who had been at a doorstep interview with Adams minutes previously, contacted me. Adams had for the first time admitted he had heard of IRA involvement in my case. I exhaled. Finally. Apparently a row had broken out in the Dáil chamber during the Order of Business. Micheál Martin had called for a debate on my case, stating: 'The story of Ms Máiría Cahill is one that has generated enormous interest on the island, created a lot of anger and touched many.'[107] The Taoiseach responded that he would like to wait to see what I said the next day when I met him.

Gerry Adams, who was in the chamber, after accusing both men of politicising the issue, instead wanted to talk about Irish water charges. The Taoiseach was not letting him off the hook that easily, saying: 'Were I standing in this position where I had to sit in the knowledge that somebody, a member of my party, had raped a woman, and were I to attend and speak to that person or in the knowledge that that person had had her abuser or rapist brought before her, I would not last five minutes in this position.'

'Neither should the Taoiseach. What is the point he is making?' Adams replied, angrily.

The Ceann Comhairle shut the row down, but not before Enda Kenny took a swing at Mary Lou McDonald: 'I merely make the point that one cannot have blind allegiance from one's deputy leader when she says she believes Deputy Adams fully and completely and can give a categoric guarantee that there is no cover-up anywhere within the Sinn Féin party about this, or within the IRA.'

It was after this exchange that Adams was doorstepped by journalists. The question from Gavan Reilly was succinct: 'Gerry, is it still your position that you never discussed these matters with Máiría Cahill when you met with her?'

Adams answered:

Absolutely. I met her at the request of a family member who was concerned about her and as I have said on quite a number of occasions, when I learned subsequently, and remember Máiría Cahill was an adult at this time and I was well intended in meeting with her, I met her to help her, anybody else she's named from Sinn Féin who I have spoken to have assured me that they tried to help her and were well intended in dealing with her. And she's acknowledged that her Uncle Joe asked her to go to the RUC and it was at my request that he did that because once it became clear to me subsequently that there was this entire situation of alleged abuse, of the IRA, of, all of this, eh, I went to Joe and said Joe, that needs to go to the RUC.[108]

Well, there it was. Adams had slipped up. Apart from the lie that I had acknowledged Joe had told me to go to the RUC, Adams's fumbling words 'it became clear to me subsequently [...] of the IRA' created a big problem for him, because he had told the press previously he didn't know anything about the IRA.

It was also a problem because of his timeline of events. Adams had already claimed he wasn't aware of anything until the newspaper article about Morris abusing children was given to him by Siobhán O'Hanlon, although he had also said that Siobhán had gone to him on an occasion to discuss me and he wasn't sure if she knew what the issue was. Siobhan knew of my abuse from its early stages in 1997. If we take Adams at his word on the latter, she could only have gone to Adams three years before he met with me, and if that was the case, she most definitely would have gone back to him to clarify once she did become aware of 'the issue'. He was tripping himself up.

Before the newspaper article was published, Siobhán had met me late that Saturday night. That evening she had gone to Joe, who was at his daughter's wedding, and quietly told him that the newspaper article was coming out the next day. Adams was not with her when she went to Joe. Adams the next day arranged a meeting with me, and I met him two days later to discuss the newspaper article and the case. He couldn't have learned of it 'subsequently', which meant that he knew about it either before the article was printed or shortly afterward. He certainly knew about it by the Tuesday because I discussed it with him, though he was still claiming now that we never discussed it.

Adams's version of events simply did not stand up to scrutiny. I just had to explain this in an understandable way so that people would not be blinded by the many details that were coming into the public domain, and point out Sinn Féin's endlessly shifting position. There was also a fatal flaw in Adams's previous argument that Siobhán had told me to go to the RUC. Years earlier, she had known of another abuse allegation against a man who was later expelled from Belfast. If she didn't go to the RUC in that case, why on earth would she expect me to do so?

43

Wednesday 22 October

The day of the meeting with the Taoiseach had arrived and I was treating it as though I was going to meet wee Mickey down the street. The papers were still covering the story: Niall O'Connor from the *Irish Independent* reported on Adams's interview the previous evening and his slip-up in mentioning the IRA, which, he wrote, was 'hugely significant'. 'Mr Adams has never before said he knew of an IRA connection when he spoke with members of Máiría's family about the abuse.'[109]

My father tweeted the link with a few thoughts of his own:

Dragged kicking and screaming towards the truth. Shameful performance from a shameless man.

Another victim of IRA abuse had come forward to Paul Williams of the *Irish Independent*. I felt sick reading about someone else who had gone through the brutal farce of an IRA 'investigation'.

After his attacker admitted the abuse, the man says he [...] was offered three options. 'We were told he could be executed and buried, or be brought to us and we could do it ourselves. The third option was that he be ordered to leave the country.[110]

Williams had contacted me the previous evening and I told him: 'Sinn Féin needs to think about the damage they are doing every time they go on radio and TV [...] dehumanising every victim out there. What this man has done is take back control over his own life by sharing painful experiences.'[111]

In the same paper, Niall O'Loughlin's half-page cartoon showed a young girl – me – clutching a teddy bear, standing in front of an IRA army council in a courtroom. Clad in balaclavas and military gear, one had his arm raised, mallet in hand, as he passed sentence. It remains probably the most powerful image of the case that I can remember.

The *Irish Times* colour writer Miriam Lord skewered Sinn Féin in two sentences: 'What do Gerry Adams and the pope have in common? To their true believers, they are infallible.'[112]

Across the water, Lord Paul Bew raised the issue in the House of Lords:

> Finally, there is the question raised very sharply – it has already been alluded to – by Mr Adams at the weekend when, under pressure, he made an important comment about the Máiría Cahill case, which has attracted a lot of attention. It was an alleged rape by a suspected IRA member in 1997. Mr Adams has been under a great degree of media pressure in both the north and the south about this. He said 'The IRA has long since left the scene so there is no corporate way of verifying'. What does this mean for any wider shared process of recovery from the past? The state definitely has a corporate memory but he is now saying the IRA has no corporate memory. It has disappeared. What can this possibly mean for a shared process?[113]

Sinn Féin had spoken *ad nauseam* about the need for a truth recovery process in Northern Ireland, similar to the South African model. Adams's 'no corporate way of verifying' had implications for every other IRA victim seeking the truth. It still does. This was missed by most other people.

Meanwhile, more Sinn Féin TDs tried to shore up the party position. Peadar Tóibín, then a Sinn Féin TD for Meath West, appeared on Newstalk with Chris Donoghue to say he had 'no doubt that the IRA moved abusers', while simultaneously also saying he believed Gerry Adams was 'telling the truth', stating that he was 'a man of integrity'.[114]

'Decency is at the very DNA of Gerry Adams and I know that to be a fact,' he said, though he also said he believed Gerry Adams was telling the truth when he stated he was never in the IRA.

He was specifically asked if he believed me. 'I don't know,' he replied. He also said something that I missed at the time, which went a bit further than the rest of Sinn Féin were prepared to go. 'Gerry understands that the likelihood is that there was an IRA investigation into her circumstances.' Adams himself wasn't admitting that publicly, and I wish now I had picked up on that statement at the time, because it would have been useful.

Labour TD Joanna Tuffy issued a press release on 23 October, calling on Sinn Féin to stand down their keyboard warriors, referring to some of the ferocious trolling I was receiving online. It was clear the party was feeding out rumours. There were attacks on my character from anonymous accounts, to the effect that I was a 'liar' and 'out to get Sinn Féin'. The court verdicts were mentioned repeatedly. It was depressing, and daunting.

My meeting with the Taoiseach was scheduled for 10 a.m., and Eilis and I were cutting it fine. We parked and walked the short distance to Leinster House, and the media cameras started moving towards us. It was starting to rain and I looked for a face that I recognised in the media scrum. Ursula Halligan was there, and I focused on her while speaking. 'All they have to do is say, yes this happened, and yes, she was telling the truth,' I said as I tried to catch my breath. I talked about Adams admitting the previous night of learning about the involvement of the IRA, and made the point to the media that I had been consistent in my account, while Sinn Féin's had changed a few times over the previous week. The media were respectful, though there were lots of them, and I felt awkward when the cameras moved in to get closer shots of me at the gate. I could hear the repetitive clicking and dug my fingernails into my skin.

I went through the gate, and we were directed to a waiting area. It was light and airy, and had a beautiful brown table with intricate carvings of what looked like a sun. I tried to breathe and get myself together. This meeting was important, and I needed not to mess it up – and I also needed to ensure that Enda Kenny understood what was at stake. I needn't have worried. He had the air of a friendly, slightly elderly pastoral figure, and a warmth that made it easy to talk to him. I think he found it hard to shut me up, so he listened with his eyebrow raised when a point came to his mind, and I found him sensitive. He explained that he had seen some accounts of the case on the TV, and that he thought I was courageous. A female official was off to his side taking notes, but I focused on the Taoiseach. In the intensity of the moment and in the rush to get out whatever I was saying, protocol went out the window and I said 'Here, Enda', before stopping and checking myself.

'Can I call you Enda?' I asked.

'Enda's my name," he said with a slight shrug of the shoulders and a smile that reached his eyes. And so, in that moment, the Taoiseach became a friend, and I was talking to him like one. I still think back to that meeting and cringe that I didn't address him by his proper title. The meeting was originally scheduled to last an hour, but it ran longer, probably because I just couldn't stop talking. I said I would make an appointment with the Gardaí and pass information in my possession about alleged abuse cases to them, and Kenny's office was going to do the same. I was relieved that he was taking the issue seriously. He explained that he was on his way to Leader's Questions in the Dáil and it was likely that Gerry Adams would be there. I requested that he ask Adams to confirm that I was brought into a room with three IRA members and my rapist, one thing that Sinn Féin were absolutely refusing to admit. As I recounted the details of what had happened to me, I could see Enda bristling with anger.

After the meeting, he walked me down a beautiful cream-carpeted staircase with gold squares designed by Mary Fitzgerald.

At the top of the stairs was Evie Hone's impressive stained-glass window, running colours of purple and red, with a gold harp and green shamrock in the bottom right panel, which Enda said was a depiction of Ireland's four green fields. The official government photographer took a photo of us, and then Enda took me over to a glass case and showed me a piece of Irish artwork.

I thanked him inside the building and then we both walked out of the door, which was a great gesture from Enda. I leaned in to thank him again, and told him I was going to give him another hug. We embraced, and I said goodbye and tried to get myself together for the media at the gate. I told them that the Taoiseach had been very sensitive and dealt with a victim of sexual abuse exactly how he should have, in stark contrast to Adams. One of the journalists told me that Adams was disputing the fact that he had discussed the details of my abuse with me. I snapped, but delivered a line off the cuff which still makes me smile when I recall it. 'I met him from 2000 right through to 2006. I mean, we were not discussing his teddy bears*.'

After the press conference, I met with Micheál Martin in his Dáil office just as the RTÉ news came on. My teddy bear quip was shown, and Micheál laughed aloud. I allowed myself a grin. I wasn't sure people had ever before seen a cheeky upstart from west Belfast take on a man who was accused of being an IRA Army Council member (which he denies). 'Fuck Adams,' I thought.

I left the meeting with Micheál Martin to go to Belfast, where I had agreed to do a pre-recorded interview with Stephen Nolan in the hotel opposite the BBC buildings. I needed to change my outfit, but didn't have time, so I stopped at a Marks and Spencers in Sprucefield, just outside Lisburn, to get a different scarf. On the way in, a woman in her sixties with short blonde hair approached and asked if I was Máiría Cahill. I confirmed I was and she

---

* Adams had made a big eejit of himself on Twitter for years tweeting about his ridiculous teddy bears, whom he referred to as Tom and Ted, presumably in an effort to change his image from mendacious and menacing IRA eminence to cuddly grandfather figure.

took my hands and said she wanted to wish me well, and what was happening to me was a disgrace. I thanked her, but I was overwhelmed that someone had recognised me. It was so lovely to hear someone on my side, but it also brought everything to the surface, and as we walked away into the shop and through the store, I had a panic attack. I was worried about the Nolan interview. Stephen Nolan had a reputation for being forensic and aggressive, and I was exhausted. I especially didn't want to panic on camera.

Once we got to the BBC make-up room and I realised that the cameraman was Bill Browne, who had filmed *Spotlight NI* and whom I liked, I began to calm down. Gwyneth Jones, the assistant editor of *Spotlight NI*, came to ask me if I had seen what had happened in the Dáil that day. She put an iPad on my knee and I watched with incredulity as Micheál Martin asked for a Dáil debate on the issue of republican sex abuse and the Taoiseach granted this. At Leader's Questions, Micheál stated:

> I have no doubt but that the Taoiseach will have been taken aback by her story and by her account of being raped as a young 16-year-old. In addition, attempts were made earlier, when this story was revealed, to undermine her credibility. The story regarding the IRA interrogation into her abuse is one that would shake any person who has had the opportunity to hear it [...]. We know that Máiría Cahill was sworn to silence by Sinn Féin-IRA. This is known and one should just read her father's testimony during the week.[115]

Enda Kenny was seething with quiet anger as he spoke in the Dáil chamber.

> I had the opportunity and privilege of meeting Máiría Cahill over the past hour and a half or so. This is a courageous, confident and brave young woman who is a force to be reckoned with. She overcame the horror of being raped and had to face down the IRA and its generals, secret or otherwise.

All Members know that the horror of rape is that it is not just a violation but it is about control or power. While in that frightening situation her own control was taken from her, she never ceded in any way her own power – when innocence is defiled, clearly there are consequences when people have the courage to speak out.[116]

I was ruining my newly applied mascara at that moment, watching Enda Kenny say those words. I didn't feel courageous or powerful, but I very much appreciated the sentiment. Micheál Martin was allowed a follow-up statement during Leader's Questions and he used it to make a stinger of a point, drawing once again an analogy with the Catholic church's treatment of abuse victims. 'The most powerful men within the IRA interrogated victims of abuse at the hands of leading members of the IRA. That happened. The most powerful men conspired to protect the abusers and swore the victims to silence.'[117]

I could not keep back my tears. It was one thing for politicians to give quotes to the media, but I realised that putting it on the record of the Dáil carried a lasting impact that wasn't achievable with column inches.

Kenny spoke again, and he lowered his voice and slowed what he was saying so that people would focus.

It is reprehensible that a young woman of this courage and bravery should have been kicked about in the last week […]
I note from Deputy Adams's comments from last night the first connection with the IRA in his statement outside the Mansion House. Perhaps when he has the opportunity he might confirm for the people of our country down here whether or not Máiría Cahill was required to attend a meeting with her rapist and three other men to discuss this matter.[118]

Enda Kenny had wrongly said there were three men in the confrontation with Morris, when it was actually two women and a man, but he got the essentials right. Adams stood up to speak.

He waffled about abuse being a 'heinous crime', and said he had acknowledged that the IRA had 'sought to deal with some cases of abuse when asked to do so by families and victims'. But I had never asked the IRA to deal with my abuse. He said the IRA was 'ill-equipped' to deal with such matters, a phrase he had used to me in 2000. He apologised to victims in general and said that Sinn Féin had not engaged in a cover-up of abuse. He went further. 'This accusation is a slur on thousands of decent Irish republicans and Sinn Féin members.'

He was accusing me of slurring Sinn Féin. Really?

Kenny got stuck into Mary Lou McDonald: 'Let us not forget that the central issue here is that a young woman was raped, sexually abused and required to go before her abuser and three other men from the IRA.' I put my head in my hands, as the unintentional inaccuracy surfaced again. 'The Deputy's (Adams) Deputy Leader does not believe this. She has blind allegiance to the Deputy...'

McDonald shook her head in disgust.

Kenny finished by asking Adams about the confrontation again, and additionally whether he had knowledge of sex offenders who were moved to Donegal or Louth. 'I think the story Máiría Cahill has to tell is not just powerful but will have serious consequences.'

Adams allowed himself to become visibly furious, and he made what any reasonable person would consider a mistake. In his anger, he asked the Taoiseach whether he would 'facilitate a meeting with those she accuses? [...] I refute the allegations that have been made about me and about other Sinn Féin members who assure me all they did in their engagements, conversations and work with Máiría Cahill was to help.' He then went from mistake to fatal error. 'The Taoiseach has heard Máiría Cahill's story. All those from Sinn Féin who have met Máiría Cahill accept and acknowledge that she was abused and traumatised. She then put a particular version of what occurred.'

'Here we go,' I thought.

'These are not nameless, anonymous people. These are decent people,' he said.

There was a gasp on the floor of the house. Enda Kenny rose, took a breath, lowered his head and eyeballed Adams. His delivery was slow and deliberate. He was going to twist the knife. 'I find it absolutely incredible that Deputy Adams would come into this house of parliament and say a man who raped a woman, who sexually abused her, is a decent person.'

Adams went what can only be described as nuts. 'I did not say that. The Taoiseach should not dare say that. Ceann Comhairle, do your job!' he raged, pointing at Seán Barrett, who looked as shocked as everybody else.* The row continued back and forth about who had said what, but the damage was done. Mary Lou McDonald looked sick, shaking her head while sitting beside Adams.[119]

---

* The Ceann Comhairle is the chairperson of the Dáil.

44

The comments online were not getting any better. A blog appeared on 21 October written under the pseudonym Ruaidrí Ua Conchobair, a disgraceful piece which alleged my abuse was

> a year- long clandestine sexual liaison between these two people ignited by a lawful but "a few cans of beer" induced seduction by a silver-tongued, musically talented, IRA-powerful type of charmer whom many a 16 year old would likely fancy.[120]

I didn't see it until the next day, but when I did, I was sick to my stomach. I read the insinuations online alleging my abuse was in fact an affair, and I was appalled that anyone would sink so low as to write the crap I was reading.

I felt ill. But I was also aware that I had to pull myself together to do an interview, and I had no idea how it would go. I resolved just to answer any question put to me honestly, and see where it went. Nolan's team had sent down a teddy bear with his name on it for Saorlaith, which was nice. I put it in my handbag and thought that I couldn't wait to spend some proper time with her. My mother had been minding her while all of this was going on, and though I knew she would be fine, I wondered what effect being apart from her mammy for this length of time would have on a three-year-old. Her mother was now embroiled in a political storm and didn't have any other option but to keep going.

We made our way to the hotel and waited for Stephen Nolan to arrive. He came in and shook hands, sat down and, after a quick camera check, we were ready to go. Stephen asked me for my reaction to Sinn Féin and the Dáil events of that day. I explained that the party had yet to admit that the IRA had repeatedly questioned me, and that they had brought me into a room to confront my abuser. 'I just think they need to admit it at this stage, I think that everybody knows that it's true and then maybe I can go back to living my life.'

Nolan kept himself protected legally when I insisted Adams knew I was telling the truth. 'But he disputes the facts,' he said to me.

'I know he does, Stephen,' I replied, 'but he disputes many facts over many things throughout his life, and I think people know that Gerry, em, clearly has trouble with some aspects of his memory.'

Stephen kept a soft tone throughout the interview. It was a masterstroke on his part, because the softer his tone, the more upset I became. I was trying not to cry, but I was shaking and on the brink of tears. He asked me about other victims, and it was enough to nudge me over the edge. 'What is striking is that it is both men and women who are contacting me, and they are in bits,' I said, my voice wobbling.

'You come across as being strong, have there been many tears?' asked Nolan.

'Yeah, and I still am very emotional,' I replied. 'I just think this week has been horrendous. I feel like I have been repeatedly kicked by denials and attacks. [...] for example, one republican wrote a piece on the internet this week and I think this is the level that this has sunk to claiming that I enticed my alleged abuser with my virginity.' It was a horrific detail, and the disgust was etched on my face.

Stephen finished the interview by asking what my message was to Adams. 'Very simple, Stephen,' I replied quietly. 'He needs to tell the truth.'[121]

After the interview, Stephen came down in the elevator with us and I thanked him for allowing me the space to speak on the issue. I had a drink in the bar and headed back to Dublin.

The blog was still playing on my mind the next day because I could see Sinn Féin representatives retweeting it, which was hurtful and enraging. I snapped when I discovered that Seamus Finucane had shared this latest insidious comment on his Facebook page.

I tweeted Mary Lou McDonald the link, and asked:

> Will you condemn Finucane for doing this and apologise to me now?'

McDonald tweeted back:

> The assertion in that blog is shameful and cruel and should not be posted anywhere by anyone.

It was her first condemnation of any of those figures, and I gave a statement to Slugger O'Toole regarding Finucane: 'Gerry Adams called this man decent. Was sharing this post a decent thing to do?'

Finucane, for his part, despite sharing the blog, later distanced himself from it.

> I did not read the blog apart from the title. It was brought to my attention later that this blog contained references to Máiría Cahill and a 'year-long clandestine sexual relationship.' I was not aware of this as I had not read the blog in full, I immediately read the blog in full and removed it from my Facebook page as I did not and would not endorse those sentiments.[122]

Meanwhile, Adams's 'decent people' remark had the press reeling. In the *Irish Independent*, Lise Hand was scathing:

Gerry Adams was on his feet and on the ropes. The high-wire upon which he has balanced with ease for the entirety of his political career bucked and yawed beneath him in the teeth of the oncoming storm. And then he lost his footing. 'These are not nameless, anonymous people; these are decent people,' he announced to a deathly-silent chamber. Decent. The dictionary definition of decent is 'conforming with generally accepted standards of respectable or moral behaviour.' And the Irish definition of decent is someone who abides by the law … someone who would never kick a man when he was down, let alone a vulnerable young woman. But here was Gerry Adams, President of Sinn Féin, offering his opinion on the three Provos who summoned Máiría Cahill before them to be quizzed by their kangaroo court over her claims that she had been raped by one of their members, in the presence of the IRA man who allegedly violated her. Adams fell.[123]

She summed up: 'This slight young woman, compellingly vulnerable and articulate, has shaken his trademark confidence and calm in a manner that seemed new. Perhaps because her story didn't rise from the dusty war archives of IRA history, but is a tale of recent outrage.'[124]

The online abuse was becoming overwhelming, and since I needed to report to the Gardaí the information I had received about suspected IRA abusers, I also decided to report the online activity. I travelled to Harcourt Street Garda Station and dealt with an experienced detective inspector, Declan Daly, who put a lot of time and effort into taking my statement, but there was little the Gardaí could do about the abuse I was getting – policing hadn't yet caught up with the social media world in Ireland, and I found that extremely frustrating.

In all of this, there were strange moments, where even at the time I had to pinch myself to make sure I wasn't dreaming. One such interview on 23 October was on *Morning Ireland* with the Catholic Archbishop of Dublin, Diarmuid Martin, who was asked what he would say to Gerry Adams on my case. 'Let the truth be investigated in a transparent, open way by the competent authorities,' he said. A church leader, with his own institution not whiter than white on kindred issues, urging the leader of Sinn Féin to 'let the truth come out' – the irony was unbearable.

Just before bed, I caught up with the newspaper coverage, to try and stay abreast of what was happening in order to answer the inevitable press queries the next day. Brendan Hughes of the *Irish News* had more on Finucane, reporting:

> Seamus Finucane also wrote yesterday on Facebook: 'Is there such a thing as a kangaroo court by media? Just asking.' Ms Cahill described the social media message as: 'completely disgusting ... I would like to ask him does he think it is right to bring an abuser into a room and interview me?'[125]

Finucane, nine years later, has still to answer that question publicly.

In the same paper, Martin McGuinness entered the fray. His statement was carefully crafted, designed to make it look as though he believed me while simultaneously blaming me for waiving anonymity and going into the public domain. 'I believe Máiría Cahill was raped,' he told journalists, then added: 'I regret that she wasn't able to go into a court and confront the person that she alleged raped her in the same fashion that republicans are being confronted now.'[126] It was a despicable thing to say, and effectively turned the IRA and Sinn Féin into victims, while publicly blaming the victim for wanting to hold them to account.

Peter Robinson again called for a personal apology to me from Adams. Peter Madden, the solicitor for four of the IRA accused, complained that 'the rule of law has been subverted by the ongoing trial-by-media' of his clients. 'Their acquittals have either been ignored or devalued,' he added.

Just after 9 a.m., Gerry Adams popped up on Twitter with a cheery message.

Out on the bike, Great start 2 the day.[127]

Uncle Gerry, blithely moving on.

Later that evening I was sitting in the living room, and Eilis was in the shower. I was trying to catch up on the Twitter activity and answer anything I had missed, when an account in the name of my abuser started favouriting tweets from my account; I had tweeted a *Belfast Telegraph* article by Liam Clarke saying I was afraid for my safety. My reaction was immediate blind panic. I tweeted a screenshot of the account and wrote 'Unbelievable. Sick', then I ran to the bathroom and banged on the door. Eilis came into the living room, sat on the sofa and put my head to her chest. Someone had opened the front door, and in my fright, I jumped.

'It's okay, Máiría, he can't get you here,' she said.

I tried to concentrate on breathing normally but I was rattled. Fine Gael's Regina Doherty was horrified and tweeted in support. Others were equally appalled, and I felt sick to my stomach at the thought that it might be Morris directly watching what I was tweeting. Even if it were someone trying to impersonate him, it was still sick. I had to try to hold myself together a little better if I was to continue with the public campaign, but I was finding it increasingly hard to do so.

Things were about to get worse. I received a call from a reporter who was writing for an American publication, stating that he had learned I had previously been a member (and briefly the National Secretary) of Republican Network for Unity. I hadn't hidden this from *Spotlight NI*, and had emailed the first reporter on the programme telling her about my involvement. The American reporter caught me at a bad time. In a panic, I told him I couldn't speak to him. I knew Sinn Féin would use my brief association with RNU to argue, wrongly, that I was opposed to the peace process and only raising my story to damage them.

The *Irish Times*'s 'Weekend Review' section carried a huge photograph of me standing outside Stormont prior to my meeting with First Minister Peter Robinson, facing a few dozen press personnel and cameramen. Their northern correspondent Gerry Moriarty outlined the issues in dispute, one of which was Adams's assertion – and my denial – that I had been told to go to the RUC. Interestingly, he had found a quote from Adams in 1995 – just two years before my abuse started, and just four years before the IRA 'investigation'. He wrote: 'in 1995, Adams said that people should not report alleged cases of child or drug abuse to the RUC because they were "not acceptable and, indeed, are using these issues for their own militaristic ends".'[128]

In his *Irish News* column, Newton Emerson, who is an acute and forensic analyst, wrote:

> It took Gerry Adams 1800 words on his blog to blame the Máiría Cahill case on 'the Orange state', providing an almost arithmetical measure of his convoluted desperation. At least one claim in this verbiage was absolutely wrong. Adams states that 'despite alienation from the RUC' some incidents of rape were reported to police by republicans during the Troubles and 'no thinking person would have made a case against that'. In fact Sinn Féin remained openly hostile to public cooperation with rape investigations until its 'acceptance' in 2010, most notoriously in the 2005 double-rape of a 15-year-old English girl in west Belfast. Instead Sinn Féin advised people to go to Community Restorative Justice Ireland, onto whose senior staff it had placed Máiría Cahill's rapist.[129]

Gerry Adams was to appear at a hastily arranged press conference packed with party supporters later that Saturday, 25 October. Speculation was rife that the party was under so much pressure that the only option he had was to apologise to me on behalf of the republican movement and admit what they had done. I knew he wouldn't. The very fact that it had been arranged, though, told me two things: that the party was indeed under pressure, and that Adams would double down amongst the Belfast faithful. I was correct, and the journalists who thought he would apologise were amazed. Adams, to sycophantic applause, told the audience: 'While I'm very mindful of the trauma she has suffered, I and the others she has named reject these allegations. And these allegations have been seized in the most cynical, calculated and opportunistic way by our political opponents.' Adams was speaking to a crowded hall, comprised of senior IRA men and women like Bobby Storey, as well as the party's assembly team and Mary Lou McDonald and Martin McGuinness. Adams also stated:

> Abuse is wrong, it cannot and must not be tolerated. Let me be equally clear. Sinn Féin has not engaged in a cover up of any aspect of abuse on any level of this party. This accusation is a vile slur on the thousands of decent upstanding republican people right across this island.

With that, he effectively threw me to the wolves howling on the internet and in the back streets of Belfast. For fourteen minutes he heaped criticism after criticism on Micheál Martin and Enda Kenny. He rejected the equivalence between Sinn Féin and the Catholic church's approach to abuse. He reserved special criticism for the *Irish Independent* group of newspapers: 'They speculate with ill-conceived glee about how much damage this controversy will do to me or Sinn Féin. For me that's not important, dealing with the issues is what is important.'

I thought to myself, if it is not important, why mention it? Clearly something had hit a nerve. He continued:

> IRA actions did fail victims of abuse. As Uachtarán Sinn Féin, I have acknowledged that. I am sorry for that. I apologise for that. This week in the Dáil, the Taoiseach disgracefully twisted and sought to misrepresent what I said on this issue. He and the leader of Fianna Fáil have shown a callous disregard for the facts, as they turn the Dáil chamber into an episode of reality television [...] they have ignored the acquittal of those they accuse.

On the one hand, Adams seemed to be doing what was required – apologising – though to victims of IRA abuse, generally. On the other hand, he was standing by those I had accused, and he was not really apologising at all. This was not lost on journalists or on the public, many of whom contacted me, horrified, after watching his speech online.

I wrote a piece for the *Sunday Independent*, and I used it to urge the republican movement to do the right thing:

> The [*Spotlight NI*] programme, and the subsequent media interest, forced Sinn Féin into the position where they had to admit that yes, the IRA did indeed investigate cases of sex abuse and in some cases moved suspected perpetrators out of one jurisdiction, and into another. Up until last week they were saying it was 'unfounded and untrue'. The consequences of that are frightening. No one has any idea who they are living beside, who has access to their children – because no child protective measures are in place in respect of these individuals – and crucially no one knows the scale. Except for the IRA, of course, and Gerry Adams told us last week that since the IRA has left the stage, there is no way of verifying this information. But there is, of course. There are republicans with this information at present, and senior at that. Hugely influential people. They need to bring that information forward in order to protect children.[130]

A major story in the *Irish Times* covered other cases of abuse. It revealed that a man was moved south by an IRA 'court martial' after he allegedly raped a twelve-year-old girl in west Belfast. This man was then appointed to a senior position within the 'southern command', which organised and carried out armed robberies and other forms of illegal fundraising for the IRA. The stones had been lifted, and unspeakable things were crawling out.

Jody Corcoran wrote an emotive piece in the *Sunday Independent* under the heading: 'The time has now come for Mary Lou to put up or shut up'. The text beneath it ran:

> The Sinn Féin/ IRA intention to help Máiría Cahill cope was for her written account to be handed to her rapist and for her

rapist to read it out loud, in an aggressive manner, in front of her and other members of the IRA – some of them experts in body language, apparently, in an upstairs room in a house in Belfast; and that the rapist would then get to pick holes in her account and shout abuse at her, and call her a liar and worse, to the point that she would vomit onto the street.[131]

Ruth Dudley Edwards remarked on my online activity: 'Sinn Féin don't know what hit them. In addition to being brave, intelligent and articulate, Máiría Cahill is well organised and a good strategist …. And Twitter is a battlefield, where, so far, she's routed the enemy.'[132]

On 26 October, the *Irish Mail on Sunday* carried a piece about my membership of Republican Network for Unity (RNU). It contained some factual inaccuracies. For example, a source told them: 'She left Sinn Féin in 2006 because of Sinn Féin signing up to policing and justice.' This was bunkum, but it showed that Sinn Féin was spinning. I had left Sinn Féin in 2001. It also wrongly claimed that my court cases collapsed in 2012, when in fact they had collapsed in 2014. The main claim in the article however, was correct: I had briefly been a member of RNU, though the paper claimed 'she is listed as a "secretary" of the splinter group in 2011 on its website'.

I was nowhere near this group in 2011. In January 2010, RNU issued a list a few hours after its Ard Fheis to a separate republican blog site and dated it 2010–2011, recording what was supposed to be a year's term for its officers. In fact, once I returned from a meeting in Derry, having been proposed without prior knowledge from the floor for the position of secretary, a journey which took around two hours, I contacted the person who uploaded the list, told him to take it down, then immediately resigned from the position, but not before Sinn Féin had taken a screenshot of the post and later peddled it to the media once I went public. The journalists in question obviously published it in good faith, but I was frustrated with their reporting.

Online, Sinn Féiners were tweeting my former links to RNU with glee, and it was gathering pace. The next day was a bank holiday, and all I wanted to do was sleep. I went to Bray and met Jennifer O'Leary in a coffee shop, but I was so distressed that I couldn't sit, and we left to walk to the promenade, me holding onto her arm mid-panic attack. We sat on a bench saying little, eating ice-cream. I put my head on her shoulder, then sat down on the cold concrete with a hoodie over my head and stayed there until Eilis collected me.

Later that evening, I issued a statement responding to the RNU allegations that were swirling around cyberspace:

> It is very strange to see myself being described as a dissident republican, when I would not even consider myself a republican anymore. The *Irish Mail On Sunday* story correctly states that I was involved with a group going by the name 'Republican Network for Unity' [....] I was opposed to 'outside influences', in what was a perfectly legal pressure group, and was extremely vocal in this regard. Indeed, this was the reason that I left. I am on record consistently as being opposed to illegal armed actions.
>
> For Sinn Féin to attempt to use this story now to smear me as some sort of dangerous dissident is particularly objectionable considering that many of them were long standing supporters of the Provisional IRA campaign which killed most of those who died as a result of the Troubles. Gerry Adams was himself a senior leader of the IRA, and again praised the organisation very strongly in his speech in Belfast at the weekend.
>
> I, by contrast with Mr Adams, have never been a member of any illegal organisation, and I do not support violence in any way, shape or form.
>
> I refer to a piece that I wrote some time ago, and which is available online, in which I heavily criticised armed dissident groups. In it I wrote, 'It's time for militant dissident republicans to wake up. They claim to be fighting for a United Ireland, yet they are the diehards, the ones who refuse to accept that support for violence in whatever name, is a thing

of the past. People just want to live their lives, and God knows it's hard enough in some parts of West Belfast to do so. They don't want to be put at risk by a few maniacs who care more about getting a 'hit', than about improving the quality of life of those around them. People just want to live. Let them.[133]

I also pointed out the following:

I have always been consistent in matters of child abuse and child protection – no person or organisation should internally investigate cases of abuse. The proper agency for doing that is the police. People should bring forward whatever information they have.

That is the issue. I raised it very publicly, at great personal cost to myself. I am now homeless and in debt. Nothing about this has brought me any personal benefit. I have been attacked for doing so and have made a complaint to the Gardaí. All manner of false rumours and innuendo and completely ludicrous allegations [...] have been peddled about. All of this is designed to increase pressure on me to go away and stop publicly raising the issue of child abuse.

It won't work. It is very distressing at times, and frustrating, moreso for my family – but I know that the people who matter know the truth. And if someone wants to peddle libellous information about me, then there is little I can do to stop it being written – but I most certainly will pursue it through my solicitor, and the police.

It says more about the motivation of the peddlers of inaccurate and in most cases completely untruthful information, than it does about me.

And I won't be silenced because of it.[134]

The statement was too long and I knew the media would only carry a line or two of it, but I needed to counter Sinn Féin's smears. I went to bed and hoped it was enough.

45

The next day, Bank Holiday Monday, was quieter. Halloween was approaching, and I was looking forward to returning to Belfast. I wanted to get back to normal life by the end of that week. On 27 October Newton Emerson tweeted (@NewtonEmerson):

> 'What political outfit were you in 13 years after you were raped?' is the new 'She was asking for it Your Honour'.

Most politicians and Irish journalists knew that the RNU angle was being used by Sinn Féin in off-the-record briefings, and by their online supporters, to smear me, as well as to distract from the real issue. Consequently, most ignored it. In contrast, the former *Daily Mirror* editor Roy Greenslade, then a columnist for the *Guardian*, wrote an online blog for the paper's website, which caused me considerable distress, especially this paragraph:

> It is further claimed that she remained a Sinn Féin supporter for many years after the alleged rape and only sought to go public with her sexual abuse allegations after she had turned against the organisation for political reasons. [...] Critics suggest that Spotlight's presenter and producer were too willing to accept Cahill's story and did not point to countervailing evidence. [...] That is not to say that she was not raped. Nor does it negate her view that the IRA handled her complaint clumsily

and insensitively. But in Northern Ireland, where almost every aspect of life has a political context, it does mean that vital information was denied to viewers.[135]

I found it outrageous that any respectable newspaper would endorse such snide tripe, and I also knew that Greenslade had been a Sinn Féin supporter for years, writing occasional pieces in the party's paper *An Phoblacht* under a pseudonym, though he hadn't declared this in his piece. The article was shared widely, including by some branches of the Sinn Féin party. In 2021, after Greenslade publicly outed himself as someone who had supported the IRA, I contacted the Taoiseach, Micheál Martin, and challenged the *Guardian* and Greenslade's editor at the time, Alan Rusbridger, who was then sitting on Ireland's Future of Media Commission. After a fortnight, though he denied knowing anything about the Greenslade blog, Rusbridger stepped down from his position, and after I engaged lawyers, the *Guardian* removed Greenslade's articles about me from their website and publicly apologised.

The media were still writing about my case. Fintan O'Toole, one of Ireland's most respected writers, was grappling with the issue of Sinn Féin's blind loyalty to Adams:

> Over the last fortnight, one after another of its smart young TDs has come out to tell us that what really matters to them – and thus what should matter to the rest of us – is not evidence about what Gerry Adams did or did not do. It is the way their personal knowledge of Gerry makes them feel, which is, inevitably, an unshakeable sense of trust. Pádraig MacLochlainn put it most touchingly: 'I know the character of Gerry Adams and I absolutely believe him.' It's that 'absolutely' that should alert those of us outside the party that we are in the realms of pure truthiness.
>
> It's no excuse for my error, but I presume you have to do some kind of course to achieve this level of truthiness, some training where you finally 'go clear' of mere concern

with objective truth and become whatever the Irish is for Operating Thetan.[136]

Meanwhile, the online abuse was continuing. An anonymous blog was circulated with untrue information about me, and fake emails were uploaded purporting to come from me. It felt like I was being attacked from all sides, and the depths people were prepared to go to were clearly sinking. The person behind the smear was not particularly clever, as they had spelled my name wrong in the fake emails. I left it to the police to discover who was behind it.

On Newstalk, I explained that I deeply regretted my attendance at RNU meetings, but that had been at a traumatic and difficult time in my life. Reporter Jonathan Healy asked me how much I thought my life had changed in the previous two weeks.

'It has been horrendous,' I said, my voice cracking with tiredness. I continued:

> the reason that those things are happening is because of the way that Sinn Féin created the conditions over the last number of weeks in which people felt that it would be fine to attack me and smear me. The behaviour of Sinn Féin members and supporters in relation to this matter which is essentially a matter of child sexual abuse…has been disgraceful.[137]

I ended the interview by stating that in my opinion, Sinn Féin could never again talk credibly about child sexual abuse.

In the *Irish News*, Seamus McKinney was reporting on a distasteful aspect of the growing online commentary, writing:

> Sinn Féin has distanced itself from comments questioning Máiría Cahill's abuse allegations which appeared to come from a former member of the party[138]

The latest comments were posted in response to a blog entry by the political commentator Jude Collins, a relentless apologist for Sinn Féin. Writing after an appearance on RTÉ's *Primetime*, Collins wrote that 'to the best of my knowledge no evidence has yet been adduced to support Ms Cahill's claims'. A contributor called Mary Nelis wrote: 'Well said Jude. No evidence. No one knows what happened unless they were present during this year-long liaison between Cahill and Morris.'

The Mary Nelis comment appeared to be from the account of former Sinn Féin MLA Mary Nelis, an elderly Derry woman I had known in the early 2000s. I was disappointed that a self-proclaimed feminist would write like this. In 2016, after another comment from Mary Nelis' Facebook account, which read 'hell hath no fury like a woman scorned', I sent her a message:

> Hi Mary. Firstly, your comments are beneath contempt. As a woman, you do a great disservice to child sexual abuse victims everywhere — and as a Sinn Féin activist and former MLA they are incredibly disturbing [...]. It is also a very clear indicator with regards to how Sinn Féin treats victims of sexual abuse who dare to expose the insidious nature of the IRA and Sinn Féin members who put the protection of their own movement above those children who were too petrified to break their silence when those who abused their positions of power took control of their bodies – and fractured their minds. As someone who professed to be a feminist yourself, your comments expose you personally — and collectively as a party for exactly who you are.[139]

The next day, Wednesday 29 October, it was announced that Sir Keir Starmer was to lead a review into the PPS handling of my cases. I didn't know much about Starmer. He was a former Director of Public Prosecutions in England, which indicated that the Northern Irish PPS were taking the matter seriously. I told various journalists who enquired that I would engage with the process and await the terms of reference.

There were exchanges in the House of Commons about the case, Nigel Dodds of the DUP asking a pointed question that further intensified the pressure on Sinn Féin.* A fortnight previously, I had been wondering if my case would have any impact. Now, I was in the middle of a political storm and my case was being mentioned in the Northern Irish Assembly, Ireland's Dáil, and Westminster. But I needed to get back to Belfast, both to see my child and consult a doctor. Jennifer O'Leary was travelling back and offered to take me with her. She allowed me to sleep in the car, and her manner was calming and kind.

My GP was concerned about the level of pressure I was under and suggested antidepressants. I didn't want to take them, but I needed something to calm the nervous feeling in my stomach, and she prescribed beta-blockers and a short-term sedative. I thought if I could just get a few nights' sleep, I would be able to bounce back with renewed energy when Sinn Féin lobbed its next smear. As I walked out of my doctor's room and down the corridor, another patient was going in to see her GP. Mindful she was in west Belfast and didn't want anyone to hear her, she simply put her head down and whispered 'well done' to me as she walked past. It took courage, and I deeply appreciated the gesture. I arrived home in time to see my daughter, sparklers in hand and in her Halloween costume, whooping with delight to see her mammy return. I thought I would be able to get some rest that would help with the fact that I was breaking inside, and planned to avoid media interviews over the next few days.

I didn't get that opportunity to rest, however, because when I woke up the next morning I discovered that Peter Madden, the solicitor who had represented four of the defendants in the IRA membership case, had been speaking on RTÉ radio. I hadn't heard him, but I got calls from journalists asking for a response. I pulled myself up out of bed and on the RTÉ website listened to what he

---

* For the full exchange, see: hansard.parliament.uk/Commons/2014-10-29/debates/14102956000011/PoliceServiceOfNorthernIreland#contribution-14102956000034, accessed 26 May 2023.

had had to say. I was taken aback but not entirely surprised when he stated:

> Well, it seems to me, having looked at the transcript of the Dáil meeting on the 22 October – last Wednesday – that the Taoiseach has already made his mind up about this. And he has already stated very clearly that he – and he states as a fact – that my clients were members of the IRA. He doesn't even state that as an allegation. What he said is – and I'm reading from the transcript. He said that the central issue here – a young woman who was raped and sexually abused being required by powerful people within the IRA to attend at a meeting and having to face her abuser. So he's taken that as a fact when in fact, it's not a fact at the moment. It's a fact – but it's a disputed fact and it's an allegation. So, it seems to me that the Taoiseach attempting to meet people in which allegations – unproven allegations actually – to meet with them is some sort of political stunt, I would say because the fact is that the, these people, my clients – there are four – four of my clients, have been acquitted by a court on these same allegations.[140]

He confirmed that he had advised his clients not to meet the Taoiseach, and then introduced the fact that I had written a letter to the Army Council of the IRA:

> But let me just ask you a question. I don't know if you're aware of it or not, but are you aware that Máiría Cahill wrote a letter to the IRA Army Council? – I don't think you would be aware of it because you wouldn't have heard about it on *Spotlight*, BBC *Spotlight*. And you wouldn't have heard about it – you wouldn't have seen it in the Sunday papers. But it's a fact. And that what she did was – she wrote a letter and this is part of the prosecution case by the way, this is in the prosecution papers. This is not a secret document. And what she said in this letter – she was complaining because she had written to the IRA

> previously and they hadn't responded. Now, she's written a letter to the IRA Army Council, believe it or not.[141]

In fact, this was partly incorrect, as I hadn't previously written to the IRA, but I had complained that I had asked for a meeting with them six weeks prior to the letter and had no response.

Madden said that the place for my credibility to be tested was in a court, and later stated:

> [...] as far as this BBC *Spotlight* programme is concerned, they will be taking action against *Spotlight* because if this is, if this is not a cover up, I don't know what is. Why this information wasn't disclosed to the public, I just don't know but it requires an investigation of its own.[142]

His clients, in fact, never sued *Spotlight NI*.

I wasn't worried about the IRA Army Council letter, as it was I who had disclosed it to the police in the first place. For me, it proved there had been an IRA 'investigation'. Madden had not released the letter, so I decided to write a statement and release it to the media myself. With reference to Madden's clients, I noted that they had 'not once made themselves available to be questioned in detail (by the media) on the issue. I have. I think that speaks volumes.'[143]

By now, there were so many details of my case in the public domain that it was hard for people to keep up, and I was mindful that I needed to keep it simple. Separately, the collapse of my court cases was of course being used incessantly by Sinn Féin members to discredit me and defend the IRA personnel who'd been part of the 'investigation'. Newton Emerson referred to this: 'The IRA membership trial that collapsed when alleged rape victim Máiría Cahill withdrew her evidence was a Diplock Court. For that reason alone it is striking that some republicans are holding it up as a final and perfect arbiter of justice.'[144]

I tweeted on 29 October in response to the online abuse I was still dealing with:

Are Sinn Féin going to admit now there was a forced investigation into my sexual abuse? Or are they going to continue publicly flogging 'the witch'?

Morris's other two alleged victims went public the next day, albeit retaining their anonymity. A report by Connla Young in the *Irish News* stated:

> The women claim that Morris sexually abused them over a period of three years from 1997–2000. They were aged just 13 and 14 years when they say it began. [...] In a statement to the *Irish News*, the two women say they 'had lost all faith in the criminal justice system' after they were told by telephone in October 2012 that the trial against Morris had been 'adjourned indefinitely to facilitate the related case' of IRA membership against him. [...] They also said the 'PPS failed to acknowledge or recognise the impact' their approach to dealing with Morris 'was and continues to have on us, particularly given the area which we live and the sensitivity of the allegations made.'[145]

I was upset on their behalf, but they were entitled to speak out. I knew how hard it had been for me, and hoped they were okay.

Mary Lou McDonald, in the midst of all this, again denied that her party was 'involved in a cover-up or was sitting on information' about my case. 'That is utterly, utterly untrue and a slur on all the women in the party.' She was quick, nevertheless, to insist that she believed I had been abused. 'What happened to her was hideous, hideous. An awful, awful thing. I absolutely believe it happened.'[146] Sinn Féin were sticking adamantly to their line that they believed I was abused, but refusing to admit there was a cover-up. By not going any further, they were continuing to fuel my determination. Any notion that I had about retiring from the public eye was gone.

My father gave an interview to Maeve Sheehan in the *Sunday Independent* that broke my heart. My father is by nature a quiet, gentle man, and I hadn't been able to have a proper conversation with him since I went public. These were hectic weeks, and my family members were finding it hard to get through to me and I had so little time. Maeve described the situation from his point of view:

> Philip Cahill has watched from the sidelines with a great deal of emotion as his daughter does battle with Sinn Féin. He is more than just an observer. He is also a crucial witness, if not to the brutal act of rape and child abuse [...] then to the ensuing heavy-handed IRA investigation into her alleged rapist. [...] Philip Cahill says he can name her alleged interrogators [...] because they gathered in his sitting room to deliver the outcome of their grotesque inquisition. 'The IRA came to my house and told me they had interrogated her. I was there and her mum was there. The republican movement knew about this long before we did. We were kept in secret while she was a minor. They did not interrogate her until she was 18. Even when she was being interrogated she was told she couldn't discuss it.[147]

I was thankful for the public corroboration, which I knew would have taken a lot out of my father, but what he said next was unbearably moving: 'I think you can detect that in Máiría they have met a formidable opponent, because she has truth on her side. She won't be hushed. They know that they dealt with it really badly. They know she's telling the truth. They are trying to defend the indefensible.'[148]

46

Eilis O'Hanlon had noticed Gerry Adams's Twitter account, and reported on some details in the *Sunday Independent*.

> Last weekend, after delivering a tub thumping speech to the party faithful in Belfast which effectively threw Máiría to the wolves, Adams went home and tweeted a link to a page from a book by Irish author Michael Harding which spoke fondly of the average man as 'a half-evolved Neanderthal with a fragrant penis'.
>
> There was nothing wrong with the passage in itself; but context is everything. Why did Adams think it appropriate that night to take a photo of that page on his phone, then link to it on Twitter? Did it never cross his mind how it might look to others?[149]

I had previously pointed out that Adams, on 5 October, the eve of his birthday, and four days after his brother Liam had been sentenced for raping his daughter Aine, tweeted: 'An early night. 2mara, le cuidiu Dhia, I am delighted 2 become a pensioner. Yeeehaaa! All things considered, not bad x'

Accompanying the tweet was a picture of the Maya Angelou poem 'Still I Rise', three lines of which really struck me:

Does my sexiness upset you?
does it come as a surprise
that I dance like I got diamonds at the meeting of my thighs?[150]

I believed that Adams should have been more cognisant of events around him that week, and more selective with his choice of poetry. He, presumably, just saw it as a chance to mark his birthday and didn't think about how some people might find it insensitive.

Adams's online activity was certainly worthy of reporting, and his tweets would have been newsworthy if it had been any other politician. He became defensive, choosing to upbraid journalists for going through his Twitter account – a bizarre accusation from a public figure about a publicly accessible form of social media.

The *Irish News* editorial the following day was very supportive, and I needed it. The piece read, in part:

> Ms Cahill has endured another appalling ordeal after telling her story on a BBC Spotlight programme last month, and had to listen to hostile figures blatantly questioning her integrity as a victim and wrongly implying that only a political motivation could explain her decision to break a perceived code of silence. A lesser person would have crumpled and retreated under the pressure, but Ms Cahill has admirably retained both her personal composure and her single-minded determination to ensure that the truth emerges over her dealings with both republicans and the state.[151]

Gerry Adams appeared that morning on RTÉ's *Morning Ireland* with Gavin Jennings. After complaining that he had been brought on under 'false pretences' and that he just wanted to talk about water charges, Jennings – who was having none of this – asked him how the republican movement differed from the Catholic church when it came to dealing with sexual abusers. Adams rejected the comparison and Jennings said: 'The republican family, with you at the head of it, allowed abusers within your ranks to roam free, to abuse with impunity. Don't you have to resign? As Martin McGuinness and others within your party called on Seán Brady* to resign at the time?'

Adams tersely replied: 'Well, first of all, there is no possibility of me resigning on this issue. I have a responsibility to those who elected me. I have a mandate. I have behaved at all times properly and with propriety and I will continue to do so.'

Jennings asked: 'In relation specifically to Máiría Cahill, do you accept now that she was made by the IRA to face her attacker?'

Adams responded: 'I don't know. That's the truth of it. I do believe that she was abused. That's my position for a very long time, but Máiría Cahill put words into my mouth that I never said and said things about me which are incorrect and that's been repeated and embellished and added to by others for party political advantage.'[152]

These interviews were frustrating to listen to, because I could not answer back, but Jennings had conducted a good interview. Later that day, Mary Lou McDonald appeared on *Newstalk Breakfast* and when asked by presenter Chris Donoghue, 'Do you agree with Gerry Adams's phrase that the people who ran these courts were decent IRA volunteers?', she answered with a straight face: 'I believe that the people who volunteered to the IRA were decent people, yes I do.'[153]

I was still receiving tweets not just from Sinn Féin supporters but from others who wanted to put their views directly to me. A woman wrote:

> In any case, having read the info, Maria Cahill doesn't appear as someone sincere to me – only someone out on a political vendetta against SF.

---

* Seán Brady was the cardinal who had, after an internal church investigation, allowed a paedophile priest to go on working with children

The tweet was retweeted by Sinn Féin Dublin councillor Daithí Doolan. On the same day, the same woman wrote directly to me:

> @Máiríac31 you're an actual complete twat. Why are you so full of hatred? Your public smear campaign isn't working so just please Shut Up.

The Assembly debate was the next evening and I was dog-tired. I was also sick with a head cold and wondered what republicans would do next. There was a motion before the Assembly to censure Jennifer McCann, the Sinn Féin MLA – a likeable and bubbly person who also possessed an ability to winkle information out of people with her friendly demeanour, as I had discovered when I knew and worked with her a decade earlier. When my story broke, Sinn Féin put her on the airwaves to say she had known about my abuse. This raised questions among her fellow opposition MLAs, who asserted that she should have gone to the police and reported it.

The motion that was to be heard that evening in the Assembly read:

> That this Assembly expresses concern at the contents of the investigation by the BBC 'Spotlight' programme broadcast on Tuesday 14 October into allegations of sexual abuse perpetrated by members of the Provisional IRA and covered up within the IRA, implicating senior members of Sinn Féin; notes Ms Jennifer McCann's admission that she was informed about the abuse that Ms Máiría Cahill suffered, yet inexplicably did not report it to the lawful authorities; further notes that Ms McCann, in her role as junior Minister in the Office of the First Minister and deputy First Minister, has responsibilities in relation to policy relating to historical institutional abuse and children; and calls for a full inquiry into the junior Minister to establish any impropriety as well as any breach of the ministerial code of conduct.[154]

Sinn Féin was angry about this debate, and that morning, Breige Wright released letters I had written to her, claiming she had been the victim of a 'media onslaught'. These letters were personal, and it was embarrassing having them in the public domain – not because of their content or tone, but because it felt like the public were going through my knicker drawer. Her statement continued:

> Due to the fact that Máiría Cahill refused to stand over her allegations against me in court where she would have been challenged, I feel that I have to release two significant letters that she sent me in 2005, and 2008. My legal team would have questioned her about these letters had there been a trial.[155]

I explained in a statement that the letters corroborated my account:

> They clearly show I was in turmoil [...] let her come out from behind her solicitor and allow herself to take questions from the media.. [...] This selective drip feeding of information without context is designed to frighten me to go away. It will not work. Although I feel like I am being abused all over again by the IRA in a very public manner, it will not deter me from continuing to deal with the serious issue of republican perpetrators of abuse being moved around this country and covered for by Sinn Féin.[156]

Some of the quotes from my letters were upsetting to reread, like this one:

> *You are never going to know how much you have helped me – through all of the shite that went on years ago, and in the aftermath, and again recently. I meant what I said before about you being the only one from that time that I trusted and for me to trust anyone after everything that happened is a major thing. I might get angry and snap, but that anger is not directed at you,*

> I'm angry at myself and at other people that I can't get at, and I'm sorry you have taken the brunt of it.

This letter was written shortly after Breige had taken me to the psychiatric unit, and I was clearly in a very bad way.

In December 2008, I wrote her a note saying that I hoped she was 'doing well' and wished her a Happy Christmas. In hindsight, I thought I was more than generous, given what the woman, along with others, had put me through. I had already acknowledged that Breige had been sympathetic at times, and the *Spotlight NI* documentary also referenced this, but this was to say the least a complicated relationship, akin to Stockholm syndrome.

I wanted to curl up in a ball and cry, but I had to keep going and travel to the Assembly for that evening's debate. It was due to start early that afternoon, but I was informed by several MLAs that Sinn Féin was filibustering an inconsequential traffic bill in order to push the debate past the evening news, thereby containing the press coverage. I sat in the public gallery facing the Sinn Féin team, which included Martin McGuinness and Michelle O'Neill, who spent most of it smiling and whispering to the person next to her and scrolling on her phone.*

The DUP's Paula Bradley looked directly at the Sinn Féin benches as she said the following:

> Ms McCann, I am sad to say, failed Máiría – Ms McCann, and anyone else with prior knowledge of the case, let a sexual predator walk amongst their community, free to carry out further crimes, and, let us not forget that this crime – child rape – is deemed by most right-thinking people to be the most depraved. I believe, given what I have said, that Jennifer McCann's position is now untenable. [...] How can any

---

* My account of proceedings is from my own notes taken at the time. See also the Hansard official reports for the Stormont Assembly debate of 4 November 2014, at aims.niassembly.gov.uk/officialreport/report.aspx?&eveDate=2014/11/04&docID=211612, accessed 24 May 2023.

survivors of such abuse have any confidence in this junior Minister, when, by her own admission, she was informed of alleged abuse and did nothing? Máiría trusted Jennifer McCann, and that trust was abused by Ms McCann's failure to act.

The SDLP's Alex Attwood spoke next, and proposed an amendment to the motion. His comments were withering:

Máiría Cahill is the latest Irishwoman who speaks truth to power. [...] She is a fearless, resilient, formidable woman. Irish democracy in all its expressions should stand with her. Those who seek to diminish her with viciousness in social media or through the releases of a Belfast lawyer must not prevail. In this Chamber in November 2009, Gerry Adams said in respect of the Ryan report [into systematic child abuse in Irish institutions] just published in Dublin: 'A just society needs decency, fairness and equality alongside accountability and transparency.' Accountability and transparency were the standard that the president of Sinn Féin said should govern these issues that face Irish society. Fast-forward not 10 years, 10 months or even 10 days ago: fast-forward to an interview that Mr Adams gave on Irish radio yesterday morning. He was asked, 'Where were abusers expelled to?' to which he replied: '"I don't know" is the direct answer to your question.' Here we are in the eye of this storm, and the president of Sinn Féin when asked where abusers were expelled to replied, '"I don't know" is the direct answer to your question.' We need to know where they were expelled to in order to assess the risk to people in this part of Ireland, across Ireland and on these islands in order to determine where they are and the level of risk. [...] Later in the same interview, Mr Adams was asked, 'Do you accept that Máiría Cahill was forced by the IRA to face her attacker?', to which Mr Adams replied, 'I don't know. That's the truth of it.' Máiría Cahill says that not only was she forced to face her attacker but she states: 'And you will remember watching as the rapist told me for hours, to my face and in front of you, that I was a liar, and that he didn't do those things to me.' [...] There is a third question when it comes to transparency and accountability. In 1999, Gerry Adams told his *Ard Fheis*: 'Scandals of child abuse have infected some of the main institutions, and the extent of the cover-ups have shocked many citizens.' That was 1999, which was around the time when the IRA was carrying out its first inquiry and interrogation of Máiría Cahill. [...] Three months later, the man who Gerry Adams and other people say abused Máiría Cahill was promoted to a post in Community Restorative Justice Ireland in west Belfast. He was given that post, which was published, publicised and promoted in *An Phoblacht*, where people were advised that the person who abused Máiría Cahill was now working on domestic abuse. If there was ever a moment that proved a point about the culture that prevailed in that organisation at that time, that was it. Based on the statements from Sinn Féin and others since the *Spotlight* programme, you have to conclude that, if an abuser, at that time, was given additional responsibilities and given all that has come to pass since, it has not yet registered with Sinn Féin.

Attwood had rattled Sinn Féin with this powerful, careful speech and had shaken some skeletons out of their closet. Martin McGuinness, red faced and visibly angry, rose to his feet: 'The motion is a wholly unjustified and unfounded attack on the integrity and sincerity of one of the most dedicated and capable Members of this Assembly, my friend and colleague junior Minister Jennifer McCann. The motion is a disgrace.' He attacked the DUP, calling them 'unrepentant bigots', and the SDLP for their amendment, continuing:

> Let me be very clear: in her contact with Máiría Cahill, seven years after the abuse occurred, Jennifer McCann acted at all times with care and compassion in attempting to support and

> assist a work colleague who, she believed, was the victim of serious sexual abuse. Jennifer McCann did absolutely nothing wrong then or since. There is absolutely no basis or substance to any suggestion that she is in breach of the ministerial code.

He confirmed that as long as he was Deputy First Minister, McCann would continue in her role.

The DUP's Paul Givan hit back directly at McGuinness:

> It is important that we treat this issue sensitively. It is a matter that should be above party political point-scoring. However, the contribution made by the deputy first minister will, I think, stand in the public record as having brought shame on the office that he holds. It is disappointing that he has continued in the same vein as the president of Sinn Féin, and that is to undermine Máiría Cahill and to seek to discredit Máiría Cahill — and to do it when Máiría Cahill is in the Gallery of the Chamber is, I think, a callous disregard for victims and their feelings.
>
> Consider how this issue has been dealt with by the republican movement: Gerry Adams has said, as others have, that he believes that she was raped. However, when it comes to the IRA interrogation — the kangaroo court that was established — he does not know whether that happened. That tells a story in and of itself. Sinn Féin is circling the wagons and using Máiría Cahill, in a way, to attack the SDLP, my party and others. Whilst this issue involves senior members of Sinn Féin, it would be wrong for all the political parties in the Chamber to ignore it just because Sinn Féin is involved in it.

After a few more interventions it was Jennifer McCann's turn to speak, and she was clearly angry:

> [...] I totally refute any inference in the motion or in what has been said that I did anything improper in the actions I took in relation to this case. I would not cover up or protect

anyone who has been accused of rape or sexual abuse; I would never do that. Máiría Cahill was a young woman of 23 or 24 years of age when she disclosed to me that she had been raped when she was 16. She told me that in 2005, some six or seven years after the abuse took place. At the time, she had recently started work in the local community forum, where I worked as a community worker. She disclosed the information to me in confidence as a work colleague, and I sought to help her in whatever way I could at that time. Anyone who has worked with people who have been raped or who are victims of sexual assault will know that that is what you do. You help the person as best you can at that time. It was very clear to me that she was quite distressed, and I was very concerned about her safety and well-being. As she appeared to be very vulnerable, I advised Máiría to seek the help of a counsellor. I spoke directly to a member of her close family to tell them of my concerns about her vulnerability, and I advised them to seek help for her. [...] At no time did Máiría indicate to me that she wanted me to report this, and I did what I would do for anyone in those circumstances and what I felt she needed at that time: I advised her to seek counselling. [...] When I first saw the motion, I was extremely upset, and I am still upset with some of the accusations that have been levelled at me. All that I did was try to help someone. I have not covered up anything or protected anyone who was responsible for sexual abuse or rape. That is not, and has never been, the case. At no time since 2005 has Máiría or her solicitor or her legal team or indeed the police approached me to ask me to make a statement on the issue. Máiría herself did not report it until 2010. When I contacted the police, they told my solicitor that I am not required to make a statement in this case, so there has been absolutely no improper conduct in my actions.

Some of this was news to me. Jennifer McCann did not explain when her solicitor had contacted the police – was it before or after the court cases collapsed? Who was the 'close family' member she said she spoke to? I also felt that her anger should be directed at her own party, because she had been put on the airwaves by them in the previous fortnight to answer questions on my case. Had she not done that, it is unlikely she would have come to the attention of her party's rivals.

The SDLP's Dolores Kelly pointed out that despite Jennifer's passionate tone, not once did she mention the name of her party president.

> Not once did she say that the principles that her colleague the deputy first minister, Martin McGuinness, applied to the then leader of the Catholic church, Seán Brady, on the cover-up of clerical sexual abuse should apply to the president of Sinn Féin. Jennifer McCann has let herself down, as has Carál Ní Chuilín and all the women in Sinn Féin who have, throughout the island of Ireland, ridiculed Máiría Cahill and, instead of trying to support her, tried to bring her good name into disrepute. You no longer have any right to stand on any platform on any feminist issue, when you cannot stand up for the victim of the most vile abuse imaginable.
>
> [...] For me, today was the day in which the IRA and Sinn Féin morphed into one organisation — they absolutely morphed. All that Sinn Féin has attempted to do over the last hour, and indeed the last number of weeks, is protect its institutions and organisation. Where were the words of condemnation of the kangaroo court and those who participated in it? Where were the words to say how the criminal justice system has failed Máiría Cahill and others? I did not hear them. All I heard was that Sinn Féin is the victim and the other parties are playing party political games with the issue. Nobody does victimhood better than Sinn Féin; nobody on this island. They are always the victims. Many of us in the House find a great deal to dispute in the definition that Mr Adams would give of 'decent' people. I heard his reply to Enda Kenny in the Dáil. I can tell you this, Mr Deputy Speaker: his words chilled me to the very core.

The question, as amended, was put. Sixty-eight MLAs voted for the motion, and twenty-seven against. Those against were the Sinn Féin members.[157]

As the speaker read the result of the vote, Jennifer McCann exhaled and slammed her file down on the desk in front of her. As I left the public gallery, Arlene Foster, a DUP MLA, came over to shake my hand. As she was doing so, Sinn Féin's Raymond McCartney passed me, smiling to himself. I couldn't contain myself and shouted something to him about his party needing to do the right thing. It startled him, and he put his head down and scurried off.

47

Gerry Adams was not at the debate, but instead was arguing in the Dáil on the order of business and criticising other parties about their highlighting of my case. Journalist Ursula Halligan, at an outdoor press conference later, asked Adams and McDonald about his Twitter behaviour.[158] Addressing McDonald, she said: 'How comfortable are you with your leader sending out tweets like this one? "Does my sexiness upset you, does it come as a surprise, that I dance like I've got diamonds at the meeting of my thighs?"'

McDonald, the sun in her eyes, looked disgusted, answering, 'I think that's a poem by Maya Angelou?' and turned to Gerry Adams, as if she was looking for him to rescue her from having to answer any more.

'Yes,' Adams interjected, 'which was sent to me by a young, eh, family member, it's a wonderful poem…'

Now it was McDonald's turn to interject: 'I like Maya Angelou,' she said.

Adams continued: 'I'm sure you would appreciate it, you picked out a particular section, eh, of it. I tweet a lot about poetry, I tweet a lot about eh books…'

Halligan saw her chance to nail him: 'Do you tweet a lot about your sexiness?'

'No, no,' Adams shook his head while, again, Mary Lou McDonald jumped in: 'That's very unfair, Ursula, tasteless.'

Adams was not happy and stated: 'I think you are being, if you don't mind, eh, provocative, eh, so take that up with the poet. Those aren't my words, those are hers.'

Halligan was not letting the matter drop: 'But there are other tweets that you've sent out,' she said.

'Well, that's fair enough,' Adams replied. 'I mean, the, the eh, are we going to have a discussion here about my tweets?'

'Yes,' Halligan replied.

'Okay,' Adams laughed nervously, while McDonald grimaced.

Halligan spoke again: 'How appropriate are they, given the number of controversies embroiling Sinn Féin at the moment, the sex abuse controversies?'

Gerry Adams's voice grew louder: 'Well, well, well, well first of all, let's put this into context if you don't mind. You talk about Sinn Féin being embroiled in sex abuse controversies. I have acknowledged very very clearly, and some people have by the way said to me you shouldn't be going off acknowledging all of this, but I think it is important to acknowledge failure and to acknowledge mistakes, when those occurred as we seek to ensure that these matters, eh, don't repeat themselves. Now there were a number of allegations made by Máiría Cahill and I have huge sympathy for Máiría Cahill and I have also acknowledged my view that she was a victim and survivor of abuse. Those allegations were then seized upon by the leader of Fianna Fáil and the Taoiseach in an attempt to smear me and to smear the Sinn Féin organisation, and most notably the Independent group of newspapers also seized upon that as well. There is no cover up. I've said this a hundred thousand times by Sinn Féin or anybody else on any of these issues.'

And with that, Adams had deftly deflected attention away from his tweets and pushed the blame for the controversy he and his party were embroiled in onto others. Though it obviously annoyed him, as he issued a statement online later that day on his *Léargas* site, stating:

> Certain media commentators have recently made an issue of the fact that some time ago, I tweeted Maya Angelou's poem

'Still I Rise'. They seem not to have the slightest appreciation of the nature of social media, the role of literature in society or indeed the character of the author who has incited their censorial righteousness. In an incredible leap of imagination they have deemed my tweet insensitive. This, because in their own fevered minds they have contrived a link between my tweet and other unrelated issues [...]. But in their zeal to propagate a vile smear against me and against Sinn Féin, these modern-day McCarthyites in the media have merely exposed their own ignorance and frightening intolerance. [...] Recent weeks have witnessed some journalists come as close as it is possible to be, to saying that when it comes to republicans, due process and the rule of law do not matter. Journalists now trawling through my Twitter account and seeking to dictate what poems I should or should not tweet brings us ever closer to the territory of book burnings.[159]

Ursula Halligan was, of course, only doing her job and raising legitimate questions which I and others had raised in the public domain.

You can imagine my feelings as I read the *Léargas* blog: Gerry Adams, defender of the rule of law and civil liberties, a martyr for free speech...

The newspapers covered the Assembly debate the following day, but the *Irish News* also reported on a memo sent by senior IRA man Bobby Storey to Sinn Féin activists. Storey was a large thug of a man who'd been at the heart of the IRA for decades, and who only months earlier had roared from a hastily arranged crowd assembled to protest the arrest of Adams in the Jean McConville case: 'We have a message for the British Government, for the Irish Government, for the cabal that is out there, we ain't going away, you know.' It was a blatant reference to the IRA. Now, here he was in a dual role as the IRA's head of intelligence and Sinn Féin's Northern chairman, issuing what John Manley of the *Irish News* referred to as an 'internal gagging order'. The memo read:

> Elected representatives approached by the media in relation to the allegations being made by Máiría Cahill should contact the press office before responding to these requests. At a wider level, party activists should refrain from making any comment on social media sites or in any other way around the issue of the sexual abuse of Máiría Cahill. Such comments are both inappropriate and elements of the media will attempt to misuse or misinterpret any comment – as has already happened. If you feel it necessary to comment on Máiría Cahill's political opposition to Sinn Féin, such media comments should only be made if they are (1) Measured, and (2) Rigorously accurate.[160]

It was clever, giving *carte blanche* to activists to say I was politically opposed to the party while also trying to limit the amount of damage their own activists were doing to them. I referred to it as 'sinister', and friends who viewed Storey's intervention as threatening asked me if I should maybe take a break. But I was not going to be bullied into silence.

Up on Stormont's hill under the shadow of Lord Carson's statue, the Northern Ireland Assembly's justice committee met, and voted to hold an inquiry into republican abuse. The three Sinn Féin members abstained and recorded a counter-proposal, saying that the focus shouldn't just be on one community.

In the early morning of 8 November, at 5 a.m., a figure dressed in dark clothing hammered on my mother's door. The person eventually left when disturbed and my mother increased security at her home. Two days later, the *Sunday Independent* reported on Adams's remarks at a fundraiser in the Sheraton Hotel in New York:

> Mr Adams hit out at media coverage of his handling of the statements made by rape victim Máiría Cahill, reserving particular criticism for this media group. In reference to Michael Collins, the War of Independence Leader, Mr Adams said: 'Mick Collins' response to the Independent's criticism

of the fight for freedom was to dispatch volunteers to the Independent's offices. They held the editor at gunpoint and then dismantled and destroyed the entire printing machinery! Now, I'm obviously not advocating that…[161]

The media saw this as a thinly veiled threat. Adams of course denied that it was, saying he was merely referencing an earlier period of Irish history and that this was clear from his comments.

48

I was utterly exhausted. Not a day had gone by where I wasn't asked for information by a journalist, or for a quote, and I was being trolled incessantly by Sinn Féin members and supporters online. One tweet read:

> Play with fire and you will get burnt.

Others were still calling me a liar. Another anonymous user wrote on YouTube:

> … sick of seeing this cunt all over the news.

Another Twitter user called me 'frigid' after I blocked the account, adding:

> No wonder the majority of Twitter fecking hates you.

The Dáil had scheduled a special debate on my case. The debate was certain to be highly charged, but I knew that it was important, and that Sinn Féin would be under huge pressure. I asked Sarah Moran, who worked in the Taoiseach's office, if they could keep me a seat in the public gallery. I wanted to sit directly facing Gerry Adams. I wanted Sinn Féin to see me when they attempted to spin and obfuscate.*

---

* To access the Dáil debate, see: www.oireachtas.ie/en/debates/debate/dail/2014-11-12/30/, accessed 24 May 2014.

I was not prepared, however, for what happened when Mary Lou McDonald took her seat. She arrived, arms full of papers, sat herself down, and immediately looked up to the gallery where I was sitting with others, including Ellen O'Malley Dunlop from the Dublin Rape Crisis center; Ann Travers, whose sister had been shot dead by the IRA; Breege and Stephen Quinn, whose son Paul had been beaten to death with unimaginable cruelty by republicans and later smeared as being involved in criminality by Sinn Féin; Eilis O'Hanlon; former senator Mary Moran; and former minister Liz McManus. McDonald locked eyes with me and gave me a look that would have turned milk sour. I refused to move my gaze, and for the next few moments we glared at each other, as if in a 'stare-out' to see who would blink first. I can still remember the intake of breath from one of the women sitting on my left, and the disbelief of those around me at what they had just seen.

The debate itself was powerful, and I was very grateful to the politicians from all parties who spoke, reminding Sinn Féin not only of the shameful way I had been treated, but about the wider issue of sexual violence and shaming. Taoiseach Enda Kenny was the first speaker:

> With their kangaroo court and their pop psychology idiocy, they inflicted on a traumatised young woman an extravagant, and for them exquisite, cruelty. Perhaps in retrospect, they can tell Members the body language for 'I am distraught' or 'I am terrified' or 'I am repulsed'. For any Sinn Féin Members, if the lexicon of such language is not to hand, they can look up into the Gallery and see one particular woman with a body, mind and spirit that states, in its dignity and inner stillness, 'you humiliated me once, you injured me once, you defeated me once but I will never give up and you will never win because I will never be silenced'.

McDonald looked distinctly uncomfortable. Kenny's speech continued remorselessly:

> [...] it is clear that in the case of Máiría Cahill, Sinn Féin and the IRA put the institution first. The allure of power and influence was just too much. They covered up the abuse and moved the perpetrators around in order that the untouchables would remain untouchable. It did not matter what terror they might cause or what damage they might do in these unlucky and unsuspecting communities. But who cared about victims once the institution, the organisation, in all its power and all its glory remained intact? It was a kind of unholy collusion. I refer to republicans who thought so much of this Republic that they would honour us with their rapists and gift us their child abusers [...]. Down here, you buried the dangerous living along with the discarded dead.

Gerry Adams sat stone-like, while McDonald put her eyes everywhere but on Kenny, until the mention of her name.

> What I cannot accept is the attitude of Sinn Féin to Ms Cahill or to the families of the country because unlike you Deputy Adams, and unlike you Deputy McDonald – your usually seismic rage and righteousness about victims now, it appears clearly to me, a pathological loyalty, your compulsive denial of a cover-up in the matter of Ms Cahill – how can you state categorically there was no cover-up of the knowledge of sexual abuse? How can the Deputy categorically state that sex abusers were not moved to safe houses...? Sinn Féin has reneged on Ms Cahill as a woman. It has let her down.

This was a passionate and devastating speech, but the most potent criticism of McDonald came from Fine Gael TD Regina Doherty.

> Let me address Deputy McDonald, who apparently likes a bit of Maya Angelou, whose most famous quotation, in my opinion, is: 'I've learned that people will forget what you said, people will forget what you did, but people will never

> forget how you made them feel.' Today I feel disgusted by
> Deputy Mary Lou McDonald's response to Máiría Cahill and
> all the other victims of Sinn Féin and IRA sexual abusers. I
> am disappointed beyond belief that she would so cheaply sell
> her integrity for political positioning, that her naked political
> ambition would cause her to fail the children of our nation,
> fail families and fail victims, all in the name of a cheap power
> grab [...] she has failed to hold her own institution to account
> and scrutinise Sinn Féin or IRA activities and actions. For all
> her rhetoric about women's rights, she did not know how to
> respond appropriately to Máiría Cahill's allegations because
> to respond or react like a woman, a human being, would have
> meant telling the truth. It actually would have meant criticising
> that chap beside her [...] I ask her sincerely to step outside the
> groupthink that obviously characterises Sinn Féin and stand
> up for victims with sincerity, not in the mealy-mouthed way
> she has done in recent weeks by saying she believes Máiría
> Cahill while undermining her at the same time.

McDonald pursed her lips and pulled her red jacket tight across her stomach.

Joan Burton of the Labour Party then spoke, followed by Micheál Martin of Fianna Fáil, the first TD to raise the issue of IRA abuse, who spoke methodically, forensically deconstructing the Sinn Féin position.

> Last November, when I stated there were many cases of child
> abuse within the Provisional movement, a succession of Sinn
> Féin leaders emerged to attack me, both the old leadership and
> the 'new faces' [...] Deputy Mary Lou McDonald said it was
> 'cynical' and causing distress. Deputy Gerry Adams said: 'Micheál
> Martin is completely out of order. A new low.' In recent weeks
> both the leader and deputy leader of Sinn Féin have accepted
> that my allegation was right. Under the force of evidence, they
> have both admitted that abuse within communities controlled
> by the Provisional movement was systematically dealt with in

the movement and kept away from the justice system. They have said that the movement handled these cases. Neither of them has said that they got this information since November, so they were clearly deliberately not telling the truth back then. They have, of course, advanced arguments to try to justify what happened while pretending not to justify it.

Martin was shrewd in pointing out Sinn Féin's tactic of doublespeak, of saying one thing and then another in an effort to deflect. He also referred to my treatment:

> After attempting to dismiss her as someone who was sick or had a political agenda, the leaders of Sinn Féin now claim that they believe her, but, of course, they actually continue to try to undermine her. How can they say they believe Máiría Cahill but dismiss what she has to say about Deputy Gerry Adams's behaviour? They are saying that everything is true but the politically inconvenient bit. It is pathetic.

Martin's words stung, and some Sinn Féin TDs shifted around in their seats. He continued:

> The basic point about the Provisional IRA-Sinn Féin cover-up of abuse is that it was not something accidental. It was not some unfortunate and unacknowledged secret; it was a standard operating procedure within the movement, directed from the top and enforced at every level. The discipline and public image of the movement came first, and non-co-operation with the justice system was an absolute principle. Deputy Adams is on the record as having supported this policy. He is also on the record, in his own words, as having participated in a 20-year cover-up of abuse. In January 1995, he told supporters in north Belfast there were counsellors who could deal with issues of child and drug abuse. He said: 'The RUC are not acceptable and, indeed, are using these issues for their own militaristic ends.' These chilling words

are reflected in his own actions and is exactly what happened to the victims I have met. Every single person who has gone public with an allegation of abuse or murder against the Provisional movement in the years since has at some point been attacked as having a political agenda, being in the hands of the 'securocrats' or been involved in criminal activity. There is no exception to this. Every single victim and family member who exposed it has been attacked or undermined. [...] Professor Liam Kennedy's report, *They Shoot Children Don't They?*, has revealed some of the scale of what was involved. Between 1990 and 2013, some 251 children were shot or beaten by the Provisionals. He stated that Sinn Féin centres acted as coordinating centres for human rights abuses against children. In addition, he showed that many of these measures happened in addition to police and judicial action – they were not a replacement for a community which supposedly refused to report anything. The *Irish News* sums it up well in its editorial today by stating:

'Anyone tempted to support this savagery needs to think about living in a society where armed gangs arrange to meet their chosen victim then shoot them in cold blood.'

There can be no ambivalence about this issue.

What we are dealing with is pure barbarity which too often goes unpunished by the legitimate forces of law and order. That also needs to change.

Adams rose to respond to these biting, scornful and lacerating analyses of him, his party and the IRA that he has consistently stated he never joined.

In the past few weeks, a barrage of malicious allegations has been made against republicans. There is one accusation that most people, including myself, accept: Máiría Cahill was the victim of sexual abuse. I believe her. There are a number of other elements to this case but at its core there is a young woman making an allegation of rape and sexual abuse. As I have said before, all victims and survivors deserve our support in bringing the abuser to justice. The other elements include an allegation that the IRA investigated the allegation of rape. This has now morphed into accusations of a cover-up by Sinn Féin and from that into a charge that we facilitate sex abusers. I reject these charges: they are not true.

For Gerry Adams, once again the poor IRA footsoldiers had been effectively forced into acting against their will:

> IRA volunteers were ordinary men and women. They had no training in dealing with criminality and no resources, legal or judicial or penal, to help respond to or to investigate allegations of anti-social behaviour, car theft, robbery, death riding, sexual abuse and rape or any of the other criminal actions that a normal police service deals with every day. When other warnings, appeals or community interventions failed, the IRA punished offenders.

There was of course no recognition that these aberrant forms of behaviour may have flourished because of the social breakdown caused by the IRA's launching of a military campaign against the state. Adams once more peddled the myth that republicans had urged me to go to the RUC:

> In dealing with these issues, I have been attempting to deal with them as they have been presented to me. On the one hand with compassion and understanding for Máiría and on the other hand robustly and honestly defending myself and Sinn Féin. Let me say clearly, if Sinn Féin or I was at fault, I would accept and acknowledge that but the republicans who played any part in speaking to Máiría Cahill, including myself, state with conviction that our concern was for her welfare. Máiría was advised to seek counselling and to go to the RUC. She was an adult at that time and refused to go to the police. That was her right.

Adams then turned savagely on Micheál Martin: 'I would also point out that despite the contrived outrage and theatrics of the Fianna Fáil leader a number of Fianna Fáil members of his team have approached me privately to say how uncomfortable they are about their leader's behaviour on these issues.'

Regina Doherty shouted across the chamber: 'Do you get a lot of that?'

Her colleague, then Justice Minister Frances Fitzgerald, challenged Adams: 'Tell us who they are.'

Labour's Eric Byrne provoked a ripple of wry laughter when he said: 'Deputy Adams is like a bishop in that everybody confesses to him.'

I sat stony-faced during the rest of his speech, but I could not contain myself when he said he wished me well. I threw my hands up in the air at that point, then put my head in my hands.

Adams's last remarks were delivered with real anger:

Let me say, and this is not part of my scripted remarks, speaking personally and on behalf of my wider family as well as my close family, we deeply reject the continuous taunts and offensive commentary by some here about what was for our family a deeply traumatic episode in our family life. I was told the rule in the South in politics and in this Dáil was that none of this should be taken personally, that none of this is personal. That is what we were told. The person who will offend one in the Chamber will sidle up to one outside and ask if one is okay. There is nothing more personal than the remarks some Deputies have made here today. I suppose I should not judge them on what they say in this particular debate as we will all be judged on what we do to protect children and the rights of women.'

And with that, Adams invited people listening to think that he was the victim.

Mary Lou McDonald's speech was an opportunity to try and claw back some of the credibility she had lost by her recent behaviour. She blew it with the following comment:

> Máiría Cahill's case follows a tragic, disturbing pattern for teenage victims. The crime was rape, the alleged perpetrator was a family member, known and trusted, and the assaults took place in the perpetrator's home. She first disclosed to a family member, someone within her circle of trust. That person was the late Siobhán O'Hanlon, her cousin.

There was no mention that my abuser was an IRA man, and no mention that Siobhán O'Hanlon was also a member of the IRA. My abuser was not a family member at the time of my abuse, but living with my aunt, while Siobhán O'Hanlon was Gerry Adams's secretary. In leaving out those details, Mary Lou McDonald was selective about facts. Later on in her speech, she continued: 'Máiría Cahill claims that she was subjected to a coercive investigation by the IRA. This version of events is vigorously contested by the women and men who stand accused of acting as interrogators. For the record, two of those so accused are women.' I wasn't sure what point she was making in bringing up their gender, but she was clearly prepared to take their side.

She continued:

> Anyone associated with the abuse of a child or the cover-up of abuse must face the full rigours of the law. That is the case irrespective of who the perpetrator may be. There are no exceptions to this rule. Nobody is exempt, nobody within any group or any organisation, and let me say explicitly that includes republicans and former members of the IRA.

This was a welcome declaration, but of course it ignored the reality that few victims of IRA abusers would ever get justice, particularly those victims whose abusers and rapists had been moved out of the jurisdiction by the IRA.

McDonald was at her most passionate making this ringing statement: 'Allegations have been made against Sinn Féin that we are party to a cover-up or conspiring to shield child abusers. This is not true and the mere repetition of this slander will never take from the fact that it is not true.' Any hope I had that Sinn Féin would simply say I was telling the truth vanished.

She ended her speech with an unfortunate choice of words, given the subject matter:

> These matters can and must be resolved. If one message goes out from this Chamber this evening, I hope it is to every victim and every person who has any information or any evidence, hard or soft, on matters relating to the abuse of a child not to delay and to come forward now.

At one point during the debate, before McDonald's contribution, I left to speak to a journalist and have a smoke outside the newer part of Leinster House. Senator Mary Moran was with me and we were later joined by Regina Doherty. As I was standing there, McDonald came round the corner, files in her arms. She smirked at me, and I exploded.

'Are you going to tell the truth today?' I shouted at her.

'I always tell the truth, Máiría, I always tell the truth,' she retorted, pushing her chin up into the air and throwing her shoulders back.

'No, clearly, youse don't,' I said, disgusted at all of the comments made about me for the previous month by her party.

'She's a disgrace,' Mary Moran said, as I tried to calm myself down before there was a worse scene.

This confrontation was reported in newspapers and radio after the debate, and I confirmed it had happened when I was contacted for a quote. McDonald, of course, denied it had occurred, stating: 'Our paths crossed momentarily yesterday, I smiled at her. I smile easily. If that was interpreted by Máiría as a smirk then I apologise to her.'[162]

Roddy Doyle wrote on his Facebook page, imagining a conversation between two people, part of which went like this:

> Máiría Cahill said Mary Lou McDonald smirked at her in the Dáil yesterday. Well, that's because Máiría Cahill wouldn't

be tha' fond of Mary Lou. Seein' as Mary Lou denies quite a lot o' wha' Máiría Cahill is sayin'. The real question is – why was Mary Lou smilin' at her in the first place?

– Why?

– Guilt.

– Cos she knows Máiría Cahill is tellin' the truth.

– That's it.[163]

*

The day after the debate, McDonald was thrown out of the Dáil. She claimed that the then Tánaiste Joan Burton had not answered questions McDonald had put to her on Irish Water, and then staged a theatrical sit-in until her questions were answered. After first refusing to resume her seat when asked to by Ceann Comhairle Seán Barrett, she then informed him she would not leave the House. He named her, and put the question to the floor, where a majority of TDs voted that she should leave.

'Deputy McDonald is suspended from the service of the Dáil. The Deputy will now leave the House,' Barrett said, his patience wearing thin.

'The Deputy will not leave the House. The Deputy is elected here to ask questions that have not been answered and I have no intention of leaving the House,' McDonald said, icily.

Fine Gael TD Patrick O'Donovan chipped in: 'Has she an objection from yesterday?'

Labour TD Emmet Stagg shouted: 'We are not in a kangaroo court now.'

Dara Murphy threw in his tuppenceworth: 'Sinn Féin is making up its own rules, its own laws, its own courts and its own version of democracy.'

Given that McDonald was going nowhere, the remaining TDs left the house and McDonald sat in the chamber on her own. As all of this was unfolding, I started tweeting that she was attempting to deflect from my case. Four hours went by, and I tweeted that if she didn't stop her sit-in, I'd go to the Dáil myself and sit in the public gallery until Sinn Féin started treating me properly. At 4.30 p.m. the Ceann Comhairle returned to the House and adjourned the Dáil.

Numerous politicians accused McDonald of deflecting from reporting on the previous day's events, which she denies. Former Fine Gael TD Jerry Buttimer issued a statement, calling it a 'stunt, directly designed to deflect attention away from the party's treatment of abuse victims', and adding: 'It disappoints me that Mary Lou McDonald, who is herself an able parliamentarian, is prepared to derail the democratic function of the Dáil in order to try and change the media agenda.'

My day was spent doing another round of media interviews with TV3 and Louth FM. The next day, I travelled from Wicklow to Dublin and went back to the Dáil to meet with all the political parties. I was exhausted, but the journalist Vincent Browne had asked me to appear on his programme on the night of the Dáil debate and it wasn't possible, so I had agreed to the evening of 14 November.

I left the Dáil to go to the TV3 studios. I had had nothing substantial to eat. The only food available was a KitKat out of the vending machine, so I grabbed one and sat in front of a bubbly make-up artist who did her best to make my pale face presentable. Vincent was in combative form and his questions to me were akin to a barrister questioning a witness. He read from my letters to Breige Wright, and from my Army Council letter. I calmly but icily explained that Breige Wright's brother was one of the 'disappeared' – people the IRA had murdered for being informers, and then hidden their bodies: 'The IRA took him away and murdered him and buried him, and he still hasn't been found to this day, and that was a very traumatic thing for [her] family.'[164]

I explained that Breige had then gone on to join the IRA, as did her sister, and that she had written a letter herself to the IRA. '[This] was published in *An Phoblacht* newspaper, where she thanked the IRA and she thanked Gerry Adams, the man who stood accused of being involved in the disappearance of some of those people – she thanked them for their efforts to find the bodies. For me, that was a very similar situation to what I was in with that woman at the time. It is a strange world to be growing up in, I've grown up in it all my life. I stand over those letters [...]. The first investigation, I was put through hell. It is still living with me to this day.'

I then told him that a psychotherapist described my relationship with her years later as 'Stockholm syndrome', and at the end of the interview, though I was upset, I explained to Vincent that 'I hope in all of this, that people remember I am a victim... I am not a politician... The people who can put a stop to this won't come on your programme, Gerry Adams will not come on your programme, because he knows he will be placed under scrutiny.'

The programme and social media were flooded with people critical of the questions I had been asked. Others thought they were fair. Vincent Browne said to his audience: 'personally, I think she dealt with them very effectively.' In hindsight, I don't think that style of questioning would now be tolerated for any other abuse victim, but Vincent inadvertently did me a favour by asking them in that inquisitorial style, because I proved that when challenged, I could answer the questions, even if it felt like a punch in the gut to do so. I received a message from a well-known feminist and Irish journalist after the programme stating: 'The interview you gave Vincent tonight was the best you've ever done – focused, credible and steady. Well done yourself.' I had never met the woman, though I had followed her life in the public arena. She wasn't known for mincing her words, and she gave me a boost when it was badly needed.

I travelled to Belfast later that evening, as I had been asked by Tim Attwood to speak at the SDLP's annual conference the next day. Shortly after I got there, people kept coming up to shake my hand as if I were some kind of celebrity, which is not how I felt. One woman came over and sat beside me, put her head on my shoulder and cried at the way I had been treated by republicans.

I didn't know how to react, so I just patted her back and told her everything would be okay.

I was speaking at a fringe event, and I wasn't expecting many people to be there. Five minutes before I was due to speak, there were only three people in the room and I left for a smoke. When I returned, some reporters asked if I would do interviews. I spoke to a BBC reporter, who asked me if I was going to run for election for the SDLP. I smiled and said to him: 'Do you not think I have enough to do at the minute?' I spoke to UTV's Ken Reid for a few minutes and he then said he didn't want to keep the people in the room waiting. I laughed and said, 'Sure there was no one there a minute ago.' Ken raised his eyebrows and told me to look around. There were people queuing outside in the corridor to gain entry, and others had moved seats into the corridor to hear what I would be saying. I was so busy I didn't have a speech prepared, but I had intended to read the statement I had given the court when withdrawing support for the prosecution. The hall was stiflingly hot, and at the end I was given a standing ovation, and a line of people asked me to take pictures or sign their conference programmes. I was appreciative, but it all felt very strange. After I left, I went home and crawled into bed.

49

That weekend, the *Sunday Independent*'s middle pages reproduced part of the Dáil debate under the heading: 'Day Dáil showed democracy with morality is invincible', and quoted Regina Doherty on Gerry Adams: 'I know I wouldn't believe the Lord's prayer from his mouth at the moment.' Joan Burton, referring to online abuse, was quoted as saying: 'The least Máiría Cahill deserves is for the Sinn Féin president to call off the dogs of war.'[165]

Willie Kealy, deputy editor of the paper, wrote about RTÉ coverage of the debate:

> What was not conveyed was the cold fury that Enda displayed, the honest emotion of Micheál Martin and the courage and conviction of Regina Doherty, who was brave enough to say she was afraid. And then the massive contrast with the cynical brass neck of Gerry Adams, who meandered through a prepared speech – prepared in advance so that none of the charges against him and his fellows could be addressed – giving the usual did-nothing, know-nothing excuses. He departed briefly to let the deputies in the other parties know that they needn't think he was going to forget this. The air of menace around the Sinn Féin leader is becoming more and more palpable.[166]

I was back in Dublin five days later, to meet with Gardaí to give them information that had come my way about suspected republican abusers. Mary Lou McDonald was due to speak at Queen's University Belfast, but a spontaneous protest had sprung up online and students had started an 'I support Máiría' campaign, urging people to change their Twitter avatars to this slogan in purple. They announced their intention to protest outside the university. My father told me that he was going to be there not only to protest, but also to thank people for their support. At the last minute, Sinn Féin announced that McDonald would not be attending after all, though the party cited 'other commitments', and Michelle Gildernew from Sinn Féin took her place, entering and leaving the university through a side entrance.

My father told the *Belfast Telegraph*: 'I am here to support Máiría, she has articulated her story and her point of view really well and there's nothing I need to add except I fully support what she says, I was there, I know it to be true,' adding: 'Despite all the abuse, the difficulties, and the position that Sinn Féin has taken there is a lot of support from very decent people and that is really appreciated.'

My solicitor Joe Rice also issued a statement, carried in the *Irish News* on 25 November, which included:

> Those found not guilty of the allegations made against them by my client still have any number of legal avenues open to them. They have complained about the contents of the BBC Spotlight programme and 'trial by media' generally and they of course can sue those they accuse of libel in the media and indeed my client.

None of them took up his invitation.

The same day, Paul Quinn's parents, Breege and Stephen, wrote an important and moving letter to the *Irish News*:

> Last week we were in the public gallery of Dáil Eireann to lend support to Máiría Cahill during the debate on her alleged rape by a member of the Provisional IRA. Máiría is a brave young woman who is being subjected to a campaign

of demonisation which we know only too well. It is a strange world when those who made victims of the innocent can then claim they are now the real victims. Our son Paul was battered to death seven years ago by a gang who told him exactly who they were, and we were accused of political attacks on SF, whose name we had never even mentioned. Worst of all, Sinn Féin spokesmen publicly accused our son of being a criminal before we even had a chance to bury him. They have never withdrawn those slanders. The campaign of demonisation against our son, our family and our support group has clearly impeded the Garda investigation and reduced the chances of bringing his murderers to justice. There was no reason for Sinn Féin to get involved in Paul's case or in Máiría's case, they chose to do so for their own reasons. Truly decent people can figure out who the real victims are in these and many other cases. We hope Máiría and those who support her will stand firm and continue to pursue justice no matter who chooses to stand with her alleged rapist.

Paul Quinn had been tortured and murdered by an Armagh IRA gang that beat him with nail-studded bars until every bone in his body was broken. He had reportedly fallen out with a republican. No one has ever been charged or convicted of his killing, although reliable reports place ten or twelve men at the scene.

Meanwhile, in the strange parallel world of Gerry Adams, he was explaining in an interview with RTÉ's Tommie Gorman how he came to be in possession of a small number of names of suspected sex offenders within the republican movement, and what he did with this information: 'It came to me anonymously,' he said. 'It was left in my letter box at home in Belfast. We have a national child protection officer, a designated person, and that's the person who brings it forward on our behalf, but I fully expect An Garda Síochána to be in touch with me.'[167]

*

An almighty row broke out in the Dáil chamber on 27 November, with Sinn Féin in the middle of it, yet again.[168] Mary Lou McDonald used her time at Leader's Questions to ask then Tánaiste Joan Burton about a review into sexual abuse allegations against the late Domhnall Ó Lubhlaí, the principal of Coláiste na bhFiann, an Irish-language college. Ó Lubhlaí had abused a whole generation of young boys at his school. He was an apparently puritanical, austere Irish-language enthusiast who was also a lifelong supporter of the IRA. Joan Burton riled Sinn Féin with her answer:

> All sexual abuse, whether of adults or children, is reprehensible. The Deputy might possibly join others in the House in condemning all sexual abuse. We recently had a discussion on that issue regarding the Máiría Cahill case. If I recall, her response regarding that case left much to be desired.

She then caused mayhem on the Sinn Féin benches when she referred to Ó Lubhlaí as 'a very significant and important republican figure', adding later in her answer:

> it was always pointed out that his links into the republican movement were of deep significance. We know from the discussion previously and the acknowledgements by the Deputy's party that in fact there has been a problem of paedophilia and sex abuse particularly of children in the republican movement [...] and cover ups.

This led to shouting from the Sinn Féiners sitting opposite; the Irish-language activist and TD Aengus Ó Snodaigh was particularly riled, shouting at the Ceann Comhairle to ask Joan Burton to withdraw her remarks. The Ceann Comhairle suspended proceedings on three occasions within an hour, telling Ó Snodaigh to complain to the Committee on Standards and Privileges if he wished.

By now, the narrative that the hard men of Belfast were running Sinn Féin had well and truly taken hold. I had just written an article that referred to 'the Belfast crew' whose support Mary Lou McDonald would need if she succeeded Adams. My reasoning was that Adams was holding back Sinn Féin's electoral prospects, and that once he went, and with Mary Lou at the helm, their vote would rise. In order for her to take over, she would have to prove her mettle to the former IRA members in Belfast. Her behaviour in my case, backing Adams to the hilt, was certainly one way of doing that, though she would no doubt deny that this was what she was doing. By defending Adams so publicly, she could be accused of putting her own political position before any question of principle.

In December I escaped to Galway for a week to recuperate. I spent the week in Renvyle, minutes from the beach. The weather was unusually warm for that time of year, and the landscape was beautiful. Rust-coloured bogland dotted with granite stones encircled black rippling lakes framed by huge green cliffs, with a few houses nestled in amongst them. The house I stayed in looked out over the Atlantic, and was the best medicine I could have hoped for. I came back to Belfast refreshed – that is, until I discovered that someone had painted in huge white letters on a wall facing the Ballymurphy estate, the area in which I was abused, 'MAIRIA CAHILL BORES ME!!'

As Northern Irish graffiti goes, it was benign enough, but the message was clear – republicans wanted me to shut up and go away. I was not going to be bullied into silence, so I decided to go to the wall, with the journalist Malachi O'Doherty, so that he could photograph me against it – though this, we both thought, might be a risky thing to do. Tensions were high and I had no idea what the reaction would be. Malachi collected me and we drove to Springfield Road. The plan was for him to cross the road first, with his camera, and once he had signalled to me, I would get out of the car quickly, let him take the photo, and we would get out of there to minimise the opportunity for trouble. This was a fine plan, but when Malachi crossed the road and signalled to me, I couldn't open his car door. He had locked me in, and had to come back to let me out. We took the photo, and I published it later on social media. Within two days, someone had painted over the graffiti.

The brutal online commentary was still continuing. In the previous week, I had been called a 'traitor' and a 'lying psycho-bitch', and a Sinn Féin councillor, Enda Fanning, had tweeted:

> The MC case is a media and politically hijacked case to smear SF under the cloak of caring.

A man tweeting from the account @bob_mcgrogan asked:

> Is @Máiríac31 really a stooge for MI5?

Others tweeted that I was a 'filthy lying scumbucket', a 'bunny boiler', 'white trash'; and one anonymous troll speculated that my rapist was my 'bit of rough' and that I liked what he did to me. I found comments like this wearying and depressing, and they did have an impact on me.

As the end of December approached, I met with Sir Keir Starmer and Katie O'Byrne for the first time, to agree terms of reference in their review into the Public Prosecution Service's handling of my court cases. I liked both of them. They appeared to be taking the issue seriously, and committed to have the review finished within six months.

50

The New Year came and went, and I was enjoying having more time with my daughter. I was also receiving messages like the following from @suzy661:

> You are disgusting #agenda.

Some republicans wrote:

> She's just an attention seeker mate cuz [sic] she hasn't been in the news for a while lol #shebores me.

A Twitter account called @MidlandCelt wrote:

> Get back in your box – Slapper.

Another wrote:

> Cahill has shown herself to be a manipulative woman. Seeking the limelight & using any story to further her career

and further:

> She's a parasite…

These types of tweet were fairly standard, and on any given day there were over fifty of them. One of the worst examples of how low people could stoop was an account set up with my head superimposed on a heavy naked woman in a string vest. There were no depths to which these people would not sink.

At about this time Adams flippantly referred to what followed my disclosures as a 'bout of reality TV'. Thus did the statesman-like president of Sinn Féin refer to a child sexual abuse case.

There were good moments too. At the end of February, the *Spotlight NI* documentary on my case won a Royal Television Society Award for Scoop of the Year, recognising the team's hard work. Jennifer told me they wished to make another documentary about the reaction to my case, and I agreed.

Also at the end of February, the Irish Labour Party asked me to accept their annual Thirst for Justice Award at their conference in Kilkenny. I was nervous about the conference, though I needn't have worried. I delivered a short speech, thanking the party for its support and detailing some of my shameful treatment online and by the Sinn Féin party. Afterwards, people in the conference hall stood and clapped, and I was swamped by well-wishers. We retired to the bar for a sing-song and let our hair down for a bit.

Within a few weeks, on 10 March 2015, my case was firmly back on the media's agenda, due to another BBC NI *Spotlight* documentary, 'Breaking the Silence', which was now not focusing on what had happened since I went public, but on a man named Paudie McGahon.

Paudie had decided to waive his anonymity in full after watching the Dáil debate on my case. Angry at my treatment, he had first spoken anonymously to Paul Williams of the *Irish Independent*, and then decided to go on television to describe what had been done to him. He had been abused as a young man by Belfast IRA man Seamus Marley, who was using Paudie's family home as a safe house.* Marley also abused another young victim. Neither

---

* A 'safe house' is a place provided by people to IRA members to stay in, to avoid arrest by the security services.

victim knew about each other until they discussed the issue years later. They told a Sinn Féin member, and this led to the IRA coming to Paudie's house and holding what he referred to as a 'kangaroo court' in 2002, in the bedroom in which Paudie had been raped.

The victims were offered three 'options' from the menu of IRA justice, of the kind with which the country was becoming very familiar. To have the offender shot, to be left in a room to beat him themselves, or to have him expelled from the country. They chose option number three as the least violent one. The story was shocking, and sent reverberations around Ireland. I felt terrible for both victims, and hoped that Sinn Féin would not treat either man as I had been treated once I went public. But before the programme had even ended, the then Sinn Féin MP Francie Molloy tweeted:

Another load of rubbish on spotlight tonight...

I was asked to go on RTÉ radio the morning after the programme aired. I lambasted Molloy for his tweet, calling it 'insensitive, crass and vile'. He later deleted it and issued a public apology. Gerry Adams appeared on *Morning Ireland* the following day. He was asked if he believed Paudie had been raped, and he confirmed that he did. He was then asked by reporter Gavin Jennings if he believed that Paudie McGahon had been subjected to an IRA court. His response, utterly predictably, was: 'I don't know', and then he said that there was a Garda investigation ongoing:

I first knew about this, somewhere between 2009 when the young man went and met with the then local TD, Arthur Morgan, and he had previously been dealing intermittently with Pearse McGeough. Arthur wrote to him, he advised him and I want to read his letter: 'I want to confirm my strong advice to you [...] to make a formal complaint to the Gardaí about these allegations. They are the competent authority to investigate these matters and, if a case can be constructed, to bring it before the courts. Such a complaint to the Gardaí would also trigger the involvement of social services as well as other services. [...] I wish to assure you again of my full support and that of my colleague councillor Pearse McGeough at all times, including accompanying you to the Gardaí if that would be helpful. Hoping you follow this course and that matters can be dealt with appropriately.' So, sometime around that time I was simply briefed, not on the detail but that there was a sex abuse allegation and that Arthur had dealt with it in that way.[169]

He was asked why he had not himself informed the Gardaí. Adams pointed out that the young man was an adult, and did not want to go to the Gardaí at that time. It was the playbook with which I had become familiar: say you believe the victim, deny it was covered up, blame them for not going to the cops.

This was a problem for Adams, however, because it was clear that this was the third sexual abuse case of which he had been aware yet did not report to police. He had known about his brother Liam since the mid-1980s, he had known about my case since the year 2000, and the public were now finding out that he had known about Seamus Marley since 2009. And he was still claiming that Sinn Féin had nothing to do with the IRA. The latter organisation sending offenders into exile, safe from prosecution, had nothing to do with him.

Alan Murray, a Northern Irish political and security journalist, went straight to the point when he spoke on Sean O'Rourke's RTÉ show on 11 March 2015, explaining:

Raymond McCartney [a Sinn Féin MLA] was making the point that Sinn Féin and the IRA were separate entities. Now, that does not stack up in terms of what was said at different Ard Fheises* [sic] through the 1980s and one remembers

---

* Ard Fheiseanna, the Sinn Féin annual party conferences.

Danny Morrison's comments about the Armalite in one hand and the ballot box in the other.*

He was correct, and in fact, Gerry Adams had previously said at the 1986 party conference: 'To leave Sinn Féin is to leave the IRA.' Indeed, the Independent Reporting Commission had confirmed that former IRA members believed that the IRA controlled Sinn Féin. One might add that the dogs in the street knew this in nationalist areas of Northern Ireland.

Fintan O'Toole wrote that week in the *Irish Times*:

> In recent Irish history, just two bodies have had the power to order a citizen into exile. No Government, no court of law, no official body, however powerful, could apply the sanction of banishment. But the Catholic church could. And so could the IRA [...]. Like all extreme powers, this one fed corruption. It was very useful indeed when either organisation needed to make an embarrassing problem go away.[170]

After the media quietened over the Paudie McGahon case, things quietened for me too. I wrote occasionally for the *Sunday Independent* and continued to highlight republican sex abuse. I also reached out across the political divide in Northern Ireland. I even attended the Shankill Road bonfire site at the request of the loyalist community, who were celebrating the Twelfth of July. It was unheard of for a nationalist to attend such events, but I was passionate about peace-building and decided that I needed to stretch myself and move outside my comfort zone. My piece on attending it was published in the *Belfast Telegraph*, where I wrote: 'When you are confident, you do not need to be triumphant, and

---

* At the Sinn Féin Ard Fheis in 1981, Danny Morrison said the following: 'Who here really believes we can win the war through the ballot box? But will anyone here object if, with a ballot paper in this hand and an Armalite in the other, we take power in Ireland?'

when you are made to feel comfortable, you do not need to feel inferior.'[171]

That piece, and another I did with the daughter of IRA murder victim Caroline Moreland, led to regular opinion pieces commissioned by former *Belfast Telegraph* editor Gail Walker and deputy editor Martin Hill. I enjoyed the work because I was asked to write about a range of subjects, aside from Sinn Féin. When I was younger, I had wanted to be a lawyer or a journalist. I was now fulfilling the latter ambition.

In May 2015, Sir Keir Starmer and Katie O'Byrne were ready to publish their report into my court cases. They met with me and my solicitors in the Public Prosecution Service's building while the press waited upstairs for him to deliver his verdict. I crumpled into tears as Keir told me that he had found I had been failed by the criminal justice system, and gave me a hug. I was relieved by the findings, which vindicated what I had been saying, and it was the best possible rebuttal to Sinn Féin's reliance on the fact that I hadn't given evidence in court.

Starmer and O'Byrne strongly criticised the Public Prosecution Service and described the cases as 'difficult, unusual and complicated'. They also crucially said that it was 'almost inevitable', given the failings of the prosecution, that the victims would 'pull out of the process'. I learned from the report that a defence request to change the order of the trials had not been opposed, which led to the membership case being put before the sexual abuse case. I met with Barra McGrory, the head of the PPS, shortly after I received the findings, and he handed me a written letter of apology. I wanted him to apologise publicly and told him so. Within thirty minutes, he stood in front of the media and said:

> One issue I'd like to make clear at the very outset is that no blame in relation to the collapse of these cases attaches to Máiría Cahill or the other two victims. In Sir Keir's words, the Public Prosecution Service let you down, and for that I wish to say sorry.

One part of the report that interested me was the following passage:

> The defence also raised an issue which appears never to have been raised before, namely that the membership trial should be heard before the sexual abuse trial. Leading Counsel later noted that a three-page written application was submitted, though this application did not appear on the prosecution file to which we were given access [...]. The defence argument appears to have been put on three bases: (1) That the defendant hoped to rely in the sexual abuse case on the evidence of the four 'investigators', but their evidence may incriminate them in the membership case[172]

The last few lines raised a question with me as to whether the IRA accused would have considered giving evidence in support of Morris. I couldn't believe that they would have, and asked the question publicly. It has never been answered.

The Starmer report contained recommendations for improvement in Northern Ireland's Public Prosecution Service, and I met with the director and assistant director on more than one occasion to ask if they had implemented these changes. I wanted to change the criminal justice system for the better for victims of sexual abuse coming after me, so that what happened to me could not happen to others. As a result of the review, a new department was established to deal with rape and murder cases. I later took part in the Sir John Gillen review into how the criminal justice system handles allegations of abuse, and he was responsive to the issues that I raised. His comprehensive report has already contributed to positive change for complainants in sexual abuse trials.

In August 2015, I was asked by Tim Attwood to speak at an event during the West Belfast Festival. The SDLP were sponsoring the annual Gerry Conlon memorial lecture and wanted me to speak about justice for abuse victims. I had met Conlon and had listened to him speak about his years in prison, after he was wrongfully convicted as one of the Guildford Four. I thought that it was important to return to the heart of the community I had been born into and tell a few home truths about Sinn Féin, the IRA and sexual abuse. Before the event, a solicitor's letter was delivered to the Festival, warning that if I said anything defamatory, they could be held liable. In response, I wrote a piece for the *Belfast Telegraph*, under the headline: 'I'll not be gagged, go ahead, sue me.'

The organisers, to their credit, allowed my speech to go ahead, and I introduced the lecture by telling the 150-strong audience that I wouldn't keep them too long, as I thought I had left my immersion heater on. The joke broke the ice. My friend Olive Buckley live-streamed the event, which I used to send direct messages to Sinn Féin suggesting that they should simply admit I had been telling the truth. The SDLP's Alex Attwood also spoke, and I left the event after receiving a standing ovation. No subsequent legal letter was ever received.

51

At the end of September 2015, I had a call from the Irish Labour Party's Deputy Leader, Alan Kelly. He was in Rome, meeting the Pope, and wondered if I would agree to the party nominating me for a Seanad (Senate) seat in the Dublin parliament. The Seanad is the Upper House of Parliament, and senators are responsible for scrutinising and revising legislation. I wasn't sure, but Alan was persuasive and, to a politics nerd, the offer was tempting. I asked for time to think about it. I had also been asked by Independent TD and journalist Shane Ross to run as an Independent candidate in the Irish General Election, and I wanted to weigh up my options.

Within a few weeks, I had agreed to Alan's offer to take up the seat vacated by Senator Jimmy Harte from Donegal, who had fallen ill during that year. I announced the Seanad run in October, and just after the announcement, a young driver accidentally crashed her car into mine, which was stationary outside my house, as I was halfway through a live radio interview. I shrugged my shoulders and wondered if it was a metaphor for things to come.

The news appeared on the front page of the *Sunday Independent* the next day, and Willie Kealy wrote: 'Joan Burton has nominated Máiría Cahill to contest the Seanad by-election following the resignation of Labour Senator Jimmy Harte. The Labour leader said yesterday she had picked the Belfast woman [...] because she was "incredibly taken with Máiría's bravery, honesty and dignity since first meeting her last year".[173]

In the *Belfast Telegraph*, the late Henry McDonald wrote, under the headline 'A Senate sniper to shoot barbs at Sinn Féin':

> Máiría Cahill has arguably more 'on the ground' knowledge about the workings of mainstream republicanism than most of the Seanad put together […]. Máiría Cahill grew up among some of the most prominent figures in the organisation and knows how Belfast still holds the centre of power in the party, contrary to [Pearse] Doherty, Mary Lou McDonald or any of the neo-Shinners who are useful in detoxifying the party's brand among Middle Ireland.[174]

The campaign itself exploded when the public was reminded of my previous links with RNU. I couldn't understand the furore, as the issue had already been discussed in public and I had given interviews addressing it, but it took me some time to realise that running for political office was different from campaigning as a victim. I found myself hamstrung by legalities. A republican online campaign that Joan Burton described as 'demonic' was flinging around libel like confetti, and my solicitor had advised me not to comment, in case I wanted to take action. Labour were reluctant to give the attacks any credence.

I had medical issues too; my folate levels had depleted, meaning that I was feeling more exhausted than I had ever felt before – which was saying something – and my beloved grandmother was in hospital. Labour were strongly of the opinion that I shouldn't give my opponents the oxygen of publicity. I was, instead, to concentrate on canvassing those with a vote, which in a senate election means parliamentarians. Faced with an abusive online campaign, I agreed, only speaking to RTÉ's Philip Boucher-Hayes on the day of the vote. In that interview, I apologised again for my previous involvement with RNU and tried to set it in the context of my life, which was chaotic and traumatic at the time.

I reported some of the online attacks to the police – attacks that included a convicted fraudster faking letters purporting to be from me to IRA prisoners, and Sinn Féin members posting pictures of a woman standing in military gear in 1981, the year I was born, which they claimed to be me. The campaign attracted online crackpots of all sorts, and for that reason, I dug my heels in and refused to respond. One relative advised me against this, arguing that I was damaging my own reputation by not just tackling all the nonsensical accusations head-on when they first surfaced. I could see her point, but this was easier said than done and I was in the eye of a storm; I just wanted to pull the duvet over my head and make the whole thing go away. It was so intense that several politicians, concerned about my safety, offered me a place to stay until things calmed down.

I was elected with what, according to my director of elections Joe Costello, was the highest vote in a by-election in the history of the state.* Unfortunately, my time in the Seanad was short-lived. Enda Kenny called a general election, and Labour's vote was significantly reduced. The more general election votes a party gets, the more senate seats it is able to occupy, and I stood aside to allow Aodhán Ó Ríordáin a clear run for the Industrial and Commercial panel. I may have only been there six months, but I loved the experience and was looked after well by my PA Aideen Blackwood, who at times went with me to and from the Seanad chamber to calm my nerves about walking through packed corridors. She also worked hard on pulling up legislation that I could speak on. She was excellent at detail, and hard-working.

During my time in the Seanad I raised issues of domestic and sexual abuse, worked on legislation and threw myself into the general election, canvassing for my colleagues. I commuted from Belfast daily, trying to get home to see Saorlaith either before she went to bed or as she got up in the morning, and my mother was a great help with minding her. I stayed in Dublin on Wednesday

---

* Seanad by election votes are restricted to Oireachtas members. I received 122 of 188 valid votes. My nearest rival, the Fianna Fáil candidate, received 38.

nights for Labour parliamentary party meetings, and enjoyed socialising afterwards with Joan Burton's daughter, Aoife, or former special adviser, Claire Power, and staff members, Mags and Seaneen – something I was unable to do at home because of the risk to my safety. All of them ensured that I was comfortable, and looked after me well.

One regret I have was a miscommunication that left me grounded in Ireland when I should have been at the White House. We had asked Enda Kenny's office if Aideen and I could go and see President Barack Obama for the St Patrick's Day celebrations. We provided our details and then waited for confirmation. Enda's office thought we knew we had clearance and so didn't confirm with us. As the days passed, we simply thought we hadn't made the cut and commiserated with each other. We were left feeling green when an email arrived from Kenny's private secretary Nick Reddy, telling us to be at the White House's Pennsylvania Avenue later that day. We were stuck in Dublin, and all the flights out were full.

It was probably just as well. The same evening, Gerry Adams was refused entry into the White House and left after waiting for an hour, while officials were trying to resolve the matter. In his usual petulant manner, he deemed this 'unacceptable' in a press statement, before bizarrely and offensively telling an administration with the first black president at its helm that Sinn Féin would not 'sit at the back of the bus for anyone'.

Joan Burton, the Tánaiste, looked after me like a mother hen in the Oireachtas. In my time as a senator, I largely stayed within the gates of parliament. Joan ditched her Garda detail one day and took me on a trip down Grafton Street. There are few countries in the world, I thought, where the deputy prime minister can casually browse the shops and be left alone to buy underwear in Dunnes Stores. I was grateful to my political colleagues, not just within Labour, but in other parties also. Fine Gael's Regina Doherty became a firm friend, Labour's Marie Moloney and John Gilroy kept me in good humour, and people like Timmy Dooley and Diarmuid Wilson of Fianna Fail and Bernard Durkan and

Martin Conway of Fine Gael would sit with me over coffee in the Members' Bar. One Fine Gael senator, the late Terry Brennan, was jovial and paternal, and the chair of the Seanad Paddy Burke gave me lots of leeway to speak, as did the Leader of the House, Maurice Cummins. David Norris, a well-known literary critic and gay-rights activist who had originally criticised my election to the Seanad, later signed a copy of his book to me, calling me a 'vital voice in Seanad Eireann'.

In the middle of the election, I found myself trending on Twitter again, due to a gaffe of Gerry Adams's during the party leaders' debate. Enda Kenny was in full flow attacking Sinn Féin and said: 'Gerry here defends Mr Murphy* but he won't defend Senator Cahill.'

Adams, smiling, turned to him and inexplicably asked: 'Who's Senator Cahill, who's Senator Cahill?'

Kenny, stony-faced, replied to him as if he was a child: 'Máiría Cahill.'

Adams realised his error, saying sheepishly: 'Oh, sorry, sorry.' But the damage was done as political correspondents live-tweeted the event.

I was watching the debate with Labour activists in the party's HQ, where reaction rippled around the room. People could not believe what they were hearing. I just rolled my eyes and tweeted out: 'What a dick', and further that this was 'selective memory syndrome'. My comments annoyed Sinn Féin activists, who complained about my use of 'unparliamentary language', and Danny Morrison tweeted:

> Nice language coming from a Senator. That will have opened a few eyes.

---

* 'Mr Murphy' refers to Tom 'Slab' Murphy, a notorious South Armagh IRA man whom Adams had called 'a good republican' in a press statement in December 2015 after Murphy was convicted for tax evasion, while also stating that 'everyone has a duty to pay taxes for which they are liable'.

I laughed, given the irony of Morrison, a former director of publicity for Sinn Féin who coined the 'ballot box and Armalite' catchphrase, clutching his pearls about a salty bit of slang. I found a video of Mary Lou McDonald in the Dáil muttering under her breath 'what a dick' at an opposing politician, and tweeted it out. Strangely, there was no criticism from any republican for her use of the same language in the actual parliament.

Kenny was asked about the election campaign later on voting day, and cited the incident as his favourite moment of the campaign. It is still mine, to this day.

52

Over the next year, I concentrated on trying to keep my head on an even keel. I worked with victims of abuse who came to me privately for help. I spoke about abuse in the public domain and tried to break down the stigma for others so they would feel more comfortable not only in getting help, but also reporting it to the authorities. I also talked about my case, because every time I drew attention to it, another abuse victim would inevitably find the courage to reach out. I was surprised by the number of male victims of abuse.

In March 2017, Martin McGuinness died. In the wake of his passing, many tributes were paid to him as a peacemaker, notably from former President Bill Clinton. His funeral was a grand state affair, and a forlorn-looking Mary Lou McDonald and Michelle O'Neill stood beside Gerry Adams, in images that looked incongruous, seeming like two lost schoolchildren being rounded up by an elderly grandfather figure. As they stood on a platform in front of the crowds on a bitterly cold day in Derry, I was asked to write a piece for the *Belfast Telegraph* on McGuinness's legacy. I described the contradiction in people's views of him and mentioned the 'families of people such as Joanne Mathers, Frank Hegarty, the Enniskillen bombing victims,* and the thousands of others who

---

* Joanne Mathers was a young mother shot by the IRA in Derry as she collected census forms; Frank Hegarty was an alleged IRA informer lured home to Derry personally by McGuinness in 1986 and then murdered; eleven people were killed in the Enniskillen bombing on Remembrance Sunday, when McGuinness was Northern commander of the IRA. Another man, Ronnie Hill, died thirteen years later, having been in a coma since the bomb.

have had their hearts ripped out of them and their minds fractured at the hands of an organisation which McGuinness led in times of war and in peace.' I also wrote about a tarring-and-feathering incident in 1971, when republican women had tied another woman to a lamp post and shaved her hair, then poured lead on her body. Her 'crime' was seeing a soldier. The women only agreed to release her after McGuinness 'arrived and gave his permission'.[175] Martin McGuinness was always the dominant IRA figure in Derry. This was a man who had held, with his comrades, the arbitrary power of life and death over his community for decades.

In 2020, Derry republicans decided to hold a poetry competition in Martin McGuinness's memory. I decided to enter it just to make a point, in full knowledge that they couldn't possibly let my entry win. Malachi O'Doherty had the same idea, separately. I emailed my entry and a polite Paul Kavanagh, an ex-IRA prisoner, emailed me back to ask if I wanted my poem included in the under- or over-eighteen category, which made me smile. This was my unsuccessful poem, 'The Fisherman':

> *They say one man's terrorist is another man's freedom fighter.*
> *Maybe that's true, though I don't remember much freedom in the initial days.*
> *Barricaded in, watching yer man swanning about with his M60 glinting.*
> *Him, his gun, and a gaggle of curious kids poking their noses into what shouldn't have been their business.*
> *Washing on the line fluttered, marking the territory of the housewife, while a few yards away he loaded the boot with a bomb and smiled for the camera.*
> *This was his area, his and the housewives.*
>
> *His life a juxtaposition. Loved and loathed in equal measure.*
> *Breaking bread for a sup of soup in one house, drawing blood in another.*
> *Courting and killing, managed like old contemporaries.*

*You'd wonder how someone could swing off the altar rails one
    minute, and kneel and tell a woman wrapping her rosary
    beads round her wrinkled hands the next –*
That her son was safe to come home.
Rose's boy, coaxed on a wing and a prayer;
*Found cocooned in a sheet with a bullet through his brain not
    long after.*
Whatever you say, say nothing.

*For decades the fisherman cast his fly and reeled in the young
    men, the madmen – and caught and dumped the dead
    men. Later, the churchmen and the statesmen tripped over
    themselves to deliver*
A eulogy fit for a peacemaker,
but not for a life-taker.

Some buried their Chieftain, others their villain.
All is not fair in love and war...
Another woman couldn't bury a body
When all that was left of her husband was a zip.
*You asked for poetry to remember his legacy. What rhymes
    with Patsy Gillespie?**

---

* 'Rose' in the poem is the mother of Frank Hegarty; Patsy Gillespie was a Derry man chained into his van with a thousand-pound bomb and forced to drive it into a fortified British checkpoint outside the city in October 1990. He was considered a 'legitimate target' because he worked as a cook on a British Army base.

53

In May 2017, I was diagnosed with Asperger's with sensory processing issues, which was a relief to me, as I finally had an explanation as to why I had found things like walking up the bustling corridors in the Irish parliament difficult, and why they had caused me so much anxiety. The diagnosis, however, also firmly focused my mind on one detail of the IRA 'investigation' into my abuse, and made it all the more horrific. How much more frightening, to an awkward teenager whose brain read human cues differently, was an IRA figure saying that he or she would read body language to see who was telling the truth?

In August 2017, Sinn Féin insider Matt Treacy broke ranks to say that at a party meeting in Leinster House words like 'witch' and 'slut' had been used about me. It wasn't surprising, but it was unusual for someone to state it on the record. He stated he left Sinn Féin shortly after the meeting. The Sinn Féin press office reaction claimed, 'These allegations are completely unfounded.'[176] In 2018, it was reported in the media that a WhatsApp group set up for members and supporters of Sinn Féin in Ballymun and Finglas to interact with each other contained a conversation from February 2017 in which a participant, speculating on another general election being called, opined that the media would be

> on the phone to Cahill [...] et al and every other waster they can wheel out with a sob story.

When contacted by journalists, Sinn Féin stated 'these comments are completely unacceptable' and that they were 'currently trying to establish the facts of the matter'. I emailed them, asking for the outcome. I received no response.

I was also provided with internal party documents by another ex-Sinn Féin activist, showing that the party had attempted to brief what their members would say about my case. These have never been published, until now.

One email, on 23 October 2014, which came from the Sinn Féin email account of Cork press officer Ruairí Doyle, told councillors:

> The party's regional organiser DJ O'Driscoll has asked me to send on the attached briefing to each of you. THIS IS AN INTERNAL PARTY BRIEFING NOTE – AND IS FOR YOUR INFORMATION ONLY. As you may be aware, The Sunday Independent is ringing some Sinn Féin Councillors on private numbers enquiring about the Máiría Cahill case. It is probably best not to engage with the Sunday Independent, if at all possible. Of course councillors need to be in contact with their local press regarding local issues and in particular the Right2Water Protest. Attached is a briefing note on the key points of Gerry's apology. It should cover any questions you are asked on local media around local issues, but any interaction with media regarding the Máiría Cahill case is best kept at a minimum.

The briefing note is a mirror image of the lines that numerous Sinn Féin representatives trotted out on my case. Interestingly, it does not deny that an IRA 'investigation' took place. One of the briefing questions asks: 'Do you believe there was an IRA investigation?' The response people are advised to make is: 'Four people were charged and acquitted in connection with the allegation of an IRA investigation. If the IRA did investigate this it was clearly wrong.' Another question reads: 'Did the IRA force a confrontation between Máiría and her alleged abuser?' The answer suggested for Sinn Féin members is: 'I have heard that allegation and if it were true it would clearly be inappropriate and wrong.' Another hypothetical question in the briefing note is this: 'Do you believe Máiría Cahill?' The answer suggested in the Sinn Féin memo reads: 'I do not know/knew Máiría but all those within Sinn Féin who have dealt with Máiría believe that she is a victim of abuse. The same people have also refuted her claims of a Sinn Féin cover up and how she has characterised there [sic] role with her.'

So much for freedom of thought.

I emailed Ruairí Doyle in 2018, asking him if he had any comment to make, 'given some of your public reps denied on air that they were instructed centrally from the press office on how to answer questions on my case'. He did not respond.

Another internal Sinn Féin briefing note about the Paudie McGahon abuse case was sent out from the email account of the then Southern Sinn Féin political manager Conor Foley, which read in part: 'These are to be used only by public representatives should you be requested for media interviews about it, and are not for wider circulation.' They were also asked to go through the regional PRO 'if any journalist contacts you about this issue'. This briefing note contained a statement sent to media from the former Louth TD Arthur Morgan, whom Gerry Adams replaced, and included the lines: 'I first met with Mr McGahon in late 2008 when he came into my office when I was the TD for Louth. At the time I advised him to go directly to the Gardaí and offered to arrange a meeting there and then.' He had also copied a letter he had sent to Paudie McGahon after the meeting. That particular briefing note did not acknowledge that other Sinn Féin representatives had been aware of Paudie's case since 2002.

The existence of these briefing notes, like the Bobby Storey memo on my case, shows a party very much trying to keep the narrative tight in the media, and to ensure that their representatives stayed on message. Every political party has briefing lines – though not every party has to put on paper a line in case their political party reps are asked if they believe a victim of child abuse. Sinn Féin is not a party known for internal dissent, to put it mildly. In draft Ard Chomhairle minutes from 2000, there is an almost comical section which reveals the influence Gerry Adams had amongst party activists (and he is still revered by them). The Sinn Féin leadership was discussing the format for their forthcoming Ard Fheis, and the section reads:

Lucy (Lucilita Bhreatnach): Party Chair opens Ard Fheis traditionally. Suggest 26-County priority candidate this year.

Micheál MacDonncha: Suggest Martin Ferris.

Alex Maskey: Suggest Seán MacManus.

Daithí Doolan: Suggest Sean Crowe, Dubliner and Euro election candidate.

Anne Speed: Suggest Michelle Gildernew. Young woman leader. Give her the opportunity.

Fra McCann: Suggest Barry McElduff, given Tyrone by-election.

Lucy: Suggest sending it back to Ard Rúnaí and Ard Fheis Committee.

Gerry Adams: We should keep the traditional form and have the National Chair open it.

Agreed.

54

In February 2018, Mary Lou McDonald became president of Sinn Féin, elected unopposed by party activists. Looking like a nationalist Margaret Thatcher in a structured green jacket, she ended her speech to the party's Ard Fheis with a shout of 'Up the rebels', to rapturous applause.

My own political career was reviving, and five months later, in July 2018, the SDLP announced that I would be joining the party and taking up a co-opted council seat on Lisburn Council. I had missed my time in the Seanad. I enjoyed talking to constituents and trying to help them with their problems, and had forged good relationships with the other parties across the political spectrum. I was particularly touched by a welcome message from the Alliance group leader on council, Stephen Martin, who handed me a congratulations card on my first night in the chamber.

Four months after I entered the council, and four years after I had fully waived anonymity, the Police Ombudsman's office indicated to me that their investigation examining police actions had been finalised, and asked me to come to their office to read their findings. I went there with my solicitors Joe Rice and Shauna Benson. I was shown into a room and given a copy of the document, referred to as a 'closure letter', and left to read it before meeting the then-Ombudsman Michael Maguire. It was 65 pages long, so we all agreed to take a section each to skim. I had started reading the line 'The findings articulated in this letter support the conclusion that you were failed by police as a victim of serious crime in a number of key areas during the police investigations...' but relief turned to disgust when Joe Rice exclaimed loudly and put a paragraph in front of me, which read:

> Of further concern is that you and other victims were failed by police in 2000. Between the summer of 2000 and 2001 the Royal Ulster Constabulary received information that Martin Morris was suspected of abusing certain children. The intelligence, which was obtained separately by both the Criminal Investigation Department (CID) and subsequently Special Branch, was sufficiently specific that had police undertaken even cursory enquiries, you would have been identified as a potential victim of this abuse. The Police Ombudsman's investigation found no evidence of any such enquiries by police, even when the intelligence indicated that the IRA were conducting their own investigation. In respect of the information received by Special Branch, the Police Ombudsman's investigation found no evidence that it was disseminated outside that department.[177]

The obvious conclusion was that had the police acted at the time, it would have saved me an awful lot of pain. But I had also spent the previous four years being bounced around by Sinn Féin, who stubbornly refused to acknowledge that an IRA investigation ever took place. All of this time, the police had evidence that there was such an internal inquiry – and nobody put it into the public domain to support my account. I was very angry, in fact so upset that I threw up in the toilet.

Another section of the closure letter read:

> RUC CID received information in 2000 that suggested Mr Morris was suspended from Sinn Féin as it was suspected that he was abusing certain children. This information was placed on police systems and shared with specific police officers within the CARE unit, CID and Special Branch. Upon request

by the Police Ombudsman, police confirmed they could find no electronic record of any actions having been taken by the police officers with whom this information was shared.[178]

And further: 'The Police Ombudsman has confirmed that RUC Special Branch also began to receive reports from 2000 alleging Mr Morris was involved in the sexual abuse of children and that the IRA were investigating the matter. This reporting continued for a number of months.'[179]

Social Services was also aware of the abuse in the year 2000, and the Ombudsman's letter noted:

> The Police Ombudsman became aware that in September 2000 the North and West Belfast Health and Social Services Trust recorded an initial referral and assessment following anonymous concerns and a newspaper article suggesting that two young children may have been sexually abused [...]. At the end of November 2000 the North and West Belfast Health and Social Services Trust Child Protection Team closed the case [...]. The Child Protection Team were in contact with a Grosvenor Road CARE Unit Detective Constable and a Detective Sergeant and kept them updated throughout the engagement. This investigation has not identified evidence of corresponding police enquiries.[180]

The Ombudsman's letter was hard to take in, and at first glance it certainly appeared that I and others had been the victims of a series of failures across a range of agencies. In relation to the treatment of Sinn Féin witnesses, the Ombudsman wrote that a number of witnesses had given statements through their solicitor:

> The PPU Detective Constable attended a solicitor's office and stated that he made it clear they were being approached as witnesses and not suspects. There was a group meeting, including their solicitor, where the PPU Detective Constable explained to the witnesses that he wanted them to provide

accounts of what they recalled. The PPU Detective Constable described the meeting as difficult and confrontational.[181]

In another section regarding Gerry Adams, the letter read:

> The PPU Detective Constable noted that on 15 August 2010 Mr Adams' solicitor informed police that a draft statement was almost ready and he would arrange a meeting to have it signed. On 10 December 2010 Mr Adams signed a witness statement in the presence of his solicitor. This statement was included in the IRA membership investigation file. At interview the MIT Detective Chief Inspector stated that none of the Sinn Féin members were going to cooperate with police and that he never expected them to provide statements confirming that the IRA had conducted an investigation. Mr Adams' solicitor informed police that the statement was all Mr Adams would provide to police…there is no evidence that police ever considered Mr Adams as a suspect and the PPS did not regard Mr Adams as a suspect….The Police Ombudsman has concluded that to treat these individuals as witnesses was a necessary and pragmatic approach by police, as to declare them suspects would have had been of no evidential value for the prosecution.[182]

There were other police failings, and these mostly related to the court process in relation to my sexual abuse cases and the IRA membership cases. Four police officers were recommended for discipline, and one retired before any sanction could be placed on him. I met the Ombudsman, Dr Michael Maguire, who gave me the option of releasing the press release on his office's findings the following day, or delaying it for a few weeks as he was going on holiday. I wanted it out as soon as possible; I was aware that a presidential election was imminent in the Irish republic and did not want to be accused by Sinn Féin of trying to deflect from it, or influence the outcome. We agreed that a statement would be drawn up and placed under embargo for two days. The

Ombudsman agreed to allow me to use his offices to meet with the media, as the closure letter was now mine, and the decision was mine as to how much information would be disclosed to the public, given the sensitive nature of the contents.

I went home and telephoned two journalists – Jennifer O'Leary and Gail Walker. I agreed to have dinner with Jennifer that evening in a restaurant on the Lisburn Road in Belfast. I met her in my car before heading into the restaurant, and showed her the document. She held me while I cried tears of frustration. When I spoke to Gail, she expressed her sympathy and we briefly discussed the Ombudsman's findings. She asked if I wanted to write for the *Belfast Telegraph* about it, and I agreed to give her something for publication in two days' time. We both laughed as she asked how I was, and I explained that as ever I was trying to pull clothes out of the washing machine to see if I had anything to wear that I could dry in time for the following day's round of media interviews.

The press, predictably, were all over the story once the embargo was lifted. Various journalists tried to get a response from Sinn Féin; their press office was silent. My *Belfast Telegraph* column allowed me to put pressure on the party. I again accused them of a cover-up of abuse, and explained why.

> At no point in the last four years since I went public did Sinn Féin admit that my abuser, as well as being an IRA man, was also a Sinn Féin party member [...]. Nowhere did it state that senior Sinn Féin members were aware from 1997 and 1998 that I was being abused by this man, but they didn't 'suspend' him from the party until 2000. Think about that for a second. Sinn Féin repeatedly stated that it had never been involved in a cover-up of abuse. Not only did they not tell the public that they allowed a child sex abuser to remain in the party for three years after becoming aware – but they didn't even admit that he was a member of their party. If that isn't cover-up, then [...][183]

Sinn Féin remained quiet while the media reported the story of police failings. I had called for a meeting with Chief Constable George Hamilton, and received a text from his deputy, Tim Mairs, to ask me to arrange a time to see him. I picked that afternoon, wanting to get the meeting done as soon as possible. I wanted an explanation as to how I was only hearing about the police intelligence now, and to ensure that there would be no repeat for other victims. I also wanted a public and comprehensive apology.

The meeting was scheduled for the PSNI's Knock Headquarters for 3.30 p.m. and I arrived to find the press waiting for me. I said that I would speak to them after the meeting and went through the security gate, where two senior police officers, Paula Hillman and Tim Mairs, were waiting to walk me to the main building to meet the Chief Constable. George Hamilton was direct, and told me that he was 'scundered' (a Belfast word for embarrassed) by the findings. He explained how the intelligence had been found 'by chance' and disclosed to the PPS as soon as police had found it, during my court cases. I was clear that I wanted to be sure that nothing like this would ever happen again to anyone else. I also wanted to meet police again to advise them of changes they could make in their treatment of sexual and domestic abuse cases. The meeting took around ninety minutes, and Hamilton agreed to my requests. As I left to speak to the media, the rain started and Paula Hillman lent me her umbrella.

I told the press that Hamilton appeared to be taking responsibility for his organisation, and that I now needed Sinn Féin to do the same. I outlined what exactly I needed to hear from the party:

> There are three aspects to it. One: Simply, Máiría Cahill was telling the truth. Two: There was an IRA investigation into this abuse. And Three: We covered up the fact that we had a party member who was an abuser for three years, and we continued to cover up in 2014 when Máiría Cahill went public.

The party has, to this day, never admitted any of the three things I asked of them.

After the meeting, Sinn Féin finally issued a statement in Mary Lou McDonald's name, which read:

> I welcome the publication of the Ombudsman's report and the fact the PSNI have accepted and will implement the recommendations of that report [...]. I have no doubt that the three women at the heart of this report have been through an ordeal. I want to commend their bravery, in particular the bravery of Máiría Cahill for waiving her anonymity. Sinn Féin has robust procedures in place for mandatory reporting of abuse. I deeply regret that these procedures were not in place at the time of Máiría Cahill's disclosure. For this I unreservedly apologise. I wish Máiría Cahill every best wish for the future.

While I recognised the party had gone further than it had ever done before, McDonald's statement failed to apologise for her party's treatment of me since I had waived anonymity, or indeed, to admit that I had been telling the truth. As I said in response, 'I think Mary-Lou's statement was cowardly and woeful, and that is me being kind to Mary Lou.'

George Hamilton's statement was reflective of what he had indicated to me he would be saying to the media:

> I was struck by Máiría's courage and resilience. I was also struck by the fact that she shouldn't have had to display that much resilience, had Máiría and the other victims been better supported by the Police Service and by the wider criminal justice system.
>
> We have all failed them and for that I once more apologise. The responsibility for the failing of these cases rests with the Criminal Justice system and not with Máiría or any other victim.
>
> I fully accept the Ombudsman Report and we discussed how the organisation, and the criminal justice system, today

is very different as a result of Máiría's courage and strength in speaking out. We discussed how the Ombudsman noted that the previous intelligence failures would not occur today.

He also noted that we'd discussed the need for improvements in the PPS and PSNI, with investigators and prosecutors working more closely together to better support victims, and that we'd agreed to keep talking about the necessary reforms. I couldn't help thinking that now that I had received an apology from the Director of Public Prosecutions and the Chief Constable, that Sinn Féin would have to go further in their half-apology. I urged Mary Lou McDonald to at last do the right thing: 'She needs to finally put abuse victims before her party's interests and step up to the plate.'

I spent that weekend filming another *Spotlight NI* documentary, which was broadcast on 18 September 2018. The programme, entitled 'The Ombudsman's report', was a thirty-minute walk-through of what had happened to me since I'd been raped, including the court cases and how Sinn Féin behaved after I went public. In the documentary, Jennifer O'Leary laid out the issue very carefully: 'As part of the original *Spotlight* investigation in 2014, we specifically asked Sinn Féin was Martin Morris a member of the party between 1998 and 2000. The party responded by way of a statement to a series of questions but we did not receive an answer to that question.' I explained that the line about him being suspended from Sinn Féin was one line in a sixty-five-page letter but that:

> [it was] a very important line. One, it provides independent information that this man was connected with Sinn Féin never mind the IRA, and two, that when I went public in 2014, Sinn Féin screamed from the rooftops 'we have not been involved in a cover up of abuse. [...]. They weren't completely open with the Irish public, they allowed a child abuser, or a suspected child abuser to remain within [the party]. Sinn Féin came out fighting on the issue and they withheld information from the general public.[184]

Sinn Féin had never disclosed that Morris was a member, or told anyone that the party only suspended him *three years* after I had revealed in 1997 that I'd been abused by him. There had also been by that time two IRA 'investigations' into the abuse. The constitution of the party at that time required that a member be suspended without prejudice the minute a member became aware of sexual abuse allegations, and it should have been reported to the party's Ard Chomhairle.

The *Spotlight NI* team had again sent Sinn Féin a list of questions to answer. The same day, Mary Lou McDonald held a press conference outside Leinster House. She was at her most blustering and robust. She said:

> The issue around Martin Morris, I have asked, and I am advised, there is no evidence or no record of him being a member of Sinn Féin. He was of course a former prisoner, he was a person who was very active on the ground, so I can't discount that he may have been a member, our record keeping was not as it is now twenty years ago, and there is no record of any suspension of him.

She was flanked by Pearse Doherty, who stood looking like a serious nodding dog. She continued: 'As regards your other question around intelligence and intelligence source, of course I'm not in a position to answer that. I'm not a spook, I'm not a spy, I'm not a police officer, I'm the leader of a political party.'

I told *Spotlight NI* that her remarks were 'cynically timed' ahead of the programme. I was asked by Jennifer O'Leary whether I had a vendetta against Sinn Féin. I answered: 'No – that's victim blaming, Jennifer. The assertion that I am somehow not supposed to criticise the Sinn Féin party who did nothing with a child abuser for three years, just in case someone accuses you of having a political agenda, is absolutely disgusting.'

The programme closed with O'Leary telling the public that on the night of broadcast, Sinn Féin issued a statement to *Spotlight NI*: 'Unusually, it was issued through a solicitor. It completely refuted any allegation of a cover-up and said it would take all steps necessary to protect the party's reputation in the event of it being attacked.' They were still doing what they do best, circling the wagons and obfuscating as hard as possible.

After the programme aired, I rejected Sinn Féin's claims that the party had no records of Morris's membership. I pointed out that unfortunately for the party, records obviously exist within RUC Special Branch intelligence. I also stated that on the wider issue of truth recovery, which Sinn Féin claimed to be so concerned about, nobody could have any confidence in participating with them in any sort of mechanism to address the past, in the light of Sinn Féin's response to the Police Ombudsman's findings.

Micheál Martin, the leader of Fianna Fáil, addressed the issue of Sinn Féin's assertion that it couldn't find records. He said that it was simply 'not credible' for Ms McDonald to claim she could not establish whether the man alleged to have abused me was a member of Sinn Féin. I agreed with Micheál, particularly because, despite McDonald's assertion that the party's record keeping in 2000 was not as good it is today, Sinn Féin was able to find detailed records of Liam Adams's membership of the party in west Belfast in 2000. But the party repeatedly refused to answer further questions about its membership records. Morris had been erased from its history.

Three days later, a row broke out when BBC journalist Mark Devenport repeatedly asked Sinn Féin's Northern Ireland leader Michelle O'Neill whether she believed the IRA had investigated my abuse. 'It's not for me to say whether I believe her,' she replied, before becoming tongue-tied and eventually saying she believed I had been a victim of abuse. Colum Eastwood tweeted again, in response:

I believe Máiría Cahill. I always have.

The Ombudsman findings and the stress of dealing with the situation had taken a lot out of me, and I woke up within days of its release unable to feel the left side of my face, lips or tongue. I was also slurring my words, and when a journalist phoned, I had to explain that I was not drunk, but I clearly wasn't well. I went to Accident and Emergency, where, after checking on a CT that I hadn't had a stroke, they referred me to neurology. I was eventually diagnosed with Ramsay Hunt syndrome, and it took around eight months for the feeling in my face to come back. I have lasting nerve damage as a result.

55

Meanwhile an Irish presidential election was under way, and Sinn Féin's candidate Liadh Ní Riada was facing questions about me. 'She was failed by Sinn Féin,' she told RTÉ radio, 'because there was no mandatory reporting at the time.' Asked whether her apology was qualified, she said: 'It's about making sure the proper procedures are in place, that such an event will never happen again and it's about trying to find some kind of reconciliation for Máiría Cahill and some sort of justice.'[185]

I thought it was unfair that Ní Riada had been put in a position by her party where she was answering for them in my case, and personally thought that McDonald, as the Sinn Féin president, should be answering the questions. Sinn Féin, as part of their campaign, were taking their battle bus to Derry in October to hold a rally for the commemoration of the Civil Rights campaign. I had been asked to speak at an event with Mark Durkan of the SDLP the same weekend, and I decided to go to the Sinn Féin rally in silent protest.

Just before the rally was due to take place, I positioned myself to the right of the stage. McDonald was to be the main speaker. The press noticed me and began to take pictures. A Sinn Féin security man in a yellow bib was visibly shocked when he realised who I was and began frantically shouting into his radio for security people to come to where I was standing. As the march progressed down Bishop Street and the Sinn Féin MEP Martina

Anderson began to sing 'We Shall Overcome' like a strangled cat through the microphone, some burly heavies ran down the street and stood directly in front of me. Malachi O'Doherty and a few other journalists were standing beside me and all I could do was look at him and laugh. I stood politely while McDonald gave her speech and then left to go and speak at my own event, my point made.

I told the media that if Mary Lou McDonald was still denying Sinn Féin was involved in a cover-up of abuse, she should meet with me and say so to my face. To my surprise, I received an email from her, asking me to meet her at Leinster House. I had been invited to attend a group photograph the next week for all past and present female parliamentarians, and agreed to a meeting on the same day. I wasn't sure I was ready to face her without letting my anger spill over, but saw no harm in seeing the 'whites of her eyes'.

I travelled down early for the photo and made my way into the Dáil chamber. Everyone was in great form, until I noticed a commotion from the corner of my eye. Mary Lou McDonald had arrived to find former minister Mary Hanafin sitting in her seat. She was not happy, and Hanafin told others Mary Lou had said to her: 'Who gave you permission to sit there?' Miriam Lord described what happened next in the *Irish Times*:

> Seating was allocated in the front row for serving and former cabinet Ministers [...] Hanafin pointed out that she had been directed to her seat by the ushers...Mary Lou replied she didn't really care where anyone else was sitting but this was her seat and she wouldn't be sitting for any photograph until she got it back.[186]

Mary Hanafin also told Miriam Lord: 'I did the gracious thing and moved when the usher asked me. I didn't want to make a scene or make the situation any more difficult for the staff.'[187]

The day was not going well for McDonald, and she was the talk of the Irish parliament as the women moved into the members' dining area for lunch. I was scheduled to do an interview with RTÉ's Aine Lawlor, and used Joan Burton's office, which was quiet, to tell RTÉ I had no great expectations or hopes of my meeting with McDonald. But I was nervous. I was too wound up to eat anything ahead of the meeting that evening and spent the rest of the day catching up with other parliamentarians, including Frances Fitzgerald, and taking calls from journalists.

Aideen Blackwood, who had worked with me in the Seanad, offered to come with me to the meeting and take minutes, and I accepted her offer gratefully. We arrived around ten minutes early in the Leinster House 2000 building, a smart, modern annex off the main parliament building. The room had soft furnishings and low lighting, and I was happy enough with it, until someone came to tell us that Sinn Féin had changed the room at the last minute, and we were to move downstairs to another, smaller room. We got there, and I extended my hand to the young man Mary Lou McDonald had brought with her. He sat in silence, not meeting my eyes, as I tried to engage in conversation about mundane things like the weather. He was clearly uncomfortable, and if my talking to him was making him more so, then I was going to keep talking. McDonald arrived shortly afterwards and extended her hand to me. I shook it, and she sat down.*

So far, so cordial. But it was about to turn politely sour, and did so fairly quickly. She opened the meeting by telling me she was there to listen. I said to her: 'Well, I'm here to listen too, so it looks like both of us are going to be doing a lot of listening.'

She apologised as leader of Sinn Féin that the party members I disclosed to in the late 1990s had not reported my abuse to the police. I then asked her if she accepted that there was an IRA investigation into my abuse. She replied that she could only deal with things that as the leader of Sinn Féin she was responsible for. I told her: 'I think in that case, there is not much point in me continuing with this meeting, because I think it will be a waste

---

* The following account is taken from Aideen Blackwood's notes made at the time of our meeting and my own notes made immediately afterwards.

of my time,' and got up to go. She asked me to stay a minute, and extended her arms in a conciliatory gesture. I agreed to give her more than a minute, aware that if I walked out, it would look terrible for her, but I also wanted to challenge her.

She said she hadn't seen the Ombudsman report, and I pointed out that she had accepted it a few weeks previously, when she issued her apology after its release. I said to her: 'The evidence is there, and I am not accepting that from you, and I mean no disrespect by saying that. You are saying you don't have access to the facts, but you were content in 2014 to say I was slurring Sinn Féin.'

She replied that saying Sinn Féin was covering up abuse was a generalised slur.

'There was a cover-up,' I said, angrily. 'What else would you call it when people deny there was an IRA investigation into abuse, or moving perpetrators around the country – I think you know there was an IRA investigation, and you are saying you don't.'

She denied that she knew that there was an IRA investigation.

I became extremely frustrated, and told her: 'And by the way, see this business about Adams and the rest saying I was told to go to the RUC? It's a load of nonsense and you know it and I know it, I was not told to go to the RUC, and even if I had gone to the RUC at the time, they would not have been able to investigate it, because the IRA involved themselves.'

She told me she wasn't there to adjudicate on the criminal justice system. Aideen was furiously scribbling away and shaking her head from time to time, while I was trying to contain my temper. Mary Lou looked distinctly uncomfortable. The following are Aideen's minutes combined with my contemporaneous notes of the meeting.

Mary Lou: I know that is your story, that is what you say happened, and if that did happen it was wrong.

Me: Not 'if it happened', it *did* happen, and I know it happened, and you know it happened.

Mary Lou: Those you say carried out this, very strongly

dispute this. The court case is the proper place to decide that.

Me: Do you believe as a human being, not as a politician, that there was an IRA investigation into my abuse?

Mary Lou: I don't know. I haven't been party to conversations about that.

This was interesting, because McDonald had appeared in the media in 2014 confirming that she had spoken to one of the women who was part of 'this kangaroo court'. I wasn't quick enough to remind her of this. Instead, I replied:

> I find that astonishing, that you have been more than happy to go out in the media over the last four years in defence of them, and you're saying you haven't had any conversations with these people, who are still members of your party? Did you not think of lifting the phone and saying 'what's the craic lads' before you did your media interviews? That's poor judgement – no offence.

'If you want answers,' she said, 'I am not the person to give them to you.'

'I don't want answers,' I replied angrily. 'I know what happened to me and I believe that you know too. These people are still members of your party.'

She told me that she had accepted 'that that is your account of what happened'.

She hadn't moved far enough, and the meeting became a quick-fire round of to-ing and fro-ing where I made points to her and she did her best to counter them.

I told her what she was saying was 'bullshit'.

'It isn't bullshit,' she shot back, before telling me that when allegations are made of a serious or criminal nature, then no action should be taken or view formed until criminal processes are complete. I thought of all of those people who had been denied due process by those 'decent' IRA volunteers.

I replied: 'Well, I think that stance from you is hypocritical because you haven't waited for results or evidence in other cases before forming a view.'

She asked me for an example. Thinking of the case of Thomas 'Slab' Murphy, the Armagh IRA commander, I said: 'Okay, you said Slab was a good republican when he was in the middle of a tax evasion case.' I also cited her raising Ansbacher in the Dáil as an example. '…and you accused Frances Fitzgerald of having knowledge of a strategy to smear an innocent man as a sex abuser, and the evidence showed she didn't.

'You didn't wait for results there, and you weren't rushing to the police with your views either.'

She bristled at this. Murphy had years ago lost a libel action against the *Sunday Times* when they alleged he was the IRA's Officer Commanding for the whole of Northern Ireland. He was arrested on suspicion of tax evasion on money owed to the Irish exchequer totalling €190,000, and found guilty in 2015. He was a fuel smuggler on a very large scale. When asked questions about him in December 2015, McDonald called him a '…typical rural man' and 'very nice', stating that she had met him two or three times. She was quick to point out that she felt all people should pay their taxes. Most people, especially in South Armagh, would view Slab as far from 'typical'. He was a feared and dangerous man.

In the Ansbacher case, McDonald had used parliamentary privilege in December 2014, and was later found to have abused it when she rhymed off a list of individuals against whom she claimed a whistleblower had made allegations of tax evasion.[188] The individuals named denied the allegations.

Frances Fitzgerald resigned as Tánaiste in 2017 to avert a general election, when Sinn Féin and then Fianna Fáil threatened to bring a motion of no confidence in her. This was a dispute about emails the Justice department had received during Fitzgerald's tenure as Minister for Justice and Equality regarding Garda whistleblower Maurice McCabe. McCabe had been falsely accused of sex abuse, due to a copy-and-paste error which originated within the child and family agency Tusla. Fitzgerald had nothing to do with any of it, yet Sinn Féin were loudly vocal in criticism of her – and were prepared to ratchet up tension which could have led to the collapse of the government during a destabilising period of the Brexit negotiations. It was an easy scalp – the Minister for Justice position is always tricky – and Fitzgerald resigned in the face of Sinn Féin's belligerence. In one of the most highly charged debates to take place in Leinster House, Mary Lou McDonald, whose tone was icy, told those present: 'This is her last chance to answer [...] questions', accused her of 'bluster', and later informed the Dáil: 'It is time for her to go.'

Fitzgerald, frustrated, countered that McDonald should not 'malign her', and pointed out that a tribunal was under way. 'Let me say one thing to the Deputy,' Fitzgerald added: 'My party has always believed in due process and I have always believed in due process. She can speak for her own party in regard to how it handles issues but I can speak for my party, and I have always followed the principle of natural process and due process.'

The minister Simon Harris also told McDonald: 'The Deputy would not want the facts to get in the way.' It was a prescient observation, as Frances Fitzgerald was found by the Charleton Tribunal in 2018 to have acted appropriately at all times. Fitzgerald had been an efficient minister and none of the parliamentarians who wanted her head, especially McDonald, had been content to await the outcome of the tribunal. Now McDonald was virtuously telling me that she needed evidence before she would pass judgement on IRA members.

When I pointed these examples out to McDonald, she drew a small breath and moved the matter on. Then I caught her in a problem of her own making. She was trying to communicate to me why she believed I had been abused, by saying that *three* people alleged abuse by Morris. I said: 'That's very interesting so just to make sure I am hearing you right. You based your decision on the fact that because other people said it happened?' She confirmed that this was her position. I knew I had her, and said: 'Okay, well are you aware that I was not the only person who told the police there was an IRA investigation?' I told her that the other two victims had *also* told police that they were questioned about their abuse. I asked her: 'Based on that knowledge now, and that you have said was based on the strength of three complainants, do you believe there was an IRA investigation?'

She said she hadn't 'seen that evidence', and I told her it was publicly available. I added:

> You continue to have people in your party who don't believe they have done anything wrong. There was a pattern of behaviour within the republican movement, I know this to be fact because I have been contacted by victims and by people across the country. And those people watched how you and your party treated me and they are too frightened to make complaints, and that is despicable, and rest assured, at some point those complaints will be made, and I have absolutely no faith in Sinn Féin procedures. No faith in Sinn Féin or IRA members cooperating with the courts.
>
> When I originally gave an interview to the *Sunday Tribune*, no one from SF denied an IRA investigation then, Adams didn't even deny it. Both [Padraic] Wilson and [Seamus] Finucane issued public statements, neither denied it then – in fact Finucane said he wished to state that he did have a role to play – on whose behalf was he acting if he wasn't acting on behalf of the IRA – Sinn Féin's?

McDonald replied: 'He was not acting on behalf of Sinn Féin. No one from Sinn Féin investigated abuse.'

That wasn't strictly true, because Siobhán O'Hanlon, who was Gerry Adams's secretary, had been pulled into both the first and second investigations. She had also made Adams's personal office available when he wasn't there, so that the IRA women could speak to me. But I had already made myself perfectly clear to McDonald, and it was obvious the meeting was going round in circles. I decided to ask her a few final questions.

'Do you accept that your party treated me badly from the point when I went public?'

She replied: 'From your point of view, yes, I can see that, I think it's fair to say that but that wasn't the intention. The whole thing got very highly politicised.'

I rolled my eyes: 'Well, what do you expect, you're a political party. If it had been a bishop and a load of paedophile priests, everyone would have been out commenting on it, including yourselves. You said I slurred your party!'

She retracted the word 'slur'. I responded: 'The very least that I am owed by SF after everything you've done is that you admit the IRA investigated my abuse and brought me into a room with my abuser, the very least.'

I became upset when she asked me something about Morris, and I faltered. Aideen, concerned, put her hand out to me in a gesture of solidarity. I held up my hand to her, indicating that I was okay to continue, and watched McDonald's eyes flick across both of our hand gestures. I told her: 'You are giving these people cover as leader of Sinn Féin. The graffiti on the walls and the online comments from your members are out of order, and not one of you, except for the time you commented about that blog has stood up and said this should stop.'

She reiterated her opposition to abusive comments.

I then asked her specifically: 'Go back to those named individuals and ask them if they investigated abuse.' She said she would not be involving herself in that. I kept talking over her: 'Come back and tell me the answers they give you – it's difficult to believe you haven't had that conversation with them. You have abdicated your responsibility as a human being and as a political leader, you've been out over and over in the media, and you are giving these people cover by doing so. And you tell Gerry Adams from me that he knows he's a liar, and I know he's a liar.'

I was getting up to leave, and lifted my handbag.

'By the way,' I said, 'I'm also not happy with how your press office dealt with *Spotlight*,' meaning that in the first programme the party had not answered the list of detailed questions they had been sent.

'Well, Máiría,' she said in what I took to be a sarcastic tone, 'I'll be sure to let them know.'

The meeting did not end with a handshake or any pleasantries, and it took me a while to calm down after it. I told RTÉ, when a journalist called me, that I had entered the meeting with low expectations and had left with even lower ones.

I returned to Belfast, and that weekend appeared as the main speaker at the Reclaim the Night rally in Belfast, where I told the feminist crowd: 'The criminal justice system is currently failing rape victims and it's time for that to stop. People should engage with the Gillen Review to support every single victim. When you come forward the criminal justice system should treat you with care and respect.' The organisers had taken some grief from republicans for inviting me to speak, but to their credit, they held firm.

Sinn Féin now appeared to have an issue with me telling the public that McDonald had retracted her assertion that I had slurred Sinn Féin. In the *Sunday Business Post* a Sinn Féin spokesperson was quoted as saying, 'With regards to the issue of the 'slur', Máiría clarified to Mary Lou that she had no intention of slurring all members of Sinn Féin. Mary Lou welcomed this clarification and withdrew her remark on that basis.' My notes record McDonald retracting the remark when I said to her: 'You said I slurred your party.'[189] The following Tuesday, McDonald appeared on RTÉ's *Sean O'Rourke Show* and described our meeting as 'very cordial'. I promptly released the records of that meeting to the *Irish Independent*, which showed clearly that we repeatedly clashed over whether the IRA had carried out an investigation.

The nature of cordiality wasn't the only issue McDonald had difficulty with. Sean O'Rourke had tackled her over the Ombudsman letter, which referred to a policeman stating that it was obvious none of the Sinn Féin representatives were going to cooperate with police. She insisted there had been full cooperation. The transcript of that particular part of the interview makes for painful reading:

> *Sean*: You accused her of casting a slur against Sinn Féin for suggesting that members of the party did not cooperate with

the inquiries by the police. Now, it appears that cooperation was quite limited. It extended only to supplying statements, signed statements, and not doing full police interviews. Is that what you call 'full cooperation'?

Mary Lou: Well, the people in question cooperated with the investigation, I think, would take grave issue with the commentary that you have made. They cooperated, they cooperated with the assistance and advice of their solicitors…

Sean: Did Gerry Adams make himself available for interview?

Mary Lou: They cooperated with the assistance of their solicitors which they are fully entitled to do and I dare say, Sean, if for any reason you were summoned to a Garda station in the morning I imagine that you would take advice from a legal person…

Sean: Absolutely. But I mean, did…

Mary Lou: …and you would be very wise to.

Sean: … just, can you just clarify, do you know, did Gerry Adams make himself available for an interview or was his cooperation limited to just supplying a written statement signed in the presence of his solicitor?

Mary Lou: Gerry Adams's cooperation with the investigation was full and was mediated through his legal representative and it's not for…

Sean: Did he answer questions about what he knew?

Mary Lou: Excuse me, excuse me, Sean. Excuse me, Sean – those questions are properly answered by Gerry Adams, not by me, not by a third party, that's entirely…

Sean: No, no, but you said there was full cooperation. I'm just asking about one particular thing that was highlighted, I think, in the Ombudsman's report.

Mary Lou: I want to take you up on your assertion, again on the radio, that Sinn Féin covered up abuse. Can you state for me, Sean…

Sean: No, I don't think I said that. I don't think I said that – I said that is the suggestion that's been made.

Mary Lou: So, yes and let me just take you back to my meeting with Máiría because we talked about that. Let me reiterate: I apologise absolutely for the shortcomings and failures in the organisation and I can assure you we have very robust procedures now and that would never, ever happen again. But I do not accept and it's entirely not true, untrue, to suggest that there was a cover-up and on the issue of the slur…

Sean: No, but I'm, no, I'm – yes, go on.

Mary Lou: …on the issue of the slur – I spoke to Máiría about that and I said to her: Look, we're an organisation of thousands and thousands of people right across the country, as she knows. When an accusation is repeated again and again in the media – and you did it again this morning – that Sinn Féin covered up abuse – that is felt by every single member of Sinn Féin and, Sean, it is felt as a slur. Máiría said to me that she certainly never intended it to be interpreted or read that way and I accept that….

Sean: …No, but I'm simply saying….

Mary Lou: …and I accept that.

Sean: Now I'd have to listen back to the tape to know if I said there was a cover-up by Sinn Féin. What I'm simply saying is the suggestion is that there was lack of full cooperation. That there was not full cooperation between Sinn Féin and the PSNI over her complaint.

Mary Lou: Well, listen to me…

Sean: …and your definition of…

Mary Lou: ….the statutory…

Sean: …And Sinn Féin's definition of full cooperation is a statement provided and signed in the presence of a solicitor, in Gerry Adams's case, but not being made available for interview.

Mary Lou: Sorry, Sean, just to remind you, the matters in question here were investigated and went to court – books of evidence were created. It was to go to trial. Unfortunately, that didn't happen for reasons that have absolutely nothing got to do with Sinn Féin – and that is the appropriate forum – with the greatest of respect to you – for evidence to be presented, for evidence to be tested and for a conclusion to be reached – not on the airwaves and not by questioning me, Sean.

Sean: No, you seem to be saying that a statement being signed in the presence of a solicitor amounts to full cooperation. I'm simply questioning that.

Mary Lou: Well, that's a matter with you. We can have a legal argument as to what, what you view as full cooperation. I would say to you…

Sean: I think it's pretty obvious – anybody would know – I mean, if you go down to a Garda station, just to go back to what you asked me earlier, and you hand in a statement and your solicitor's there and said: 'Right. That's it. That's all you're getting from me. Good-bye!' Do you call that full cooperation?

Mary Lou: I call that cooperation with an investigation – yes. If you're called, if a charge is put to you, that's a different matter. If you're called as a witness, that's a – you know – all of these things is different stages to any investigation or any judicial process and every citizen is absolutely duty-bound to fully cooperate, to fully and fulsomely cooperate, and they're also, they're also entitled to the protection of the law and to the protection of their good name and their liberty if a charge is put to them.

Sean: Okay.

Mary Lou: No charge was put in the case of Gerry Adams – just for the purposes of clarity… [crosstalk] …in case of any of your listeners are…

Sean: … Oh, I was never suggesting that – everybody knows that…

Mary Lou: Well, I'm not sure anymore what everybody knows. What I'm doing is taking the opportunity to be absolutely clear – as you've asked.

Sean: Okay. Mary Lou McDonald,…

Mary Lou: …Thank you.'

Clarity, Sinn Féin style.

For myself, I now needed time to represent people on the local council, and to deal with my own health. Disaster struck in April 2019 when, after the SDLP had placed my election posters on lamp posts and I was about to hand in my nomination papers, the party discovered that I would have to publish my home address so that anyone could see it. This was impossible, because quite apart from being threatened by republicans, I was also in receipt of a restraining order for life against an individual and I was not about to place my family's lives in jeopardy. I would now be unable to run for election, and would have to stand down from a position into which I'd been co-opted. This was a bitter disappointment.

Colum Eastwood told the *Irish News* that it was 'a disgrace that a victim whose safety would be jeopardised by publication of her address is not afforded the same protection in a local government election that every assembly and Wesminster candidate can avail of'. I contacted the Equality Commission and took the British government to court to change the law, and in 2020, they settled the case with me, and indeed, changed the law so that no council candidate now has to publish their address when running for election.

*

In May 2019, Seamus Marley was convicted of sexual abuse. This was some compensation for Paudie McGahon and another victim abused by him. Marley, the son of Larry Marley, who had masterminded the largest prison escape in Irish history, when 38 IRA prisoners escaped from the Maze, had been extradited from Spain. The other victim, who wished to remain anonymous, told the court in an emotional victim impact statement that his house was beside a graveyard and they had 'quiet neighbours, dead ones'. After the abuse, he learned that it is 'not the dead we should be afraid of, but the living'. Both victims had suffered a great deal, and I was happy for them.

Mr Justice Paul McDermott told the court that Marley 'used his standing in a republican movement, which was well capable of clandestine killing, and through that he threatened one victim by saying: "Touts end up on a border road".' Marley was sentenced to seven years in prison. Paudie said afterwards:

> The final straw for me came in October 2014 when I saw the way Máiría Cahill was treated by Sinn Féin after she came forward [...]. The minute I heard her description of what happened I knew she was telling the truth – it was exactly like what we had experienced. The moment I decided that I was going to the Gardaí was while watching the debate around the Máiría Cahill situation in the Dáil. I was taken by Mary Lou McDonald's demeanour – I wanted the world to know that Máiría Cahill was not the only one.

In July that year, the RTÉ journalist Barry Cummins reported on *Prime Time* that a senior republican who had been charged with alleged sexual offences had skipped bail and Gardaí were unable to locate him. I knew who the man was – his name was one of those I had given to detectives in 2014, though reporting restrictions prevent me from naming him here. Once Cummins's report aired, I called on Sinn Féin to appeal to the man to give himself up to Gardaí. They did not do so. This man had simply vanished into thin air, and none of his former associates appeared to have a clue where he was.

Such is the magical world of the republican movement.

56

The Northern Irish writer and winner of the Man Booker prize, Anna Burns, in her novel *Milkman*, wrote an extraordinary piece of fiction about a young woman living in 'totalitarian run enclaves' where brutality was as rife as the rumours which centred on her and where 'one quarter rape kangaroo courts' took place, where forces dominated and wielded power over people simply trying to get on with life.

Burns was not writing about me, but I couldn't help seeing some similarities with my own life and I wrote in the *Belfast Telegraph* that the book brought 'alive experiences of women like me who have lived through appalling measures of mind and bodily control, without fully recognising the enormity of trauma it brings'.[190]

As I write this in 2023, I am still dealing with the effects of what happened to me, and I still grieve for the young woman I was before someone decided to forcibly breach the most sacred boundary of the human body, and others decided to breach her psyche by forcibly invading her life. I look back at videos and pictures of me around that age – childlike and, despite everything, smiling. To see her, my earlier self, is to mourn for what might have been; and yet I recognise that to be here today – and to have a good life – is an achievement in itself. I have many people to thank for that, people who have helped me with kindness and care – the antithesis of how I have been treated by republicans.

One person changed everything when she came along and gave me purpose: my lovely daughter Saorlaith, who will, in a small matter of years, make her own journey towards and through adulthood. I hope it is a smooth one. I was pregnant with her when I made my police complaint in 2010, and her whole life has spanned my time either in the criminal justice system or in the public eye, trying to drag accountability kicking and screaming out of officialdom, or from Sinn Féin.

To put it like this is to starkly illustrate for people the extraordinary commitment some abuse victims have to make in order to simply try to get people to admit the truth. It's not acceptable that they should have to make such painful sacrifices. All over the world, there are organisations who would rather not admit responsibility when it comes to the heinous matter of abuse. In Ireland, we have several. What sets Sinn Féin apart is that for decades they had a military wing which should never have been anywhere near the issue of child sexual abuse. An 'army' that used the party's political offices to hold 'meetings' in the course of these 'investigations'. That makes the party both culpable and responsible for providing answers. They have never done so.

Had I gone public now, after the #MeToo movement, rather than in 2014, it is doubtful Sinn Féin would have attempted to treat me in the way they did. It was shocking at the time for people to see a victim of sexual abuse trashed so shabbily in public by a political party – and it would be, I hope, intolerable now. And yet, there are those who were disgusted by my treatment then who can now go through all kinds of mental contortions to offer their support to a political party which is easing inexorably towards power in the southern part of Ireland, while retaining its governing grip on the northern side of the border. So-called feminists, up in arms at rape and the covering up of violence against women in every other case, happily pose for pictures with Sinn Féin representatives who sought to cast doubt on my credibility when speaking of my own experiences. Others will cast their vote for the party in the ballot box, as is their right. But to do so means either to support, or give a free pass to the party's appalling track record on child abuse. As one person put it to me when I lamented this fact: 'What's a little child abuse, if they can turn a blind eye to murder?'

There are others, like Mary Lou McDonald, who still believe that IRA volunteers were 'decent'. I would like to ask her a few questions. Is it *decent* to hold kangaroo courts into child abuse? Is it *decent* to bring an abuse victim face to face with her rapist? Is it *decent* to deny it, and allow the victim to be reabused in the public sphere? What about shooting young people in the knees? Is that decent? Kidnap? Robbery? Torture? Can all this be made retrospectively 'decent'?

In recent years, former IRA members have worked hard at changing their image. Padraic Wilson, for example, wrote a cookbook in collaboration with Gerry Adams. Seamus Finucane, the brother of murdered solicitor Pat Finucane, regularly attends Time for Truth rallies, though he has never admitted the truth about bringing me face to face with my abuser. Even the dead can't escape the kindly effect of Sinn Féin rose-tinted glasses. Bobby Storey, once the IRA's director of intelligence and probably the organiser of the biggest bank robbery in our islands, died in June 2020. He was best remembered by the public for roaring through a microphone like a thug when in 2014, Gerry Adams was arrested and questioned (and later released without charge) about the murder of Jean McConville. Within twenty-four hours of Adams entering a PSNI custody suite, a mural sprang up in west Belfast, yards from Divis Flats where McConville was abducted in 1972. In a manner reminiscent of Kim Jong-Un, hordes of republicans were shepherded in front of a makeshift stage, where a six-foot portrait of a smiling Gerry adorned a wall beside the words 'Fear an Phobail [man of the people], Peacemaker, Leader, Visionary'.

'How dare they touch our leader, the leader of Irish republicanism!' Storey shouted, veins pumping in his neck with rage.

When Storey died, Gerry Adams described him as 'kind, thoughtful, loyal and very giving'. After I waïved anonymity, my granny Nora and I were shopping in a local supermarket in west

Belfast when we rounded the aisle and encountered Storey. He put down his shopping basket then stood slowly to his full 6 foot 5 inches' height and stared menacingly at me, only stopping when my brilliantly fearless four-foot-nothing grandmother shouted that if he continued, she would put her 'toe up his hole'.

Myths and legends are spun about 'chieftains' and 'heroes' like Bobby Storey who took on the might of the British state. Sinn Féin need such myths in order to equate the Provisional IRA with the old IRA in people's minds – shadows whose collective narrative shaped the foundations of the Irish state. They want to shift popular memory from murder to martyrdom.

Few acknowledge that as a group the IRA was responsible for the murder of more members of their own community than any other entity.

That's not to say that loyalist paramilitary murders were not despicable, nor that the British state has no serious questions to answer about its collusion with armed groups and in some cases killings in Northern Ireland. Bloody Sunday, Ballymurphy, Springhill: these are unforgettable and atrocious events. The Irish state also has questions to answer regarding its slow release of files and lack of support for extradition of IRA people who went on the run.

But in this instance, since I have seen at first hand the internal workings of the republican movement, there are certain things that I believe Sinn Féin should do. They should admit the truth in relation to those people who were deeply hurt by republican kangaroo courts into sexual abuse – and by the IRA. Gerry Adams wrote in 2014 that there was no 'corporate way' of verifying what the IRA actually did. I disagree. All it entails is that some republicans hold a mirror up to themselves, examine their consciences, and provide an honest account of their activities. It is maddening to listen to the Sinn Féin party preach about 'truth and justice' and call on the British government to provide a full account of their role in the Northern Irish conflict, without a hint of irony about their lack of candour on the role of the IRA and its actions. They are unwilling, or incapable, of providing comfort to the victims of republican violence, and vicious in their response to anyone from within their own community who challenges them.

Sinn Féin has still yet to admit that I was ever 'investigated' by the IRA for my abuse, or apologise properly for the way in which I was treated. They have never admitted that I was brought into a room by three IRA members to face my abuser. Until they do so, they can never speak credibly about the issue of child sexual abuse. They are on course to be elected to govern the Irish Republic, whose 1916 Proclamation of Independence states that we should treat 'all the children of the nation equally'. Sinn Féin have sadly proven again and again that they value their own reputation and that of their leaders over the protection of children.

I still receive online abuse, though these days it usually follows a newspaper article I've written. On just one day in August 2022, after I wrote about crowds in west Belfast singing IRA songs at the West Belfast Festival, the following comments appeared:

> I wouldn't give her the oxygen, she's actually demented.
>
> Narcissist through and through
>
> She's an embarrassment
>
> Maybe she should stop attention seeking!
>
> Cahill is trash.
>
> Maria Cahill carries no credibility. She is consumed with and blinded by vitriol and vindictiveness.
>
> Oh please! The disaffected Máiría.
>
> Rent a mouth!
>
> Drag yon cvnt out again why not its nearly Christmas.
>
> This useful idiot again.
>
> there's literally wiser eating grass!
>
> She likes being manipulated and abused by some people.
>
> A wannabe victim.

Such abuse does not affect me in the way that it once did, and I tend to respond to it less, though it is frustrating that Sinn Féin does little about their abusive trolls. The current president of Sinn Féin, Mary Lou McDonald, stands a good chance of becoming Taoiseach after the next Irish election. Her counterpart, Michelle O'Neill, will become First Minister of Northern Ireland if the Democratic Unionist Party ever agree to re-enter a power-sharing executive. In August 2022, O'Neill told a BBC journalist that there had been 'no alternative' to the IRA becoming involved in the conflict – something that caused uproar amongst victims and politicians, who accused the party of rewriting history. That this is O'Neill's view is not surprising; McDonald herself has stated that the IRA campaign was 'justified'. Her predecessor, Gerry Adams, is in the background these days, but the party's views have not shifted one iota from Gerry Adams's previous comments on the IRA. In 2018, he insisted that 'armed actions were a legitimate response'.

The Irish Republic stands at a crossroads and looks set to elect a political party that the Garda Commissioner and Chief Constable say is still directed by the IRA. McDonald has been moulded by the party to lead a political movement that advocates for 'change', yet is no more than a facade for populist rhetoric. Like other countries who have seen a rise in toxic politics after the financial crash of 2008–2009 and the pandemic of recent years, Ireland is desperate to improve its housing and health, and the country will elect politicians who haven't yet been tested. Sinn Féin have convinced a mainly young electorate with no memory of IRA violence that the IRA really has 'left the stage', and less importance is attached in voters' minds to the carnage they caused over decades in the northern part of this island.

To this victim, and others, the past is very much the present when it remains unresolved, and Sinn Féin fails to take responsibility for their past and for what they did to us. Their record in government in Northern Ireland in a power-sharing arrangement has allowed them to hide behind their partners. They escape scrutiny on the 44,000 people on waiting lists for doctors and hospitals, a health service almost on the point of collapse, a sewage system that pumps over seven million tonnes of waste per year into our rivers and seas, and a cost of living crisis. The party single-mindedly prioritises Irish unification over every other policy. Meanwhile, there has been a rise in sectarianism to levels that haven't been seen in decades.

Irish voters may well find that the grass isn't greener in the hands of a republican party that tramples and devours everything in its wake. How could it possibly treat the electorate properly, when it treats abuse survivors and those bereaved by the IRA like dirt it would like to wipe off its shoe? As Yeats wrote in his poem 'The Second Coming':

> *Things fall apart; the centre cannot hold*
> *Mere anarchy is loosed upon the world*
> *The blood-dimmed tide is loosed, and everywhere*
> *The ceremony of innocence is drowned.*

About the Author

MÁIRÍA CAHILL is a former Irish Senator and Councillor. At the age of sixteen she was abused by a member of the IRA and waived anonymity in 2014. This led to a furore in the Irish media and debates in Dáil Éireann and the Northern Irish Assembly, culminating in an investigation by Sir Keir Starmer and the NI Police Ombudsman, resulting in apologies from the DPP and PSNI Chief Constable. Cahill writes a political opinion column for the *Sunday Independent*, has written for the *Belfast Telegraph* and *Fortnight Magazine*, and regularly appears as a media commentator. She has been described as "a force to be reckoned with" by former Taoiseach Enda Kenny and "incredibly courageous" by former Northern Ireland First Minister Peter Robinson. Cahill lives in Northern Ireland.

Acknowledgements

This book has been, at times, tough to write, and difficult to read. It was also cathartic, and the initial pieces of writing were typed at night-time in 2012 when my then two-year-old daughter went to sleep. I was halfway through a four-year court process that would eventually collapse and needed an outlet for my frustration. In 2022, I pulled it out to look at it again in the course of writing something else. This is the result. *Rough Beast* publishes as Saorlaith becomes a teenager, and her entire life has spanned the second and third parts of this memoir. She has been a delight and the saving grace in my life. And so, my greatest thanks goes to her, for understanding that her mammy sometimes had to interrupt our plans to write, or to do interviews, or to take phone calls, and that, for safety reasons, her life is a bit different to that of her peers. She would not forgive me if I did not also mention our cat Milo, who provided regular distraction from writing the rest of this memoir by dangling like an acrobat off the living room window, looking for more food.

I have chosen deliberately not to go into too much detail about the sexual abuse I was subjected to, because I am conscious it can be triggering for other victims, and that perpetrators sometimes seek out such material to re-abuse others. It is also impossible to include every 'meeting' with the IRA, due to space, but I have sought to portray the main events. I have also kept details about my abuser's other victims to a minimum to protect their identity. I have similarly used (very few) pseudonyms in order to protect others who are not central to this story. Likewise, I have chosen not to give too much oxygen to those who trolled me on social media (or who I argued with) – had I done so, it would have been a very different book with little space for anything else. Maybe next time.

There also isn't enough room to thank everyone who has ever helped me, and I am terrified of leaving someone out, so, if I have done so, please know that it isn't intentional and your help has been greatly appreciated. To all those who have been named in this book who raised my case, who championed the truth, and who encouraged me to keep going, I do not have the words to convey just how much you helped. To those who have not been named due to lack of space, please know I am deeply appreciative.

My story would not have been covered to the extent that it has been were it not for the BBC NI *Spotlight* programme *A Woman Alone with the IRA*, so thanks to all the editors, producer Chris Thornton and cameraman Bill Browne. Special thanks goes to reporter Jennifer O'Leary, the journalist whom I am now proud to call a friend, who stayed the course through thick and thin, whose kindness and tenacity when reporting sets her apart and whose empathy lifted me when things got rocky. To the media outlets who covered it, and continue to, thank you; and to every journalist who treated me with respect, and as a person and not just a story, it was noted and appreciated.

To all the politicians in Dáil Éireann, the Northern Ireland Assembly and Westminster who raised my case and highlighted the issue – it could not have found traction without you and this was vitally important. Some of those politicians went above and beyond; it will always be deeply appreciated. I especially want to thank Tim and Alex Attwood, Mark Durkan, Micheál Martin, Mike Nesbitt, Jim Allister and Naomi Long, all of whom listened to me with concern during my court processes and were there when I went public. Similarly, Enda Kenny and Peter Robinson, who both allowed their parliamentary offices and time to be given to my case once I waived anonymity. Without that, I would not have been able to highlight the issue of paramilitary sexual abuse as effectively. To Joan Burton and Pat and Aoife Carroll, who took me and Saorlaith under their wing like extra members of the family, thank you for your generosity and friendship. To Kathy Sheridan and Patsey Murphy for everything. To Olivia O'Leary for her extraordinary kindness to me and about the book (and many other things above and beyond) and Emily Tansey, who graciously shared her mother, and her lovely self. Thank you both. To Regina Doherty, who championed me from the start and was abused mercilessly for doing so, and remained a good friend, thank you for always doing the right, but not necessarily the most comfortable, thing. To Frances Fitzgerald MEP, for friendship and for continuing to legislate to protect victims from sexual and domestic violence, and Martin and Breege Conway, who never forget to send a Christmas card, and to Baroness Arlene Foster.

To all of those people who have provided me with support and stood up for the right thing on and off social media, who have read articles and who will buy this book, thank you.

To my editor Neil Belton, who has the patience of a saint and who ended up with many more written words than he initially bargained for, thank you for trusting me and for being a great editor. To Jane Anstey for the herculean task of copyediting; sorry about all those missing references. To Kathyrn Colwell for your PR expertise, and to all at Head of Zeus. To Declan Heeney and Simon Hess at Gill Hess Ltd, and Cormac Kinsella, thank you for your encouragement and for your expertise in helping me to release this memoir. To Matt Bray, thank you for designing the cover. To Kayrn and Lesley at Dentons, thank you for your attention to detail and wise advice.

To Anne Harris, the first editor who encouraged me to write and who was incredibly supportive. To all at the *Sunday Independent* and *Belfast Telegraph*, and my past editors, Willie Kealy and Martin Hill, and current, Jody Corcoran and Alan English. To Gail Walker, the second editor to take me on as a political writer, and who gave me my first front-page byline in the *Tele*, thank you for your friendship, laughter, trust and kindness since. To all at the *Stephen Nolan Show* who regularly cover stories that others shy away from, and who have allowed me a voice, thank you.

To Paudie McGahon, who suffered horrendously along with another victim of IRA man Seamus Marley, thank you for using your voice in a difficult climate, and to all of the other victims of abuse who contacted me privately, keep going. To other victims of IRA abuse and cover-up, I hope that you have support to heal.

Because of the nature of where I came from and the issues I was dealing with, I have lost some friends along the way, but there are those who have stayed the course with me, through thick and thin since the early days in west Belfast and beyond. To Julie-Ann and Anna, Grant, Rab and Paul, Alice and Michelle and Lucy, Maria, Elaine and Jennifer, Sharon, Sheila and Paddy, and in memory of Olive Buckley and Lily Hall, all of whom put friendship before politics or pettiness and have provided me with love and many laughs over the years.

To good neighbours and friends in lots of different places, Cathy and Sally, Betty, Pamela, Catherine, Dermot, Sean and Leo, Una, Sinead and Johnny and Margaret and Brian, Julie and Paul, Carmel, and to family friends Mary Jo, Máire and Paul, Terri, Eileen Brian, who I have known since I was born and who always have a smile. To Michael and Sandra, thanks for the love and fun. To the Cahills who remain in our corner, thanks. To those who refused to stand against the IRA, perhaps, on reading, you realise how wrong that decision was.

To the legal eagles who have helped me over the years: Joe Rice, Leona Askin, Frank O'Donaghue, Eithne Ryan, the solicitors at JJ Rice and Co, Aidan Eames, Diarmuid Cohen, Brett Lockhart, Trevor Ringland and all at Macauley & Ritchie.

To Roddy Doyle, who has been extremely generous with his time in reading this book, and in providing a quote, I will always be profoundly grateful. To Maureen Boyle, for reading the first three chapters of this memoir and encouraging a love for GCSE English many years ago. Also, to my A-level Politics teacher Mr Scott, who taught me how to argue, and more importantly how to listen. I got there in the end. To Malachi O'Doherty and Ruth

Dudley Edwards for friendship, laughter and encouragement, to Damian McAteer, whose advice was always helpful, and to Damian Smyth, whose knowledge on the writing process was invaluable at this book's conception, as was that of Eoghan Harris when I mentioned I was writing a book. To Orla in Derry for her kindness at an incredibly pressured time. To all the people who provided me with a place to stay and other help, thank you. To Anthony and Carrie, Dixie, and other republicans who spoke out on the issue of abuse from within their community, and those who came privately to me with knowledge of other cases. And to Julian Smith MP for friendship and for caring about NI, particularly institutional and other abuse victims.

To the wonderful author Flynn Berry for her encouragement and friendship, and her selfless help at the start of this process and throughout.

To Sarah Moran, Kevin Dillon, Ronan Farren and Claire Power, all of whom were instrumental in facilitating access for me to politicians and who all treated me well. Ronan and Claire became friends as I moved through Labour and along with Mags, Seaneen, Amy Rose, Dermot, Niamh, Aideen, Elaine, Billie, Noreen, Cathal, Siobhán, Alan Kelly, Joe and Emer Costello, and everyone else at Labour staff who took me under their wing, thank you. To Shane Ross, who once asked me to run for election (and had a lucky escape), thank you for your help and knowledge of the writing process.

My deep appreciation to Breege and Stephen Quinn, who, despite the traumatic loss of their son Paul, have been supportive of my case right from the start, as has Ann Travers, whose sister Mary was cruelly taken from her by the IRA.

To Elliott's, who provide a refuge after a windy day on Dooey and wifi to send writing from when my own in Donegal is temperamental.

To all the booksellers who stock and recommend *Rough Beast*, thank you.

A special thanks to all of those from the unionist community, and particularly my friends on the Shankill Road, who took time to come and speak with me over the years. To Charlie Lawson and Debbie Stanley for their friendship, and to Eamonn McCann and Goretti Horgan for standing up for me and the issue.

To three women who head up organisations helping abuse victims, Ellen O'Malley, Mary Crilly and Marie Brown, thank you for your colossal work to make society better, and for your personal support.

There are, of course, some people who would rather this book was not written. I hope they realise that I have been fair in my approach to this writing and will learn something from reading it. Like everyone, I am not perfect, and I have tried to convey how people can be shaped by their surroundings and make choices in life they may otherwise not have made. I have also, I hope, demonstrated that setbacks do not mean your life should be written off, and that everyone has the capacity to change. To that end, I still hold out hope that those republicans who treated me badly will, one day, admit what they have done, and that the Sinn Féin party will finally tell the truth and apologise for giving them political cover.

Last but not least, to my parents Noreen and Philip, who I gave a few grey hairs to over the years. No one could have predicted the way in which life has twisted and turned, but I could not have taken all of this on without the support of both of you. Thank you for your love, and for being there, and for standing up to the IRA, when the easiest thing to do would have been to do what others did and capitulate. We have all suffered as a result, but gained much more strength than anyone could have realised. I love you both very much. Here's to the next chapter.

Notes

1. Triple FM interview, July 1998.
2. Triple FM interview, July 1998.
3. W. B. Yeats, *Easter 1916*, ll. 68–80.
4. Volunteer Rights (issued in 1988), excerpt from the IRA's Green Book.
5. Gerry Adams speaking at the West Belfast Festival, footage from: 'We won't be kept down easy', Laurence McKeown, Aug 1997, viewed June 2023.
6. 'Sinn Féin force closure of Castlecourt RUC barracks', *An Phoblacht*, 14 Jan 1999.
7. 'Timing of meeting with corporals killer Maguire a genuine oversight, says PSNI chief', *Belfast Telegraph*, 7 May 2021. At www.belfasttelegraph.co.uk/news/timing-of-meeting-with-corporals-killer-maguire-a-genuine-oversight-says-psni-chief/40398865.html, accessed 25 May 2023.
8. 'Fr Des Wilson: A Priest of the people', *An Phoblacht*, 22 April 1981, reproduced in 'Obituary: A Spiritual Revolutionary', 6 Nov 2019, at www.dannymorrison.com/a-spirtual-revolutionary/, accessed 25 May 2023
9. Triple FM interview, July 1998.
10. Triple FM interview, July 1998.
11. 'A new police service – This is our goal', *An Phoblacht*, 10 Aug 2000, at www.anphoblacht.com/contents/6549, accessed 25 May 2023.
12. 'Dúirt siad…', *An Phoblacht*, 10 Aug 2000, at www.anphoblacht.com/contents/6549, accessed 25 May 2023.
13. 'Fund women's support services – Mayo Sinn Féin', *An Phoblacht*, 24 Aug 2000.
14. Tom Travers, 'Letters to the Editor', *Irish Times*, 8 Apr 1994.
15. Freya McClements, 'Forty years after Sands's election as an MP and death by hunger strike, what is his legacy?', *Irish Times*, 3 Apr 2021, at www.irishtimes.com/culture/heritage/what-bobby-sands-means-to-me-the-hunger-strikers-chose-to-die-daddy-didn-t-1.4525223, accessed 25 May 2023.

16 Henry McDonald, 'Republicans feud over hunger striker's legacy,' *Guardian*, 18 Mar 2001, at www.theguardian.com/uk/2001/mar/18/northernireland.northernireland, accessed 25 May 2023.
17 'Hunger strikers died for gay rights, claims Sinn Féin senator Fintan Warfield,' *Belfast Telegraph*, 15 Aug 2016, at www.belfasttelegraph.co.uk/news/politics/hunger-strikers-died-for-gay-rights-claims-sinn-fein-senator-fintan-warfield/34965230.html, accessed 25 May 2023.
18 Sinn Féin (@sinnfeinireland), 8 Aug 2021.
19 Paul Hosford, 'Sinn Féin defends tribute to hunger striker who was convicted of manslaughter,' *Irish Examiner*, 9 Aug 2021, at www.irishexaminer.com/news/politics/arid-40355906.html, accessed 25 May 2023.
20 Ógra Shinn Féin (@Ogra_SF), 8 Aug 2021.
21 Philip Bradfield, 'Máiría Cahill expresses sadness after reading last wishes of hunger striker Thomas McElwee – "sacrificed by republicans for their aims"', *Belfast News Letter*, 12 Aug 2021, at www.newsletter.co.uk/news/politics/mairia-cahill-expresses-sadness-after-reading-last-wishes-of-hunger-striker-3343082, accessed 25 May 2023.
22 Aidan Lonergan, 'Sinn Féin removes controversial IRA-themed merchandise from its website after backlash,' *Irish Post*, 19 Feb 2018, at www.irishpost.com/news/sinn-fein-removes-controversial-ira-themed-merchandise-website-backlash-150051, accessed 25 May 2023.
23 Personal communication to the author.
24 Máiría Cahill, 'What the Hunger Strikes mean for young people', *Republican News*, 22 Feb 2001.
25 Suzanne Breen, 'Grand-niece of Provo legend endured horrific sexual abuse,' *Sunday Tribune*, 17 Jan 2010.
26 The Pensive Quill (TPQ) blog, 'Ballymurphy rape,' 18 Jan 2010, at: www.thepensivequill.com/2010/01/ballymurphy-rape.html, accessed 25 May 2023.
27 Press release, Seamus Finucane, 21 Jan 2010.
28 Press release, Padraic Wilson, 21 Jan 2010.
29 Comment section, (O'Bhrad) 'Grand-niece of Provo legend endured horrific sexual abuse', (tribune.ie), 18 Jan 2010, 10:49pm, accessed 7 June 2023
30 Sir Keir Starmer KCB QC and Katherine O'Byrne, *Independent Review of the Prosecution of Related Sexual Abuse And Terrorism Cases Report*, 6 May 2015, p. 18, Section 5.8(4).
31 Aaron Tinney, *Sunday Life*, 18 July 2010.
32 John Cassidy, *Sunday World*, 10 Oct 2010.
33 E-mail to the PPS, 12 Aug 2011.
34 Allison Morris, *Irish News*, 1 Aug 2012.
35 *Belfast News Letter*, 31 Aug 2012.

36 Starmer and O'Byrne, *Independent Review*, 2015, p. 14.
37 Allison Morris, *Irish News*, 11 Sep 2012.
38 Martin McGartland, *Fifty Dead Men Walking* (John Blake Publishing, 1998), pp.37, 47.
39 Jim Cusack and Alan Murray, 'Gerry Adams reported only head lice not sex abuse at sister-in-law's house,' *Sunday Independent*, 13 Oct 2013, at: www.independent.ie/irish-news/gerry-adams-reported-only-head-lice-not-sex-abuse-at-sister-in-laws-house/29655391.html, accessed 25 May 2023.
40 Eilis O'Hanlon, 'Adams' plea for privacy and space over Aine is just a self-serving ploy', *Sunday Independent*, 5 Oct 2013.
41 See: https://publications.parliament.uk/pa/cm201314/cmhansrd/cm131016/debtext/131016-0001.htm, accessed 23 May 2023.
42 'Gerry Adams to meet woman "raped by top republican"', *Irish Independent*, 1 Dec 2013, at: www.independent.ie/irish-news/gerry-adams-to-meet-woman-raped-by-top-republican/29798826.html, accessed 25 May 2023.
43 'SF knows that republicans "investigated" cases of abuse. I know, because it happened to me,' *Irish Independent*, 1 Dec 2013, at: www.independent.ie/irish-news/sf-knows-that-republicans-investigated-cases-of-abuse-i-know-because-it-happened-to-me/29799024.html, accessed 25 May 2023.
44 Ibid.
45 Allison Morris, 'Former Adams bodyguard was "never a witness in Cahill case",' *Irish News*, 13 Nov 2014.
46 'PIRA accused freed', *Irish News* report, 9 May 2014.
47 Jim Allister, 'Starmer shows catastrophic failure', Traditional Unionist Voice, 22 May 2015 at https://tuv.org.uk/starmer-shows-catastrophic-failure/, accessed 28 July 2023.
48 'Sue Ramsey: Sinn Féin MLA to stand down for health reasons,' BBC News online, 7 Oct 2014, at: www.bbc.co.uk/news/uk-northern-ireland-29531024, accessed 25 May 2023.
49 Ann Travers, 'Spotlight shines on "abuse" handling, Vixens with Convictions', online blog, 12 Oct 2014.
50 Mike Nesbitt statement, 14 Oct 2014.
51 from @Máiríac31 to Gerry Adams Twitter account, 14 Oct 2014, 11.24 p.m.
52 Transcript: 'A Woman Alone with the IRA', *BBC NI Spotlight*, 14 Oct 2014.
53 Gerry Adams statement: www.sinnfein.ie, 15 Oct 2014, accessed March 2022.
54 from @Máiríac31, 15 Oct 2014.
55 Ibid.

56. Gerry Adams interview with Richard Crowley, *RTÉ News at One*, 16 Oct 2014.
57. Ibid.
58. Ibid.
59. Hugh Jordan, *Sunday World*, 6 Aug 2000.
60. Ibid.
61. Máiría Cahill, press conference, 16 Oct 2014.
62. Ibid.
63. Micheál Martin, press conference, 16 Oct 2014.
64. Fionnan Sheehan, 'The Making of Mary Lou McDonald,' *Irish Independent*, 14 May 2022.
65. 'A Conversation with Sinn Féin leader Mary Lou McDonald,' on YouTube, at: www.youtube.com/watch?v=mZo2hRglTmk&t=1094s, accessed 25 May 2023.
66. Mick Fealty, 'Micheal Martin claims Sinn Féin's cover up of sexual abuse goes beyond the Adams case,' Slugger O'Toole blog, 28 Nov 2013, at: sluggerotoole.com/2013/11/28/micheal-martin-claims-sinn-feins-cover-up-of-sexual-abuse-goes-beyond-the-adams-case/, accessed 25 May 2023.
67. 'Martin claims Adams aware of other abuse cases,' *Irish Times*, 28 Nov 2013, at: www.irishtimes.com/news/politics/martin-claims-adams-aware-of-other-abuse-cases-1.1610341, accessed 25 May 2023.
68. Mary Lou McDonald, interview with Rachel English, *Morning Ireland*, 28 Nov 2013.
69. Mary Lou McDonald, 'Today with Pat Kenny', *RTÉ Radio One*, 22 Jan 2010.
70. Suzanne Breen, 'Today with Pat Kenny', *RTÉ Radio One*, 22 Jan 2010.
71. Mary Lou McDonald, interview with Rachel English, *Morning Ireland*, 28 Nov 2013.
72. 'Cross examination of Gerry Adams by Ms McDermott QC', BBC News NI transcript of first trial of Liam Adams in Belfast Crown Court on 22 April 2013, supplied by the office of the Lord Chief Justice, available at: 08_10_2013_cross_exam_gerry_adams.pdf (bbc.co.uk), accessed 7 June 2023.
73. Ibid.
74. Press Release: 'RTÉ must explain failure to interview Mairia Cahill', Joanna Tuffy, Irish Labour Party, 17 Oct 2014.
75. Máiría Cahill interview with Richard Crowley, *RTÉ Radio One,* 17 Oct 2014
76. Ibid.
77. Ibid.
78. Gerry Adams statement, 17 Oct 2014.
79. Máiría Cahill interview with Brian Dobson, *Six One News*, 17 Oct 2014.

80 Email from Máiría Cahill to Mary Lou McDonald, 17 Oct 2014, 19:42pm
81 RTÉ's *Saturday with Brian Dowling* show, 18 Oct 2014.
82 Ibid.
83 Pearse Doherty on RTÉ's *This Week*, 19 Oct 2014.
84 Máiría Cahill, 'I actually worked out what would be the best way for me to be killed. Shot, not beaten', *Sunday Independent*, 19 Oct 2014.
85 Ibid.
86 Eoghan Harris, 'RTE gives Sinn Fein a soft ride on Cahill case', *Sunday Independent*, 19 Oct 2014.
87 Una Heaton, 'Try to help her, Liz', 'Letters to the Editor', *Sunday Independent*, 19 Oct 2014.
88 Nick Sommerlad, 'British spies recruited paedo IRA chief: Spooks used pictures of Joe Cahill to "turn him"', *Daily Mirror*, 19 Oct 2014.
89 Máiría Cahill, 'Uncomfortable truths for Sinn Féin', 20 October 2014; Máiría Cahill: Uncomfortable truths for Sinn Fein – Slugger O'Toole blog (sluggerotoole.com), accessed 5 June 2023.
90 Gerry Adams, 'How republicans dealt with allegations of child abuse', *Léargas* blog, 19 Oct 2014.
91 Ibid.
92 Ibid.
93 Máiría Cahill, 'Uncomfortable truths for Sinn Fein', 20 October 2014, Slugger O'Toole blog.
94 Ibid.
95 Máiría Cahill speaking at press conference outside Stormont, Parliament Buildings, Belfast, 20 Oct 2014.
96 Jennifer McCann, media interview, 20 Oct 2014.
97 Niall O'Connor, 'Taoiseach made "politically motivated" remarks over Mairia Cahill affair – Adams', *Irish Independent*, 20 Oct 2014.
98 Mary Lou McDonald, speaking on Newstalk's *Ivan Yates* programme, 20 Oct 2014. All references to this programme here come from this transcript.
99 Ibid.
100 Dessie Ellis interview with Gavin Jennings, *Morning Ireland*, 20 Oct 2014. All references to this programme here come from this transcript.
101 Ibid.
102 Brian Campbell, *Irish News*, 20 Oct 2014.
103 Gerry Moriarty, *Irish Times*, 21 Oct 2014.
104 'PPS announces review of Mairia Cahill cases', *BBC News NI*, 21 Oct 2014; PPS announces review of Maíria Cahill cases – BBC News, accessed 8 Jun 2014.
105 *Irish Times* editorial, 21 Oct 2014.
106 Letters page, *Irish Times*, 21 Oct 2014.
107 Houses of the Oireachtas debates, at: www.oireachtas.ie/en/debates/

debate/dail/2014-10-21/18/, accessed 23 May 2023. All the quotations from this exchange during the Order of Business on 21 October 2014 are from this source.
108 Gerry Adams press conference, Leinster House, 21 Oct 2014.
109 'Adams says he knew of IRA connection to Máiría Cahill abuse claims', *Irish Independent*, 22 Oct 2014, at: independent.ie irish-news/politics/adams-says-he-knew-of-ira-connection-to-mairia-cahill-abuse-claims/30683626.html, accessed 23 May 2023.
110 Paul Williams, 'New victim breaks his silence on "Kangaroo IRA Irish courts"', *Irish Independent*, 22 Oct 2014.
111 Ibid.
112 Miriam Lord, 'Cahill allegations hang heavy in the air', *Irish Times*, 22 Oct 2014.
113 The Lord Bew, contribution to Haass Talks debate, 22 Oct 2014, at: hansard.parliament.uk/Lords/2014-10-22/debates/14102295000249/details#contribution-14102295000047, accessed 24 May 2023.
114 Peadar Tóibín, Newstalk, 23 Oct 2014.
115 Houses of the Oireachtas debates, at: www.oireachtas.ie/en/debates/debate/dail/2014-10-22/17/, accessed 23 May 2023.
116 Ibid.
117 Ibid.
118 Ibid.
119 Ibid.
120 Quoted by Niall O'Connor, *The Herald*, 24 Oct 2014.
121 Máiría Cahill interview, *Stephen Nolan Show*, BBC One, 22 Oct 2014.
122 Brian Byrne, 'Former IRA man distances himself from Cahill blog', *Irish Independent*, 27 Oct 2014.
123 Lise Hand, 'Gripping exchanges as Kenny plunges home the knife and claims SF leader "laughing"', *Irish Independent*, 23 Oct 2014.
124 Ibid.
125 Brendan Hughes, 'Cahill: A whole weight of evidence yet to be revealed', *Irish News*, 24 Oct 2014.
126 Claire Simpson, 'McGuinness: I believe Máiría Cahill was raped', *Irish News*, 24 Oct 2014.
127 Quoted by Lise Hand in the *Irish Independent*, 24 Oct 2014.
128 Gerard Moriarty, 'Weekend review', *Irish Times*, 25 Oct 2014.
129 Newton Emerson column, *Irish News*, 25 Oct 2014.
130 Máiría Cahill, 'In a split second I remembered what it felt like to be frightened beyond belief', *Irish Independent*, 26 Oct 2014.
131 Jody Corcoran, 'The time has now come for Mary Lou to put up or shut up', *Sunday Independent*, 26 October 2014.
132 Ruth Dudley Edwards, 'Party Leader Gerry Adams' Twitter teddy bears have gone strangely quiet', *Sunday Independent*, 26 Oct 2014.

133 Máiría Cahill, 'A Statement,' Slugger O'Toole blog, 26 Oct 2014, at: Máiría Cahill – A statement – Slugger O'Toole (sluggerotoole.com), accessed 6 June 2023.
134 Ibid.
135 Roy Greenslade, 'BBC programmme on IRA rape allegations flawed by lack of political balance', *Guardian* online blog, 27 Oct 2014.
136 Fintan O'Toole, 'Never mind the evidence, feel the "truthiness" of what Gerry Adams says', *Irish Times*, 28 Oct 2014.
137 Máiría Cahill interview with Jonathan Healy, Newstalk, *Lunchtime*, 28 Oct 2014.
138 Seamus McKinney, 'SF distanced itself from "Nelis" blog comments', *Irish News*, 28 Oct 2014.
139 Máiría Cahill to Mary Nelis, Facebook message, 28 Oct 2014.
140 Peter Madden, speaking on RTÉ radio, *Morning Ireland*, 29 Oct 2014.
141 Ibid.
142 Ibid.
143 Máiría Cahill, press statement, 29 Oct 2014
144 Newton Emerson column, *Irish News*, 1 Nov 2014.
145 Connla Young, 'Abuse case "transformed into a politically charged matter"', *Irish News*, 1 Nov 2014.
146 Jerome Reilly, 'Mary Lou: cover-up claims "a slur" on Sinn Fein women', *Sunday Independent*, 2 Nov 2014.
147 Philip Cahill, interview with Maeve Sheehan, *Sunday Independent*, 2 Nov 2014.
148 Ibid.
149 Eilis O'Hanlon, '"Hey bby gurl": How Gerry Adams is serially insensitive to abuse victims', *Sunday Independent*, 2 Nov 2014.
150 Maya Angelou, 'Still I Rise', *And Still I Rise* (Virago, 1986), pp.41–42.
151 *Irish News* editorial, 3 Nov 2014.
152 Gerry Adams, interview with Gavin Jennings, *Morning Ireland*, 3 Nov 2014.
153 Mary Lou McDonald, interview with Chris Donoghue, *Newstalk Breakfast*, 3 Nov 2014.
154 Stormont Assembly motion: 'BBC Spotlight Programme 14 October 2014', debated 4 Nov 2014, at: aims.niassembly.gov.uk/officialreport/report.aspx?&eveDate=2014/11/04&docID=211612, accessed 24 May 2023.
155 Breige Wright, statement, 4 Nov 2014.
156 Máiría Cahill, statement, 4 Nov 2014.
157 Stormont Assembly debate, 4 Nov 2014.
158 Press conference with Mary Lou McDonald and Gerry Adams, Leinster House plinth, 4 Nov 2014.
159 Gerry Adams, Léargas website, 4 Nov 2014.

160 Quoted in John Manley, *Irish News*, 5 Nov 2014.
161 Jody Corcoran, John Drennan, Philip Ryan, *Sunday Independent*, 8 Nov 2014.
162 '"I smile easily" – Mary Lou denies "smirking" at Máiría Cahill during abuse debate', *The Journal*, 13 Nov 2104, at: www.thejournal.ie/mairia-cahill-mary-lou-mcdonald-1777561-Nov2014/, accessed 26 May 2023.
163 Roddy Doyle, Facebook, 13 Nov 2014.
164 Máiría Cahill, interview with Vincent Browne on RTÉ, 12 Nov 2014.
165 'Day Dáil showed democracy with morality is invincible', *Sunday Independent*, 16 Nov 2014.
166 Willie Kealy, 'Gerry Adams now exudes a palpable air of menace', *Sunday Independent*, 16 Nov 2014.
167 Gerry Adams interview with Tommie Gorman, *RTÉ News*, 24 Nov 2014.
168 Houses of the Oireachtas debates, at: www.oireachtas.ie/en/debates/debate/dail/2014-11-27/26/, accessed 25 May 2023.
169 Gerry Adams, interview with Gavin Jennings, *Morning Ireland*, 11 Mar 2015.
170 Fintan O'Toole, 'On a wing and a prayer – how the IRA banished abusers', *Irish Times*, 14 March 2015.
171 Máiría Cahill, 'I took my daughter to a Twelfth bonfire party and she loved it', *Belfast Telegraph*, 13 Jul 2015.
172 Starmer and O'Byrne, *Independent Review*, 2015, p. 31, Section 5.81.
173 Willie Kealy, 'Labour chooses Máiría Cahill for Seanad seat', *Sunday Independent*, 4 Oct 2015.
174 Henry McDonald, 'A Senate sniper to shoot barbs at Sinn Fein', *Belfast Telegraph*, 7 Oct 2015.
175 Máiría Cahill, 'Martin McGuinness and Me', *Belfast Telegraph*, 23 Mar 2017.
176 Niall O'Connor, 'Sinn Féin hits back at former member in Cahill row', *Sunday Independent*, 10 Aug 2017, at: https://www.independent.ie/irish-news/sinn-fein-hits-back-at-former-member-in-cahill-row/36017624.html
177 Closure Letter from the Police Ombudsman for Northern Ireland (PONI) to Máiría Cahill, Oct 2018.
178 Ibid.
179 Ibid.
180 Ibid.
181 Ibid.
182 Ibid.
183 Máiría Cahill, 'I told truth about what happened to me 20 years ago… I'm angry I've been let down by almost everybody in relation to my case', *Belfast Telegraph*, 13 Sep 2018.

184 Máiría Cahill, BBC NI *Spotlight* documentary, 18 Sep 2018.
185 RTÉ Radio One, *The Sean O'Rourke Show*, 16 Oct 2018.
186 Miriam Lord, 'Mary Lou McDonald takes "sitting TD" a little too far', *Irish Times*, 21 Nov 2018.
187 Ibid.
188 'Committee says McDonald abused privilege in remarks on alleged tax evasion,' Newstalk, 8 Apr 2015, at https://www.newstalk.com/news/mary-lou-mcdonald-parliamentary-privilege-committee-on-procedures-and-privileges-abuse-ansbacher-662790
189 Hugh O'Connell, *Sunday Business Post*, 25 Nov 2018.
190 Máiría Cahill, '*Milkman* may be fiction, but its depiction of how paramilitaries use control to prey on vulnerable young women is strikingly accurate… I know because I've lived through it', *Belfast Telegraph*, 19 Oct 2018.

Image Credits

Page 1

(*top left*) Cahill family collection
(*top right*) Cahill family collection
(*bottom*) Cahill family collection

Page 2

(*bottom*) Cahill family collection

Page 3

(*top*) Julie Ann Rogers, 2011
(*middle*) Author collection
(*bottom*) BBC NI *Spotlight*

Page 4

(*top*) Kelvin Boyes / Presseye.com
(*bottom*) PA Images / Alamy Stock Photo

Page 5

(*top*) PA Images / Alamy Stock Photo
(*bottom*) Shauneen Armstrong

Page 6

(*top*) Malachi O'Doherty
(*bottom*) Niall O'Loughlin

Page 7
(*top*) Photo by Artur Widak/NurPhoto via Getty Images
(*bottom*) Mags Murphy

Page 8
(*top*) Author collection
(*bottom*) Saorlaith Ní Chathail, Feb 2022